God's Englishwomen

*Seventeenth-century
radical sectarian writing
and feminist criticism*

God's *[...]* *[...]* enth
centur *[...]* these
remar *[...]* ween
femini *[...]* urces
and p *[...]*

This *[...]* ed by
Quake *[...]* s was
produ *[...]* terial
throu *[...]* texts
and r *[...]* previ-
ously *[...]*

Hilar *[...]* ligher
Educ *[...]*

God's Englishwomen

Seventeenth-century radical sectarian writing and feminist criticism

Hilary Hinds

Manchester University Press
Manchester and New York

distributed exclusively in the USA and Canada by St. Martin's Press

Copyright © Hilary Hinds 1996

Published by Manchester University Press
Oxford Road, Manchester M13 9NR, UK
and Room 400, 175 Fifth Avenue, New York, NY 10010, USA

Distributed exclusively in the USA and Canada
by St. Martin's Press, Inc., 175 Fifth Avenue, New York, NY 10010, USA

British Library Cataloguing-in-Publication Data
A catalogue record for this book is available from the British Library

Library of Congress Cataloging-in-Publication Data
Hinds, Hilary
   God's Englishwomen : Seventeenth-century radical sectarian writing and feminist criticism /
   Hilary Hinds
      p.   cm.
   Includes bibliographical references (p.   ) and index.
   ISBN 0-7190-4886-9 (hard). — ISBN 0-7190-4887-7 (pbk. : alk. paper)
   1. Christian literature, English—History and criticism. 2. Dissenters, Religious, in literature.
      3. English literature—Early modern, 1500-1700—History and criticism. 4. English literature—
      Women authors—History and criticism. 5. Feminism and literature—England—History—
      17th century. 6. Women and literature—England—History—17th century. 7. Christian sects in
      literature. 8. Authorship—Sex differences. 9 Radicalism in literature. 10. Renaissance—England.
      I. Title
   PR438.D57H56   1996
   820.9'382'082—dc20   95-41310
                                                                CIP

ISBN 0 7190 4886 9 *hardback*
ISBN 0 7190 4887 7 *paperback*

First published 1996

00 99 98 97 96   10 9 8 7 6 5 4 3 2 1

Typeset in Great Britain
by Koinonia, Manchester
Printed in Great Britain
by Bell & Bain Ltd, Glasgow

Contents

Acknowledgements

The research upon which this book is based was undertaken in the Department of English at the University of Birmingham, under the percipient supervision of Tony Davies. The research was funded by the British Academy, and conducted with the support of Birmingham University Library, the Bodleian, the British Library, Friends' Library, and Woodbrooke College Library. Fircroft College of Adult Education in Birmingham generously granted me a sabbatical in the summer of 1994 to complete the writing of this book, and the staff and students showed patience and forebearance in the spring of 1995 during its final stages. Joan O'Hagan in particular has taken on many an extra responsibility to facilitate the production of this publication.

Elspeth Graham and Martin Pumphrey convinced me of the worth of transforming the thesis into a book. During its writing and rewriting, the following people have contributed their time and thoughts, for which I am very grateful: Maureen Bell, Pam Lunn, Lyndal Roper, and Helen Wilcox. In particular, I would like to thank Kathryn Perry for her critical interest and much-valued support, and Elaine Hobby, who got me started on this work, and whose unfailing faith in it has been a sustaining force.

Like all researchers of the seventeenth century, I am indebted to the extensive scholarship of Christopher Hill. In particularly, however, I acknowledge his *God's Englishman* (1971), to which the title of this study refers.

Earlier versions of Chapter 6 appeared in S. P. Cerasano and Marion Wynne-Davis (eds) (1992) *Gloriana's Face: Women, Public and Private, in the English Renaissance*, Hemel Hempstead, Harvester Wheatsheaf, and as Occasional Paper No. 7, University of Birmingham: Institute for Advanced Research in the Humanities.

Finally, my thanks go to Jackie Stacey, who kept me on course. Without her clarity, her powers of synthesis, her resolution, her good humour, and above all her energy, the transition from doctorate to book would never have been completed. The importance of her contribution cannot be exaggerated.

A note on quotations

Where I quote from seventeenth-century texts, I have modernised the spelling, but changed the punctuation only where to leave it unaltered might have been confusing for a twentieth-century reader. I have retained the original spellings of all titles in the bibliography, to facilitate further reference. Where I include quotations from seventeenth-century texts cited in other books, I have changed nothing: they appear as they were quoted.

A more detailed explanation of the editorial policy I have followed can be found preceding the appendices.

1

Sectarian writing, the literary canon, and feminist criticism

This book is a study of writings by women from the seventeenth-century radical religious sects, analysed in relation to a number of key debates and theories within contemporary feminist literary criticism. Prophecies, spiritual autobiographies and short tracts, perhaps warning readers of their impending damnation, or exhorting them to turn to God, all written by Quaker, Baptist, Independent and Fifth Monarchist women, comprise my object of study. They are examined through a range of late twentieth-century literary concerns such as the character and impact of silence in a text, the critical function of the author, or debates about language, all of them inflected through the specificities of a feminist approach.

The women writers discussed in this study were prolific and polemical, and their work was at the heart of seventeenth-century upheavals, religious, linguistic and political. They engaged critically with questions of the changing social order – the law, the church, the family and the state – and they debated the relationship between women, men and the divine. Calling for radical transformation, many of these women challenged existing authority and questioned long-standing beliefs. They broke loose from expected social conventions, often leaving familial duties in order to pursue their callings. They risked ridicule, violence and even imprisonment in order to speak their words and publish their texts. Not only did they offer listeners and readers new ideas about how to live, but they did so with an audacious claim to godly authority: many of them claimed to be prophets, speaking God's word and fulfilling their duties in his name. Indeed, many of them devoted years of their lives, undergoing extreme hardships and retributions for so doing, in order to complete their divine mission. The texts that have remained often demonstrate sophisticated linguistic and rhetorical manoeuvrings, playing with readers' expectations and undermining their assumptions. Across the complex range of styles and genres discussed in this book, these women exercised not only their devotion to God's new order, but also their imaginative and creative abilities in the production of these texts.

Refusing the traditional constraints of gender at this time, these women writers insisted upon their right, indeed their duty, to be heard. Despite severe punishments for so doing, many of them continued to participate in the revolutionary transformations and struggles which have come to characterise this turbulent century. Leaving husbands, children and fathers, many of them fought for their independence in

1

God's name. Travelling widely through England, and in some cases also through Europe, America and the Caribbean, these women endured physical privation, social ridicule and stigmatisation. Contributing to important and influential social movements, these sectarian women played a central role in transforming the relationship of religion and politics in England at this time. Through their struggles with the limitations of their place in the social and spiritual orders they called into question the meanings of gender, power and participation in the public sphere, and in so doing refigured the limitations of the social ascriptions of femininity as a vantage point from which to participate in religious discourses at this time.

Given their contribution to fundamental social changes at this time, one might well ask why so little is known of them by contemporary feminist critics. At the cutting edge of profound transformations, and transgressing the gender norms of the day, one might expect such women to have taken their rightful place in the feminist hall of fame alongside Sappho, Joan of Arc, Mary Wollstonecraft and the Pankhursts. Obvious role models, or even heroines, for a movement predicated upon radical social change such as feminism, these women might well have become familiar names to students of women's literary and cultural history.

And yet only readers who are specialists in this field will recognise the names of Mary Cary, Anne Wentworth or Joan Vokins. What has prevented them from achieving the kind of status of other writers of their time, or of other women famed for their refusals of the constraints of patriarchal demands? Why does traditional literary history honour the Baptist sectary John Bunyan and not Anna Trapnel? And why has feminist literary history rehabilitated Aphra Behn, but passed over Jane Turner? The answer to the first of these questions might be seen to lie in the much-criticised patriarchal character of the literary canon,[1] and indeed this may well be the case. The second question, however, complicates such straightforward ascriptions of guilt, by requiring us to examine the precepts upon which the construction of a feminist literary history are based.

The inclusion of these women writers within English literary studies, and my insistence upon their relevance and significance to feminist literary studies, is a challenge to the limits not only of the literary canon in all its pomp and solemnity, but also to those of feminist scholarship, which has tended to set the starting-point of women's writing in the eighteenth century. These seventeenth-century women writers are both of literary and political importance, and, as we shall see, challenge the notion that there was only one woman writer of interest in that entire century, or that a concern with gender relations started at the beginning of the eighteenth century.

For too many students in English departments, the works of Shakespeare, Donne, Marvell, Milton and Dryden have remained the sum total of their contact with seventeenth-century writing, and too often these texts have been discussed only as a part of the great forward march of English literature: examples of the flowering of Renaissance drama, the wit of Metaphysical poetry, the profundity of epic verse or the bite of early Augustan satire. Only recently has such writing started to be informed by any of the developments within contemporary critical theory which have so transformed studies of more contemporary literature in the last twenty years.[2] In part, at least, the lateness of this change might be ascribed to feminist neglect of this century in its reworking of the canon. Typically, women's writing/reading/feminist literary criticism courses have seen 'women's writing' as starting in the eighteenth century, usually with Jane Austen or with Mary Wollstonecraft, sometimes with less well-known names such as Sarah Fielding and Charlotte Smith. Seventeenth-century women writers such as Aphra Behn or Katherine Philips remain relatively well referenced but frequently unstudied, partly, no doubt, because so much of their writing is still out of print, though the fact that it is out of print is largely due to the paucity of demand for it from within teaching institutions. The mere inclusion of some of these women-authored seventeenth-century texts within the curriculum would in itself, then, counter the continuing impression that there was no women's writing of note before the mid-eighteenth century.

More recently, however, feminist interventions in seventeenth-century studies have begun to change this picture.[3] Part of a more general concern to question the constitution of the literary canon and the values embedded within it,[4] this represents a challenge not only by reviewing the date by which 'women's writing' can be said to have existed (and thereby questioning the whole notion of 'starting dates'), but also by necessitating a re-evaluation of the notion of 'literature' itself. The inclusion of writing by women such as Behn or Philips may occasion a revision of the prevailing definitions and characterisations of seventeenth-century literary genres such as drama and poetry, but it leaves the generic base and status quo of literary studies intact. However, the inclusion of texts by women from the radical religious sects (a body of writing which constituted the majority of women's published writings in the seventeenth century) would extend the challenge to the established canon and cur-riculum still further by necessitating a questioning of just what kinds of writing constitute 'literature': what happens to the canon if we include not only the drama, poetry and romances of the seventeenth century, but also the tracts, prophecies and spiritual autobiographies that formed such a major part of women's published output of this time? Such writing has usually been excluded from literary consideration on a whole range of grounds: it is ephemeral, it is political, it is religious, it is too topical, too inaccessible, it is not 'good' writing: in short, it is not recognisable as the stuff of 'great literature' on which literary studies have come to depend. Even some apologists of seventeenth-century women's writing at times rather sheepishly suggest that while such texts might hold historical and political interest, they have a limited amount to offer on a 'literary' level; even Germaine Greer, in the introduction to her anthology of seventeenth-century women's poetry, describes 'the women who *tried* to write poetry in the century of Donne, Milton, and Dryden' as 'untrained, ill-equipped, isolated and vulnerable' (Greer *et al.* 1988: 1; my emphasis). Such res-ponses demonstrate the endurance of the notion of the literary canon, a desire for certain boundaries to be drawn around the object of study, and a continuing search for criteria by which literary value can be assessed and established.

The literary canon has been the foundation on which the edifice of 'English literature' has been built and which has supported it as an academic subject through

3

most of the twentieth century. From the inception of 'English literature' as an object of curricular study in schools, institutes, colleges and universities in the late nineteenth and early twentieth centuries, definitions of literature drawn from founding fathers and exemplars, such as Matthew Arnold's 'the best that has been known and said in the world, ... the history of the human spirit' (Arnold 1873), or, later, F. R. Leavis's notion of a 'Great Tradition' of supreme and enduring literary geniuses, have informed both the rationale for literary study and the selection of texts that have become the object of that study. Whilst the precise terms and character of these definitions might differ, they could all be said to rely on three fundamental underlying and interconnected criteria by which the status of a piece of 'literature' could be judged: its qualities of transcendence, of universality, and of endurance.

For a text to be considered truly great, a 'classic', and therefore worthy of critical attention, traditional literary studies have required that it produce feelings of transcendence in the reader. What this is usually taken to refer to is some kind of profound experience which takes 'man' beyond his everyday context and confronts him with the essence of human existence. This is effected through the generation of intense emotions which connect the reader with the heights, the depths and the limits of experience, enabling him to leave behind the mundane, routine and trivial details of material life. Truly 'great literature' thus reaches not just the intellect, or even the emotions, but somehow speaks to and enriches our souls, confirming our place in the order of things. In this way literature, like other forms of art, has been one means of experiencing 'the sublime': that combination of fear and awe which connects us to an unrepresentable sense of divine and natural majesty. Texts which qualify for such acclaim do so through the author's masterly compositional powers: words are combined through the inspired and imaginative exercise of the author's genuis, which allows him to move and inspire, rather than just to describe or inform. Such literary power is the enviable property of the chosen few; it is not a skill to be learnt, but a gift to be nurtured.[5]

Such texts (and their authors) are not only praised by traditional literary critics for their transcendent qualities, but also, and consequently, for the universality of their greatness. Dealing as they do in the common currency of human universals, they speak to experiences which are said to unite humankind, dissolving superficial, local and insignificant cultural differences. Such universals are said to include not only emotions such as love, hate, desire, jealousy, loss, sorrow and fear, which may be engendered by and represented in the text itself, but also to refer to metaphenomena such as 'Truth' and 'Beauty' which the text both captures and for which it inspires reverence. The true measure of the universality of great literature is the extent to which it stands the test of time. The claim upon which these ideas about such literature are based is that the recognition of its greatness will continue beyond the life of its author, and indeed for centuries to come. Thus, endurance is seen to be the final confirmation of the literary value of a great piece of writing.

According to these criteria, none of the texts discussed in this book would be likely to qualify as literary works worthy of sustained critical attention. Despite the fact that many of them deal with issues of enduring and, according to the above criteria, even 'universal' significance, such as liberty, justice and godliness, they nevertheless fall outside the remit of the traditional literary canon. The reason for this is both because they are female-authored (so few being seen to rise above the disqualifying sex of their authors[6]), and because they are considered too topical and ephemeral. They speak very much from a particular place and to a specific audience. The context of their production could not contrast more starkly with the Romantic myth of literary creativity: these are texts written from within a collective movement, not composed by the solitary genius in his garret. Moreover, the forms they take do not conform to the traditional genres which have come to comprise the canon of seventeenth-century writing: poetry and drama. Instead, as I shall detail later in this chapter, they take the form of spiritual autobiography, prophecy and conversion narratives.

The limits of the traditional literary canon begin to become clear when considering the exclusion of such a proliferation of diverse and innovative forms of writing. The texts discussed in this book constitute a wide-ranging and substantial body of seventeenth-century writing which, taken together, transforms the traditional picture of textual production at this time. Indeed, their forms and their subjects might be read as a challenge to the boundaries which have been erected around the canonical literary genres. Limiting the seventeenth-century literary remit to poetry and drama rules out of bounds a whole range of texts whose conventions have not been canonised and whose forms are therefore unfamiliar to the twentieth-century critic. Recent challenges to the generic boundaries of the canon have criticised the restricted generic principle which has reproduced a rather conservative version of English literature. Instead, such critics have argued for the inclusion of texts such as autobiography within literary studies. The success of such challenges has opened up the space for studies such as this to be included within this much more pluralistic version of English literature.

As well as the generic exclusions which characterised canon formations for so long, the identification of 'the literary' with 'imaginative' writing, and hence as distinct from overtly political or religious texts, has also functioned to establish a particular notion of classic texts. Even literary critics writing of the seventeenth century – a period in which religion was so integral to the imaginative possibilities of the era, and indeed which constituted a key site of political struggle – have traditionally maintained a clear distinction between literary, religious and political writings, dealing with the latter two categories, if at all, in terms of their 'literary' qualities. More recently, however, critics have begun to initiate debate about the appropriateness of such retrospective classifications, questioning the criteria whereby these designations of the literary have been demarcated. In this respect, it becomes pertinent to ask the following questions. Why should Shakespeare's history plays, with their overt concern to construct a fitting genealogy for the glories of the reign of Elizabeth I, or his Roman plays, with their direct and unmistakable political commentaries, be accepted as being at the heart of English literature, whilst sectarian texts are excluded on the basis of their political character? Why are Ben Jonson's highly topical social comedies, dealing as they do in the specificities – and the argot – of Jacobean city life, endowed with literary value, when sectarian writings have been excluded

5

precisely on the basis of their topicality and the 'difficulty' of their idiom? Why are the devotional poems of John Donne seen as literary masterpieces, when sectarian writings are dismissed as being of a narrowly religious interest?

All these questions point to the problem of how the canon legitimates its authority and justifies its inclusions and exclusions. We might highlight the ways in which the literary values of transcendence, universality and endurance are deeply embedded within a very particular cultural construction of taste. Denying their own cultural and historical specificities, literary critics have turned their judgements of what constitutes 'Truth and Beauty' into would-be objective criteria by appealing to notions of universality and enduring worth. Those keen to open up the canon for critical and ideological inspection have stressed the extent to which its arbitrators have avoided questions of their own cultural construction and of their investments in particular representations of the world. Is it a coincidence that those authors elevated to canonical heights bear a remarkable resemblance, in terms of their social status, to their judges? Why are certain groups of people more fully represented in the canon than others? Is this a sign of their inherently superior powers of creativity, or rather yet another indication of an exercise of power over cultural taste and judgements?

In relation to the seventeenth century, I shall argue that the definitions of litera-ture, religion and politics need to be carefully examined, and the rigid distinctions between them called into question. In one sense, the case for the intensely religious and political character of seventeenth-century 'literature' can be made quite simply by reference to a few well-known canonical texts. The 'political' character of Shake-speare's history and Roman plays has already been noted, as has the religious character of much of Donne's poetry. To these we could add, under the 'political' heading, Spenser's *Faerie Queene* (1589-96), Marvell's 'An Horatian Ode upon Cromwell's Return from Ireland' (1650), or Dryden's 'Absalom and Achitophel' (1681), and, under the 'religious' heading, much of the work of Vaughan, Herbert and Milton, and also Butler's *Hudibras* (1663-78). This list alone highlights how certain manifestations of political or religious concerns have long been acceptable within the canon, provided that they are recognisably 'literary' in their form and style.

Yet even these classifications begin to alert us to the other side of these problem-atic categorisations: namely, the distinction between the categories 'religion' and 'politics' themselves. Milton, for example, could have been included just as easily under the 'political' as under the 'religious' heading, and not only for his overtly political prose writings such as 'Areopagitica' (1644), 'Tenure of Kings and Magis-trates' (1649) and 'Eikonoklastes' (1649), but also for those very same works that are classifiable as 'religious', such as 'Paradise Lost' (1667), 'Paradise Regained' (1671) and 'Samson Agonistes' (1671), for these have been widely read as extended allegori-cal treatments of Milton's analysis of, and response to, the failure of the revolution-ary decades to transform permanently the English social, political and religious order (Hill 1993: 32). This mingling of religion and politics is by no means exceptional; indeed, the notion of a distinction between the two had little meaning until the later years of the seventeenth century. Until then, the two were seen as aspects of the same concern: that is, with the fulfilment of God's plans for his people. There were certainly debates and disputes about the precise character of that plan, about the best way to effect it, about the correct interpretation of various indicators of God's wishes, and these took place within contexts that we would now designate as both 'religious' – such as in sermons or other devotional writings – and 'political' – such as in parliamentary debate or petitions presented to parliament. As Christopher Hill has suggested, it was not so much that religion and politics informed each other, but that together they comprised a single discourse:

> when scholars laboriously demonstrate that Levellers or Milton were 'primarily motivated by religon', they have proved no more than that these thinkers lived in the seventeenth century. Then the Bible was the source of virtually all ideas; it supplied the idiom in which men and women discussed them. Hobbes and Filmer used the language of the Bible no less than Levellers or Milton or Winstanley. Jesuits and radical Parliamentarians alike defended their causes with Biblical arguments. To say that the English Revolution was about religion is tautologous; it took place in the seventeenth century. (Hill 1993: 34)

Religion, then, was the foundational discourse on which politics – or economics, or science, or history – was predicated. The struggles and events of the seventeenth century which we would probably characterise now as 'political' – the civil wars of the 1640s, the formation of the New Model Army, the execution of Charles I in 1649, the accession to power of Cromwell through the early 1650s, the restoration of Charles II to the throne in 1660 – are all articulated through the language of religion. The king was not only head of state, but also 'defender of the faith', head of the Church of England. His power to rule was accorded him by God himself, through 'the divine right of kings', a power which not only justified his position and actions in relation to the state but also was thought to give him the power to heal scrofula, by means of 'the king's touch'. Cromwell justified the severance of relations with Charles I through reference to the Bible (Hill 1993: 33), and drew on the prophecies of the books of Daniel and of Revelation in his inaugural speech to Parliament in 1653. It is, therefore, confusing, not to say profoundly misleading, to try to separate and compartmentalise the discourses of religion and politics; they were one and the same.

To call religion a foundational discourse, however, is not to say that it was monolithic, speaking with only one voice. Religion spoke in, and was spoken in, many voices, discussing, debating, disputing, challenging and vilifying each other. What was at issue was God's plan for the world and for his people: what kind of society was closest to his vision? Was it a strictly hierarchical and demarcated one, or was it one in which the only distinctions were spiritual rather than social, not between rich and poor, men and women, master and servant, the educated and uneducated, but between the godly and the ungodly? The king's answer to these questions was not the same as that of Cromwell, nor was Cromwell's the same as that of all the different groupings within Parliament, or within the army. Most significant in terms of this book, however, was the proliferation of religious groups, now generally known as 'radical sects',[7] in the middle years of the seventeeth century, whose answers to these questions in some senses could be said to be in agreement, whilst in others were at odds with each other's priorities and understandings. I shall explore in more detail in Chapter 2 some of the commonalities between the various sects; however, for those readers unfamiliar with these groups, I want now to sketch out the origins and characteristics of those sects most important for this study: the Independents, the Baptists, the Fifth Monarchists, and the Quakers.[8]

Whilst it was not until the 1640s that these groups could be said to have proliferated, the first Independent congregation is actually credited with having been established in London as early as 1616, although other separatist congregations had existed since the reign of Elizabeth. 'Independency' was a loosely applied, generic name under which a number of different separatist congregations were grouped, but this term did not so much indicate a federation as serve as a catch-all for a collection of splinter groups, with different and sometimes opposing priorities, interpretations, and emphases. In common with each other, though, were their arguments that the state should have no power in ecclesiastical matters, and that each congregation should be separate, managing its own affairs without the interference of external, national ecclesiastical bodies. Their stress on the spiritual equality of all allowed some women to debate these issues in print and sometimes to preach.

The General and the Particular Baptists have, despite their similar names, quite distinct origins and histories. The General Baptists originated from exiled separatist groups in Holland; they believed that Christ died for all, not just an 'elect': a select few chosen by God for salvation. More numerous were the Particular Baptists, who arose from splits within an Independent church in the 1630s, and held a Calvinistic belief in restricted atonement: only the elect, foreordained by God, would be saved. Generally, both groups were opposed to infant baptism, believing the only true baptism was through immersion, freely chosen by the individual. This in itself was subversive of a state church, for it denied that every child born was automatically a member of the Church of England; this in turn meant that they opposed the tithing system which supported the national church. Congregations were still self-governing, so that it is difficult to generalise on such matters as their attitudes to women preachers and writers. However, the Baptists relied the most heavily of all the sects on a literal interpretation of the Bible, and thus were tied most tightly by the scriptural strictures against women's public spiritual activity.

The Fifth Monarchist movement had its origins in the millenarian ideas circulating in the 1640s, predicting the imminent second coming of Christ and the establishing of the New Jerusalem on earth, or, more precisely, in England. Most importantly, these beliefs involved a notion of the centrality of prophecy, the reading and interpreting of the Scriptures as a guide to the understanding of current and future events (see below for fuller discussion of prophecy). The movement began to gain momentum in 1651, when a number of prominent Baptists and Independents drew up a list of objectives and beliefs. They argued for non-hierarchical organisation amongst the saints – God's elect – and took as a basis for action a literal interpretation of the biblical prophecies of Daniel and Revelation. This entailed belief not only in the imminent arrival of King Jesus, but also in the duty of the saints to eliminate any hindrances to this event, using physical force if necessary. This sanctioning of

8

the use of violence (rather than any actual manifestations of violence) also contributed to the widespread alarm and opposition to the movement. They were at their
most influential in 1653, when there were a number of Fifth Monarchist sympathisers in the so-called 'Barebones Parliament'. After Parliament's dissolution at the end
of that year, Fifth Monarchists continued to voice their opposition to Cromwell and
the Protectorate, but after two unsuccessful uprisings in 1657 and 1661, the movement declined and had disappeared by the end of the century.

The Quakers originated in the north of England in the early 1650s. By 1656 they
had moved south and gained in numbers and influence, particularly in Wales,
Gloucestershire and Cornwall. They came together principally from the New Model
Army and from other radical groups such as the Ranters and Baptists. It was only
after 1660 that the movement took on the quietist and pacifist stance now associated
with Quakerism, before this being one of the most radical and militant groups. They
argued against tithes, the supremacy of the clergy and the restoration of the monarchy, as well as refusing hat honour[9] and insisting on using 'thou' (rather than the
more respectful 'you') to all, irrespective of their position in the social hierarchy.
They relied on the 'inner light' of God within them as their ultimate guide, above
even the scriptures, and this enabled women to justify their writing, prophesying and
travelling, despite the disapproval and hostility of many men. Unlike most of the
other sects, the Quakers survived the Restoration and the persecution that followed
it, albeit in a more restrictive and conservative spirit: later Quaker women's writings
show a much greater concern with the internal workings of the movement and its
ability to retain its members than did texts from before 1660, when there was a much
greater tendency to debate such matters as tithes, the clergy and the irrelevance of
the universities.

These sects and groupings were notable, to a greater or lesser degree, for the
numbers of women active within them. Bernard Capp, in his misleadingly entitled
The Fifth-Monarchy Men (1972), notes that 'in the church lists which have survived,
women easily outnumbered men' (Capp 1972: 82); more than 7,000 Quaker women
put their names to a petition against tithes presented to parliament in 1659 (Forster
1659: 1); and it seems that high numbers of women were common in other sects as
well, commentators often noting that they made up of 'chiefly women' or 'most silly
women' (Thomas 1958: 45). Nor was women's involvement in religious dissent
something entirely new; there are numerous instances of women in the fifteenth and
sixteenth centuries being brought to trial for their religious activities (Thomson
1965). The innovatory aspect, therefore, was not that women were involved in the
sects, but on the one hand the scale of that involvement, and on the other hand the
textual output that it generated.[10]

The centrality and diversity of religious practice to seventeenth-century culture,
therefore, cannot be overestimated; moreover, its impact upon the forms of writing
available to women at this time was extraordinarily significant, and requires some
readjustment from the late twentieth-century reader approaching the texts discussed
in this book. For the majority of us in Britain now, religion, or more specifically
Christianity, tends to be seen as either outdated and irrelevant to contemporary

circumstances, or as functioning as a reassuring but rather marginal insurance policy against the terrors of disease, distress and death, or as a hopelessly conservative rationalisation of worldly suffering. When organised religion does intervene in socio-political debate, as in the Church of England's contentious publication *Faith in the City* (1985), the advice of politicians to clergymen is, by and large, to tell them to mind their own business; religion, quite clearly, is now not expected to meddle in public affairs. Such a separation of politics from religion forms a stark contrast, almost a polar opposite, to the circumstances of the mid-seventeenth century, and it is one of the tenets of this study (and one to which I return in more detail in Chapter 2) that the texts under consideration here cannot be understood outside this context in which religion was the organising principle of social and cultural life.

This is important not so much because these circumstances *contextualise* the sectarian writings, but because they are *constitutive* of them: they produced a range of different kinds of text that are no longer familiar to us, and which, as I have already suggested, do not conform to the conventions of the literary canon as it has been formed, and, just as the sects themselves warranted some introduction, so too do the writings produced within them. The texts with which I am concerned here can be grouped under such generic titles as prophecy, spiritual autobiography, conversion narrative, scriptural commentaries, and general exhortations, warnings and advice. Whilst these are no more watertight than any other generic categorisations, they do none the less allow readers to map out and classify the textual territory.

Prophecy is perhaps the most complicated of these categories, for it can be said both to subsume all the other genres, and to describe the more familiar kind of prediction that we now think of as 'prophecy'. As Diane Purkiss has written, for sectaries 'prophecy was any utterance produced by God through human agency' (Purkiss 1992a: 139); in this, they were following the scriptural deployment of the term: 'As he spake by the mouth of his holy prophets, which have been since the world began' (Luke 1:70). What was spoken by the prophet was 'not so much the mere prediction of happenings in the near future', but visions of 'the certainty of the overruling of the universe on the part of God' (Clow 1962: 299). As I shall demonstrate in subsequent chapters, virtually all sectarian writing by women – whether autobiography, warning or prediction – conformed to this definition: it was glossed as the work of God, with the human author as no more than a medium for its dissemination. All this writing, therefore, was in this sense 'prophetic', and indeed the consequent status of its authors as 'prophets' was highly significant for their representations of themselves, their justifications for their writing, and their relationship to religious discourse. As prophets, they were uttering God's word verbatim; as women, their lowliness, their irrationality and their despised condition made them (in scriptural terms) closer to God, more likely to be chosen by him to speak.[11] In relation to the figure of the author as prophet, then, femininity could, unusually for the seventeenth century, function to legitimate and authorise women's public and spiritual activities.

However, as well as this broad interpretation of 'prophecy', there were also writings by sectarian women that conformed more closely to the definition of prophecy as prediction, and it is in this sense that I have used the word to designate a generic category. Predictions might concern the future of an individual (such as Cromwell), a particular community (such as the inhabitants of certain towns, such as Oxford, Cambridge or Aylesbury) or a particular group (such as priests). Such predictions, however, relate closely to the more general definition of prophecy in that they were not random prognostications, but were systematically rooted in the word of God, in scriptural analysis and interpretation, which were then carefully related to contemporary circumstances and events. In Anna Trapnel's *The Cry of a Stone* (1654), for example, she predicts that God had 'finished the greatest business that he would employ him [Cromwell] in' (Trapnel 1654a: 10), and in Mary Cary's *The Little Horn's Doom and Downfall* (1651) she identifies Charles I with the 'little horn' amongst the ten horns of the fourth beast of Daniel's vision (see Daniel 7, and Appendix A in this volume). Prophecies were sometimes uttered verbally in the first instance, and transcribed by an onlooker (*The Cry of a Stone*, for example, or Elinor Channel's *A Message from God* (1654), reproduced in Appendix B); in some of these cases, they were accompanied by an ecstatic trance, in which divinely inspired and hence legitimating state the words of the prophecy were uttered. Other prophecies (such as those of Mary Cary) originated in a written form. In all cases, however, references and allusions to the Bible structure and justify the predictions being made.

Prophecy, in both the broader and the narrower sense, forms an important element of what I described above as a separate generic category: that of texts offering warnings and advice, and promising retribution unless speedy repentance on the part of the readers/hearers follows. The vast majority of these kinds of prophecies were written by the early Quakers; many are very short broadsheets or pamphlets, no more than two or three pages, and their admonitory character is encapsulated in such titles as Priscilla Cotton and Mary Cole's *To the Priests and People of England* (1655) (reproduced in Appendix C in this volume), Grace Barwick's *To all present Rulers* (1659), Hester Biddle's *Wo to thee City of Oxford* (1655) and *A Warning from The Lord God* (1660), Mary Adams's *A Warning To The Inhabitants of England* (1676), Ann Gargill's *A Warning To all the World* (1656), Elizabeth Hooton *et al.*'s *False Prophets and false Teachers Described* (1652), and Dorothy White's *An Alarum Sounded Forth* (1662). These texts, even more than the prophecies to which I referred above, engage with a specifically identified audience or readership – anything from 'all present rulers' to 'all the world'. As dependent on biblical authority for their messages as any of the other prophecies, these texts have an unambiguous mission to warn these various constituencies of what will befall them if they do not turn away from their sinful ways and towards God. Whilst these texts are prophetic in both senses – their authors claim them to be the word of God, and they interpret the scriptures in such a way as to authorise a particular prediction for the future – I have distinguished them from other prophetic texts in order to highlight their directly confrontational character. Whilst the prophecies of Trapnel and Cary, for example, are lengthy works, comprising many forms and styles, at times apologetic, at others angry or celebratory, sometimes written in verse, sometimes including passages of spiritual autobiography and conversion narrative, these texts are in prose, each tending to have one key, and very clear, message to communicate. This is not to deny the complexity of these texts: as I shall explore later in the book, the ways in which the reader is addressed, for example, or in which the author-figure is constructed, are as multi-layered as in any other of these genres. It is, however, to suggest that this particular group of texts has enough in common in terms of form, tone and address to distinguish it as a distinct kind of prophetic writing.

The other two main genres with which I will be concerned – the spiritual autobiography and the conversion narrative – are, similarly, highly interrelated. The principal distinction between the two is that the former originated as a written text, whilst the latter generally refers to a spoken testimony given before the congregation – usually Baptist or Independent – of which the speaker was seeking membership. These spoken conversion narratives were sometimes collected and published by the minister of the congregation (such John Rogers's *Ohel or beth-shemesh* (1653) or Henry Walker's *Spiritual Experiences of Sundry Believers* (1653)). When accounts of conversion were written by the subject as longer narratives, they tend to be referred to as spiritual autobiographies. The distinction between the two, however, is once again not absolute, and the term 'conversion narrative' is at times used to refer to the written spiritual autobiography. It is unhelpful, then, to seek to distinguish absolutely the one from the other, particularly since all these accounts followed, at greater or lesser length, the same narrative trajectory. The author recorded his or her journey through sin, false confidence, doubt, conviction, faith, temptation and assurance, deploying a conventional framework that gave a structure and chronology to a range of events and experiences. Moreover, adherence to these conventions confirmed and valorised the godliness of the author: 'For an experience to be accepted as a genuine guarantee of salvation, it would have to fall within a specific pattern: otherwise the conversion might be a false one, and the sinner caught in the hypocrisy of a false confidence in their salvation' (Hobby 1988: 66). Of the texts discussed in this book, Jane Turner's *Choice Experiences* (1653) is a key example of the spiritual autobiography, whilst Joan Vokins's *God's Mighty Power Magnified* (1691), a much later account, follows this conventional structure in its early part, whilst incorporating into later sections a number of the author's letters to her family and fellow Friends written on her travels. Anna Trapnel's prophetic *The Cry of a Stone* also conforms to the pattern in its account of her coming to faith.

This returns me to the fact that none of these generic labels, for all their usefulness as broad-brush classifications, is absolute; all the texts considered here are, to some extent at least, hybrids. Trapnel's writings are mixes of prophecy, autobiography, admonition and warning; many of the prophecies discussed in this book, such as Elinor Channel's and many of the Quakers', mix autobiograpical elements with their biblical interpretations and predictions; Dorothy Waugh's short account (included as Appendix D in this volume) is autobiographical, but does not follow the typical generic pattern of the spiritual autobiography, concerned instead to record, and draw out the spiritual significance of, just one incident from her life; Jane Turner's spiritual autobiography combines accounts of her own experiences with careful scriptural reference. This hybridity is a reminder of the provisional character of any generic designation. With respect to these forms of writing, however, a careful introduction to the genres in question (however qualified they might be) is crucial for the twentieth-century reader who is unlikely to be familiar with such forms.

The purpose, then, of this brief detour into the typicalities of these distinct yet overlapping forms is twofold: first, to familiarise the reader with the kinds of writing under consideration in this book; and secondly, to pinpoint precisely the inappropriateness of applying existing canonical judgements in respect of a large body of women's writing from the seventeenth century. Indeed, the limits of the canon may be nowhere so clear as here. For how are we to judge the merits of such work by the criteria of a canon which has not begun to address the 'value' of such forms of writing? How might we satisfactorily define 'the literary' (not to mention rank the comparative 'greatness' of its component texts) if 'the literary' itself defies such rigid separation from other aspects of seventeenth-century culture? Whereas religion, politics and literature are categories whose separation may be convenient for twentieth-century classification, this is by no means the case in the context of the seventeenth century.

It is my contention that these forms of women's writing from the radical sects both challenge the conventional understanding of literary genres and cannot be understood outside the very specific contexts of their production. One of the yardsticks of canonical judgement has been the very reverse of this: a text's perceived autonomy from its context of production has been seen as a mark of its transcendence, its occupation of a plane higher than the mundane and material. The very enmeshment of certain texts in the circumstances of their days, such as Restoration comedies or Victorian melodramas, has in itself been enough to relegate these writings to the margins of the canon. This has, of course, necessitated the active denial of the glaringly apparent social and political origins of certain of the 'classics', such as the epics of Milton and the history plays of Shakespeare. Just as New Historicism has insisted on the importance of refusing this asocial and apolitical reading of, in particular, Renaissance drama, I would suggest that, similarly, we need to make sense of these sectarian writings as a part of the cultural specificities of their moment.

It has long been argued, for example, that the proliferation of autobiography in the seventeenth century has its roots on the one hand in the Protestant emphasis on the responsibility of each believer for his or her salvation, and in particular in the spiritual self-examination required by Puritan ministers, and on the other hand in the associated rise in bourgeois individualism in the same period. What, though, of the 'self' constructed in these autobiographical accounts? Do we find a solitary and autonomous individual reflecting on the condition of his or her soul? Do we find representations of fixed and stable identities, weathering spiritual storms but remaining essentially unchanged by them? Or do we find more relational models of the self, contingent upon interaction with the divine, certainly, but also with the human: family, friends, community? And if so, what does this do to our sense of a 'core self' running through and holding together an autobiographical text? And, importantly for this study, what about the gendering of the self? In all contexts, whether spiritual, social or political, differential notions of gender were key; so in what ways was

13

this binarism written into the 'selves' represented? Furthermore, how does the sectarian emphasis on community, on 'brothers and sisters', impact on Protestant notions of individual responsibility, and on the autobiographical project?

Similar questions can be framed around the 'prophetic' texts. Whilst these writings may be quite expicitly rooted in the political and religious circumstances of the time, they constitute a very particular kind of site for the examination of the interrelation of the social and the spiritual. Do we conclude that one is 'really' just a guise for the other, or do we instead have to find a new way to conceptualise this religio-political discourse? In what ways were the changing political circumstances – the execution of Charles I, for example, or the rise of Cromwell, or the anti-sectarian legislation of the post-Restoration period – written into these prophecies? How does the 'self' posited in autobiography function in the more explicitly social and dialogic genre of prophecy, in particular when the two genres merge with each other? How did ideas about the significance of gender impact on these writings, in comparison with their impact on more explicitly autobiographical texts?

And throughout all these considerations, we need to locate not only the texts under consideration, but also make explicit our own contexts and agendas. In writing this book I have been wary of the potential pitfalls of a search for a transhistorical dialogue, such as projection and anachronism, and have attempted to locate texts and readings in such a way as to argue for the importance of seventeenth-century women's writing, without simply subsuming it within a universalising literary project. We need to remain aware of our own, and various, stakes in investigating these questions. As literary critics, we need to recognise that the kinds of questions that we ask of these texts are as rooted in our own interests and concerns, as the genesis of the texts themselves is rooted in those of their own time. As feminists, we need in particular to be conscious of the temptation of searching for a genealogy, a history: the desire for feminist foremothers is beguiling but fraught with untenable premises, of unsubstantiated continuities and of the denial of just the kind of historical location for which this book is arguing. Moreover, for some readers, the combination of these apparently disparate perspectives and discourses might seem to constitute a rather risky enterprise: what could the two worlds, of seventeenth-century devotional and doctrinal texts and twentieth-century feminist literary criticism, have in common?

This book works through the implications of precisely this question. Indeed, in the next chapter I go on to explore in greater detail the debate about the historical (dis)continuities in the meaning of the category 'woman', and raise questions about some of the problems with historical contextualisations which may, more or less, explicitly, assume a continuity across time in the meanings of gendered categories. How might it be possible to avoid *both* the pitfalls of straightforward ahistoricism, through which these texts might be decontextualised and read purely in the light of contemporary feminist concerns, *and* some of the limits of an empiricism which ignores the textuality of historical constructions of the past? Having situated my project in relation to one of the key debates within feminist historical and literary studies, I then offer a detailed analysis of the discourses through which femininity was constructed in seventeenth-century England. Arguing that apparently disparate notions of femininity were rooted in a common construction of women's bodily inferiority, I analyse a number of sources, including legal handbooks, domestic conduct books and popular political pamphlets. Whilst such discursive representations designate a constrained and docile place to femininity, some space for negotiation can none the less be found within the domain of spirituality. Here, I develop Riley's argument (1988) that the 'ungendered soul' opens up the possibility of women's participation in certain forms of social communication through religious beliefs and practices, thus transforming the rather monolithic and inescapable version of gender relations suggested within the above discourses.

In Chapter 3, I consider the production of women's writing in the context of its cultural prohibition: if writing was seen to be immodest and reprehensible (as outlined in the previous chapter), in what conditions and with what justifications did women break the prescribed silence, and speak, write and publish? Such a question involves an engagement with theories of silence and prohibition. The chapter investigates feminist work on this subject, highlighting both the usefulness and the limits of such critiques of women's silence in patriarchal culture for an understanding of the problems faced by seventeenth-century women writers, and considers a number of examples of the ways in which women negotiated such prohibitions. I then turn to rather different theoretical models, which argue for the productiveness (as opposed to the straightforward repressiveness) of textual and extratextual silences. Whilst these extend our understanding of how silence operates in relation to writing, they do not do so in relation to the question of gender. The rest of this chapter thus discusses how such approaches might be extended to take account of gender. I go on to consider the meaning of silence in a specifically seventeenth-century context through the analysis of a number of seventeenth-century texts, asking questions about the place of gender in our understanding of the significance of speech, silence and writing in this context, and relate the silences that I have identified running through these texts back to the conflict between the 'unequal bodies' and 'equal souls' discussed in Chapter 2.

Chapter 4 moves on to address a debate consequential to questions of silence: namely, authorship. Since Barthes pronounced the death of the author in the 1970s, the discipline of literature has wrestled with questions of the ownership and meaning of literary production. This questioning has opened up a disciplinary and political can of worms concerning the authenticity of the self and its mediation in textual representations. Having evaluated these debates and problems at the beginning of the chapter, I then relate them to a consideration of seventeenth-century women's writing from the radical sects. Looking at a wide range of examples, I examine the shifting and elusive textual presence of the female author-figure in these writings. Central to this discussion is the repeated and puzzling (for contemporary criticism) denial of authorial responsibility in the writings by women in the sects. How do such denials of authorship function, and how can we account for their prevalence in these writings? And if the authors deny responsiblity for their writings, with whom does this responsibility lie? By means of an analysis which demonstrates the relationship between gender, religion and writing, I explore possible resolutions to these questions.

Next, Chapter 5, with its concern with language, style and textuality, engages with crucial debates about the relationship between representation and 'reality' which have been so radically challenged by recent structuralist and poststructuralist interventions in literary studies. More specifically, it focuses on issues of language and representation in the seventeenth century. The politics of language took on a new symbolic significance after the Restoration, with calls for a clarification of style both in accordance with the needs of 'the new science' and as a guard against the linguistic, spiritual and political excesses of the preceding years of the revolution and commonwealth. Clarifying expression was seen to be a desirable and stabilising political end in itself, and contemporary critics criticised the sectaries' style as 'feminine' and manipulative. These debates formed part of a 'revolution' in the perception of the relationship beween language and the material world, the texts of these sectarian women writers exemplifying the tension of conflicting under-standings and raising questions about its gendered significance. In the light of these debates, I examine how this changing linguistic style helped these writers negotiate the problematic act of writing. I conclude that both these phenomena facilitated the relocation of responsibility for writing with God identified in the previous chapter.

Chapter 6 completes the narrative trajectory of literary production with a discus-sion of its reception: how were the texts of sectarian women writers received, and how did their authors anticipate their reception? In this chapter, I examine the almost uniform hostility encountered by women writers from the sects, and identify the authorship of the texts, rather than their subjects, as the underlying common denominator in relation to these reactions. Moreover, in anticipating this hostility, these texts might be read through Bakhtin's notion of 'hidden polemic' to be in dialogue with condemnatory masculine readers and discourses. I end this chapter with an exemplification of the ways in which these texts both negotiate this oppro-brium in an attempt to defuse its power prior to its articulation, and also covertly address a sympathetic sectarian audience.

Finally, in Chapter 7, I bring together the the main arguments of the previous chapters by means of a detailed reading of one text not discussed in the rest of the book. Using Priscilla Cotton and Mary Cole's *To the Priests and People of England* (1655) (a short pamphlet reproduced in full in Appendix C), I exemplify the impli-cations of these arguments by offering a thorough textual analysis which enables the reader to appreciate the interconnections between the theories developed in each of the preceding chapters. Arguing for the impossibility of understanding this text outside the historical location of its production, I demonstrate the changing meanings of authorship, textuality and reception. In particular, I show the speci-ficities of the gendered meaning of such concepts at a time when religious discourses played a central role in defining notions of femininity, writing and the production of texts.

The appendices provide a selection of edited and footnoted extracts from a range of the texts discussed in this book, in order that the reader may have direct access to these writings and test out more fully the theories and analyses offered in the book. Given the relative scarcity of the primary texts under consideration in this project, the inclusion of a range of seventeenth-century women's writings here proved necessary to guarantee the availability of such work to readers. The contrast between writing a book about these texts as opposed to one concerned with accepted canonical works is thus drawn into sharp focus by precisely such a necessity.

It is not only the subject of the book, then, that addresses the frustrations of a narrow canon, but also its structure (and in particular its appendices) which itself demonstrates the continuing importance of feminist interventions into definitions of 'English literature'. This book, together with a growing number of others,[12] seeks to expand seventeenth-century studies and to open up definitions of the literary to critical scrutiny. Perhaps future feminist scholars writing about the seventeenth century might find themselves surrounded by easily available primary texts by women writers of this period. I look forward to such a time, and hope that this book plays its part in hastening its arrival.

2

Configurations of femininity:
the bodies and souls of seventeenth-century women

The researcher of seventeenth-century sectarian women's writing is faced with a dilemma: having identified her 'primary sources' – the prophecies, exhortations or spiritual autobiographies produced by women in the sects – where does she then turn in order to try to make sense of them? Or, more specifically, how might she begin to build up a sense of their authors and the circumstances in which these texts were produced? For, inevitably in a study predicated on notions of *women*'s writing, the concept of the author remains important, though by no means uncomplicated (see Chapter 4); and thus in trying to understand these writings we may also be concerned with who the authors were, how they lived and under what kinds of circumstances they came to write. Furthermore, as well as wanting to find out about the conditions under which women were producing texts, the feminist researcher also needs to convey some idea of what the gender relations were more generally during this period. Where, then, are we to find the 'seventeenth-century women' with whom we are concerned?

Answering this question is not as easy as it might once have seemed. Whilst the long-standing (and, over the years, very productive[1]) aim of feminist history may have been both a 'retrieval' of women from the past – those 'hidden from (patriarchal) history' – and a reshaping of our sense of the past through a gendering of the historical process, many critics have now started to call into question the epistemological basis of some of this kind of historical practice. They have argued that feminist history (whether a social history, political history or literary history) is not a question of 'gaining access' to women in past centuries, for this phrase implies that they have, somewhere, a quantifiable, material reality, to be unearthed through extensive reading, diligent research, immersion in the material. Whilst none would argue with the desirability of such painstaking research practices, there is for many an increasing doubt that they will yield up the 'authentic' defining characteristics of seventeenth-century women and their experiences, allowing us an insider's view of what it meant to be a woman at that time. At issue here are two very different matters. First, the sources that we have are of necessity partial, incomplete, and strange or foreign to us, separated as we are by 350 years of change, whether linguistic, social, economic, political or ideological. Secondly, even if we could clarify the occlusions resulting from this partiality, we would still be left with the immoveable

18

fact that written accounts are always representations, and have a highly complicated relationship with what we might think of as 'history', 'reality' or 'lived experience'. Rather than approaching contemporary seventeenth-century texts as if they offer up straightforward 'facts' about women's lives in the past, then, some recent critics have instead emphasised their *textuality* and have analysed the ways in which this produces particular forms of knowledge about women from previous centuries: for example, in relation to the seventeenth century, they might emphasise that the texts were produced within certain generic conventions; that they were written for particular audiences and not for others; that they drew on and were shaped by particular linguistic patterns, or scriptural narratives, or sectarian arguments; that they engaged with, and were part of, a network of interlocking debates, no element of which is the definitive or authoritative one. From the point of view of constructing a 'literary history', as I am here, the cautions offered by those highlighting textuality (as opposed to facticity) are particularly important. Sensitised to the significance of the textuality of writing, the literary historian is likely to approach such sources (perhaps seen from a more empirical standpoint as 'evidence' or 'facts') with a caution that might stem from a disciplinary concern with the processes of representation itself. By this account, then, history is complicated by the textuality of its sources: rather than these writings providing us with a window through which to look at 'real women' in the past, they are instead revealed as a set of patterns and conventions that tell us as much about the history of writing as about the history of women.

In addition to this, some feminist historians have argued that instead of looking at women in history, we should look at how history has constructed the category of 'women'. This not only requires attention to 'textuality', but further problematises the assumptions about the continuity of the category of women throughout history, and the claims which might be made about them on the basis of current readings of past texts. This move might be characterised as a more poststructuralist approach to the writing of history, premised on the Foucauldian notion of 'discourse':

> A discourse is not a language or a text but a historically, socially, and institutionally specific structure of statements, terms, categories, and beliefs ... Discourse is thus contained or expressed in organisations and institutions as well as in words; all of these constitute texts or documents to be read. (Scott 1988: 35)

This discursive approach suggests that there is no separation between 'reality' and the structures, apparatuses and languages through which we make sense of it: 'Discourses are perhaps best understood as practices that systematically form the objects of which they speak' (Sarup 1988: 70). From this perspective, then, 'reading around' our primary sources would not function to provide us with a 'background' or context for the *real* object of study, the 'writings by seventeenth-century women'; instead, this whole mesh of different discourses – here the texts from the sects, the marriage manuals written by Puritan clergymen, the documents that set out the legal position of women, enclosure riots, popular festivals and rituals, and so on – together *constitute* the object of study. According to this approach, there is no locus for the existence of 'sevententh-century women' other than these discourses. Through an analysis of

19

these discourses, then, it is argued, we can attain specific and localised understandings of gender as a discursive relation in particular places at particular times.

Before relating this specifically to my own object of study, I want first to elaborate
the impact of these theories on feminist history more generally. Some feminist
historians have welcomed the perspectives and possibilities offered by such a discursive approach; Joan Scott, for instance, found that it offered 'a new way of analyzing
constructions of meaning and relationships of power that called unitary, universal
categories into question and historicized concepts otherwise treated as natural (such
as man/woman) or absolute (such as equality or justice)' (Scott 1988: 33-4).

Whilst embracing such deconstructionist readings, which emphasise the contingency of meaning and the fluidity of identity, for the possibity of change that they
seem to offer (if gender identity is not fixed, then maybe we can transform its
meanings in the future), these critics have also been alert to the possibility that such
practices risk throwing out the (feminist) baby with the (humanist) bathwater. Mary
Poovey has expressed concern about what this might mean for feminism:

> To take deconstruction to its logical conclusion would be to argue that 'woman' is *only*
> a social construct that has no basis in nature, that 'woman,' in other words, is a term
> whose definition depends upon the context in which it is being discussed and not upon
> some set of sexual organs or social experiences. This renders the experience women
> have of themselves and the meaning of their social relations problematic, to say the
> least. (Poovey 1988: 52)

Without 'woman' – that is, some kind of concept of a unified category – Poovey
wonders what would happen to our notion of feminism, founded as it is (particularly
in the United States and Britain) both on notions of gender identity and on the
significance of 'women's experiences'.

Some of Poovey's anxieties about the implications of this approach to history for
feminism seem to be exemplified in the writings of other feminist deconstructionist
historians. Denise Riley, for example, questions not only the nature of historical
knowledge but also the usefulness and tenability of 'women' as the feminist object of
study. She suggests that an acceptance of the 'ordinary, innocent-sounding' term
'women' – its grammatical plural form reassuring us that we are acknowledging the
cultural plurality of women, and not making any unsubstantiated generalisations
across the various axes of difference – leads us into a morass of pitfalls and assumptions as dangerous as the banished universalisms contemporary feminists typically
seek to overcome. She sets out her definitions of the term 'women', definitions which
she suggests are obscured or denied by the implications of its general usage:

> To put it schematically: 'women' is historically, discursively constructed, and always
> relatively to other categories which themselves change; 'women' is a volatile collectivity
> in which female persons can be very differently positioned, so that the apparent conti-
> nuity of the subject of 'women' isn't to be relied on; 'women' is both synchronically and
> diachronically erratic as a collectivity, while for the individual, 'being a woman' is also
> inconstant, and can't provide an ontological foundation. (Riley 1988: 1-2)

In a statement that seems to be the fulfilment of the Poovey's prediction of the 'logical conclusion' of feminist deconstructionism, Riley here suggests that perhaps the only way to avoid the lingering convictions about 'women's natural dispositions' that lurk in the contemporary implications of the word 'women' is to 'stand back and announce that there *aren't any* women' (Riley 1988: 2; original emphasis). She defends this as a properly feminist project, involving the careful scrutiny of all definitions of gender, wherever they occur, and asserting that it avoids the Scylla of 'neutral deconstruction' and the Charybdis of a feminism which identifies itself with 'the camp of the lovers of "real women"' (Riley 1988: 3); indeed, she suggests that the 'instabilities of the category ['women'] are the *sine qua non* of feminism' (Riley 1988: 2).

Riley's position is, in a nicely poststructuralist way, both the same as and different from those of other feminist deconstructionist historians. Scott, for example, differs from Riley in arguing that deconstruction is not opposed to other feminist practices, but just an extension of it:

> [Deconstruction] means analyzing in context the way any binary opposition operates, reversing and displacing its hierarchical construction, rather than accepting it as real or self-evident or in the nature of things. In a sense, of course, feminists have been doing this for years. The history of feminist thought is a history of the refusal of the hierarchical construction of the relationship between male and female in its specific contexts and an attempt to reverse or displace its operations. (Scott 1989: 92)

What is new, she argues, is that historians can now *theorise* this practice. Poovey, too, differs from Riley: she insists on the importance of retaining a notion of 'real historical women', and argues that feminism's task is to work through the retention of this notion in relation to poststructuralism: 'The challenge for those of us who are convinced both that real historical women do exist and share certain experiences *and* that deconstruction's demystification of presence makes theoretical sense is to work out some way to think both women and "woman." It isn't an easy task' (Poovey 1988: 52-3).

However, what these historians have in common is a desire to use deconstruction's refusal of notions of stability of identity and historical continuities to feminist ends. Riley, for example, anticipating feminist objections to the dissolution of an identity which many would argue has been the basis for a collective politics, clarifies how deconstructionist history can also be feminist history:

> It's not that our identity is to be dissipated into airy indeterminacy, extinction; instead it is to be referred to the more substantial realms of discursive historical formation. Certainly the indeterminacy of sexual positionings can be demonstrated in other ways, most obviously perhaps by comparative anthropology ... But such work is often relegated to exoticism, while psychoanalytic investigations reside in the confined heats of clinical studies. It is the misleading familiarity of 'history' which can break open the daily naturalism of what surrounds us. (Riley 1988: 5)

Riley argues that her insistence on taking account of the different 'temporalities' of women – the fluctuating definitions, understandings and deployments of the term which mean that '"women" are only sometimes "women"' (Riley 1988: 96) – differs from what she calls a 'Women Through the Ages approach' in that 'nothing is assumed about an underlying continuity of real women, above whose constant bodies changing aerial descriptions dance' (Riley 1988: 7). In practice, she suggests that this engagement with the 'temporality' of women might be undertaken through examining 'the changing relations of "woman" and her variants to the concept of a general humanity'; most pertinently for this study, she suggests looking at the 'history of an increasing sexualisation, in which female persons became held to be virtually saturated with their sex which then invades their rational and spiritual faculties' (Riley 1988: 8).

Poovey similarly makes specific claims for the feminist possibilities of a deconstructionist history. Although she is critical of many aspects of current deconstructionist work (she suggests it is generally politically conservative, and that it refuses to deconstruct and historicise its own processes), she suggests that it can make three key contributions to feminist history. First, deconstruction demystifies and denaturalises categories such as 'nature' and 'gender'; this emphasis 'could enable feminists to write a history of the various contradictions within institutional definitions of woman that would show how these contradictions have opened the possibility for change' (Poovey 1988: 58). Secondly, through challenging oppositional or binary logic (in which everything is seen as inherently either one thing or the other: either male or female, natural or unnatural, radical or conservative), deconstruction 'makes visible the artifice necessary to establish, legislate and maintain hierarchical thinking. Given this emphasis, deconstructive strategies could enable us to chart more accurately the multiple determinants that figure in any individual's social position and (relative) power and oppression' (Poovey 1988: 58). Third, and related to the second point, by revealing binarism as an artificial construct, 'the identity of the two, apparently fixed terms and the rigidity of the "structure" that prevents other possiblities from being formulated could be destabilized'. This would enable us to reconceptualise the workings of 'power' and denaturalise its unequal distribution between different groups (Poovey 1988: 59). She suggests that we need to recognise that binary logic has dictated, and still does, aspects of women's social treatment, but also that, given that these binarisms are arbitrary, that they cannot form a basis for feminist political action of the future:

> Real historical women have been (and are) oppressed, and the ways and means of that oppression need to be analyzed and fought. But at the same time, we need to be ready to abandon the binary thinking that has stabilized women as a group that *could* be collectively (although not uniformly) oppressed. (Poovey 1988: 62)

Scott, too, welcomes deconstruction's refusal of binarism as a potentialy fruitful feminist strategy – in one article, for example, she painstakingly deconstructs the binary opposition of 'equality' and 'difference' and shows how the foundations of this supposed antithesis are untenable (Scott 1988). Further, she suggests that a specifically *feminist* deconstructive history could reconfigure notions of power as they pervade all aspects of the social formation, including not only those discourses that very obviously relate to notions of gender (discourses of the family or sexuality, for example) but also those that at first sight might seem outside the reach of feminist history because of women's non-participation in their workings, such as discourses of government and 'high' politics. Scott argues that all these, because of their reliance on binary oppositions and the way that these are coded as masculine and feminine within their configurations, demand a theorisation of gender based in a deconstructionist feminist history.

How might such theoretical arguments be extended to the subject of our search for what it meant to be a woman writing in the seventeenth-century radical sects? What are the methodological implications of these manifestos for the feminist literary historian? Are the historical and analytical methods, as well as the object of study, implicated by the uses of poststructuralism? With respect to this study, for example, it might be argued that the focus of this project, 'seventeenth-century women writers', is already problematic, since it appears to take as given precisely the group which it should be deconstructing. Furthermore, a 'context' chapter such as this might be seen to reinforce the illusory division between 'real women' and their 'society', reproducing the misconstrued empiricist assumption that the meaning of the category of women can be taken for granted so long as it is made sense of through contextual 'scene-setting', and positing the job of the feminist historian as being to trace the impact of their context on 'women' at a particular historical moment.

The deconstructionist challenge, then, problematises the role of the feminist historian as the archaeologist of the truth about women in the past. Such a perspective can be a welcome one for a researcher burdened with the task of retrieving a comprehensive and overarching truth. Letting go of the truth, and settling for more localised 'truths', or accounts of particular dynamics based on an analysis of certain discourses, can feel like a relief. To see texts as not relating to some absolute external reality, but as *constituting* the meanings of gender – to see discourse as all there is – can help iron out some of the tortuous wrinkles of historical readings. However, for many feminist historians this reconfiguration continues to raise as many questions as it answers: after all, what precisely constitutes the difference between 'context' and 'discourse'? Do feminist historians of the 1990s feel a compulsion to substitute terms such as 'discourse' for those such as 'context' in an attempt to keep up with the debates, whilst not actually changing their methods of analysis? Indeed, looking critically at deconstructive methods, we might ask to what extent and in what ways they differ substantially in their method and their execution from more empirical procedures, even if the overall theoretical perspective motivating their analysis is indeed fundamentally opposed to such empirical accounts. Grounded as they are in the careful reading and analysis of a range of historical documents, they perhaps differ from other kinds of feminist history principally in the specific relating of these readings to particular theoretical questions of epistemology and subjectivity.

Like many others working at this historical juncture, my work combines elements of these different feminist epistemological 'traditions'. Originally motivated by a desire to bring to light and analyse a body of long-forgotten texts – texts whose radical origins and subsequent disappearance from both history and 'literature' seemed to speak to late twentieth-century feminist concerns – I began this project as both archivist and literary critic equipped with skills in textual analysis which might seem well suited to the poststructuralist clarion call: for many of the techniques which a literary critic such as myself brings to historical research are indeed compatible with a desire to highlight the textuality of historical documents and the partiality and contingency of their 'truths'. Furthermore, methods such as 'discourse analysis' (advocated by Riley, Scott and others) might function well in such a project, given my approach which foregrounds the detailed operations of language, power and authority within and around the texts. Later chapters, for example, analyse the ways in which discursive constructions of authors, divine sanctions, apparent prohibitions and spiritual equality function to legitimate particular kinds of knowledge and regulate others.

However, as well as such readings of these texts, my argument about their significance also crucially hinges upon understanding them in relation to the specificities of their social, religious and political circumstances of production. Hence the importance of the present 'contextualising' chapter. But what does a literary critic doing historical work mean by 'context'? Some contextualisations might offer the reader a backdrop of life in these times culled from fragmented historical sources which have been rationalised and synthesised in order to present a smooth and unified picture. Whilst these may make enjoyable narratives and colourful snapshots of life in a given period, they nevertheless sometimes fall into the trap of presenting themselves as 'fact' against which the 'fiction' of the linguistic structures of the text are then read: in poststructuralist terms, ignoring the discursivity of both sets of sources; in literary critical terms, ignoring the intertextualities at work. Perhaps a more appropriate conceptualisation of a 'context' chapter for my purposes here might be one in which the production of gender as a category is analysed in a range of other texts as well as the 'literary' ones which form the basis of this study. Part of this chapter then, investigates how legal, political and religious texts discursively constitute the meanings of masculinity and femininity through the use of particular metaphors and foundational belief systems. Thus, textual analysis can be widely employed to decode the historical significance of changing definitions of gender. In addition to these sources, I nevertheless *also* draw upon the work of empirical historians in order to examine the different activities of men and women as accounted for in a variety of historical records. Here, then, representations are not being matched against reality, but rather accounts of practices (such as those drawn from court records and parish registers) are seen to be as constitutive of gender and power relations as their more obviously textual counterparts. My sources for such a 'contextualisation' are thus as diverse as the prescriptive rhetoric of Puritan marriage manuals and estimates of literacy levels based on signatures of deponents in London courts during the seventeenth century.

In this chapter I will begin to define and locate my object of study – writings by Englishwomen in the seventeenth-century radical religious sects – by reference to one of its main constitutive elements: the gender of the authors. Without dealing with questions of authorship here (see Chapter 4), I shall analyse both seventeenth-century discourses of femininity, and social historians' analyses of the specific conditions of women during those years, in order to answer my own original question: where are we to find 'seventeenth-century women'?

The 'well-broken horse'?: seventeenth-century figures of the feminine

The special natures of women and men, and the specificities of the differences between them and the relationships between them, were well documented both before and during the seventeenth century; yet they were rarely described in isolation from relationships between other human and natural phenomena. Many of the attempts to define and delineate these natures and the relationship between them are reinforced with, or explained through, the use of metaphor, metonymy or simile: linguistic figures that structure, explicate and nuance these discourses. In a culture where the world was understood as a great text waiting to be read, a set of signs or marks which corresponded with each other through analogy and similarity and which, justly interpreted, could speak of God's scheme for the world,[2] both the density of figurative language and the textual preoccupation with their exploration, commentary and interpretation is to be expected. This leaves us with a literature particularly rich in tropes that figure a world founded in sets of interlocking oppositions: male and female, mind and body, reason and passion, divine and profane, superior and inferior, dominant and subordinate. Examples of three such tropes will illustrate some of the ways these binarisms intersected and mutually defined each other and, in particular, set forth the proper relationship between women and men: figures of rationalisation, of domestication, and of dissolution.

The human body provided the terms for what was perhaps the commonest comparison that was used to delineate the relationship between the sexes. Whilst it is a comparison founded in the body, and hence indicative of a natural order, its authority is confirmed through reference to the divine by its use in the Bible (1 Corinthians 11:3; Ephesians 5:22-4). In many sixteenth- and seventeenth-century writings, it sets the terms for the ordering of the relationship between husband and wife: 'The man is as the *Head*, and the *woman* as the body ... And as it is against the order of nature that the body should rule the head: so it is no lesse against the course of all good order, that the *woman* should *usurpe* authoritie to her selfe over her husband, her head' (Gataker 1620, in Findley and Hobby 1981: 12). Just as the head, the highest part (both literally and figuratively), the ruler and legislator, was to control the desires of the body, the lower passions, and just as reason was to hold sway over unreason, madness and disorder, so men were ordained to be the natural guardians of, and legislators for women: it was men's duty to provide the rationalising check or curb to women's unreason, which was rooted in their bodies and their resulting passions. Gataker's simile echoes a metaphor employed by James I in advice to his son: 'Ye are the head, she is your body: It is your office to command, and hers to obey; but yet with such a swete harmonie, as shee should be as readie to obey, as ye to commaunde; as willing to follow, as ye to go before' (James I, in Smith 1982: 51). The emphasis here is on harmony: in this preordained order, every element has its place, whether higher or lower, ruler or ruled. Just as the body recognises its dependence on the head, so women should comply with the parallel pre-eminence of men, for on such harmony good order depends.

Seventeenth-century commentators who made this comparison did not leave it to speak for itself: they were apparently conscious that the trope was fragile, unstable, open to variant readings and dissent, to critics arguing either that it was not an apt comparison, or that it 'meant' something other than the meaning being drawn forth by the author. William Gouge, for example, in his conduct book *Of Domesticall Duties* (1622), recognises the currency of the metaphor, and embarks on an extended justification of it:

> [The husband] is the wife's head, which is also urged to this very purpose in other places.
> This metaphor showeth that to his wife he is as the head of a natural body, both more eminent in place, and also more excellent in dignity: by virtue of both which, he is a ruler and governor of his wife. Nature teacheth us that this is true of the head of a natural body ...
> Were it not monstrous for the side to be advanced above the head? If the body should not be subject to the head, would not destruction follow upon head, body, and all the parts thereof? As monstrous, and much more monstrous, is it for a wife to be above her husband: and as great, yea and greater disturbance and ruin would fall on that family. The order which God hath set in would be clear overthrown thereby: and they that overthrow it would show themselves oppugners of God's wisdom in establishing order. (Gouge 1622: 343-4)

Gouge here anticipates the prospect of a body at war with the head, and the wife having pre-eminence over her husband, and suggests that each case would be evidence of the victory of irrationality over reason, and would result in the destruction of the ordered system of which it was a part – a system which is founded on divine order. Gouge makes this clear by compounding and ratifying the bodily metaphor through giving it a divine equivalence:

> in being an head, he is like Christ. So as there is a kind of fellowship and copartnership betwixt Christ, and an husband, they are brethren in office, as two kings of several places.
> *Objection*: There is no equality betwixt Christ the Lord for heaven, and an earthly husband: the disparity betwixt them is infinite.
> *Answer*: Yet there may be similitude, resemblance, and fellowship: inequality is no hindrance to these.
> ... So then a husband resembleth not only the head of a natural body, but also the glorious image of Christ, and is that to his wife which Christ is to his church. (Gouge 1622: 344)

Several things can be adduced from Gouge's exploration of his trope – an exploration which is reliant on its being a simile rather than a metaphor, in fact, for this avoids the potentially blasphemous metaphorical formulation of saying that a husband *is* Christ, saying instead that he is *like* Christ. The comparison of a husband and wife with a head and body is extended and buttressed through reference to another fundamental relationship, that between Christ and his church. These are not discrete metaphors, then, but each links with and is underpinned by reference to others. These may be religious, as here, or, elsewhere and equally frequently, be founded in notions of social order: 'he is the household prince, the domestical king' (Whateley 1617: 42). All are legitimised by a common referent: the natural order established by God on earth, where everything has its place in the great harmonious hierarchy. To challenge the order, then, is to challenge not only the familial or social order, but to challenge the divine order, and to risk incurring the wrath of God. Rebellion against this order tells nothing of the iniquity of the order, but speaks instead of the unnaturalness and ungodliness of the warring element.

Use of this figure was clearly current amongst all social ranks, as is demonstrated by its use in one of the prophecies of Elizabeth Poole, delivered to the Council of the Army and published in 1648, and concerning the future of Charles I. The prophecy is structured through reference to a series of mutually reinforcing comparisons, of head and body, husband and wife, ruler and ruled:

> And although this bond [of fatherhood to the country] be broken on his part; you never heard that a wife might put away her husband, as he is the head of her body; but for the Lord's sake suffereth his terror to her flesh, though she be free in the spirit to the Lord; and he being uncapable to act as her husband, she acteth in his stead ... And accordingly you may hold the hands of your husband, that he pierce not your bowels with a knife or sword to take your life. Neither may you take his ... (Poole 1649: 5)

Poole's conclusions about the proper fate of the king here depend on her elision of the three tropes: the king is to the nation as the husband is to the wife and the head to the body; and just as the body cannot be severed from the head, so, by analogy, the interdependence of the elements of the other binarisms is assured. The integrity founded in nature is a guarantee of the other integrities. Interestingly, when it fell to others to justify the execution of the king, this was effected principally through another analogy, this time a biblical one: that between the king and the 'man of blood' of Numbers 35:33, whose own blood had to be spilled in order to cleanse the land of the defilement caused by the blood of those whom the king had unjustly slaughtered (Crawford 1977; Hill 1993: Chapter 15).

One writer, however, whilst not contesting the authority of this comparison, reinterprets it to emphasise the consequent responsibilities of men rather than the necessary obedience of women. Rachel Speght, in *A Mouzell for Melastomus* (1617), a pamphlet written in reply to Joseph Swetnam's misogynist *The Arraignment of Lewde, idle, froward and unconstant women* (1615) (see pp. 28–9 below), allows that it is 'a truth ungainsayable' that the man is the woman's head. She goes on to argue, however, that this is not a reason to dominer, 'but hereby is he taught the duties which he oweth to her'. Having set these out, she concludes that: 'if men would remember the duties they are to perform in being heads, some would not stand a tip-toe as they do, thinking themselves lords and rulers, and account every omission of

27

performing whatsoever they command – whether lawful or not – to be matter of great disparagement and indignity done them' (Speght 1617, in Shepherd 1985: 72). Men, she continues, should honour women, as in doing so they are honouring God's handiwork, and 'What greater discredit can redound to a workman than to have the man for whom he hath made it say it is naught?' (Speght 1617, in Shepherd 1985: 73). Whilst the trope of the man as head has in no sense been overturned by Speght, she reworks its meanings to provide a warning to men about respecting the divine origins, and hence limitations, of their power. This to some extent confirms Gouge's concern about the instability of the trope, as we see it deployed to justify a range of positions from husbandly pre-eminence to husbandly duty.

Another and related common metaphor, favoured in particular by the Puritan authors of domestic conduct books (guides for the proper governance of the family and household) is one of domestication, where the relationship between husband and wife is explicated through reference to that between a horse and its rider:

> Then it is laudable, commendable, a note of a virtuous woman, a dutiful wife, when she submits herself with quietness, cheerfully, even as a well-broken horse turns at the least turning, stands at the least check of the rider's bridle, readily going and standing as he wishes that sits upon his back. (Whateley 1617: 43)

Here the implications of the metaphor are markedly different from those of the head and body; they suggest that there is nothing 'natural' about the subservience and compliance of the wife to the husband; on the contrary, it is something that needs to be achieved by the husband, working to contain or 'break' the independence of his wife. Any harmony between husband and wife, then, is founded in a struggle for power, the triumph of the husband, the vanquishing of the wife, and thus it is an *enforced* docility. Not all women, however, will need the same kind of 'breaking':

> The breaker of horses, that use to ride and pace them, doth handle the rough and sturdy colt, with all craft, rigour, and fierceness that may be: but with the colt that is more tractable, he taketh not so great pains. A sharp and shrewd wife must be pleased and mitigated with love, and ruled with authority: and the more gently thou dost use and shew thy self unto her that is meek and honest, the more benign and meek thou shalt find her. (Cleaver and Dod 1621: sig. L5^{r-v})

Whilst all women needed taming, then, some needed taming more than others; the technique must be adapted to fit the woman, otherwise the process might prove counterproductive. Sometimes, husbands failed satisfactorily to 'break' their wives: evidence of an 'unbroken' wife included the kinds of activities engaged in by women in the radical sects. Of them, the Puritan divine Daniel Rogers wrote that women who wrote or prophesied had 'shaken off the bridle of all subjection to their husbands' (Rogers, *Matrimoniall Honour* (1642), in Yoshioka 1977: 425).

Swetnam, in the popular and rabidly anti-women pamphlet he produced and to which Speght produced the reply discussed above, was even less sanguine about the possibility of 'breaking' wives than Rogers. In a passage that exploits the trope of horse-breaking specifically in relation to women's purportedly unfettered tongues,

Swetnam concludes that women have only their own lack of restraint to blame for any violence they receive at the hands of their husbands:

> Is it not strange of what kind of mettle a woman's tongue is made of, that neither correction can chastise nor fair means quiet; for there is a kind of venom in that neither by fair means nor foul they are to be ruled. All beasts by man are made tame, but a woman's tongue will never be tame ... Therefore as a sharp bit curbs a froward horse, even so a cursed woman must be roughly used; but if women could hold their tongues, then many times men would hold their hands. (Swetnam 1615, quoted in Shepherd 1985: 195)

For Swetnam, it is the bit in the mouth that seems to constitute the most suggestive element in the comparison: the figure is here extended from a concern with rendering the beast tractable in terms of its docility and submissiveness to a specific focus on the need to 'tame' women's tongues through the use of the bit. The versatility and multi-nuanced possibilities of the comparison perhaps help to explain its popularity, for metaphors of horse-breaking were, like metaphors of the body, very common: Kathleen Davies notes that instances of their use can also be found in the conduct books of Heinrich Bullinger (1543), Henrie Smith (1591) and William Gouge (1622), whilst Robert Snawsel (1610), rather more imaginatively, used comparisons with the taming of other beasts, including lions, bulls and elephants, to make a similar point (Davies 1977: 572, 567).

Although marriage manuals are some of the most fruitful sources of such prescriptions and their attendant tropes concerning the proper relations of husband and wife, they are not the only ones. Legal documents can also provide some telling statements; in particular, T. E.'s *The Lawes Resolutions of Women's Rights* (1632) provides an extended consideration of the subject. It is from here that I want to draw my final metaphor, embedded in a detailed exposition on the marriage partnership:

> All [women] are understood either married or to be married, and their desires are subject to their husbands; I know no remedy, yet some can shift it well enough. The common law here shaketh hand with divinity.
>
> ... in this consolidation which we call wedlock is a locking together. It is true, that a man and wife are one person; but understand in what manner.
>
> When a small brook or little river incorporateth with Rhodanus, Humber or the Thames, the poor rivulet loseth her name; it is carried and recarried with the new associate; it beareth no sway; it possesseth nothing during coverture. A woman as soon as she is married is called 'covert'; in Latin 'nupta', that is, 'veiled'; as it were clouded and overshadowed; she hath lost her stream. I may more truly, far away, say to a married woman, her new self is her superior, her companion, her master. (T.E. 1632: 6, 124-5)

Here we see references to secular law commingling with divine law, which is also manifested in natural law, all reinforcing the point made most strikingly by the metaphor of the river and the tributary: marriage for a woman involves dissolution of her own identity, as she is subsumed in her husband's; it is not that she has no identity, but that his replaces hers. As well as losing her identity, she loses any sense of tracking her own course: from now on, she will go in the direction determined by 'her superior', as she has 'lost her stream'. Despite this being sanctioned by divine law, there is also a clear sense that this godly state is not always problem-free: as T.E. puts it, there is no 'remedy' for this situation, but, none the less, some can 'shift' it well enough: hardly terms suggestive of a thoroughgoing celebration of marital harmony.[3] This seems to conform much more closely to the sense of achieved docility suggested in the trope of domestication than it does to its accompanying trope of dissolution – for this, in contradistinction, suggests a sense of a 'natural order' to the relationship betwen men and women. Certainly, all rely on binary oppositions of superiority and inferiority; but the way that these translate into the relationship between men and women, it seems, is the subject of some figurative (at least) uncertainty.

'Strive to subdue your passions':[4] women's disorderly nature

Although these figures of feminine submission take different and sometimes contra-dictory forms – is, for example, the subordinate woman submissive by nature, as the tropes of rationalisation suggest, or submissive through training and regulation, as implied by the tropes of domestication? – they have in common a unifying founda-tion in a discourse of bodily difference. Women's bodies, the argument goes, are physiologically and compositionally different from men's bodies, and it is in these material differences that we can find a basis both for the arguments made by means of these linguistic figures and for the contradictions in the ways these set forth the character of the relationship between men and women.

Since classical times, women had been represented as being of a quite different physiological constitution from men: according to Galenic medicine, still pre-dominant in the early part of the seventeenth century, in women, two of the four fluids or 'humours' of which the body was said to be constituted were understood to be pre-eminent: the cold and the wet (as opposed to men's typically hot and dry humoral composition). The combination and balance of these humours was taken to determine temperament and character: so that women's combination not only endowed them with 'a changeable, deceptive and tricky temperament', but also with a lustful one: a woman's 'womb was like a hungry animal; when not amply fed by sexual intercourse or reproduction, it was likely to wander about her body, over-powering her speech and senses' (Davis 1975a: 124, 128). In short, a woman's 'physiology and humours seem to destine her to be the inferior of man, both physically and mentally' (Maclean 1980: 44):

> woman is considered to be inferior to man in that the physiological effects of her cold
> and moist humours throw doubt on her control of her emotions and her rationality;
> furthermore, her less robust physique predisposes her, it is thought, to a more pro-
> tected and less prominent role in the household and in society. Although apparently not
> bound by the authority of the divine institution of matrimony, doctors nonetheless

produce a 'natural' justification for women's relegation to the home and exclusion from public office, and provide thereby, as well as coherence with a central tenet of theology, an important foundation on which arguments of ethics, politics and law are based. (Maclean 1980: 46)

Perceptions of women's bodies, then, are taken to form the foundation (in nature, and therefore also divine) for a whole series of justifications, judgements and prescriptions concerning a range of powerful social institutions.

If women's bodies are naturally disorderly, however, how can submissiveness be their proper 'natural' state? This contradiction can only be understood in the context of seventeenth-century distinctions between what we might term 'the essential' and 'the natural'. Whereas in twentieth-century feminist debates about femininity, essentialism has been typically located in forms of biological determinism, in which the body is the guarantor of woman's naturally inferior place to man, in the seventeenth century such elisions functioned differently. Here, woman's essential nature threatened her place in the natural order, thus necessitating social intervention to secure appropriate gender relations. In the above examples, then, disorderliness can be seen to define women's nature: for in their bodies, the lower, carnal elements ruled the higher, rational ones, and, if not strictly contained, women would strive to reproduce this physiological disorderliness in society by dominating men. This helps explain the manifold warnings, exhortations, prescriptions and instructions for women published at this time: for the 'good' woman was not the 'natural' woman; on the contrary, she was the one who managed to contain her baser nature through religious training (which taught modesty and humility), through selective education (which taught her her moral duty), through honest work (to busy her hands), and through laws and constraints (to make her subject to her husband).

This distinction between the 'good', constrained and modest woman and the unruly woman in the grip of her baser passions forms yet another of the binarisms which structured so many seventeenth-century debates. This opposition is manifested most clearly in an extensive popular controversy in the late sixteenth and early seventeenth centuries over the nature of women, known variously as the 'querelle des femmes' or the controversy over women.[5] Within this controversy, women were represented as conforming to one of two sharply differentiated types:

Women are of two sorts, some of them are wiser, better learned, discreeter and more constant than *a number* of men; but another and worse sort of them, and *the most part*, are fond, foolish, wanton flibbergibs, tatlers, triflers, wavering, witless, without council, feeble, careless, rash, proud, dainty, nice, talebearers, evesdroppers, rumour-raisers, evil-tongued, worse-minded, and in every way doltified with the dregs of the devel's dunghill. (Bishop Aylmer, in Powell 1917: 147; original emphasis)

Coming as this does from a sermon preached before Elizabeth I, it is perhaps surprising that Aylmer did not enthuse at somewhat greater length about the first sort of woman, of whom presumably Elizabeth was the pattern and apotheosis. Instead, however, the full extent and variety of his adjectival vocabulary is reserved for the

31

second sort of woman; he clearly finds much more of interest to be said about 'the worse sort of them, and the most part'.

This division of women into two types set the terms of the controversy over the nature of women. As the debate became popularised (it had an earlier counterpart in scholastic works), publishers put out poems, ballads and pamphlets both attacking and defending the archetypal 'woman' and her position in society. Women's supposed increasing freedom alarmed conservative commentators so much that in 1547 a declaration was issued forbidding women to 'meet together to babble and talk', and ordering husbands to 'keep their wives in their houses' (Wright 1935: 467). Women's words, particularly those addressed to other women, were actively discouraged, and women, it was urged, should be isolated within their proper sphere, their own houses. Attacks were published against women's vanity, talkativeness, extravagence and faithlessness, by the end of the sixteenth century focusing specifically on the increasing affluence of the middle-class woman and thus on the sins of pomp and pride:

> Yet we see how proud many, especially women, be of such bables: for when they haue spent a good part of the day in tricking and trimming, pricking and pinning, pranking and pouncing, girding and lacing, and brauing vp themselues in most exquisit manner, then out they come into the streetes with their Pedlars shop about their backe, and carrie their crests very high, ... And truly wee may thinke the very stones in the streete, and the beames in the houses do quake, & wonder at their monstrous, intollerable, and excessiue pride: for it seemeth that they are altogether a lvmpe of pride, a masse of pride, euen altogether made of pride, and nothing else but pride, pride. (Arthur Dent, *The Plaine Mans Path-way to Heaven* (1601), in Wright 1935: 478-9)

The controversy continued and intensified into the seventeenth century, with the attacks on women reaching their popular zenith in Joseph Swetnam's most famous pamphlet, published in 1615, *The Araignment of Lewde, idle, froward and unconstant women*; this sold well for over half a century, and was reprinted ten times by 1634 alone. For Swetnam too, the sins of extravagence and pride were the principal targets:

> Eagles eate not men till they are dead but women devour them alive, for a woman will pick thy pocket and empty thy purse, laugh in thy face and cutt thy throat, they are ungratefull, periured, full of fraud, flouting and deceit, unconstant, waspish, toyish ... and yet they were by God created, and by nature formed and therefore by pollicy and wisedome to bee avoyded, for good things abused are to be refused. (Swetnam 1615: 16)

The text's misogyny is uncompromising: 'it is said of women that they have two faultes, that is, they can neither say well nor yet doe well'. Yet it is also suggestive of fear and awe at the power and influence women were perceived to have: 'What is it that a woman cannot doe, which knowes her power?' (Swetnam 1615: 28, 22).

The controversy was not confined to pamphlets: plays and ballads were often directly or indirectly concerned with this issue, as were sermons:

> Our pulpits ring continually of the insolence and impudence of women: and to helpe the matter forward the players have likewise taken them to taske, and so the ballads and ballad-singers, so that they can come no where but theyre eares tingle: and yf all this

will not serve the King threatens to fall upon theyre husbands, parents or frends that have or shold have powre over them, and make them pay for yt. (Chamberlain 1620, quoted in Woodbridge 1984: 143-4)

Defences of women were as varied as the attacks on them. Anthony Gibson, in *A Woman's Woorth* (1599), gives examples of famous and virtuous women from history and the classics to prove that women's souls are the 'treasurie[s] of celestiall and divine vertues' (Wright 1935: 479). Men must acknowledge the divinity of women, thereby proving their own excellence and virtue: 'the most parte of excellent and vertuous men, have attributed all tytle of honour to Women, daylie becomming their servantes in hart, yea even humble in prostration (as it were) to adore them, as if in some sorte they tooke parte with the highest divinitie' (Gibson, in Wright 1935: 479-80). Swetnam's popularisation of the controversy was matched by a number of pamphlets in reply to his arguments. Some of these, such as Rachel Speght's (see p. 27 above), were female-authored, whilst others were clearly written under pseudonyms, such as Ester Sowernam's and Constantia Munda's. These last two take on Swetnam on his own terms, denouncing masculinity in as damning terms as he has femininity, and Purkiss argues that it is this, rather than the gender of the authors, that is important:

> These representations of women on top offer a figure for women to read with pleasure even as they also represent that figure as an outsider ... the placing of a discourse of invective and experience in the mouth of a woman, however fictional, creates a spectacle of female power which displays precisely what Swetnam fears: the strength of knowledge as a means to curtail pleasure. (Purkiss 1992b: 89-90)

The definition of women's temperament as distinct from, inferior to and more carnal than men's had an impact in areas other than this primarily literary debate: discourses of witchcraft, for example, also relied on this characterisation. The most well-known published attack on witchcraft was that produced by two German Dominicans, Jakob Sprenger and Heinrich Kramer: *Malleus Maleficarum* was published in 1486, and its popularity continued unabated for 200 years, there being five editions in English alone between 1584 and 1669 (Feder 1980: 112). In this attempt to destroy witchcraft, they report on the characteristics and crimes of those accused of practising it, as well as means of detecting, exorcising and punishing it. For them, although in theory either sex could be a witch, in practice they found the character of women synonymous with that of a witch: the first woman, Eve, had also been the first witch, since she had made a pact with the devil, and Eve was the model for all fallen women thereafter. At the root of this link was the disorderly nature of women, for 'all witchcraft comes from carnal lust, which is in women insatiable ... For the sake of fulfilling their lusts, they consort even with devils' (quoted in Yoshioka 1977: 127). Other books appeared, both in support of and in opposition to these views. One of the most influential, Reginald Scot's *A Discovery of Witchcraft* (1584), was dismissive of Sprenger and Kramer's claims, saying instead that witchcraft was largely a matter of superstition. He did not underestimate, however, the strength of belief in their powers: 'Witches deceive. They make of God a willful magician whose power is at their disposal. Though they profess otherwise, they have become servants of anti-Christ – the Devil' (quoted in Yoshioka 1977: 130). Examples are legion, but the general consensus was that women were more susceptible to the wiles of the devil because of their lustful, greedy, ignorant, hysterical, ambitious and generally inferior nature. Unsurprisingly, accusations of witchcraft multiplied with the proliferation of the radical sects in the middle part of the century and the acceptance in some cases of prophecy, visionary trances and healing powers: the manifestation of religious experience seemingly differed little from that of diabolical possession.[6]

If witchcraft could be read as a manifestation of femininity untrammelled, then the plethora of marriage manuals and domestic conduct books from this period can be seen as instruments for the proper management and constraint of women, and in particular married women.[7] These were generally written by Puritan ministers, and set out the 'right ordering' of families, for this was seen as both the foundation and reflection of a well-ordered commonwealth (Ingram 1987: 142). These ideas concerning the nature of women were expressly founded in theology: by the Middle Ages, men's superiority over women had been systematised and justified in four main ways: men were active, women passive; women were subordinate because they were cursed at the Fall; women were less robust than men; and the spiritual signification of sex difference was seen to lie in the parallel between women and the soul and the man and Godhead (Maclean 1980: 10). Above all, women were associated with sensuality, and were feared for their incitement to lust and concupiscence in men. By 1600, with the shift towards Puritanism, there had been a gradual shift in the conceptualisation of women: from the views of Bishop Aylmer (see p. 31 above), where the 'most part' of women were castigated as immoral, immodest and unruly, the predominant Puritan view emphasised the dignity of the married woman as the ideal for which women were to strive. This was in sharp contrast to the old model of Roman Catholic origin, whereby virginity was the ideal against which other states were measured and found wanting. 'In the society they [Puritans] were helping to shape, the family household, with its extensions in the farmstead and shop and in its relation to religious life, was assuming an importance it had not had in feudal, monastic or courtly society' (Haller and Haller 1941-42: 247). With the Puritans, then, marriage changed from being a necessary evil for the containment of the baser passions to an honourable and natural union between men and women, where children were the proper result but not the prime cause. Milton summarised this view of the marriage relationship as 'the crown of all our bliss / Ordained by thee' in an appropriately celebratory passage in *Paradise Lost* (1677):

> Our maker bids increase, who bids abstain
> But our destroyer, foe to God and man?
> Hail wedded love, mysterious law, true source
> Of human offspring, sole propriety
> In Paradise of all things common else.
> (Milton 1667: Book IV, ll. 728-9, 748-52)

Within the marriage relationship it was the role of the wife that the conduct books were particularly concerned to delineate. The family was represented as a 'little church' or 'little state', and thus unquestionably patriarchal and authoritarian, but the role of women was none the less focused on increasingly within it.[8] Once again, nature was invoked to help to define the marriage partners' respective duties: 'Nature hath placed an eminency in the male over the female: so as where they are linked together in one yoke, it is given by nature that he should govern, she obey' (Gouge 1622: 270). Forced or grudging submission, however, was not sufficient. The woman's willingness to submit was as important as the submission itself:

> The whole duty of the wife is referred to two heads. The first, is to acknowledge her inferiority: the next, to carry herself as inferior. First then the wife's judgement must be convinced, that she is not her husband's equal, yea that her husband is her better by far; else there can be no contentment, either in her heart, or in her house. (Whateley 1617: 36)

This acknowledgement of inferiority and the resulting necessity of obedience was important because all the other prescriptions for the marriage relationship hung on it: 'Unless the women freely acknowledged obedience to be their first duty, there could be no assurance that they would fulfil faithfully any other' (Haller and Haller 1941–42: 249).

The conduct books not only urged subservience, they also defined and anatomised its forms exhaustively. If a woman's nature could be characterised by reference to her unruly physiology, her duty could be summarised by reference to the concept of her 'honour'. This was a term used almost interchangeably with others, such as honesty, modesty and chastity; and yet each had a series of precise, and gendered, associations and meanings, quite distinct from the meanings they had when used in relation to men.

A concern with 'honour' was not confined to women, nor was it confined to the upper ranks of society: 'sexual "credit" and "honesty" – the lower class equivalents of gentry notions of honour – were an important touchstone of respectability, certainly among the middling ranks of yeomen, husbandmen and substantial craftsmen, and to an extent even lower down the social scale' (Ingram 1987: 165). In general, a man's honour depended on his actions in the public sphere:[9] his work, his loyalty to his master or his sovereign, the dependability of his word. For a woman, her reputation was dependent principally on sexual matters:

> Women were more sensitive, and probably more subject, to sexual slander for two main reasons. First, fornication and adultery were more seriously regarded in the female than the male. Secondly, the fact that contemporaries conventionally assigned passive, dependent, home-based roles to women, in contrast to the active, extra-domestic functions of the male, meant that sexual reputation was more central to the female persona. The nature of slanders alleged by men in the common law courts, concerning probity in business dealings, social rank and status, and 'honesty' in its modern sense, were probably a fair reflection of the central issues around which male reputation revolved ...

The pattern of cases in the church courts reflected the fact that for women the central issue was that of 'honesty' in its now obsolete sense of 'chastity' – was she an honest woman or a whore? (Ingram 1987: 302-3)

Ingram has traced those accusations of sexual impropriety that occasioned counter-accusations of sexual slander and thus reached the ecclesiastical courts; the sheer number of cases that he identifies, and the predominance of female plaintiffs, testify to the significance of sexual reputation, most especially for women, and to the extent it was 'of real significance in everyday life' (Ingram 1987: 302, 318).

This identification of 'separate spheres' and the consequently differing codes of morality was well established before the seventeenth century. Vives, in his *Instruction of a Christian Woman* (1540) summarised it thus:

though the precepts for men be innumerable: women may yet be informed with few words. For men must be occupied both at home and abroad, both in their own matters and for the common weal. Therefore it cannot be declared in few books, but in many and long, how they shall handle themselves, in so many and divers things. As for a woman, she hath no charge to see to, but her honesty and chastity. Wherewith when she is informed of that, she is sufficiently appointed. (Vives, in Watson 1912: 34)

Despite his claim that women may 'be informed with few words', the conduct books were concerned to define in the greatest detail just what comprised a woman's 'honour'. Whilst her sexual reputation – virginity until marriage and unwavering sexual fidelity to her husband thereafter – was a key component, it was not the only one. A married woman should not only be sexually faithful, but she should also maintain a demeanour fitting for a wife: submissiveness, deference, loyalty and silence unless spoken to. Robert Cleaver defined this a little more fully, giving six rules a man should follow when choosing a wife. He recommended that she:

should have a good report among her acquaintances; that she should have a good countenance, neither given to angry glances, vain immodesty, nor proud looks; that she should be of modest talk, 'for she which is full of talke, is not likely to prooue a quiet wife'; that she should wear modest apparel, 'beseeming her estate and condition: to wit, honest and sober raiment'; that she should keep good company; and finally, that she should have a useful education. (Wright 1935: 213-14)

Women writers engaged, sometimes directly, with these prescriptions and definitions. Margaret Cavendish, Duchess of Newcastle, for example, summarised the virtuous woman as 'Modest, Chast, Temperate, Humble, Patient and Pious: also to be Huswifely, Cleanly, and of few Words' (Cavendish 1662, quoted in Riley 1988: 27). Cavendish also sets out the terms of the double standard resulting from these gender-distinct definitions of 'honour':

It is the greatest Dishonour for a Man to be called a Coward, for a Woman to be called a Whore; and nothing will satisfie a Man that is called a Coward, but the Life of him that doth it, so Tender is he of his Honour, and so Revengfull doth the Law make him; But a Woman can give no Honourable Revenge; if she be disgraced with Words, she must only mourn over the Loss of her Honour; she may weep Funeral-tears over it, or curse or sigh for it; but when it is once Dead, it hath no Resurrection. (Cavendish 1655, in Hobby 1979: 32-3)

For a woman, then, honour challenged is honour lost. According to Cavendish, there can be no recourse, no defence, for to defend would be to act and thereby break the bounds of modesty and silence. Ingram's analysis of the ecclesiastical court records suggest that *some* form of redress was possible, but in general his accounts of the degree of distress caused by assaults on a woman's sexual reputation tend to reinforce rather than undermine Cavendish's general argument (Ingram 1987: 311-14).

Nor was it only aristocratic women such as Cavendish who discussed the significance of the notion of honesty. The Quaker Mary Mollineux included two poems in her collection *Fruits of Retirement* (1702) on the subjects of modesty and chastity, again describing the different implications of the terms for men and for women. For men, renown depends on 'valour'; chastity is not essential to it, simply serving to add 'A more ennobling lustre to their name' (Mollineux 1702: 90). For women, however, chastity is indispensable:

> Then for the blushing sex, what tongue can tell
> The infamy that on her name shall dwell,
> That wants the ornament of chastity?
> 'Tis a reproach unto her memory:
> But she that keeps her mind retired and chaste,
> Her Praise shall flourish; fame nor envy's Blast
> Can never blemish it ...
> (Mollineux 1702: 90)

Without chastity, then, infamy attaches to the woman's name, and does so permanently, for her 'memory' will be sullied. Chastity flourishes on privacy, reticence, a 'mind retired'; it is impervious not only to 'envy', but also to 'fame', which embraces not only infamy but also the opposite of the 'mind retired': a concern with 'public' issues. Modesty, too, is something that Mollineux writes of as integral and indispensible to a woman, but a mere asset to a man:

> Then why should either sex claim liberty,
> Beyond the confines of sweet modesty?
> It seasons words, and fairly regulates
> Deportment, both to high and low estates;
> It crowns the man with comeliness: But she
> That wants it, deserves shame and infamy.
> (Mollineux 1702: 145-6)

For the man, modesty is a crown, an external indicator of his inner 'honesty', but it neither determines nor defines that 'honesty'. For a woman, however, it determines her character; its absence indicates that any 'shame and infamy' that may attach to her is thoroughly deserved.

37

These assertions of women's natural dependence on men, the necessity of curbs and controls on their rebellious spirits, the absence of an independent identity for wives, and the necessity of separate moral codes to inform the conduct of men and women are given further substance through reference to the manifestations of these sentiments as enshrined in the law: 'in Renaissance legal tracts, the same underlying association of physical and mental weakness in the female sex can be detected as is in evidence in theology, medicine and ethics' (Maclean 1980: 72). T.E.'s statement (see p. 29 above) that all women 'are understood either married or to be married' (T.E. 1632: 6) is no flight of rhetoric, but a factual statement of the law's formal conceptualisation of women. Women in the seventeenth century still had no independent legal status; first their fathers and then their husbands had legal responsibility for their actions, and their persons were these men's legal property: 'In English law, the married woman is treated as a wife, not as an *individuum*, since she is "of one flesh" with her husband (Gen. 2.24)' (Maclean 1980: 76). Quoting Matthew Bacon's *A New Abridgment of the Law* (4th edition, 1778), Ingram has summarised women's position thus:

> the common law was strongly biased in favour of the husband/father. Despite legal modification based on decisions in equity, it was still essentially true that married women had no proprietary rights independent of their husbands; while the law prescribed that 'the husband hath ... power and dominion over his wife, and may keep her by force within the bounds of duty, and may beat her' (albeit not in 'a violent and cruel manner'). (Ingram 1987: 143)

Just what constituted a 'violent and cruel manner' clearly exercised the minds of some commentators: one deemed the beating was acceptable provided the stick 'was no thicker than a man's thumb' (Ferguson 1992: 22). A woman's 'lack of proprietary rights' extended both to her own person (her husband could legally confine her) and to her children (he could remove his wife's children from her and refuse her access to them). Despite this lack of legal status, however, women were tied to the law's decrees as firmly as were men: 'women have no voice in Parliament, they ... have nothing to do in constituting laws, or consenting to them, or interpreting of laws or in hearing them interpreted at lectures, leets or charges, and yet they stand strictly tied to men's establishments, little or nothing excused by ignorance' (T.E. 1632: 6, 2).

The picture constructed by these discourses of women's lot is a gloomy one: it is one of constraint, repression, powerlessness, docility, and restriction, where women, it would seem, are positioned either as submissive inferiors of their husbands and fathers, as passive victims of laws and prescriptions, or as disorderly creatures (whether scolds, witches, or wantons), in the thrall of their carnal natures, and beyond the bounds of social respectability. This, however, relies on a very top-heavy model of power, where those 'with power' (in this case, men) systematically and successfully suppress and oppress those 'without power' (here, women). It is important, then, to interrogate the extent to which this model of power is appropriate for an understanding for these seventeenth-century discourses of femininity. Did all the discursive constructions of 'women' conform to this monolithic and univocal model; or can we find other models, that construct a different version of 'women', 'men' and of the power relations betwen them? Foucault's characterisation of power as being 'exercised from innumerable points, in the interplay of nonegalitarian and mobile relations' (Foucault 1979: 94) perhaps offers a way both to retain a sense of the unequal distribution of power and to conceptualise the complexities of its generation and manifestation. And if, indeed, this model proves more appropriate, do we read these reconfigurations of femininity and power as constructed in opposition to this 'dominant' version, or are they constructed along its flaws and faultlines? It is to these questions that I shall now turn.

'Hiding behind their sex': reconfigurations of the feminine

The discourses of femininity set out so far, then, are suggestive of limits, constraints, restrictions and denials: the curbing of the woman's 'nature' in order to fit her for her 'duty'. However, the anxiety that Gouge expressed about the aptness of his metaphors for the proper relationship between men and women can be read as indicative of the contested, uncertain status of these characterisations: for they were by no means the only ones circulating at the time. This is not to deny the significance of it as, in some senses, a 'dominant' or hegemonic version of the meanings and nature of femininity, but it is to draw attention to the ways in which it was in constant dialogue with other characterisations: a dialogue that constantly engaged with, challenged, countered, rewrote, or contained this definition. These counter-discourses might be more properly said not to be constructed in opposition to the dominant discourse, but constructed through its reconfiguration. These discourses, then, could be said to be founded in what Jameson has called 'the general unity of a shared code' (Jameson 1981: 84): within this shared code, he argues, are fought out two opposing discourses. He takes as his example of this the struggles of England in the 1640s, where the opposing sides in the Civil War fought their battles through the common language or 'shared code' of religion (Jameson 1981: 84); equally, however, we could argue that struggles over the definition of femininity were conducted by means of a 'shared code' of women's bodily inferiority. It is the ways in which that code was differently interpreted and deployed that I will consider now.

Gender, the law and the state

T.E.'s suggestion (p. 38 above) that women were not excused from the law's strictures by their exclusion from its formation is categorical in its assertion that women and men are equally tied to the limits set by the law. However, historians have found that in many instances this was not the case: men and women were not held accountable in the same ways for their actions. What lay behind this discrepancy between the letter of the law and its implementation? It seems that at the root of it were differing interpretations of the significance of women's bodily inferiority to men. Since women were seen to be in thrall to their baser, carnal passions, and because, as

39

a result of this, they were subsumed in the persons of their fathers or husbands, it was not they who were held wholly responsible for their actions, but the men of whom they were a part:

> In England, in most felonious acts by a married woman to which her husband could be shown to be privy or at which he was present, the wife could not be held entirely culpable. If indicted, she might be acquitted or receive a lesser sentence than he for the same crime. In Normandy and Brittany, the husband might have to answer for her crimes in court, and everywhere the *sexus imbecillus* might be punished less severely. The full weight of the law fell only on the ruling male. Small wonder that the husband sometimes thought it safer to send their wives out to do the rioting alone. Small wonder that the Star Chamber grumbled in 1605 that some women who had torn down enclosure fences were 'hiding behind their sex'. (Davis 1975a: 146)

At times, this feminine irresponsibility was exploited by men to their own advantage: sometimes they found it beneficial to adopt the identity of women through cross-dressing in order to mitigate their own disobedience and riotous behaviour.[10] Examples have been found in both England and France of cases were men dressed in women's clothes in order to defend their rights to wood and pasturage, or in a grain riot, or in assaulting a dissenting meeting-house (Davis 1975a: 148). Cross-dressing seems to have authorised resistance:

> On the one hand, the disguise freed men from full responsibility for their deeds and perhaps, too, from fear of outrageous revenge on their manhood. After all, it was mere women who were acting in this disorderly way. On the other hand, the males drew upon the sexual power and energy of the unruly woman and on her licence (which they had long assumed at carnival and games) – to promote fertility, to defend the community's interests and standards, and to tell the truth about unjust rule. (Davis 1975a: 149-50)

The licence afforded by a female gender identity provided latitude for women in rather different ways. Within their own homes and communities, for example, there seems to have been an increase in various sorts of unruly behaviour in the period prior to the Civil War, between 1560 and 1640: 'Women scolding and brawling with their neighbours, single women refusing to enter service, wives dominating or even beating their husbands: all seem to surface more frequently than in the periods immediately before or afterwards' (Underdown 1985a: 119). All of these carried the risk of retaliation. Some of this was formal and effected through the legal system (Underdown, for example, draws his conclusions from the local court records for the period), and took the form of, for example, duckings for scolds, or 'cartings' around the town or village for whores. Some responses were informal and community-based, such as the 'skimmington ride': a noisy, mocking demonstration which 'characteristically took place when a wife had beaten her husband, thus subverting the conventional ideal of "right order" within the family' (Ingram 1987: 144). Ingram suggests, however, that such retributions did not meet all breaches of the norm, but were reserved mostly for extreme violations of the patriarchal schema; indeed, he concludes that, far from the rise in court cases during these years marking a more rigid enforcement of patriarchal norms, on the contrary, 'the authoritarian ideal was much modified in everyday life' (Ingram 1987: 144). This licence also extended outside the family and relationships with neighbours. Davis has found instances where:

> women turn up telling off priests and pastors, being central actors in grain and bread riots in town and country, and participating in tax revolts and other rural disturbances. In England in the early seventeenth century ... a significant percentage of the rioters against enclosures and for common rights were female. In Calvinist Edinburgh in 1637, the resistance to Charles I's imposition of the Book of Common Prayer was opened by a crowd of 'rascally serving women' at St Giles' Church, who drowned out the Dean's reading, threw stools at the Bishop of Edinburgh, and when evicted, stoned the doors and windows. (Davis 1975a: 146)

Davis's findings are confirmed by the work of Patricia Higgins, who has written of the long tradition of women's involvement in enclosure and fen riots, and how this contin-ued and expanded in the Civil War period: women put pressure on the Lords and Commons both by taking a leading part in London's mob, and by presenting numerous petitions to Parliament on matters of state. These petitions initially concerned the decline of trading, or protested against the papists and Archbishop Laud, but later they concerned the war, some petitioning for peace and others against it. They were connected also with the Leveller petitioners, and in 1659 there was a mass petition of Parliament signed by 7,000 Quaker women, calling for, amongst other changes, the abolition of tithes (Hobby 1988: 16-17, 39; Higgins 1973; McArthur 1909).

These petitions challenged the representation of women constructed through the marriage manuals and legal documents, in that they openly asserted that women had political rights, including the right to present their views to Parliament. These con-ventional representations are upheld to a certain degree: women are, the petitions concede, the 'weaker sex', and of 'frail condition'; they are concerned that such petitioning should not be interpreted as coming from 'self-conceit or Pride of Heart'. None the less, they argue the case for their interest both in concerns of the state and of religion:

> in the free enjoying of Christ in His own laws, and a flourishing estate of Church and Commonwealth, consisteth the happinesse of women as well as of men ... women are sharers in the common calamities that accompany both Church and Commonwealth ... and an unlimited power have been given to Prelates to exercise over the consciences of women as well as men. (McArthur 1909: 700)

This constitutes a direct challenge to T.E.'s assertion that women are both excluded from the formulation of the law yet responsible before it: instead, it suggests that as subjects of both Church and Commonwealth, they have the right to participate in their decisions, with their voices if not with their votes: 'Have we not an equal interest with the Men of this Nation in those liberties and securities contained in the Petition of Right and other the good Laws of the Land?' (McArthur 1909: 708).

Although such licence was justified through recourse to a sense of women's lack of agency and responsibility before the law, based in notions of their bodily inferiority,

41

these same attitudes governed the kinds of responses with which they were met. Just as it was 'mere women' rioting, and thus not deserving of too great a reaction, so it was 'mere women' presenting the petitions, a 'company of Gossops' whose husbands should give them 'fitter employment' (Higgins 1973: 213). On 26 July 1653, women petitioners were told that 'the House could take no cognizance of their petition, they being women, and many of them wives, so that the Law took no notice of them' (Higgins 1973: 213). The legal non-recognition of women is here manifested in a very material way: as the law 'took no notice' of women, the Commons would do likewise.

It is clear, then, that there was no single, univocal, definitive discourse of femininity in the seventeenth century. Whilst ideas about subordination and dependence, underpinned by reference to the divinely ordained natural order, constructed women as passive and compliant, the arguments made in women's petitions (and, indeed, by the very existence of women's petitions), and the evidence of court records, construct a very different version of women, in opposition to these prescriptions. They do, however, operate within the 'shared code' of women's bodily inferiority, using the familiar claims of feminine weakness and frailty and consequent lack of responsibility before the law to underpin and ground their own arguments and justify their own activities.

Just as the official exclusion of women from the processes of the law could be interpreted, through reference to the inherent irresponsibility of women rooted in their biological constitution, to give licence to women as well as limiting them, so the relationship between women's perceived 'nature' and the social and familial expectations of them could be ambiguous. Davis suggests that the very same images and definitions that were used to justify the subjugation of women could also be deployed to expose the contradictions of women's social positions. She argues that the image of the disorderly or unruly woman, the 'woman on top', was 'a multivalent image and could operate ... to widen behavioural options for women within and even outside marriage, and to sanction riot and political disobedience for both men and women in a society that allowed the lower orders few formal means of protest' (Davis 1975a: 131). Davis substantiates this by reference to a range of sources. From literature, she cites women who are happily given over to the sway of their bodily senses, such as the Wife of Bath or Rabelais's Gargamelle, and a whole host of other husband-dominators who are by no means wholly condemned. She cites Rosalind from *As You Like It*, who 'teaches' her future husband wisdom, and also the popular image of Phyllis riding Aristotle, symbolising the triumph of youth over age, nature over reason, and female over male. She gives examples of transvestism and role-reversal at popular festivals from all over Europe, which she suggests acted not only as a release from the stable hierarchical social control, but also as an expression of the struggle over change, and over the location of power and property within the family and within society more generally (Davis 1975: 140a. See also Reay 1985a; Stallybrass 1986: 142). In short, she argues that 'Play with the various images of women on top ... kept open an alternate way of conceiving family structure' (Davis 1975a: 143).

Reshaping the family

'Alternate way[s] of conceiving family structure' were important, then, as a means of countering the construction of women as operating legitimately only within a domestic and familial framework. This reconfiguration of the family could function in a number of different ways for women writers. For some, it meant extending the notion of domestic duties to include activities usually seen as in opposition to the domestic, such as writing: Anne Fanshawe, for example, claimed that the writing of her autobiography fell within the range of her feminine duty to the family, arguing that it was written for her son in order to offer him advice on how to lead his life (Fanshawe 1676: 31). Margaret Cavendish, the Duchess of Newcastle, took a different tack: rather than writing in service to her family, she claims that her particular family circumstances exempted her from the more common run of wifely duties: 'I have no Children to imploy my Care, and Attendance on; And my Lords Estate being taken away, had nothing for Huswifery, or thrifty Industry to imploy my selfe in; having no Stock to work on' (Cavendish 1653, quoted in Hobby 1979: 34). This justification, based on the absence of domestic duties, is backed up with another, more directly protective of her modesty. Her desire to write, she claims, has consistently been 'Lawful, Honest, Honourable, and Modest, of which I can avouch to the world with a great confidence, because it is a pure Truth' (Cavendish, quoted in Findley and Hobby 1981: 31).

Writers who fell outside the boundaries of the 'family' altogether were a rather different case. Women who were 'masterless', particularly those who were unattached to a particular household through service, were anyway of special concern to the authorities: 'A society held together by the cement of the household required that everyone have either a parent or master. Seventeenth-century court records are littered with orders to masterless individuals, frequently women, to put themselves into service' (Underdown 1985b: 36). As Underdown says, this concern was not just because they might become a burden on the poor rates, but also because their conduct 'defied conventional assumptions about women's dependence' (Underdown 1985b: 37). Women, then, who fell outside the bounds of the family were able to argue their own special circumstances without (directly) countering the idea that women's primary duty was to the family. The Fifth Monarchist Anna Trapnel, for example, argued that she had been free to travel to Cornwall because she was unmarried and therefore had no conflicting demands on her; as she put it, 'having no hindrance, why may not I go where I please, if the Lord so will?' (Trapnel 1654b: 26).

For women writing specifically religious works, the reconciliation of the demands of the family with those of writing was fortified by reference both to God's will and to the writer's relationship with God. The Quaker spiritual autobiographer Joan Vokins, for example, wrote that it was necessary for her to leave her family in order to travel and minister abroad, despite its being against her husband's wishes, for otherwise her whole family might suffer from her disobedience: 'if I had disobeyed the Lord to please them, I might have provoked him to have withholden his mercies from us all, and to bring his judgments upon us' (Vokins 1691: 23). Sectarian writers also expand and reform the notion of the 'family' to include a range of different kinds of relationship: fellow sectaries are 'brothers and sisters', and all are the 'sons and daughters' of God; Joan Vokins's maternal care extended from her own family to other young Friends: 'She was a nursing mother over the young convinced, and in her own family' (Vokins 1691: sig. A2^r). God himself was also frequently a 'nursing mother' (Hincks 1671: 24; see also Hobby 1988: 42, Purkiss 1992a: 152-3) as well as the more usual father. Sometimes different familial roles merge in one trope: Purkiss has noted how the use of food imagery in the prophets Sarah Wight and Anna Trapnel positions them as at once infants and mothers, as they are 'nourished by the always plenitudinous maternality of God', and yet in turn themselves 'provide nourishment for a hungry congregation'; she suggests that 'this undoing of important hierarchical categories also depicts the possibility of moving from infancy to maternity without passing through marriage' (Purkiss 1992a: 147). Marriage itself was also recast in these writings: Christ was Anne Wentworth's 'heavenly bridegroom' (Wentworth 1677); and the Quakers Katharine Evans and Sarah Chevers wrote about their relationship to each other in terms that quite clearly echo the marriage service: 'I took her by the arm and said, "The Lord hath joined us together, and woe be to them that should part us"' (Evans and Chevers 1662, in Graham *et al.* 1989: 125). Such reworkings of familiar relationships were not confined to sectarian writers: for example, for the more conservative poet who wrote *Eliza's Babes* (1652), a book of devotional poetry, the 'babes' of the title are her own poems, the fruit of her union with God (Hobby 1988: 54-9).

It has often been noted how seldom sectarian writers, even (and particularly) autobiographers, mention their families (Watkins 1972). It is not, however, that familial relationships are excluded from these texts, but more that they are refigured to refer to the relationship of the writer with God and with her fellow sectaries, or with her spiritual work. Sectarian references to the family generally allude to very different set of relationhips from the usual 'carnal' family ones. Whilst notions of marriage, motherhood, filial responsibility and sibling allegiance are all central to the discourses produced by sectarian women writers, they are almost invariably metaphorisations of a whole series of other relationships, relationships which transgress the boundaries produced by women's positions within their earthly families. These familial metaphors thus foreground and familiarise a range of *extra*familial activities and relationships.

Unequal bodies, equal souls

Trapnel's final clause quoted above – 'if the Lord so will' – is suggestive of another way in which the 'shared code' of bodily inferiority was reconfigured in ways that undercut the dominant interpretation. This reconfiguration was effected through reference to religion, the soul and salvation, and proved to be a key component in the discourses that challenged the dominant construction of femininity, and is of particular sigificance for this study of women writers from the radical sects. This religious discourse shared the dominant conception of women's *bodily* inferiority in comparison with men; but, crucially, it matched this with a belief in their *spiritual* equality. Thus, although Puritan ministers preached the necessary subservience of women to their husbands on the basis of their inferior natures, they also noted that the difference between men and women in which this subservience was rooted was in itself so minor as to create confusion: 'Woman is less than man, but so little less that it is easy to fall into the error of supposing that she is not less at all' (Gouge 1622, quoted in Haller and Haller 1941-42: 250). And in one crucial respect, women were not inferior at all, but were equal with men:

> Since they are equal in sin and alike in their appointed inheritance of death, therefore they are the heirs together of the grace of life. The husband, that is to say, notwith-standing his superiority in other respects, had no better title to salvation than the wife who submitted to him. (Haller and Haller 1941-42: 250-1)

Women's bodily inferiority, then, was justification for their earthly subjection; because of the equality of their souls with men's, however, this subjection did not extend beyond this life:

> like woman's subordination to her husband and her disqualification from full participation in the spiritual life, this inequality attached to this life only, and all commentators stress that she will share equally in the joys of paradise. In theological terms woman is, therefore, the inferior of the male by nature, his equal by grace. (Maclean 1980: 22)

The soul, then, escaped the limitations and penalties of gender. Why, though, did this notion of the 'ungendered soul', as Riley calls it (Riley 1988: 42), prove to be so central to discourses of femininity at this particular time, when Christianity had always allowed men and women equal access to the possibility of salvation? The answer lies principally in the combination of specific religious and political developments in the years leading up to the mid-seventeenth century: namely, the increasing influence of Puritan notions of individuality and the proliferation of the radical religious sects in these years.

Perhaps the most well-worn word associated with Puritanism[11] is 'individualism', used to indicate the direct relationship of the individual believer with God, unmediated by any priest, so that each becomes responsible for his or her own soul and salvation. Tawney has suggested that this characterisation is too simplistic, ignoring the many contradictions to be found in Puritans' attitudes and origins:

> There was in Puritanism an element which was conservative and traditionalist, and an element which was revolutionary; a collectivism which grasped at an iron discipline, and an individualism which spurned the savourless mess of human ordinances; a sober prudence which would garner the fruits of the world, and a divine recklessness which would make all thing new. (Tawney 1926: 212)

Nevertheless, the notion of individualism combines a number of elements that are important when considering the reconfigurations of the feminine effected through the radical sects, the religious groups who shared (and modified) certain Puritan beliefs. Tawney describes the centrality of this concept and the manner in which it coloured all aspects of Puritan doctrine:

> While the revelation of God to the individual soul is the centre of all religion, the essence of Puritan theology was that it made it, not only the centre, but the circumference and substance, dismissing as dross and vanity all else but this secret solitary communion. Grace alone can save, and this grace is the direct gift of God, unmediated by any earthly institution. The elect cannot by any act of their own evoke it; but they can prepare their hearts to receive it, and cherish it when received. They will prepare them best, if they empty them of all that may disturb the intentness of their lonely vigil. (Tawney 1926: 227)

This individual relationship with God challenged many of the old traditions of the established church, and not least the authority of the clergy: for if all individuals were responsible for the well-being of their own souls, then all needed to settle their account with God for themselves; no one else could do it for them. Whilst this individual and direct relationship between the believer and God in no sense challenged the discourse of women's bodily inferiority and the resulting sexual hierarchy, it did mean that in spiritual matters God was no longer considered a respecter of ecclesiastical and social hierarchies: the words from Acts 10:34, 'God is no respecter of persons', were often quoted. Instead, he was perceived as taking account of only one distinction: that between the elect (or the saints, as sectaries usually referred to them) and the unregenerate. This egalitarianism allowed the Puritans to challenge institutional hierarchies, particularly those that related to the relationship between church and state; it left, however, those hierarchies within the home and family largely untouched. The individualisation, then, of the relationship between the believer and God is at the heart of many of the phenomena that this book will investigate. As Christopher Hill summarised it: 'The protestant doctrine of the priesthood of all believers opened doors to innovation, because it was ultimately an appeal to individual interpretation of the Bible, to the consciences of (some) lay men and women' (Hill 1993: 416). Time and time again, the texts from the radical sects bear out Hill's argument: writers justify their actions both on the basis of their understanding of the scriptures and on the communication they have had with God concerning the progress of their own salvation.

Whilst the activities of women preaching, prophesying and writing from within the radical sects in the middle years of the seventeenth century are striking in their sheer volume and high public profile, they were not without their precedents. A religious justification for 'disorderly' women's activities was not an entirely new phenomenon: the ungendered soul of Christianity had long been referred to in order to vindicate women's participation in religious affairs of all kinds. There are, for example, many instances of women involved in 'heretical' activities in pre-revolutionary England. Thomson gives example after example of women brought to trial in the fifteenth and sixteenth centuries for their religious activities. In January 1510, for example, Joan Baker admitted in court that she had unlawfully determined on matters of faith; in April 1494 Joan Boughton, who was over eighty years old, was burnt at Smithfield for heresy; in 1491 Alice Hignall was charged on the subject of images, which she maintained should be chopped for firewood; and proceedings of

1511 and 1512 showed that Alice Rowley had been active for over twenty years teaching her views on the sacrament (Thomson 1965). Ludlow suggests that this religious activity increased as the sixteenth century progressed, with the Protestant stress on every individual's responsibility for their own salvation, with more and more women rejecting a passive role in spiritual matters: 'women, of all religious persuasions, were as willing and able as their male counterparts to protest againt religous practices and doctrines which were not in accordance with their own beliefs' (Ludlow 1978: 163-4). There were references to women preaching and prophesying in tract and sermon literature from early in the seventeenth century, but, since theology, and in particular St Paul, demanded silence of women, then any public utterence could be seen as a breach of this ordinance against women's preaching:

> Contemporary reference to women preachers, therefore, although often applied specifi-
> cally to women who openly expounded Scriptures in public, was also used in the
> generic sense to describe a general class of activity which consisted of any voicing of
> religious opinion – in print, in the church or congregation, in the company of others
> anywhere, and even in the home in disagreement with one's husband. (Ludlow 1978: 8)

Women of the revolutionary period represented the culmination of a long-estab-
lished tradition of dissent in England, just as the women petitioners of the period were in the tradition of women protesters against enclosure, or bread rioters. The difference was perhaps mostly one of scale: 'there had been isolated social and politi-
cal rebellion, but [medieval society] proved capable always of containing discontent and absorbing the restless in the old order of things' (Rowbotham 1972: 19). What differed in the middle years of the century, then, was not that an entirely new phenomenon was manifested, but that the particular combination of political and cultural circumstances permitted the radical sects to proliferate and take root to an unprecedented extent.

It was the first Civil War in the early 1640s that marked the emergence of these groups in any significant number: 'With only a handful of separatist churches in the 1630s, and perhaps a population of 1,000 separatists in 1641, London could by 1646 boast thirty-six gathered churches; while by 1670, London Quakers alone possibly numbered between 8,000 and 10,000' (Reay 1984a: 12). Although numerically too insignificant to influence the events leading to the outbreak of the war, the sects none the less benefited from the conditions created by it. As Reay notes, the 1640s saw the demise of the Star Chamber, the Court of High Commission, the Councils of Wales and the North, episcopacy, the church courts, the House of Lords, and censorship, as well as the executions of the Earl of Strafford, the Archbishop of Canterbury and the King. New bodies created included the county committees, which had the power to call 'errant ministers and politically suspect landlords' before them and to deprive them of their parishes and lands. The testimonies of artisans, labourers and women before these committees, concerning the competence and political respectability of their hitherto superiors, were now permissible. Tithes were never abolished, but many people simply stopped paying them; there were enclosure riots in at least twenty-six counties betwen 1640 and 1644; and people petitioned, agitated and demonstrated. 'Popular agitation', as Reay says, 'forced the pace of the English Revolution' (Reay 1984a: 4-6). This helped constitute a context in which the sects could flourish and gain influence: 'The reluctance of the peers to enforce the law against dissent from the established church, coupled with the prospect of the imminent collapse of episcopacy, led to the proliferation of conventicles in London' (Watts 1978: 79). In addition, McGregor points out that 'local magistrates were generally uncertain of the law and lacked confidence in their power to deal with lay preachers' (McGregor 1984: 32). The harsh penalties previously imposed upon dissenters, then, were no longer an effective discouragement.

Another decisive factor in the growth of the sects was the New Model Army. By 1642 most of the orthodox ministers accompanying the regiments had gone home: 'the soldiers were thus left largely to their own devices, and the army became a training ground of lay preachers whose activities Parliament laboured in vain to suppress' (Watts 1978: 107). Nor was this influence confined to the army: as the soldiery travelled the country, the ideas being discussed by them were disseminated amongst the people they met. Thomas Edwards, a vehement anti-sectarian, attributed the spread of sectarianism in large part to the movements of the army: 'Every taking of a town or city [by the Parliamentary army] … is a further spreading over the kingdom the gangrene of heresy and error, where the errors were never known nor heard of before' (Edwards, quoted in Watts 1978: 111).

Religion, in one form or another, was at the heart of the revolution for all parties involved; it was 'both the legitimizing ideology of the rulers and … the revolutionary idiom of the ruled' (Reay 1984a: 3). It was, however, an idiom that was not consistent or uniform amongst all the sects: Reay comments that the 1640s saw not only the disintegration of the Church of England but also of Puritanism (Reay 1984a: 9-10). The resulting plethora of groupings, alignments and sympathies are hard not only for twentieth-century historians to distinguish from one another; the difficulty was shared by seventeenth-century commentators:

> It was difficult for contemporaries to differentiate between millenarian Quakers and millenarian Fifth Monarchists, whose social programmes and aggressive foreign policies were so similar … [B]efore 1661 this distinction [between sects] did not exist. A government spy reported in 1657 'it is said that the Anabaptists and Quakers were chiefly active' in the Fifth Monarchist conspiracy of that year. (Hill 1993: 310)

This crossover helps explain why there are so many, and such important, continuities between the different sects. Reay has identified some 'radical themes' common to all of them. These, he suggest, included an emphasis om immediate contact with the divine; stress on experienced truth against established, given truth; rejection of the distinction between layman and priest, and of the notion of an established church; hostility to tithes; speculation about the existence of heaven and hell; and the advocacy of human effort as a means of salvation, or at least as an attempt to control the Calvinist doctrine of predestination. He also notes a theme of practical morality; of treating others as you would wish to be treated, amongst Levellers, Diggers and Quakers; and an emphasis on action against oppression amongst Levellers, Diggers,

Quakers, some Ranters, and Fifth Monarchists; a strong sense of community; a general desire to see law reform; and, for most, criticism of the monarchy, nobility and gentry. Yet he notes that only the Diggers were out to overthrow property (Reay 1984a: 14-18).

This is not to suggest a homogeneity amongst the sects that did not exist.[12] The identity of each group was not dependent only on its own beliefs and practices, but on distinguishing them from those of the other sects: George Fox, for example, noted that many Quakers were drawn from 'shattered' Baptist communities, but he was careful to dissociate the Quakers from the Ranters. The emphasis changed, too, as different groups were to the fore: in Reay's words, the 1640s were dominated by the Levellers, who were superseded by the Fifth Monarchists in the early 1650s, until they were eclipsed in the mid-1650s by the Quakers. The Baptists were 'a kind of common denominator of radicalism' (Reay 1984a: 20), and survive the whole of the 1640s and 1650s and beyond. Thus Puritanism did not simply evolve into a set of groups united in their opposition to the monarchy and the Church of England, but diversified and divided into different tendencies, influential at different times, putting forward different analyses and proposing different solutions to their definitions of the nation's problems.

It was under these circumstances and in this context that notions of spiritual equality came to be of such significance for the proliferating sects. The 'ungendered soul' on which this equality depends is key to an understanding of both the proliferation of writings by women from the sects in the mid-seventeenth century, and the dynamics of the textual processes themselves, for it offered a discourse that was both oppositional to and rooted in the status quo, both subversive and conservative. In other words, it took as its foundation the discourses of feminine subservience, inferiority and obedience, which were founded in, and justified by, women's inferior or unequal bodies and minds, and manifested most clearly in theological, medical and legal writings. It also, however, crucially, clearly and absolutely placed limits on this subordination: for the inferiority related to this life and this body only. The woman, then, was subject to her husband in earthly matters and to God in spiritual matters; in neither case was her 'self' or her own will of importance: 'She may do nothing against God's will; but many things must she do against her own will if her husband require her' (Gouge 1622: 337). In general, no conflict would arise between these two loyalties to God and to her husband, for 'a woman who truly loved God would be sure to love God's image in her husband' (Haller and Haller 1941-42: 257). It was this dual, but none the less hierarchical, loyalty, however, that generated a conflict that proved to be so productive for women writers from the radical sects: for if a husband forbade his wife from performing a godly duty, she should, after proper prayer and reflection, follow God's will. Her loyalty to her husband, then, should be absolute in matters temporal; but in spiritual matters, because of the 'ungendered soul', women's equal inheritance of grace and salvation with men, and the consequent responsibility of each individual for the salvation of her or his own soul, women's duty to their husbands stopped at the point where it conflicted with their spiritual well-being. This discrepancy between what was due to God and what was due to a husband was productive of some of the most forceful and persuasive justifications for the immodest act of writing (amongst others) offered by women writers from the sects. If a woman's writing was interpreted by her husband as transgressive of her proper, modest, silent and submissive familial role, and he consequently tried to prohibit her from continuing with it, then she had incontrovertible religious grounds for defying her husband and continuing in her obedience to God's will with this work.[13]

The ungendered soul, then, was at the heart of women sectaries' reconfigurations of femininity, a reconfiguration that is articulated again and again in justification of the texts that they produced. Alongside this, and indeed as a part of it, the 'shared code' of bodily inferiority remains – just as it does for the reconfigurations of the feminine through legal and familial discourses – unchallenged and unquestioned. It is in the dialogue conducted through the varying interpretations of this code – the limits of legal responsibility, the boundaries of the family, the implications of the ungendered soul – that we can begin to chart the meanings of femininity within the context of the seventeenth-century radical sects. It is with the articulation, deployment and refiguring of these interpretations that the rest of this book is concerned.

3

'By the dumb she meaneth herself':
silences in radical sectarian women's writing

The seventeenth century is newly discovered territory for contemporary feminist literary critics and historians. Until five or ten years ago, one might have been forgiven for inferring from the body of feminist work on women's writing from previous centuries that there really was nothing of significance dating from before the end of the eighteenth century, bar the odd footnoted writer such as Mary Sidney, Margaret Cavendish or Aphra Behn.[1] Latterly, however, studies such as Elaine Hobby's (1988), Phyllis Mack's (1992) and Barbara Lewalski's (1993), and the collections edited by Isobel Grundy and Susan Wiseman (1992) and by Clare Brant and Diane Purkiss (1992), have not only largely scotched the idea that the seventeenth century forms a kind of prehistory to women's writing, but they have also set the record straight concerning the extent and forms of women's literary production during this century, and have testified to the richness of the material for a feminist analysis.

Of continuing interest, however, is what lay behind the critical silence of the 1970s and much of the 1980s concerning this body of writing. What was it that meant that, whilst the late eighteenth and the nineteenth centuries were easily – and quickly – recognised as the seed-bed and forcing-house of women's literary achievement, the seventeenth century was largely unrecognised and undocumented,[2] apparently offering little to the feminist researcher interested in the history of women's writing? As we now know, it was certainly not a lack of material produced by women at this time that occasioned such an oversight: both Hilda Smith and Susan Cardinale's annotated bibliography of women's writings from the seventeenth century (1990), and Maureen Bell, George Parfitt and Simon Shepherd's *Biographical Dictionary of English Women Writers 1580-1720* (1990), have demonstrated the profusion of texts by women, in particular during the latter half of the century.

Although an absence of 'primary' material, then, cannot account for the silence surrounding the seventeenth century, perhaps its location and inaccessibility can, to some extent, do so. Even now, the vast majority of the literary production by women during these years is located only in academic libraries and archives, never republished since its original appearance in print. This is certainly a barrier to be overcome by the cub researcher: I recall clearly my own rather bemused negotiation of identity cards, the checking of *bona fides*, and the intimidating, if flattering, assumptions of enthusiast librarians that I was some kind of expert before even the first page of the first book had been turned. But this in itself cannot fully account for these silences: feminist researchers of eighteenth- and nineteenth-century writings will have encountered similar impediments at the outset of their projects, yet the task of recognition was accomplished some ten or fifteen years earlier. The archival locations of this material, then, are no more than an expected first hurdle in any literary historical investigation.

Perhaps a more convincing explanation for this silence can be found in the forms of the writing and the prevailing literary institutions and contexts of the seventeenth century. Feminist researchers investigating the eighteenth and nineteenth centuries have been aided by the familiarity of the forms and genres deployed and developed by the objects of their research. Not only did these writers work within modes still current, or at least recognisable, in the twentieth century – the novel, poetry, drama, the essay – they have also been recognised (again, largely thanks to the work of feminists)[3] as being instrumental in the development and transformation of genres, in particular the novel. Whilst there is a body of seventeenth-century women's writing that conforms to these familiar generic forms (such as the the poetry of Katherine Philips and the drama of Aphra Behn), and whilst it was indeed this work that was the first to be unearthed and republished, it is none the less the case that the majority of the published output by women writers of the seventeenth century is (as was discussed in Chapter 1) in forms unfamiliar and inhospitable to twentieth-century eyes focused on canonical works: for most of this writing was generated within the context of the radical religious sects that proliferated in the middle years of the century, and takes the form of conversion narratives, spiritual autobiographies, prophecies, and pamphlets urging their readership to repent or warning them of impending retributions if they fail to do so. In the late twentieth century, where religious discourse is widely seen either as liberal philanthropising or as reactionary fundamentalist cant, such material might at first sight seem to constitute an unpromising subject for a feminist analysis.

The increase in the numbers of the radical sects and of the people active within them (see Chapter 2), together with the breakdown of the system of state-regulated censorship between 1640 and 1660, then, helps to account for this proliferation of writings by women. As I discussed in the previous chapter, the sects' stress on the accountability of the individual before God facilitated the increased production of such writings, in which they anatomised and negotiated their relationships with God and with the world. In addition, the *kinds* of writings – the characteristic forms of sectarian texts – and their lack of familiarity can also be understood in the context of the development of what is now generally understood as the institution of 'literature'. Clearly the term itself is now fiercely contested within the academy: debates about 'classic' or 'great' literature versus popular or mass literature (in other words, about the constitution and politics of the object of study) have been well rehearsed (see Chapters 1 and 4); having said that, its still widely accepted definition as creative or imaginative writing remains in currency in many contexts. This, however, is a relatively recent definition, stemming from (argues Terry Eagleton) the Romantics:

prior to this, 'literature' referred to 'the whole body of valued writing in society', so that the criteria of acceptability were not primarily aesthetic but ideological (Eagleton 1983: 17). The weightiness and fixity of what has been deemed enduring or great writing for the most part of the twentieth century simply did not attach to seventeenth- or eighteenth-century ideas about writing. For writing to be acceptable in the seventeenth century, then, it did not of necessity conform to the accepted literary genres that have structured twentieth-century ideas about literature. Instead, alongside the proliferation of the sects, we see a proliferation of these different kinds of writing, conforming to a set of prescriptions quite other than the 'literary'. The absence of continuity in the *forms* of writing available for study, then, may also help us account for the feminist silence around seventeenth-century women's writing: it was, perhaps, hard to know what to do with a set of texts concerned with the intricacies of the preparations for the establishment of the New Jerusalem or the iniquity of the inhabitants of Oxford (Cary 1651; Biddle 1655).

Even this, though, does not fully explain the silence since, for many years, critics had been analysing and commentating the writings of men from the radical sects, making sense of their pronouncements on issues similar to those engaged with by the women writers. Critics considered such matters as the origins of the spiritual autobiography (Ebner 1971), the defining characteristics of Puritan writing (Watkins 1972), and the language of Quakerism (Cope 1956; Bauman 1983) or of the sects more generally (Smith 1989). The unfamiliarity of the genres and forms was clearly no barrier here. So it was not that there was no precedent for looking at this work, no body of criticism to engage or enrage the feminist researcher; it was more that there was a lacuna when it came to that body of writing produced by *women* from the sects.

Whilst there was for a long time little investigation of seventeenth-century women's writing amongst feminist scholars, there was none the less curiosity about what was perceived as that century's 'missing writing'. Rather than looking at the material that did exist, feminists instead tended to ask why we did not have a *different* kind of women's writing to investigate, why we did not have (for example) a female Shakespeare. Olive Schreiner asked this question in the 1880s:

> What of the possible Shakespeares we might have had who passed their life from youth upward brewing currant wine and making pastries for fat country squires to eat ... stifled out without one line written, simply because being of the weaker sex, life gave no room for action and grasp on life? (Schreiner 1883, quoted in Olsen 1980: 6)

Similarly, and more famously, Virginia Woolf suggested that, had Shakespeare had a sister as gifted as he, her talents would have come to nothing, for 'all the conditions of her life, all her instincts, were hostile to the state of mind which is needed to free whatever is in the brain' (Woolf 1928: 52). Such questions begin from the premise that there is an absence of writing, and that this absence is of importance: in other words, it is the consequence of a particular configuration of circumstances and not just an accident of history or an indicator of an inferior intellect or creative faculty.

This line of questioning has implications for how the silence around women's writings of the seventeenth century might be understood, for it starts from the

53

premise that there was both a silence and a silencing in that century itself: in other words, both an absence and a suppression of women's writings. Much feminist work of the 1970s and early 1980s was concerned to expose the absences and explore the dynamics and processes of these phenomena in relation to women's writing in general. Tillie Olsen's book *Silences* (Olsen 1980) is the most well-known and exhaustive example of this concern. Her whole argument, a collage of quotations and meditations on this theme, aims to challenge the idea that silence is indicative of a lack or absence; instead, Olsen suggests that silences are produced by particular sets of hostile circumstances:

> These are not *natural* silences – ... that necessary time for renewal, lying fallow, gestation, in the natural cycle of creation. The silences I speak of here are unnatural: the unnatural thwarting of what struggles to come into being, but cannot. In the old, the obvious parallels: when the seed strikes stone; the soil will not sustain; the spring is false; the time is drought or blight or infestation; the frost comes premature. (Olsen 1980: 6; original emphasis)

Although she documents both women and men who experience such circumstances, she argues that the specificities of women's social positions and psychic formations mean that such conditions have a particular impact on women's relationship to writing: 'women are traditionally trained to place others' needs first, to feel these needs as their own (the "infinite capacity"); their sphere, their satisfaction to be in making it possible for others to use their abilities' (Olsen 1980: 17). Olsen goes on to document evidence of these silences and to chart the ways in which they functioned. Either, she suggests, conditions were so unfavourable that women did not write at all; or, if they did, then the condemnation they received meant that they tended not to write again; if the work got into print, then it was seldom referred to (unless negatively) and even more rarely was it ever republished. This, then, is an account of devaluation, dismissive critical attitudes, a hostile literary climate, restriction, and constriction (Olsen 1980: 40-1); these, according to Olsen, explain and account for women's silences.

Whilst Olsen writes more about the forces which maintain women's silences, Joanna Russ, in *How to Suppress Women's Writing* (1984) is more concerned to anatomise the silencing of women: the processes which ensure the dismissal and disappearance of women's writing if and once it finds its way into print. Thus, she is concerned to trace 'patterns in the suppression of women's writing':

> The methods ... are varied but tend to occur in certain key areas: informal prohibitions (including discouragement and the inaccessibility of materials and training), denying the authorship of the work in question (this ploy ranges from simple misattribution to psychological subtleties that make the head spin), belittlement of the work itself in various ways, isolation of the work from the tradition to which it belongs and its consequent presentation as anomalous, assertions that the work indicates the author's bad character and hence is of primarily scandalous interest or ought not to have been done at all (this did not end with the nineteenth century), and simply ignoring the

works, the workers, and the whole tradition, the most commonly employed technique and the hardest to combat. (Russ 1984: 5)

Chapter by chapter, Russ goes on to detail how each of these methods operates, offering detailed evidence culled from an enormous variety of sources.

Work such as Olsen's and Russ's has been extremely important for feminist scholars seeking to engage in the debate as to why 'there has never been a female Shakespeare', or, more precisely, why there is not a body of work written by women to parallel that produced by men. Their accounts of exclusion, prohibition, control and prevention confront us with the range and complexity of the barriers to be circumvented or surmounted by women writers of the present as well as of the past. In the context of the seventeenth century, these arguments have been fundamental for exposing the very specific impediments encountered by women writers at that time.

First, these discussions have enabled critics to recognise the extent of the 'silencing' of women during this time. Just as recent work has been concerned to correct the notion that there was no seventeenth-century women's writing, so the work of Olsen and Russ reminds us to look at this profusion of texts by women in the middle years of the century in the broader context of a continuing 'silence'. It is certainly true that the number of texts produced by women increased greatly in the course of the century. Patricia Crawford outlines the changes in this way:

> The impact of the Civil Wars and Interregnum upon women's publications was re-markable. The quantity of publications increased ... to sixty-nine new editions in the half-decade 1646-50, which was the greatest number of women's first editions in any half-decade of the century. In addition, after 1640 there was an expansion of the range of women's publications. They began to publish in political controversy, and wrote prose fictions. Increasingly, women wrote of their personal experiences and published lives and letters. (Crawford 1985: 213)

Crawford relates this eruption into print quite directly to the political events of the time:

> The Civil War and Interregnum were the high points of women's publication ... Two things were important. First, the Wars forced women to act in a number of unaccus-tomed roles. With husbands, fathers and sons away fighting or in exile, women were defenders of their homes, petitioners for estates and generally responsible for their families' survival. Secondly, in order to debate political issues, they had to engage in political controversy. The experience of opposition and hostility forced them to refine and sharpen their arguments, and so led to further publications. (Crawford 1985: 213)

These statements give a good sense of the richness, newness and profusion of the material available for study, and offer a convincing and generally accepted explana-tion of why this proliferation should have happened when it did. However, what is obscured by accounts such as this is that, owing to the general increase in published work during this period, the proportion of publications produced by women writers remains almost unchanged. For example, even within sects such as the Quakers, in which all members were, at least in the early years, seen as spiritually equal and therefore equally likely to be called to witness to the inner light, only 82 of the 650 writers recorded as writing between 1650 and 1700 were women: less than thirteen per cent (Barbour and Roberts 1973: 14). Similarly, in relation to the spiritual auto-biography, a genre often discussed for its centrality in the process of women's 'coming to voice' in the seventeenth century, women's autobiographies 'make up roughly ten per cent of the total produced in the seventeenth century' (Pomerleau 1980: 21). Taking the totality of women's published work, the picture shows even less cause for celebration: Elaine Hobby has calculated that less than one per cent of published writers between 1649 and 1688 were women (Hobby 1988: 6). Statistics such as these are salutary reminders that silences, as anatomised by Olsen and Russ, need to remain as a constituent of any discussion of seventeenth-century women's writing: for whilst there was an *overall* rise in women's published output, in terms of it as a *percentage* of the total output, very little changed.

In addition to this, and perhaps more importantly, Olsen and Russ's work use-fully reminds us that we should not take all such silences as absences, and that there are many different kinds of silence and silencing. They insist that we take account of the long tradition of male hostility, both explicit and implicit, to women's writing, and that even writing that did find its way into print will bear the marks of its context of production. Within the texts written by women in the sects, for example, there are a number of indications of this that give a sense of the barriers to writing encountered by their authors, some of which I want now to outline: self-depreciation and reluctance to publish, 'ownings' by husbands and fellow sectaries, and endorse-ments that serve to denigrate other women.

'She was backward to appear': reticence and self-depreciation in sectarian women's writings

Self-depreciation takes many forms in these writings; one important manifestation of it, however, can be found in the repeated claims that the author was reluctant to publish. Mary Mollineux, for example, wrote that she wanted to publish her poems, all of which were concerned with some aspect of her Quaker beliefs, but knew that others' reactions to this lack of modesty would invalidate anything she might other-wise achieve. She therefore confined the exercise of her 'peculiar gifts' to within her immediate circle of Friends and family, and, as this constituted another way of serving them and so maintained her work within the private sphere, this allowed her modesty and honour to remain uncompromised. Once dead, however, her modesty could no longer be assailed by publication, as others took over responsibility for this:

> she was not then free that her name should be exposed; she not seeking praise amongst men, but to communicate the exercise of peculiar gifts amongst her near friends and acquaintance; but now ... I think it would be ungrateful to her memory, and also a wronging of others, to keep such worthy things unpublished. (Mollineux 1702: 'Testi-mony' by Tryal Ryder.)

Mollineux's memory could be elevated in death in a manner which, in her lifetime, would have been a sure way of damning it. The demands of modesty and respectablility outlined in the previous chapter, then, ensured the 'silence' of Mollineux in her own lifetime.

A similar kind of reluctance, even self-censorship, can be found in the testimonies preceding the Quaker Elizabeth Stirredge's work. It was written of her that 'altho' the Lord had given her a large gift, and a good utterance, she was not forward to appear in her public service' (Stirredge 1711: 'Testimony from Several Friends'); John Thornton similarly notes in a separate preface that 'altho' the Lord had given her a large gift in verbal testimony, yet she was backward to appear therein, except she found it was immediately required of her' (Stirredge 1711: 'Testimony ... by John Thornton'). Silence (particularly for a Quaker, and particularly for a woman) was a mark of godliness; to break it by preaching and writing demanded a particular kind of certainty and confidence that the words did indeed come from God. Although we cannot take such testimonies as necessarily offering straightforward access to the truth about these authors' attitudes to their writing (for there were a series of generic and sectarian conventions that comprise an important part of their production), it is none the less significant that in these cases, and elsewhere, the assertion of reluctance to publish on the part of the author was clearly seen to function as a commendation of her honour and worth, confirmation of her modesty and retiring nature, and thus as a recommendation of the work as worthy of attention.

A particularly striking example of this kind of relationship between silence and publication can be found in the work of the more conservative Presbyterian Mary Simpson, whose *Faith and Experience* was published after her death in 1649, together with the sermon preached at her funeral by John Collings. In her own text she wrote that all she desired was to be 'serviceable' and to submit to God's will, but it is in Collings's sermon that this idea is clarified: the one trait of her character that he repeatedly praises is her self-abasement: 'I must not exalt her, whose constant design and practice, was so much to debase her self'; 'her God had subdued her spirit to the feet of his own will' (Collings, in Simpson 1649: 67, 71). As with Mary Mollineux, Simpson is praised by Collings for limiting the exercising of her gift for preaching to her immediate circle: 'she preached by privately instructing others in the ways of God' (Collings, in Simpson 1649: 66-7).

This reluctance to publish was not confined to the authors themselves, but can also be found in the accounts of fellow sectaries' attitudes to these texts. For example, in R. T.'s (her fellow-Quaker, Rebeckah Travers's) testimony prefacing Alice Curwen's spiritual autobiography, she writes that 'in my mind I had not much for printing it, there not being much prophecy in it' (Curwen 1680: 'R. T.'s testimony'). Jane Turner met with discouragements from her fellow Baptists on the publication of her spiritual autobiography, which compounded her own misgivings: 'as I had some discouraging thoughts as to my writing of it at the first, so I have met with the like as to my giving way to the publishing it' (Turner 1653: 'A word from the Author to the Reader'). Anne Wentworth, another Baptist but writing much later, in the restrictive climate of the 1670s, similarly records opposition, in this case not only from her fellow Baptists but also from her husband: she records 'the bitter zeal of several eminent professors of religion, commonly called Baptists, who have most unjustly and unchristianlike caused all their pretended church power to wait upon and serve the wrath of my oppressors', as well as her need 'to finish a work which my earthly husband in a most cruel manner hindered me from performing, seizing and running away with my writings' (Wentworth 1677: 1, 5).

These examples illustrate the pressures to remain silent, not to speak or write, that existed in the seventeenth century and that were, as Olsen suggested, quite clearly gendered. As I outlined in the previous chapters, exhortations to remain silent were quite explicitly directed at women, anything else entailing the risk of compromising or jeopardising their modesty and honour. Many women, however, did both write and publish; and the following examples focus more on the 'silencing', what happenened to contain or diminish women's writings once they did find their way into print.

An indicator of one form of 'silencing' can be found in the way that so many of these texts by women in the sects are prefaced by testimonies or epistles by family or fellow-sectaries validating or 'owning' the work.[4] These have the express intention of vouching for the spiritual authenticity of the text by confirming the moral worthiness of its author. Typically, then, we find texts – particularly spiritual autobiographies, where the identity of the author is so explicitly implicated in the text – hedged in with two, three or more of these testimonies.[5] One key example of this occurs in the spiritual autobiography of the Baptist Jane Turner, *Choice Experiences* (1653). In this, Turner drew a series of moral precepts from the principal events of her coming to faith; however, preceding this account, Turner's husband wrote a lengthy explanatory dedicatory epistle:

> I know it would seem very strange to you, if this following treatise should come to your hands without my public owning of it, as indeed well it might, considering my near relation to the author; it is no small joy to my heart that the Lord is pleased in these our days any way by any means to put his people in mind of that which they are so prone to forget.
>
> ... Beloved brethren, you have here the labours of one of the weakest sex, which I trust will occasion you the more to give glory to God, in that his strength appear in weakness ... Let her works praise her; only I have this I cannot but say, it was not her desire to publish it, her reasons she hath expressed. Secondly, so far as one can speak for another, I can say for my wife, in this work she hath had little help from men or things, but I believe much from the Lord ... At my first sight of it, which was when it was near finished, though I believe I was the first that saw it, next herself, I was so surprized, knowing nothing of it before, that I knew not what to say of it; but upon consideration, and reviewing of it, I was very much pressed in spirit to publish it.
> (Turner 1653: 'Epistle Dedicatory' by Captain John Turner)

This narrative offers a fascinating account of the processes whereby John Turner gained control of his wife's unsolicited and errant text. First, he addresses his words to his 'Beloved brethren', rather than, as was more common, to both 'brothers and sisters'; this suggests that the textual processes of his epistle had a particular relevance for a male readership, as indeed is confirmed by his opening sentence. John Turner predicts such a readership would find it 'strange' if the text were not accompanied by a 'public owning of it' from the author's husband. As a woman, Turner's actions and writings would have implications for not only herself but for her husband, who was legally responsible for her; her words, in other words, were also his. He recognises this situation, but also its instability, when he writes 'so far as one can speak for another, I can say for my wife': legally and socially he can indeed speak for her, but the reason for his speaking (or writing) now was precisely because he has found her to be speaking/writing for herself. He therefore needs to 'own' the text both in the sense of publicly declaring his support for its precepts, and also in the sense of taking control of it and its destiny: as well as speaking for his wife, it is also he, after all, that 'considers', 'reviews' and is 'pressed in spirit to publish it'. Part of this process of 'owning' the text involves confirming the conformity of his wife to contemporary descriptions and prescriptions of weakness and unworthiness: she is one of 'the weakest sex', and he expresses his joy that God is prepared to communicate his message 'in these our days any way by any means' – even, he implies, by making use of one such as his wife. Although he suggests that the work alone is sufficient testimony to its own worth, he none the less finds it necessary to add two more justifacatory riders: first, that she was against the idea of publishing the work, her modesty, as was appropriate, restricting her ambitions to the private sphere. Secondly, he confirms that the work was executed with the help of God, not of 'men or things': this guarantees its spiritual origins by denying its material ones, and also, perhaps, reassures his readers that his wife has not been seeking out the company of others during the writing of the text. John Turner's epistle, then, moves towards the owning or appropriation of Jane Turner's writing, and casts it in a such a way as to render it compatible with the demands of respectability. His acknowledgement of his own surprise at learning of the text's existence – a discovery which resulted in his own temporary silence ('I knew not what to say of it') – disrupts the smooth surface of his account, however, and makes clear why he went to such lengths in his preface to contain and defuse the possible implications of his wife's self-inscription.

One way in which these dedicatory epistles construct a validation of the texts' authors is through praising them. However, even the praise that is meted out to women writers from the sects can be seen as a form of silencing: for the praise it accords to this writer is very often at the expense of all other women; in other words, it is the contrast between this woman and most other women that is noteworthy. Frances Owen, for example, wrote of her cousin Mary Mollineux that she was 'quick, witty and studiously inclined, [so that] her father brought her up to more learning, than is commonly bestowed on our sex' (Mollineux 1702: 'Testimony from … Frances Owen'). Theophila Townsend wrote that Joan Vokins, another Quaker, who had crossed the Atlantic to spread the Quaker faith, served God, 'not sparing her weak body, which in appearance, was fitter to keep her chamber, than travel as she did; who left husband and children, and all other outward enjoyments for the truth['s] sake, and went over-sea to answer the Lord' (Vokins 1691: 'Testimony ... by Theophila Townsend'). Elizabeth Stirredge was 'gifted for the ministry, and acquainted with the wiles and subtle devices of the enemy, was made a serviceable instrument in our defence and preservation; being attended with power, wisdom, and true zeal for the prosperity of the truth, and people of God' (Stirredge 1711: 'Testimony from several Friends'). Hugh Peter, in his praise of fellow Fifth Monarchist Mary Cary's works of prophecy, establishes her in opposition to all the rest of her sex, and implies that religion is a way to keep women out of mischief if they refuse to keep to their household duties: 'she hath taught her sex that there are more ways than one to avoid idleness ... They that will not use the distaff may improve a pen' (Cary 1651: prefatory epistle by Hugh Peter; see Appendix A below). He describes Cary as singular in her holiness, in contrast with the manifest unfitness of all other women for this kind of work: a 'holy, modest and painful spirit' runs through her writing; 'in this dress you shall neither see naked breasts, black patches, nor long trains, but only words of the coming of Christ and the comfort of saints'. He goes on to suggest that Cary's work is so well written that it is hard to believe that it is written by her at all: 'you might easily think that she ploughed with another's heifer, were not the contrary well-known' (Cary 1651: prefatory epistle by Hugh Peter). For a testimony seeking to recommend the work of a woman writer, what is most noteworthy about Peter's statement is how double-edged all the compliments are: in praising her, he both denigrates other women (both in terms of social rank and of sex), and concurs with the projected reaction that it is extraordinary that a woman should write as well as this. His praise sets Cary apart from all other women, reinforcing the idea that she is an anomaly, and that women in general are unfitted for this kind of work. His validation of Cary is dependent on the silence of other, lesser, women.[6]

Such readings, then, demonstrate how work such as Olsen's and Russ's has been invaluable for feminist scholars addressing both textual presences and absences from past centuries. Their significance lies partly in that they have contributed to the move towards retrieval, the refusal to accept that the silences surrounding women's writing from the seventeenth century was a reliable indicator that no such writing existed, and partly in that they began the work of anatomising and analysing the structures and functioning of women's silences and silencing. Silences, they stressed, take many forms, and can be traced by means of careful attention to the many clues embedded in the texts that we do have, as well as in the responses to these texts, the circumstances of their publication and in their subsequent disappearance.

Whilst these theories of silence and silencing offer us a valuable perspective on the relationship between gender and writing in the seventeenth century, there is nevertheless a limit to their usefulness in the analysis of contemporary seventeenth-century gender/power relations. Although they alert readers to many of the complexities of the relationships between silence, silencing, writing and publishing, and in particular to the gendered character of the power relations operating here, their model suggests that there is an absolute distinction between the 'dominant' and the 'oppressed', in this case the silencer and the silenced, and consequently it posits a rather monolithic notion of power, in which it functions endlessly and successfully to constrain women writers. This conception of power might lead us to ask how we can account for the existence of any writers at all at this time, if these processes of silencing served the dominant patriarchal order so well. Furthermore, to locate power solely in the hands of those opposed to such textual productions may well misleadingly deflect attention from the processes of power operating within the texts themselves.

Olsen and Russ's approaches can be seen to tend towards an implicit reinforcement of what Foucault (1979) termed 'the repressive hypothesis': the idea that mechanisms of repression, suppression, denial and censorship function to silence whatever the dominant order perceives as threatening, disruptive or subversive. What is needed instead, perhaps, is a model that can take account of the textual mechanisms whereby women writers negotiated power and resistance, and that can examine how these discourses of denial or repression might function as a constituent in the production of the very thing that they seek to deny. It is to this issue that I now want to turn. How might the silences and silencings of seventeenth-century radical sectarian women writers identified in this chapter so far have been productive of the very texts or utterances against which they were apparently pitted? And how might this change the way that we understand these texts in the context of seventeenth-century gender/power relations? In order to explore the implications of these questions, I want first to discuss aspects of the work of three theorists who have conceptualised silence in rather different ways from those discussed above: Macherey, Jameson and Foucault. I shall examine how their ideas about silence, writing, discourse and power might extend our understandings of writings by seventeenth-century women.

Macherey, Jameson and Foucault: making the silence speak

> The speech of the book comes from a certain silence, a matter which it endows with form. Thus, the book is not self-sufficient; it is necessarily accompanied by a *certain absence*, without which it would not exist. A knowledge of the book must include a consideration of this absence. (Macherey 1978: 85; original emphasis)

This quotation is suggestive of how Macherey's arguments concerning silence and writing both extend and change the perspectives I have outlined so far in this chapter. Like Olsen and Russ, his concern here is with 'silence'; like them, he argues that silence is not something diametrically opposed to writing, but, rather, that it is something that forms a part of the writing itself, and can be detected within it: 'in its every particle, the work *manifests*, uncovers, what it cannot say. This silence gives it life' (Macherey 1978: 84).

Unlike Olsen and Russ, however, he is not concerned with the manifestation within the text of the silencing of the *author*, but with *textual* silences, the text's unarticulated ideological concomitants. This, he suggests, is not something undesirable, a manifestation of a hostile repressive force attempting to deny or silence the impulse to expression, but more of a necessary condition of *any* text. All writing, he argues, is composed of both what is said and what is unsaid; the unsaid is manifested in gaps, contradictions, omissions in the said, characteristics which are symptomatic of what he terms the text's 'unconscious' (but not, he underlines, of the author's unconscious), its 'repressions'. The revelation of the text's unconscious within the writing, it is argued, will help us to understand the 'history of ideological themes':

> This is not a question of introducing a historical explanation which is stuck on to the work from the outside. On the contrary, we must show a sort of splitting within the work: this division is *its* unconscious, in so far as it possesses one – the unconscious which is history, the play of history beyond its edges, encroaching on those edges: this is why it is possible to trace the path which leads from the haunted work to that which haunts it. Once again it is not a question of redoubling the work with an unconscious, but a question of revealing in its very gestures of expression that which is not. Then, the reverse side of what is written will be history itself. (Macherey 1978: 94)

For Fredric Jameson, too, as for Macherey, the notion of a text's 'unconscious' is central; his conceptualisation of this unconscious, whilst similar to Macherey's in terms of its mechanisms and manifestations, is articulated very explicitly as a *political* phenomenon. He suggests that the text's unconscious can be thought of as that which links it with all other texts and maintains them within the 'unity of a single great collective story', which he identifies as the 'collective struggle from freedom from necessity': 'It is in detecting the traces of that uninterrupted narrative, or restoring to the surface of the text the repressed and buried reality of this fundamental history, that the doctrine of a political unconscious finds its function and its necessity' (Jameson 1981: 20). This formulation is a useful addition to Macherey's in that it clarifies the notion of a textual as opposed to an authorial unconscious; whilst the authors may be as much produced by, or in oppositon to, the ideology of that political unconscious as anybody else, the text is not seen as revelatory of their individual psyche but of social, political or ideological forces. For both Macherey and Jameson, then, the idea of a text's *unconscious* provides a key to its interpretation: for, in Macherey's terms, it is the detection and reading of this unconscious that constitutes the task of the critic. Making the silences, absences and contradictions speak serves to make explicit the repressed textual awareness of the ideology that it embodies and that has shaped it.

Macherey's proposals for the critical project are important for the way in which they insist on the interrelationship between the said and the unsaid in the text: in other words, that these are not two discrete phenomena, but that each is shaped by, and is an aspect of, the other. Silence, according to this model, can take many forms and be found in many locations. Certain *extra*-textual silences, for example, might be produced by certain writings (just as certain writings might be produced by certain silences), but also *within* given texts it would be possible to trace the silences, the necessarily unspoken concomitant (since nothing can say everything) of that which is articulated. Moreover, these silences are not conceived as lacks, the blank spaces between the words of the texts; instead, they are seen almost as in dialogue with the 'spoken' of the text, actively moulding and directing it as each engages with the terms and implications of the other. This extends the analysis of Olsen and Russ in that it posits the *productiveness* of the silence, and suggests a way in which we can take account of the impact it might have on the writing (and vice versa), rather than perceiving it as symptomatic only of repression, denial and prohibition. This, I would argue, is not antithetical to the work of Olsen and Russ, but takes it in a new direction. Whilst they would recognise and advocate similarly the detection and 'reading' of silences embedded in texts, they would, however, read them as symptomatic of the power relations governing the gendered right to legitimate authorship, whereas for Macherey the gender of the author is immaterial, privileging instead the internal and indeed unconscious textuality of writing.

Foucault, in turn, takes the notion of the detection and reading of silences in a somewhat different direction. In *The History of Sexuality: An Introduction* (1979) he explores the relationship between power, discourse and silence in relation, specifically, to changing ideas about sex and sexuality, but positing more general models as a result of this analysis. His principal concern is to counter the idea that the Victorian age represented the zenith of secrecy, censorship, repression, and silence about sexuality, with sexuality construed as 'a rebellious energy that must be throttled' (Foucault 1979: 81) by repressive and puritanical religious and cultural mechanisms. He argues instead that the eighteenth century and beyond saw a proliferation of discourses on sexuality: 'Western man has been drawn for three centuries to the task of telling everything concerning his sex ... A censorship of sex? There was installed rather an apparatus for producing an ever greater quantity of discourse about sex' (Foucault 1979: 23). Despite this emphasis on the articulation or the 'spokenness' of discourses of sexuality, however, Foucault suggests that this was predicated on an array of silences. Whilst, then, these discourses were explicitly concerned with the regulation and harnessing of sexuality, he argues that it was that which was *not* explicitly addressed, the implications of the unspoken, as well as the profusion of the discourses and the kinds of addressees to whom they were directed, rather than their expressed 'intention', that need the closest attention.

Foucault begins by justifying his claim that what we have is a profusion of discourses of sexuality, rather than a lack of them. He characterises the sixteenth and seventeenth centuries as times when the verbal or written articulation of feelings and experience were being increasingly emphasised and exhorted, suggesting that this urge to 'confess' was the common inheritance of both Catholicism and Protestantism:

> An imperative was established: Not only will you confess to acts contravening the law, but you will seek to transform your desire, your every desire, into discourse. Insofar as possible, nothing was meant to elude this dictum, even if the words it employed had to be carefully neutralized. (Foucault 1979: 21)

This imperative to speak (here, specifically of sex) was, he argues, not in order for it to be theorised, but for it to be classified, quantified, analysed, administered and managed, policed not in the service of a taboo, but in order that it might be regulated through 'useful and public discourses' (Foucault 1979: 25). These regulatory discourses, he argues, did not mean that less was said, just that it was said differently,

63

and by different people. Whilst Macherey urged that readers pay attention to the manifestations of the unsaid in the said, or the inscription of the silence in the text, Foucault goes further and suggests that the silences embedded in these discourses are both productive and constitutive of them:

> Silence itself – the things one declines to say, or is forbidden to name, the discretion that is required between different speakers – is less the absolute limit of discourse, the other side from which it is separated by a strict boundary, than an element that functions alongside the things said, with them and in relation to them within over-all strategies. There is no binary division to be made between what one says and what one does not say; we must try to determine the different ways of not saying such things, how those who can and those who cannot speak of them are distributed, which type of discourse is authorized, or which form of discretion is required in either case. There is not one but many silences, and they are an integral part of the strategies that underlie and permeate discourses. (Foucault 1979: 27)

Like Macherey, then, Foucault urges readers to pay attention to the unsaid as well as to the said; to discern and characterise the different kinds of silence just as one would do with different kinds of utterance.

Foucault goes on to explore the operation and interaction of different kinds of discourse, power and silence, at each stage outlining and then countering the 'dominant' versions of the history of these forms in relation to discourses of sexuality. He argues that confession, for example, is now generally understood as something that frees, whilst 'power reduces one to silence'; he suggests that the common-sense understanding of confession is as the expression of truths 'lodged in our most secret nature', which '"demands" only to surface':

> if it fails to do so, this is because a constraint holds it in place, the violence of a power weighs it down, and it can finally be articulated only at the price of a kind of liberation. Confession frees, but power reduces one to silence; truth does not belong to the order of power, but shares an original affinity with freedom. (Foucault 1979: 60)

In opposition to this 'repression–liberation' model of confession, he argues instead that confession is 'the effect of a power that constrains us':

> It plays a part in justice, medicine, education, family relationships, and love relations, in the most ordinary affairs of everyday life, and in the most solemn rites; one confesses one's crimes, one's sins, one's thoughts and desires, one's illnesses and troubles; one goes about telling, with the greatest precision, whatever is most difficult to tell. One confesses in public and in private, to one's parents, one's educators, one's doctor, to those one loves; one admits to oneself, in pleasure and in pain, things it would be impossible to tell to anyone else, the things people write books about … Western man has become a confessing animal. (Foucault 1979: 59)

In short, he argues that 'the confession became one of the West's most highly valued techniques for *producing* truth' (Foucault 1979: 59; my emphasis). He demonstrates just how he sees confession as being productive of truth by anatomising its specific forms and conventions. Rather than the straightforward expression of the 'truth' about the subject, it is played out within a very particular set of power relations:

> The confession is a ritual of discourse in which the speaking subject is also the subject of the statement; it is also a ritual that unfolds within a power relationship, for one does not confess without the presence (or virtual presence) of a partner who is not simply the interlocutor but the authority who requires the confession, prescribes and appreciates it, and intervenes in order to judge, punish, forgive, console, and reconcile; a ritual in which the truth is corroborated by the obstacles and resistances it has had to surmount in order to be formulated; and finally, a ritual in which the expression alone, independently of its external consequences, produces intrinsic modifications in the person who articulates it: it exonerates, redeems and purifies him; it unburdens him of his wrongs, liberates him, and promises him salvation. (Foucault 1979: 61-2)

The very forms and structures of the ritual of confession, then, construct its discourse as 'truth'; they produce the conditions whereby the discourse meets the demands, the criteria, of something recognisable as true, accurate, reliable. We may take confession as opening a window on the soul, but Foucault argues that the process of confession itself is productive, in the first instance, of both the window and the soul.

The other set of common-sense understandings in relation to the 'repressive hypothesis' that Foucault is concerned to counter is that concerning the operation of power. He summarises what he sees as the five key, defining ways in which power is seen to operate in relation to sex. First, 'the negative relation': all connections between power and sex are negative. Second, 'the insistence of the rule': power lays down the rules in relation to sex. Third, 'the cycle of prohibition': in order to regulate sex, power lays down a series of prohibitions, enforced through the threat of punishment. Fourth, 'the logic of censorship', in which censorship takes three forms: it affirms that something is not permitted; it prevents something from being said; and it denies that something exists. Fifth, 'the uniformity of the apparatus': the apparatus of power controlling sex acts in uniform and comprehensive ways, and operates according to endlessly reproduced mechanisms of law, taboo and censorship (Foucault 1979: 83-5). These systems of domination, the repressive institutions and mechanisms and the modes of subjugation implicit in this model, do not characterise power itelf, but instead are just the 'terminal forms power takes' (Foucault 1979: 92). In contrast, Foucault proposes a quite different model for the operation of power, one which begins from the premise that 'power is everywhere; not because it embraces everything, but because it comes from everywhere'; it is 'exercised from innumerable points, in the interplay of nonegalitarian and mobile relations' (Foucault 1979: 93, 94):

> Relations of power are not in a position of exteriority with respect to other types of relationships (economic processes, knowledge relationships, sexual relations), but are immanent in the latter; they are the immediate effects of the divisions, inequalities, and disequilibriums which occur in the latter, and conversely they are the internal

65

conditions of these differentiations; relations of power are not in superstructural positions, with merely a role of prohibition or accompaniment; they have a directly productive role, wherever they come into play. (Foucault 1979: 94)

By Foucault's account, then, power does not exist anterior to the structures and
discourses that characterise it, but is constructed through and by means of these.
Resistance to power is, likewise, not exterior to that power or arising after the fact, as
a response to it, but, just as silence structures discourse, so resistance structures
power relations:

[Resistances] are the odd term in relations of power; they are inscribed in the latter as
an irreducible opposite. Hence they too are distributed in irregular fashion: the points,
knots or focuses of resistance are spread over time and space at varying densities, at
times mobilizing groups or individuals in a definitive way. (Foucault 1979: 96)

What Foucault's account offers, rather than a series of binary oppositions (silence/
discourse, power/resistance), is a series of networks of power relations, passing
through and over groups, individuals, institutions and apparatuses, at once producing, destabilising and threatening manifestations of power:

Discourse transmits and produces power; it reinforces it, but also undermines and
exposes it, renders it fragile and makes it possible to thwart it. In like manner, silence
and secrecy are a shelter for power, anchoring its prohibitions; but they also loosen its
holds and provide for relatively obscure areas of tolerance. (Foucault 1979: 101)

This model of power has several implications for a consideration of silence and
expression. Because it recognises both the 'nonegalitarian' relations between different
social groups and different subject positions, and the multiple mechanisms of the
power relations that constitute those groups and positions, neither silence nor its
opposite are seen as the prerogative of any one group or position. Moreover, as for
Macherey, silence is seen as constitutive of discourse, and differently constitutive in
relation to different discourses; for example, that of the conversion narratives is both
different in form and effect from that of warnings to repent.

The work of Macherey, Jameson and Foucault extends the possible analyses of
silence available for a reading of seventeenth-century radical sectarian women's writing. First, it urges us to look at silence as a condition and factor of all writing: it is
not only those texts that allude to forms of silencing in relation to their authors that
yield up these silences, but all the others, too, bear witness to their own 'unsaid' in
the gaps and omissions of their 'said'. Furthermore, the unsaid is as productive, as
communicative, as constitutive of the meanings of the texts as is the said.

Secondly, Foucault's analysis of the structures and operation of power relations
suggests that we can detect both power and resistance within the said and the unsaid
of discourse, that these are not polarised into different texts, different authors, but
cross and recross different texts in different ways. This has the advantage, when
reading women's writings, of moving us away from conceptualising women only as
victims of male omnipotence, where all we can see is constraint, silencing, oppression
and powerlessness. Instead, it postulates a constant and productive negotiation of

both power and resistance across all the relationships implicit in the production of texts and meanings. It is thus important not to lose sight of the *patterned* inequalities in the distribution of power in these relationships, when extending Foucauldian insights to seventeenth-century women's texts: combining feminism and Foucault in this way we might advocate an analysis of the intersections of both power and resistance. Such a combination mitigates against a monolithic approach to silence which can cause us to overlook some of the subtleties and complexities of both female authors and their texts.

Lastly, Foucault's analysis of the productive character of confessional discourse has a particular resonance for the seventeenth-century sects, with their characteristic textual mechanisms of conversion narrative, spiritual autobiography (with its formalised stages of sin, conviction, faith and doubt) and self-surveillance (both individual and sectarian). As I go on to discuss, many of the forms of writing produced by women during this period were indeed 'confessional' texts in which their subjects were constituted by prohibition and restraint.

As many feminists have now detailed, however, there are numerous problems with Foucault's analysis of power, not least the relativising tendency of his insistence on its dispersed character. It is possible to come away from reading Foucault with the sense that the operation of power is something like so many simultaneous games of pass-the-parcel, where power is tossed playfully and indiscriminately from person to person and group to group, with everyone as likely or unlikely as everyone else to get hold of it, at least for a short time. In his desire to reject certain kinds of Marxist functionalism, Foucault perhaps neglects the ways in which power is productive according to certain repeated configurations: in other words, that the paths or channels through which power travels form patterns and thus become, to some extent at least, predictable. More specific, in terms of a feminist critique, has been the often reiterated insistence that, no matter how valuable his analysis of power relations and his insights about the constitutive forces of power, these still require gendering, much as do the models of power which preceded them. Diamond and Quinby, for example, argue that not only does his work 'gloss over the gender configurations of power' (Diamond and Quinby 1988: xiv), but it also fails to take account of the contributions made by a substantial body of feminist work concerned with many of the same issues. In particular, his theorisation of the body remains uninformed by feminist analysis of the medicalisation of women's bodies and of the mutilation of women's bodies for the sake of 'beauty' (Diamond and Quinby 1988: xv), and by feminist linguistic theory which has demonstrated how women have been 'trivialised and degraded through derogatory metaphors, deprived of access to sacred languages, or silenced altogether' and feminist literary theory which has shown how women have been excluded from written discourse; moreover, 'his almost exclusive focus on works by men pushes women's discourses of resistance to the margins of his texts' (Diamond and Quinby 1988: xv, xvi). Similar criticisms have been made by many other feminists (Morris 1988; Bartky 1988; Bordo 1993; Ramazanoglu and Holland 1993). Thus whilst our analysis may indeed benefit from adopting certain of Macherey's arguments about the silence in the text and Foucault's about the productivity of such silence, as feminist literary critics we might nevertheless continue to insist upon the gendering of both processes.

'The reverse side of what is written': silences in the radical sects

For silences to be read – and here the arguments of Olsen, Russ, Macherey and Foucault would coincide – they must be read in context, whether textual, historical or social. Detailed work on the significance of silence in a specifically seventeenth-century context has been undertaken by Richard Bauman (1983), in an ethnography of speaking and silence among seventeenth-century Quakers. Here, however, rather than reading the silences of Quaker texts, he is investigating the significance of silence in Quaker doctrine and practice more generally. His work is an invaluable starting-point in any attempt to move away from understanding silence as

> merely an abstention from speaking, or as an empty interval between utterances ... the Quaker case not only helps to suggest how richly textured and multidimensional the kinds of meanings of silence can be, but also underscores the need to examine the patterns, functions, and meanings of silence, like speaking, in ethnographic, culture-specific terms. (Bauman 1983: 11)

Quaker silences differ from others in that they were theorised and institutionalised within their practice and religious tenets. Whilst this may make the silences easier to observe and analyse, it does not necessarily follow that Quakers were exceptional in having silence structure their discourse; it may be that it just does so more explicitly.

Silence, for the early Quakers, was the fundamental precondition of godly communication, for it was in a state of silent attentiveness that the voice of God within would be heard: the 'inner light' – the usual Quaker visual metaphor for the presence of God within each individual – manifested through an aural metaphor as the voice of God. 'Carnal speaking', a concern for human communication on worldly matters, was a distraction from this voice, so the suppression of the self and the will, the rejection of all that was corrupt in the world, was also implicit in the Quaker embracing of silence. Silence, then, was not an end in itself, but 'a means to the attainment of the defining spiritual experience of early Quakerism, the direct personal experience of the spirit of God within oneself' (Bauman 1983: 23).

It was this regard for silence that structured the Quaker meeting for worship, an event that, 'in ideal terms, ... could be held in complete silence without a word being spoken aloud. God's word, manifested in the inward experience of his presence and the communion of the congregation, was sufficient' (Bauman 1983: 122). This 'communion' between worshippers could be attained in complete silence: a 'collective spiritual force generated by the group' was sufficient to refocus a wandering mind or calm a Friend who was caught up in the 'outward' business of the world: 'the heightened spiritual awareness of the other worshippers made them exquisitely sensitive to the distressed spiritual state of one who was not caught up in their communion, opening the way for God to answer his travail' (Bauman 1983: 122). Moreover, any Friend who broke the silence in meeting, whether through prayer or through preaching, did so only *by means of* silence and the workings of God therein: 'Silence was necessary for the worshipper to be open to the Word of God within, to be spiritually prepared to receive it and speak it forth' (Bauman 1983: 124). Silence, too, was the desired outcome of speaking, both for the speaker and for the auditor, for it was directed towards a greater capacity for the apprehension of the voice of God within, the voice heard only in silent watchfulness (Bauman 1983: 125).

Far, then, from words being the essence of communication and communion, they were seen as being a distraction from the attainment of true spiritual experience, and at the root of the downfall of the world's religions and their priests with their 'trade of words' (Bauman 1983: 123). In a reversal of the norm, silence is understood to be more reliably communicative, the guarantee of godliness and spiritual truth, and words are the signifiers of emptiness and meaninglessness, the absence of godliness, or at least potentially so: words are pitfalls, always fallible, to be avoided unless there is the conviction that the 'motion' and 'opening' to speak are from God.

Whilst Bauman's analysis is both fascinating and significant for the ways in which it anatomises some of the many forms and functions of silence within seventeenth-century Quakerism, what it does not do, however, is take account of the gendered character of silence in the seventeenth century, and relate it to Quaker formulations of the significance of silence. The Quakers were not building into the foundations of their faith a gender-neutral practice, but one that was the cornerstone of discourses of acceptable femininity, and more specifically definitions of femininity that were enunciated in the Bible. As I detailed in the last chapter, women were exhorted to silence, through legal, religious and social discourses; silence was a basic constituent of a woman's honour, her respectability, her modesty, and it was one that had its incontrovertible formulation in the Scriptures, the textual authority for so many of the activities undertaken by women from the sects. Biblical exhortations related quite specifically to women's place within the spiritual order, and were referred to frequently in the sectarian texts. Paul's statements on the matter are the most commonly cited. His letter to the Corinthians, for example:

> Let your women keep silence in the churches: for it is not permitted unto them to speak; but they are commanded to be under bedience, as also saith the Law.
> And if they will learn anything, let them ask their husbands at home; for it is a shame for women to speak in church (1 Corinthians 14:34-5)

and his instruction to Timothy:

> Let the woman learn in silence with all subjection.
> But I suffer not a woman to teach, nor to usurp authority over the man, but to be in silence (Timothy 2:11-12)

comprised the orthodoxy with which all women sectarians had to deal if they were to speak, write or publish and yet remain 'modest' and 'holy'. These biblical references were, in turn, buttressed by the *contemporary* exhortations to silence emanating from the clergy and finding their most extensive exemplification in the conduct books of the period. Cleaver and Dod's *A Godly Form of Household Government* (1621), for example, contained the following statement on women's silence: 'Now silence is the best ornament of a woman and therefore the law was given to the man rather than to the woman, to shew that he should be the teacher, and she the hearer; and therefore she is commanded to learn of her husband 1 Cor.14.34.35' (Cleaver and Dod 1621: n.p.). Whilst this is explicitly founded in – indeed, is a bare paraphrase of – Paul's first letter to the Corinthians, its reiteration in a contemporary context (this section forms part of a long section warning women against gossiping) is important. It serves to underscore not only the ancient and divine origins of the call to silence, but also the continuing fundamental centrality of this tenet to seventeenth-century religious practice.

Silence, then, was unquestionably a condition that was profoundly gendered, both in its scriptural origins and in its seventeenth-century meanings. For Quaker men and Quaker women, therefore, the systematic adoption of the principle and practice of silence would certainly have had very different meanings. It might, for example, have been taken to feminise the men, by making them take on what was perceived as an essentially feminine mode of behaviour. Was this an element either in Quaker men's self-analysis, or in non-Quaker commentators' critiques of Quakerism? As for Quaker women, how did this Quaker endorsement of 'feminine' silence impact upon their representations of themselves or their sectarian practice? Did it reinforce in them a sense of passivity, receptivity and lack of agency? Or, by reversing silence's common associations with limitation, repression and lack, and by making it the foundation of *all* godly communication, were women 'released into language'[7] by the *ungendering* of silence? I will return to these questions of the specific relationship between Quakerism, silence and gender through the analysis of one particular Quaker text of the 1650s in Chapter 7. Already, though, it is clear that whilst in many respects a contextualised reading such as Bauman's answers the need for a localised, specific understanding of the operations of power within a text, it is still itself necessarily partial, with its own silences and omissions. Without an overt gendering of questions of silence within the context of the seventeenth century, such readings will remain unable to engage with one of the key constituents – that of femininity – through which silence was produced and understood in this period.

How, though, can we relate these particular meanings of silence to the silences embedded in texts produced by women in the seventeenth-century radical sects? How do these textual silences (what Macherey called the 'reverse side of what is written') relate to the textual considerations of the meanings of silence so important to Quakers? How can Foucault's characterisation of power inform a reading of these texts? And how does gender function in relation to all of these? This is not an entirely uncharted area: the work of 'making the silences speak' in relation to seven-teenth-century radical sectarian women's writing has already begun. For instance, Moira Ferguson quotes Elaine Hobby's reading of the silence of the Quaker Joan Vokins's text concerning the specific role of women Friends, written at a time when separate meetings for women and men were being instituted. Hobby argues that separate meetings constituted a move which arguably spelled the apparent downgrading of female Friends. Vokins left husband and family behind in England during her voyages. What is silenced among them is an explicit defense and interrogation of women's role in their [Friends'] work. But they do not ally themselves with the new conservative tendency either: they are simply silent on the issue and thus their recorded actions speak, as it were, on their behalf. Their near-silence in this matter and their near-silence on questions of race and slavery might be linked; certainly they constitute absent centres in their texts. (Hobby, in Ferguson 1992: 66)

Here the silence in Vokins's text on the issues of women, race and slavery are read as integral to the contemporary discourses on these topics, not as mere absences of engagement with them. This exemplifies well the importance of reading intertextually, of locating texts historically very precisely, and of reading them as in dialogue with contemporary issues and debates, which together produced, as Jameson put it, a collective story.

Already, then, it is clear that the emphasis on the multiplicity of silences is critical: we may, as in the above example, find the 'silence' of a non-engagement with a particular debate forming an 'absent centre' to a text. We may, rather differently, find a silent dialogue embedded in, and resulting from, specific sectarian conventions, such as, for example, the habitual prefacing of texts with biblical quotations. These frequently seem to have little direct connection with the overt subject of the work, or with the professed status of the writer; more often they seem to be a covert indication of the position of the text or of the writer in relation to contemporary expectations of them. Katherine Chidley, for instance, prefaces her *Justification of the Independent Churches of Christ* (1641) with a quotation (Judges 4:21) describing the killing of Sisera by Jael: 'Then Iael, Heber's wife took a nail of the tent, and took an hammer in her hand, and went softly unto him, and smote the nail into his temples and fastened it into the ground, (for he was fast asleep and weary) and so he died.' This unequivocal example of a woman seizing control and exacting vengeance through violence precedes a text in which the author represents herself as 'a poor worm, and unmeet to deal with you [Thomas Edwards, whose views she is disputing in this text]' (Chidley 1641: 81). Yet the inescapable implication is that Chidley is going to deal as summarily with Edwards as Jael did with Sisera. Anne Wentworth's *The Revelation of Jesus Christ* (1679) has a cluster of similarly provocative prefatory biblical quotations, which begin with Jeremiah 13:15: 'Hear ye, and give ear, be not proud, for the Lord hath spoken' and end with Matthew 12:37: 'By thy words thou shalt be justified, and by thy words thou shalt be condemned.' For a writer asserting both that her words emanate direct from God and that her enemies' words betray their ungodliness, these can be seen to be highly apposite quotations. Anne Audland's *A True Declaration* (1655) provides another, though more understated, example. Within the main body of her text, she asserts only circuitously that her authority to write comes from God: 'And *from the Lord I declare*, that he will visit for these things, and plead with you for all your hard speeches, and all your ungodly deeds' (Audland 1655: 3; my emphasis). Her prefatory quotation, however, from Acts 2:18, specifies and clarifies the direct and immediate nature of this relationship between the author and God: 'And on my servants, and on my handmaidens, I will pour out in those days of my spirit, and they shall prophesy.' As a Quaker prophet, Audland is arguing that she is central to the fulfilling of this promise, the realisation of God's plan for the world as laid out in the Scriptures. This is no private escapade on which she has embarked, but part of the working through and realisation of scriptural prophecies. This, in turn, is reminiscent of the Baptist Anne Wentworth's assertion of the public necessity of her continuing to write and publish, since it constituted the 'more than ordinary call and command of God to publish the things which concern the *peace of my own soul*, and *of the whole nation*' (Wentworth 1677: 6; original emphasis): these events in her life signify at one and the same time on a spiritual and national/political level.

The 'silence' of these examples, then, is the silent, unremarked, uncommented juxtaposition of materials in very different registers. Read together, these raise questions about the status of the register of the main body of the text: what, for example, are we to make of the claim of an author to be a 'poor worm' who prefaces her text with the story of Jael and Sisera? We certainly read such a claim differently than we would if no such prefatory quotation were present. Such juxtapositions thus produce a composite complete text that is rather different from the sum of its parts. The lack of an easy 'fit' between so many of these pairings – the often outspoken and always resolute tone of the quotations paired with a frequently understated or apologetic text – testifies once again to the importance of paying attention to the textual 'gaps and contradictions' in the tracing and reading of texts' silences.

Silence, speaking and gender: Channel, Beaumont and Turner

As well as the silences discernible through reading across the whole tradition of sectarian writing, there are also those very particular silences that are detectable within certain texts. I shall now extend these readings of textual silences by offering a detailed analysis of three texts written by women from the sects, in order both to analyse the multiplicities of their forms and to assess the impact they variously have on the writings in which they are traced.

A Message from God, by a Dumb Woman (1654; see Appendix B) is Elinor Channel's account of her call from God, the resistance she met to her endeavours to fulfil his commands, and the means by which she finally communicated her message. Channel received a call from God one night, 'as she was in bed in a slumber', commanding her to go to London with a message for Cromwell. Her husband tried three times to prevent her from going, until

> her mind was sore troubled that her sleep went from her; and at some times she was speechless: whereupon your petitioner's husband seeing her restless condition, contented to let her come to London, that she might express her mind to your highness [Cromwell] and have rest in her spirit. (Channel 1654: 2)

Her message for Cromwell concerned the state of the nation: 'she is to say to you … the God of Jacob hath opened the mouth of the dumb to speak for peace. The sword must be stayed' (Channel 1654: 3). A marginal note provided by her editor and publisher, the royalist prophet Arise Evans, provides a gloss to this: 'By the dumb she meaneth herself, 'cause she had been dumb.' When she arrived in London, she was unable to see Cromwell, so 'she came to the city of London, and wandered up and down to see if she could get anybody to take it from her mouth, and publish it in print ... but of a long while, she being a stranger, she could get none to hear or regard her' (Channel 1654: 5). Evans, who presents Channel's case on her behalf, concludes:

> Now this woman was very sensible and profound in what she spake to me but as she said, when she is dumb, all her senses are taken up, and then the matter which troubles her mind, is dictated and made plain to her by the spirit of God, so that when she comes to herself, she has it by heart. (Channel 1654: 7)

This account is predicated on, and structured by, many different silences. The first is indicated by the author's name: Channel. For a body of writers so committed to denying their own authorship through asserting their own instrumentality in the hands of God (see Chapter 4), the fact that this writer's name should in itself be indicative of a conduit, a means of conveyance from one place to another, sets the tone. Channel's silence is confirmed in two ways: first, her message is not her own, but comes direct from God, so that, in effect, Channel herself remains silent throughout the whole interaction; and, second, on her husband refusing to give her permission to speak God's message in London, she became literally 'speechless'. It was this 'silence' of speechlessness that finally accorded her her means of communication, for it persuaded her husband, 'seeing her restless condition, to let her come to London, that she might express her mind' (Channel 1654: 2). However, on arrival in London, it is Arise Evans who takes her up and becomes her mouthpiece, because she can find no one to 'hear or regard her'. Evans, however, proves to be no neutral 'channel' for her words: her prophecies served his own political purposes very well, and he plays her words off against those of the Fifth Monarchist prophet Anna Trapnel: 'you shall find more truth and substance in it, than in all Hana Trampenel's songs or sayings, whom some account of as the Diana of the English' (Evans in Channel 1654: 7). Here her gender is of prime importance for the making of his case: the comparison is generated by the fact that both prophets are women, and this allows him to compare Channel directly with Trapnel, to the detriment of the latter. The significance of the gender dimension is further emphasised through the reference to Diana, goddess of the moon and of chastity, and archetypal femininine symbol.[8] Important for Evans too is Channel's dumbness: 'by this dumb woman, God will put all talkers to silence, 1 Cor. 1. 27.28' (Evans in Channel 1654: 109); her speechlessness is confirmation both of her docile femininity and of her godliness. Her gender and her speechlessness, then, are deployed by Evans to effect his own speech: just as without him she was dumb, so he without her was less able to communicate. Thus Channel is a channel for God's word to Cromwell and beyond; she is also a channel by which Evans's views can reach a wider audience; and Evans, in turn, is a channel for her words. None of these channels, however, is the neutral conduit that the word implies. For Channel herself to communicate God's word, she has to negotiate and overcome her husband's opposition and then find a further mouthpiece for these words once she is London; and Evans, far from simply reproducing Channel's words, glosses and commentates them throughout.

Quite clearly, then, questions of power, silence and utterance are not straightforward here; there are no simple binary oppositions between power and its absence, speech and silence. Silence is productive of Channel's discourse, her dumbness 'empowering' her to speak as its lack had constrained her. Not only does it persuade her husband to withdraw his opposition to her leaving her home and family, it is also the means by which Channel secures the attention of Arise Evans, by then a well-known figure; through him her message does indeed get published. Here, then, power and agency could be argued to adhere within a form generally associated with passivity or lack: as Purkiss puts it, '[w]e could read Channel's dumbness as female resistance to her husband's patriarchal authority' (Purkiss 1992a: 144). However, it is also possible to read the same words in a quite different way, and to see Channel's text as a record of one denial of her after another: first her husband, who refuses to let her go to London; next, Cromwell, to whom she is denied access; and finally Evans, in his appropriation of her message for his own ends; so that in the end Channel might be represented as entirely vulnerable to the vagaries of men's permissions, refusals and decisions. This indeed is Purkiss's conclusion: she suggests that the 'dramatic silencing of Channel seems to stage on her body the same erasure of female subjectivity' as she argues we find in other texts (Purkiss 1992a: 144). I am not sure, however, that the erasure is as complete as Purkiss suggests; it seems to me that the tension between these two readings, a tension which seems to undermine the opposition between 'speech' and 'silence', precludes such a firm conclusion because it never resolves that tension. The tension, in other words, between these two kinds of silence produces a complicated inscription of the author's subjectivity, alternately, or at the same time, present and absent throughout its presentation and negotiations of these constantly fluctuating silences. Whilst the text might set out the various silences that Channel inhabits, produces, or to which she is subject, it does so in such a way that her (textual) agency pulls against her obliteration.

Another instance of a text that centres on such productive ambiguities as those of Channel's is the autobiography of Agnes Beaumont, a young Baptist who was a member of the same congregation as John Bunyan, and who encountered concerted opposition to her sectarian allegiances from her father. He forbade her to attend any more Baptist meetings, which he saw as no more than an excuse for her to pursue Bunyan, on pain of being thrown out of her home and disinherited. This produces a struggle between the pull to obey her earthly father and the related concern for her own material welfare after his death, and the pull to follow her heavenly father's commands, a struggle which structures her narrative. She asserts that there is no real contest between the two: "'Father," said I, "you cant Answere for my Sins, nor stand in my steed before god; I must look to the Salvation of my Soul, or I am undone for ever."' (Beaumont 1929: 40). Despite the clarity of this assertion, her text bears witness to a continuing struggle between the two sets of incompatible demands, the narrative culminating in her father's sudden death shortly after she defies him and goes to the Baptist meeting. Following this, she is accused of murder by a neighbour, Mr ffeery, an accusation that seems to rest on nothing more than the fact that she and her father disagreed on matters of religion. The logic seems to be that a woman who would defy her father would be quite capable of taking the next step of patricide. Later, she writes: 'Now my fathers Will was made three yeares before he dyed, and mr ffeery made it. And then he put my father on to give me more than my Sister because of some designe that he had then, but afterwards when I came to goe to meetings he was turned against me' (Beaumont 1929: 86). It seems probable that Mr ffeery's 'designe' was marriage, hence his urging Beaumont's father to give her a larger portion than her sister in his will. He subsequently 'turned against' Beaumont when she 'came to goe to meetings' and then, later still, accused her of murdering her father. No explicit connection is made between these events, yet their textual proximity suggests a connection, linking one form of 'disobedience' to the father with the ultimate filial transgression.

The silences of this text are again various. On the one hand, there is the silence of this unarticulated connection between Mr ffeery's hostility to Beaumont's defiance of her father's wishes and his subsequent accusations of patricide. This particular silence speaks more loudly of thwarted interests and authority undermined than anything expressly articulated in the text. In addition, the text is 'silent' concerning both the irreconcilability of the earthly and spiritual demands on Beaumont and the impossibility of wholly aligning herself with one or the other of these sets of demands. Whilst she makes the unequivocal statement quoted above, asserting that in fact there is no contest and she must of necessity follow God, the text hereafter is none the less a catalogue of the material or earthly privations and condemnations that she undergoes as a result of her decision. Whilst the needs of her 'ungendered soul', a soul thus equal in the eyes of God (see Chapter 2), are clear, her text also bears witness to the continuing hold of the 'unequal body' – a body whose needs were not obliterated by spiritual allegiances, but whose dependence was rendered more problematic by it. Whilst the text does not explicitly address the impossiblity of resolving the dilemma posed by the dual claims of the equal soul and unequal body, it nevertheless silently plays out this contradiction: the drama of the irresolvable emerging through a narrative of spiritual resolution.

The Baptist Jane Turner's autobiography reverberates with the same kind of ambiguities and contradictions. It is worth quoting her introductory 'A word from the Author to the Reader' at length in order to work through these fully:

These notes in the following discourse are some of the fruits of my labours written at several times in my husband's absence, which may be some satisfaction as to my spending that time. I did intend them only for my own private use, as a remembrancer of the old loving kindness of the Lord towards me, and 'twas not in the least in my thoughts that ever it should have been presented to a public view, but after I had written the greater part of it, shewing it to my husband, he had some thoughts to publish it, judging it might be profitable to some precious souls which, though it be written but in a broken, scuttering[10] way, and I am conscious to myself of too much weakness and unworthiness to be an instrument for the good of souls, or to propagate the least truth of the Lord Jesus, yet I shall be willing to submit to better judgements, hoping through the blessing of God it may be useful, knowing from my own experience I have received much from the Lord by reading: but besides the sense of my own unworthiness, as I had some discouraging thoughts as to my writing of it at the first, so I have met with the like as to my giving way to the publishing of it. At first I thought I might seem to some to walk in an untrodden path, having never seen anything written before in this manner and method. (Turner 1653: n.p.)

In many ways this provides a complementary account of the genesis of *Choice Experiences* to that offered by her husband, John Turner (see pp. 58–9 above), reiterating the narrative of the process of writing the text, though with some significant additional details. Turner implicitly confirms that it was written without her husband's knowledge – she showed it to him once it was nearly completed; but she also offers two palliatives for having written it at all. First, it was done in her husband's absence, 'which may be some satifaction as to my spending that time', suggesting that to write it at a time when her husband was at home would indeed have been an infringement of the proper behaviour of a wife; time is a commodity, or currency, to be 'spent' wisely and appropriately. Second, she reassures the reader that it was written only for 'my own private use'. The meaning of an act of writing, then, was not absolute or fixed: there were clearly degrees of acceptability and unacceptability associated with the different circumstances of its production. Turner here claims the most private and solitary of contexts for her own work. This justification is fortified further by the invocation of God: the text is written to testify to God's grace to Turner throughout her life. Moreover, it becomes clear that what is at stake is the publication of the work more than the writing of it, for her justifications do not extend to an active decision to publish it. Instead, at the point of completion of the manuscript and prior to the text entering the public domain through publication, her husband takes over and 'owns' the work, assuming responsiblity for it himself and thereby detaching the author from its public fate.

This, however, is a very passive construction of Turner's self-representation; it is possible instead to read it as the account of an author in control of her text and her all-important reputation from beginning to end. She writes it during her husband's absence, concealing its existence from him until it is almost complete; she then relinquishes the text to him, enabling him to 'own' it once he knows of its existence; it thus becomes his decision to publish it. She therefore plays an active part in her own passivity; by putting herself in a position whereby she is no longer in control of the text, she not only facilitates its passage into print, but is also able to maintain her good name by not inititating this process herself. According to this reading, she both has her cake and eats it: through careful manoeuvring and management of the circumstances of the text's production, she can both assist and manage the publication of the text and preserve her own reputation. Alongside this assertion of modesty, however, runs something quite different: a tone of excitement and anticipation. She describes the form of the text – a combination of autobiographical accounts of her own experiences and the precepts she draws from them – as innovatory: 'I thought I might seem to walk in an untrodden path, having never before seen anything written before in this manner and method', and this from a woman who by her own account had read widely ('from my own experience I have received much from the Lord by reading'), and who is aware of the subtleties and complexities of reading practices (see Turner 1653:49–61)). She is writing, then, from within an explicitly literary, as well as sectarian and social, context, negotiating a complex set of personal and sectarian demands, all of them refracted through an insistence on the gendered character of these demands: her text is predicated on the implicit premise that silence is the ideal of wifely behaviour from which she is digressing.

These three examples relate to the multiplicity of textual and authorial silences in rather different, if equally complicated, ways. None, clearly, is reducible to the 'silence' of complete non-articulation, for each exists as a fully expressed textual entity. These, however, travelled very different routes into textual articulation: Channel's words are not only mediated by Evans, but come to us only through his reiteration of them; Beaumont's words remained only in manuscript form, unpublished until 1929; and Turner's words are (to a degree, at least) dissociated from their author and appropriated by her husband by means of the prefatory epistles. Each text, moreover, offers a different kind of utterance against and within which to trace and measure its own particular 'silence'. Channel's prophecy is structured through reference to her own authorial silence, whilst Beaumont and Turner's autobiographies manifest an embedded textual silence, an 'absent centre', which offers an important commentary on their overt subject-matter.

These examples do, however, have two things in common. First, in each of these three examples, the *origin* of the silence, whether authorial or textual, can be seen to be in a collision between earthly and spiritual demands – whether between God and husband, or God and father. Second, each text manifests a *negotiation* of its own particular silence, whereby the 'said' of the text can be read as in dialogue with the 'unsaid' of its own silence.

Elinor Channel's text, for example, negotiates the silence that is the consequence of prohibition, a prohibition that exemplifies a conflict between her duty to her husband and her duty to God. In many ways these were incompatible and irreconcilable demands, and the outcome of this tension is not its resolution but its circumvention through silence. It is the speechlessness that results from her husband's attempt to silence her message (which she experiences as emanating from God) that precisely *produces* her text – its form and its organisation – in an exemplary Foucauldian way. Through the silence, Channel finds a way to communicate; and so without the silence, *this* text would not have existed; perhaps the prophecy of Elinor Channel would have taken another form, found another way into print, but it would necessarily have looked very different from this one. Prohibition and silence, then, can be seen to be directly constitutive of the text; they do not suppress or erase it, but they generate and shape it, and form its substance and texture as well as its boundaries. However, whilst the text is generated by this 'silence' that results from prohibition, it is also important not to lose sight of Channel's own lack of agency: her authorship is displaced, both on to God and then on to Evans. This displaced authorship thus functions simultaneously both to confirm and undermine her authorial status, thereby silencing her and allowing her to speak.

Agnes Beaumont's text's relation to silence is less immediately apparent, for the text itself brims over with the 'outspokenness' of Beaumont, making explicit in ways that usually remain only implicit in other texts just how critical was the choice beween obedience to God or obedience to her 'earthly' father, and emphasising the necessity to follow God. However, in a text that (as was conventional in the spiritual autobiography) asserts the primacy of the spiritual, and the transience and irrelevance of the earthly, it is possible to trace a silence, a 'reverse side' to the text, which exposes and details the *material* consequences of her refusal to comply with her father's demands. The clash, as with Channel, is between the spiritual and the earthly demands, here literalised as her earthly and her heavenly fathers. Rather than this clash silencing Beaumont, however, it generates a silent commentary on the implications, and the limits, of a rejection of the 'carnal' or material. The narrative, through its 'silent' juxtapositions of apparently unrelated events, culminating in the accusation of patricide from her neighbour, suggests that these material factors profoundly determine the conditions of her life, and are in no sense as easily dismissed as the 'spoken' of the text might assert. Indeed, the extensive detailing of privations visited on her by her father is suggestive of a resistance to, even an outrage at, the injustices that result from her dependence on her father. It is this resistance that gives shape to the 'silence' of the text, the silence around the irresolvable clash of earthly and spiritual allegiances.

Jane Turner's text, in turn, whilst overtly concerned with the processes of the production of her text and its passage into print, is none the less once again negotiating the silence regarding the gendered character of the dynamics that constituted and directed these processes. As with the other texts, the conflict is between the earthly and the spiritual: the social prescriptions concerning women's relationship with the printed word, the need for modesty, the requirements for a woman to act only within the boundaries of the familial and the spiritual requirement that she communicate God's grace clash with each other. The prefatory epistle defuses, circumvents or subverts these absent, unarticulated, but nevertheless centrally formative strictures concerning women's duties. Turner's text is structured around these prescriptions, is in silent dialogue with them, and both complies with and refuses their demands. The textual stance of the author here, then, is negotiative; whilst the two sets of demands may at one level be irreconcilable for Turner, they are none the less negotiable or manageable on a textual level, and it is this process of negotiation that is effected through her prefatory epistle.

In each case, then, we can identify silences arising from the conflict of demands between the unequal bodies and equal souls of seventeenth-century women (see Chapter 2), silences, and processes of silencing, that take many forms, and function in different ways in relation to the text itself. In each case, though, the silence is a critical and integral part of the negotiation of this conflict, and helps constitute the space in which the text is produced. These discourses of silence, then, engage fundamentally with both the bodies and the souls of women, and with the contradictions that this dual engagement engenders, and they are thus indicative of the fundamentally gendered power relations through which women's writing in this century was constituted. Moreover, these gendered power relations are negotiated not only through various forms of silence, but also through the author – also, of course, an undeniably gendered figure. As we have seen in these three examples, the textual construction of the author can vary widely, from the displaced authorship of Elinor Channel, to the resistant authorship of Agnes Beaumont and the negotiated authorship of Jane Turner. Just, then, as the silences discernible in these texts can vary from authorial manifestations to the 'absent centres' of that which remains unarticulated in the text, so the author-figure herself comes in many guises. It is to a consideration of the shifting definitions of these, and other, author-figures that I shall turn in the next chapter.

4

'There is no self in this thing': the disappearing author

If, as I argued in the previous chapter, so many texts from the women writers in the radical sects demonstrate the negotiation of some form of silence – whether the representation of an authorial silencing, or the 'absent centre' of a textual silence – then the primary sites for this negotiation are the textual manifestations of the figure of the author, and the textual constructions of the origin and status of the text itself. 'Authorship' and 'ownership', as we have already seen, were implicated in the forms that these silences took. The 'displaced authorship' of Elinor Channel functioned as a means for her prophecies to get into print; the 'resistant authorship' of Agnes Beaumont shaped the record of her conflict between her earthly and spiritual duties; and the 'negotiated authorship' of Jane Turner structured the balancing act of her prefatory epistle in which she moved back and forth between acknowledging the demands of wifely propriety and managing the passage of her text into print. At the same time, I argued that questions needed to be addressed concerning the 'owner-ship' of the text: was the text owned by the author, who wrote it; by God, who commanded it be written; or perhaps by the husband, who authorised its publication?

In order to address these questions more comprehensively, I shall in this chapter turn to a consideration of the 'author-figure'. I use this term to suggest the textually constructed persona of the 'author' as distinct from the ultimately unknowable and irretrievable living and breathing writer, and to avoid a misleading elision of the two; and yet I use it also in order to suggest a sense of the necessary – though very complicated – relationship between the two. The aim of this is to avoid the pitfalls of an approach that focuses exclusively on the *textuality* of the former to the exclusion of the sense of the *historicity* of the latter, thereby cutting off the text from the circumstances of its production. As I shall go on to demonstrate, this is crucial in the context of considering texts that rest on very specific 'truth-claims' about the role of authorship in textual production. Furthermore, the texts considered here, whether conversion narratives or prophecies, are all more or less overtly autobiographical, and thus a serious analysis of the connections between what we might call 'the historical author' and 'the textual author' are of central concern. My use of the term 'author-figure' is intended to refer to precisely such connections. This figure's relationship with the text which she produces and in which she is produced is fundamental to the ways in which these texts negotiate a space for themselves in a context which, in the main, found the notion of women's writing unacceptable because it did not respect the boundaries of 'modest' femininity.

The issues of authorship emerging from an analysis of these texts necessitate a critical rethinking of the contemporary debates about authorship within literary criticism more generally. The last twenty years or so have seen a thoroughgoing re-evaluation of the notion of authorship together with a debate about the significance and implications of this re-evaluation. However, both Roland Barthes, with his pronouncement of the 'death of the author', and Michel Foucault, in his investigation of what he called the 'author-function' (critics who are usually identified as the progenitors of a particular critique of authorship, and to whom I return below), were analysing and challenging concepts of authorship that had developed in relation to the classic realist novel of the nineteenth century. Such conceptualisations cannot be transferred unproblematically on to other kinds of texts produced in other times and places – on to, for example, the texts written by women in the radical sects of the seventeenth century. Instead, they need to be tested out, and perhaps reconfigured, in relation to a set of texts that made very different assumptions about the nature and function of authorship than those generally cited as evidence in these debates. What I propose to do in this chapter is to discuss how critical debates about authorship in current literary studies do or do not relate to such a body of writing. Having introduced some of the main premises and terms of the current critical debate about authorship, I will outline why authorship needs to be considered a significant issue in relation to seventeenth-century writings, and then examine how these contemporary debates impact upon specific constructions of the author-figure in seventeenth-century sectarian texts.

Death and resurrection: the author's progress

Twentieth-century literary criticism has been dominated first by the elevation of 'great authors' and more recently by their vigorous deconstruction. The celebration of authorship took the form of detailed readings of certain privileged works of literature through the critic's knowledge of the author's life, beliefs, habits and intentions. Central to the constitution of the literary canon in English studies has been a concern to establish the link between the writer and his (*sic*) text. Literary criticism before the 1970s might be characterised by its concern with these canonical authors and the reflection and expression of their lives, beliefs and individual genius in their work. Whilst this critical practice still to some extent continues, our contemporary understandings of authorship have been profoundly altered by the impact of the work of theorists such as Roland Barthes and Michel Foucault, who have interrogated the category of 'the author' and challenged some of the most potent assumptions behind its canonical status.

In particular, their concern was to challenge the taken-for-granted conception of the author as sole originator of his texts, expressing his quintessential self by means of his fictions, whereby his life, his experiences, his artistic development and influences provided the rationale, the coherence and the key to his *oeuvre*. Barthes sums up the impact of this approach to literary criticism:

The *author* still reigns in histories of literature, biographies of writers, interviews, magazines, as in the very consciousness of men of letters anxious to unite their person and their work through diaries and memoirs. The image of literature to be found in ordinary culture is tyrannically centred on the author, his person, his life, his tastes, his passions, while criticism still consists for the most part in saying that Baudelaire's work is the failure of Baudelaire the man, Van Gogh's his madness, Tchaikovsky's his vice. The explanation of a work is always sought in the man or woman who produced it, as if it were always in the end, through the more or less transparent allegory of the fiction, the voice of a single person, the *author* 'confiding' in us. (Barthes 1977: 209; all emphasis in quotations is Barthes's)

In what has now become a recognisably poststructuralist move, Barthes reversed the common-sense assumption about the source and production of textual meanings: namely, that the author's intentions determine the meaning ultimately produced. In opposition to this, he suggested that 'it is language that speaks, not the author' (Barthes 1977: 209): since our subjectivities are constructed in and through language, a text can be no more than 'a tissue of quotations', and an author's only power:

is to mix writings, to counter the ones with the others, in such a way as never to rest on any one of them. Did he wish to *express himself*, he ought at least to know that the inner 'thing' he thinks to 'translate' is itself only a ready-formed dictionary, its words only explainable through other words, and so on indefinitely. (Barthes 1977: 211)

For Barthes, this theoretical position necessitated the 'death of the author' as a critical construct. This demise was represented as an entirely liberating prospect, for it freed the text from the shadow of this author/authority-figure, which had long served to close down its meanings and to impose a single, fixed, unchanging and definitive 'interpretation', which it was then the job of critics to discover. With the removal of the author, Barthes suggested that texts became open to plural, contradictory and ever-changing readings:

everything is to be *disentangled*, nothing *deciphered*; the structure can be followed, 'run' (like the thread of a stocking) at every point and at every level, but there is nothing beneath: the space of writing is to be ranged over, not pierced; writing ceaselessly posits meaning ceaselessly to evaporate it, carrying out a systematic exemption of meaning. In precisely this way literature (it would be better from now on to say *writing*), by refusing to assign a 'secret', an ultimate meaning, to the text (and to the world as text), liberates what may be called an anti-theological activity, an activity that is truly revolutionary since to refuse to fix meaning is, in the end, to refuse God and his hypostases – reason, science, law. (Barthes 1977: 212)

The death of the author, then, implied a renewed and intensified focus on the text, not as offering access to some external 'reality', but as a complex and self-referential (or intertextually allusive) sequence of words. Moreover, the plurality of readings that Barthes envisaged also necessitated another important shift of emphasis within literary studies, from the author to the reader – or, more precisely, to the reader as author, for it is with the reader (or readers) that this multiplicity of meanings resides. Barthes thus concludes his polemic with a clarion call for reading practice of the future: 'we know that to give writing its future, it is necessary to overthrow the myth [of the writer]: the birth of the reader must be at the cost of the death of the Author' (Barthes 1977: 213).

At around the same time that Barthes was arguing for the redundancy of the concept of the author, Foucault was also investigating, elaborating and recasting prevailing conceptions of the 'author'. In 'What is an author?' (Foucault 1977), he, like Barthes, counters the idea that the meaning of the text is isomorphic with the author's intentions/psyche/preoccupations, and, also like Barthes, he starts from the premise that texts have no inherent meanings, only those assigned to them through various interpretive techniques. One of these techniques is what he calls the 'author-function' – not the flesh-and-blood individual who wrote the text, but a cultural/ literary construction that functions 'to provide an explanation for the work's exist-ence, a framework for its interpretation and a method for considering it as a coherent whole' (Lury 1992: 381). Foucault set out the various ways in which the 'author-function' is used to elucidate a text:

> The author explains the presence of certain events within a text, as well as their transformations, distortions, and their various modifications (and this through an author's biography or by reference to his particular point of view, in the analysis of his social preferences and his position within a class or by delineating his fundamental objectives). The author also constitutes a principle of unity in writing where any unevenness of production is ascribed to changes caused by evolution, maturation or outside influence. In addition, the author serves to neutralise the contradictions that are found in a series of texts. Governing this function is the belief that there must be – at a particular level of an author's thought, of his conscious or unconscious desire – a point where contradictions are resolved, where the incompatible elements can be shown to relate to one another or to cohere around a fundamental and originating contradic-tion. Finally, the author is a particular source of expression who, in more or less finished forms, is manifested equally well, and with similar validity, in a text, in letters, fragments, drafts, and so forth. (Foucault 1977: 287-8)

Because the art-work is traditionally seen to be solely the product of the author's aesthetic intentions, and is interpreted only in relation to these imputed intentions, the author-function also provides the means by which to distinguish between artistic activities and other, more instrumental and less highly-valued (by certain groups, at least) activities.

Like Barthes, Foucault also argued that this author-function served to limit the polysemous nature of fiction, but unlike him he focused more on the political impli-cations of such limitations. He suggested that it restricted access to positions of authorial autonomy in such a way as to exclude certain groups from cultural produc-tion altogether, or else it denied the work of particular groups the status of 'true art'. As well as providing the means to distinguish between artistic and other kinds of activities, it also provided the means of making distinctions between different kinds of art-work, such as, in the nineteenth century, the realist novel ('high culture') and the romantic novel ('popular fiction').

Barthes's and Foucault's critique of the author highlighted not only its function in canonical traditions, but also the ways in which the apparently universal conception of the author was actually one that developed through a particular set of historical and cultural formations. The construction of the notion of 'the author' as critiqued by Barthes and Foucault has been identified as originating in the later sixteenth century, when the work of authors began to be distinguished from that of other artisans. Whereas artisans used their technical skills to make products demanded by someone else, creative activity came to be defined by its relative freedom from the demands of patrons and audiences; instead, artists produced work that could sell through the market. This shift was both consolidated and modified by the discourse of Romanticism of the late eighteenth and early nineteenth centuries, which affirmed the artist as an autonomous, individual producer, but denied the role of the market in the production of texts. Instead, the creative artist was free to express himself in whatever way his aesthetic impulses and integrity demanded.[1] It is often noted that the development of this Romantic conceptualisation of the author coincided with, and was part of, the rise of bourgeois culture and the development of capitalism. The enthusiasm with which Barthes's and Foucault's critiques were taken up in many circles in the 1970s and 1980s was in part, then, motivated by a wider desire within Marxist criticism to anatomise and challenge bourgeois culture, a primary element of which was individualism, by exposing the mechanisms of literary elitism. If the author belongs to the cult of individualism so central to this kind of dominant culture, then what could be more welcome than to abandon this category altogether? Whilst often set in opposition to each other, Marxist and poststructuralist perspectives in this respect share a common desire to challenge the individualism of the very underpinnings of bourgeois literary criticism.

For feminist critics, amongst others, there has been much to be gained from this dethroning of the author, for it has removed the justification for the primacy of the 'great men of literature' who have dominated English studies since their inception. By exposing their pre-eminence as a symptom of the inequalities of patriarchal bourgeois culture, the critique of authorship has challenged the Romantic construction of the author as the isolated individual whose suffering is productive of his genius, a construction which has long inhibited women in their creative endeavours.[2] It has shown the literary canon to be a cultural construct which has functioned to maintain the dominant positions of particular social groups, rather than the 'natural' emergence of 'the best that is known and thought in the world'.[3] With the dismantling of the authorial canon, surely, at last, the politics of English literature as a discipline might be made incontestably explicit, and those hitherto excluded by these disciplinary boundaries could now find a place in the academy? Moreover, the 'death of the author' also seemed to promise a more democratic reading practice, whereby a multiplicity of interpretations of texts would be validated: feminist readings might now be taken as seriously as other readings, without any having to establish its ultimate, singular and definitive interpretive status. The critical acceptance of the possibility of multiple readings thus seemed to be a significant part of the process whereby feminist criticism was creating a space for itself in the academy.

However, certain misgivings were also voiced about the ramifications of this critique: if authorship were irrelevant, on what grounds would it now be possible to argue that it mattered whether *women*'s writing was read and studied? How might the canon be extended and transformed to include those texts that had traditionally been excluded, if not on the grounds of authorship? If *how* we read was more important than *who* or *what* we read, what was to guarantee that it was not just the same old male-authored canonical texts that were studied, albeit in a more reader-centred and polysemic way? Nor was the irony lost on critics that it was two of the most culturally authoritative, renowned, lionised, commentated and interpreted critical author-figures of the later decades of the twentieth century who were busy proclaiming the death of the author. In short, critics from a variety of perspectives traditionally marginalised or altogether excluded from mainstream academic disciplines began to delineate some of the problems associated with the wholesale abandonment of the author-figure. Such debates took on a particular significance in the context of what have come to be known as 'identity politics': the claiming of personal experience as the authenticator of public representations of oppression. In the context of such politically contentious 'authorisations', who has the right to speak or write on behalf of others, and how their intentions might be interpreted, is in excess of purely literary concerns. Synthesising the contradictions of the abandonment of the author-figure for those groups traditionally excluded from such a construction, Andy Medhurst has summarised some of the key issues relating to authorship for feminist, black and gay cultural commentators in a series of apposite quotations:

'the postmodern decision that the Author is dead, and subjective agency along with him, does not necessarily work for women and prematurely forecloses the question of identity for them. Because women have not had the same historical relation of identity to origin, institution, production that men have had, women have not, I think, (collectively) felt burdened by too much Self, Ego, Cogito, etc.'

'It never surprises me when black folks respond to the critique of essentialism, especially when it denies the validity of identity politics, by saying 'Yeah, it's easy to give up identity when you got one'. Should we not be suspicious of postmodern critiques of the 'subject' when they surface at a historical moment when many subjugated people feel themselves coming to voice for the the first time ...'

'Narrative identification ... is being rejected ... at a point in time when gays can claim they still have not had it. An initial period of identification is important to a repressed group that has never had adequate self images.' (Medhurst 1991: 206-7)[4]

Whilst welcoming the critique of the white, male, bourgeois author as the only writer worth studying, such critics, as well as many others,[5] have refused the more totalising and monolithic critique of the author which might discount or overlook the relevance of including those hitherto excluded from the curriculum of literary studies. As a result, they have begun to insist not on the uncritical reintroduction of the author-figure as the defining interpretive strategy of literary criticism, but on a reappraisal and redefinition of the notion of authorship in relation to particular kinds of texts, particular kinds of authors, and particular moments of cultural production.

For the participants in the twentieth-century authorship debate, then, whether they are defending or deconstructing the notion of the author, there are a number of recurrent issues that are clearly at stake: namely, definitions of the author, the self, the text and the reader. For Barthes, Foucault and other poststructuralists, dominant conceptions of the author as the source of meaning of a text depend upon, and privilege, the existence of an authentic, fixed, fully-formed, coherent and knowable self that can be expressed through writing. Here, the text is little more than a version of the authorial self in words, and the task of the reader is to decipher the words in order to imbibe fully the author's vision and the text's unchanging meaning. In place of this, they posit a model whereby the author is all but irrelevant; where the self is a contradictory, shifting, elusive structure, inscribed in language rather than existing in the world; where the text, too, is a complex linguistic structure, referring to itself, to other texts, but not to a pre-existing external 'reality'; and where the reader and text together can produce a multiplicity of meanings, eternally changing, never completed, never definitive. For feminist and other critics whose work is more clearly rooted in specific political agendas, the retention of the author-figure, and with it the concept of the social identity of an author (whether women, black, gay, lesbian, or working-class), ensures that groups usually marginalised in literary studies can no longer be excluded. The 'self' may be acknowledged as an endlessly complicated and contradictory structure, but it is none the less assumed to connect to at least some kind of social and political identity; the text, in similarly complex and contradictory ways, is seen as bearing some kind of relation to these identities; and the reader has to negotiate a way through this mix of social, historical, political and textual specificities in order to produce readings of the text. The 'self' and its textual expression/articulation is thus centrally at stake whichever way the issues are argued.

What, then, might be the significance of these literary debates about authorship in the particular instance of cultural production with which this book is concerned: writings by seventeenth-century Englishwomen in the radical sects? If we dismiss authorship as the poststructuralists would have us do, what then happens to the texts by women that have for so long been excluded from any serious or extended critical comment? If, on the other hand, we endorse the retention of the author-figure, as many feminist, black, and lesbian and gay critics have counselled, three issues concerning seventeenth-century sectarian writings by women emerge: first, in what ways is their authorship different because of their gender? Second, how do these contemporary debates relate to the seventeenth century? And third, do the authorial voices of these texts share these contemporary critics' enthusiasm for their new-found authorial status, and celebrate their coming to voice? More generally, how might the specific questions of authorship discussed above be reformulated and transformed both by the specificities of the author-figure in these texts and by the historical and geographical location of such work? Turning to the texts themselves, I shall now investigate an issue that in many ways exemplifies and anatomises the complexities of seventeenth-century gender politics: namely, notions of authorship in sectarian women's writings.

The disappearing author

The complexities of authorship signalled above are amplified when we examine seventeenth-century sectarian women's writing, in which very particular formations of the author/text/reader configuration can be seen to be operating. Understandings of the self, the relationship between this and the 'author', and between the author and her text, are articulated in almost every text, by means of a more or less extended positioning of the 'author-figure' in relation to her 'self', her decision to write, her relationship with the text, and her expectations of her readership. It is in these negotiations that the complexities of the construction of the authorship can be discerned, in particular in the paradoxical coincidence of both assertions and denials of authorship.

One key site for the investigation of the formations of the relationship between author, self and text is the discussions of how the writer came to write her account. Most texts from the sects, whether spiritual autobiographies, prophecies, or debates on particular religious precepts, tended to include some account of the process whereby the authors came to write and publish. In contrast, however, to the characterisation of authorship by twentieth-century feminist writers as a triumphant and liberating declaration of selfhood, seventeenth-century women writers construct a starkly different version of their transitions to authorship. Typically, this was not described as a *decision* or desire to write, but as a *call* or command to write, emanating from God and requiring obedient acceptance. This call, however, was rarely straightforward for those so called: the Quaker Dorothy White was exceptional in recording her call in the following terms: 'The word of the Lord came unto me, saying, "Write, and again I say, write with speed, to the heads and rulers of this nation;" oh! earth, earth, earth, hear the word of the Lord' (White 1659: 1). For White, the recording of her call to write is immediately followed in her text by her own call to her readers to heed the word of God; there is no mediating indication of the impact of this call on her. Such a straightforward acceptance of the command to write is notable most for its atypicality;[6] much more characteristic are the expressions of self-depreciation touched on in the last chapter. Cumulatively, these are so varied and apparently so comprehensive that they might make a twentieth-century reader wonder how these authors ever managed to write at all. There are protestations of unworthiness, of excessive weakness, much denigration of the self and even, in some cases, an association of the act of writing with illness, or a description of what is constructed as self-dissolution as a prerequisite to the acceptance of the call to write.

One such protestation of unworthiness is to be found in the work of Elizabeth Stirredge, a Quaker born in 1634, whose autobiography was published in 1711. Here she detailed her feelings of inadequacy and unworthiness when she first received God's call to preach and write:

there fell upon me another greater exercise and travail of spirit, which seemed so strange and so wonderful, that I could not believe that ever the Lord would require such a service of me that was so weak and contemptible, so unfit and unlikely, my understanding but shallow, and my capacity but mean, and very low and dejected in my own eyes; and looking so much at my insufficiency made me strive so much against it; crying often times within myself, 'Surely this is something to ensnare me, for the Lord does not require such things of me; seeing that there are so many wise and good men that are more honourable, and fitter for such service than I; oh Lord, remove it far from me, and require anything else of me, that I can better perform.' (Stirredge 1711: 37)

It is clear that a major element in Stirredge's reluctance to write and publish was her gender: as a woman she was doubly unfit to undertake God's work, for not only was she not 'wise and good', but neither was she a man:

Oh Lord, why wilt thou require such hard things of me? Lord look upon my afflictions, and lay no more upon me than I am able to bear. They will not hear me that am a contemptible instrument. And seeing they despise the service of women so much, oh Lord make use of them that are more worthy. (Stirredge 1711: 70)

'Anxiety of authorship' could certainly be said to characterise Stirredge's text here. Worthiness is articulated as being synonymous with masculinity, and leaves Stirredge in an apparently untenable position. She writes of managing to resolve the situation only by 'giving up to obey the Lord in all things he required of me': once God had shown her that he would choose the 'weak and dejected, and them that were nothing in their own eyes, and that could do nothing, no not so much as to utter a word but what the Lord giveth into their mouths' to do his work, then she could 'freely give up to obey the requirings of the Lord with peace and comfort' (Stirredge 1711: 37). Stirredge's call to do God's work, and in particular to authorship, was, then, quite clearly a source of conflict, anxiety and pain, something to which she needed to become reconciled, a cause for regret rather than celebration.

Stirredge here effects a number of assertions in relation to her own textual status as author. First, she is at pains to deny any desire to undertake such a public calling as preaching and writing; her reluctance and resistance are the overt subject of this section of her text. Second, she relocates the desire for her entry into this realm of activity with God; it is with him, not her, that this move originates. Third, she makes clear that the words that God wishes her to speak are not to be her own words, but are to be his: as she says, she cannot 'utter a word but what the Lord giveth into [her] mouth'. All these three elements are characteristic of much of the women's writings from the sects: other writers frequently voice misgivings and reluctance similar to those delineated by Stirredge, suggesting, as she does, that their own part in the production of the text is minimal, non-existent or simply irrelevant. Stirredge's expressed attitude to her writing is summarised by means of a single image, that of the 'contemptible instrument'. Whilst the adjective clearly carries associations of unworthiness and self-abnegation, the noun 'instrument' has implications of passivity, powerlessness, lack of agency, dependence on another to wield and control it; and it is a noun that is deployed again and again by women sectarian writers to describe their relationship to God in general, and to the act of writing in particular. In short, as instruments in God's all-controlling hand, they will follow his commands, and record his words; but this act of following will be passive, as instruments rather than as active agents. So, for example, Barbara Blaugdone, a Quaker, wrote 'as an instrument in the hand of the Lord, to do his work, I was faithful and obedient unto his power' (Blaugdone 1691: 35); the Baptist autobiographer Jane Turner wrote that 'I am conscious to myself of too much weakness and unworthiness to be an instrument for the good of souls' (Turner 1653: 'A word from the Author to the Reader'); and Mary Mollineux is described by her cousin Frances Owen as 'a good instrument in the hand of the Lord to me' (Mollineux, 1702: 'Testimony from ... Frances Owen').

In similar but more expansive vein, Mary Cary, a Fifth Monarchist prophet, prefaced her work (a detailed and extended exposition of Charles I's downfall and the prospective establishing of the New Jerusalem) with a statement stressing that she is not chosen by God through any particular fitness of her own character:

> I am a very weak, and unworthy instrument, and have not done this work by any strength of my own, but have been often made sensible, that I could do no more herein (wherein any light, or truth could appear) of myself, than a pencil or pen can do, when no hand guides it. (Cary 1651: 'To the Reader'; see Appendix A below.)

As a denial of a writer's fitness for her work, as a denigration of the particularity of the 'self' of the author, this is both striking and unequivocal. The writing, she suggests, is not her own, but something produced by God through her; she is no more than a medium, a means of expression. Anything useful or worthwhile in the writing comes from God; he is the active creative force, the 'author', she no more than the passive amanuensis or 'instrument'.

The image of the writer as 'instrument' is a useful example through which to anatomise the language of self-depreciation. This single image provides both a means by which to efface the significance of the author-figure, and a way of relocating the responsibility for the writing with God, whose hand guides and shapes her literary activities; in one move, the authorship and the ownership of the text are transferred from their earthly author to their divine one. The image of the instrument seems, then, to serve a dual purpose: its frequency makes it a rather standard expression of self-abnegation of the individual in the sight of God; but the image further functions to reduce the significance of the author by ascribing authorship to the ultimate male author-of-all: God.

Nor is the image of the instrument the sole one to recur that exemplifies and characterises these protestations of unworthiness; another, still more disturbing, with which women describe themselves is the image of the author as worm, the lowest and most despised of God's creatures. Anne Wentworth, a Baptist writing in the 1670s, described how she had met with many kinds of opposition and persecution, from friends and enemies alike; she continues, 'I am sensible any of these things would be too strong for me, a worm of no might or strength; but I have renounced myself, and laid down my own wisdom and will in this matter, and am given up to the will of God herein' (Wentworth 1677: 9). Not only is she without self, will and wisdom, she is also a 'poor worm', a rhetorical flourish that takes her beyond self-denial to the realms of the despised. Katherine Chidley, writing some some thirty-five years earlier, shares Wentworth's self-characterisation. Having challenged a religious opponent, Thomas Edwards, to a debate on the subject of congregational independence, Chidley then denies herself any status or opportunity as a combatant: 'But if you overcome me, your conquest will not be great, for I am a poor worm, and unmeet to deal with you' (Chidley 1641:81). Similarly, the Fifth Monarchist prophet Anna Trapnel adopts the image of the worm to describe herself. On leaving Plymouth, as she is being transported back to London to face imprisonment in Bridewell, she writes that some people 'were sorry to have me go from their quarters, not that I was anything, but the Lord did their souls good through a worm' (Trapnel 1654b: 34–5). Such an image is striking for demonstrating the lengths to which these authors appear to go to circumvent any possible suggestion of self-worth or achievement, thereby warding off the possibility of accusations of vainglory or immodesty being levelled at them for their entries into authorship: Chidley is not a fit opponent for Edwards; people do not regret Trapnel's departure for her own sake but because of the good that has come from God through her.

Such tortuous self-denials can be found in many guises throughout these texts, the need to deny the work of self-will at times engendering circuitous and convoluted disclaimers. One such can be found once again in Anna Trapnel's *The Cry of a Stone* (1654); at this point she is describing, in a now quite familiar way, how the work she has been called to do by God is antithetical to her own nature, but endurable since it is done in God's name:

> If the body suffer never so much, if it be for thyself, thy saints,[7] thy kingdom, it is better for her than to be in her own habitation, and in pleasant gardens; and when thy servants [*sic*] has done thy work, she shall be willing to lock up herself in her closet again, and not to be seen of men; oh Lord thy servant knows there is no self in this thing. (Trapnel 1654a: 42)

This statement takes the form of the by now familiar denial of authorial aspirations: Trapnel's work is for God, not herself; she is prepared to go out into the world and to suffer for him; once his work is done, she will once more confine herself to a woman's proper place, her own home, away from the public eye. Trapnel rounds off the statement with a catch-all safety clause, and one that could equally well describe the attitude towards their authorship of most of the women writers from the sects: 'there is no self in this thing'; this, in short, is God's work, his word spoken through the passive instrument of a reluctant woman.

Far, then, from entry into authorship marking a triumphant transition from the restrictions of women's allotted private, domestic and familial role into the public world of published writing and political and religious debate, it is instead clearly a problematic transition, often characterised not only by textual denials and refusals, but at times also by a period of protracted illness. This connection between writing and illness is manifested in several ways. In some cases, a life-threatening illness served as a rite of passage preceding and accompanying the call to write, whereby the writing is facilitated and legitimated; Jane Turner, for example, was 'under a bodily affliction' when the Lord visited her. She enjoyed 'sweet communion' with him for seven or eight weeks, whilst she was ill, and then, worried that she might forget the particulars of this 'continual converse', she decided to write it down (Turner 1653: 1,2; see p. 000 below). For other writers, a period of illness was a punishment for resisting or refusing God's command: the Baptist Anne Wentworth seems to have been in continual struggle against God's call for many months. She records how she begged God to spare her from the duty of writing, for she knew her work would give offence. She resisted for eleven months, until God threatened to kill her, and took her sleep from her, so that 'the terrors of the Lord forced me to obey the command'. For Wentworth, the command to write had come after eighteen years of marriage to a 'hard-hearted yoke-fellow', when

> I was consumed with grief, sorrow, oppression of heart, and long travail in the wilderness, and brought even to the gates of death, and when past the cure of all men, was raised up by the immediate and mighty hand of God. And being thus healed, I was commanded to write, and give glory to him who had so miraculously raised me up from the grave. (Wentworth 1677: 7)

For others, faith and 'public service' in the form of preaching, prophesying or writing emerged out of the suffering of illness: Anna Trapnel, the Fifth Monarchist prophet, for example, related how 'seven years ago I being visited with a fever, given over by all for dead, the Lord then gave me faith to believe' (Trapnel 1654a: 3). Once she had proved this faith, God promised to make her 'an instrument of much more; for particular souls shall not only have benefit of thee, but the universality of saints shall have discoveries of God through thee' (Trapnel 1654a: 3). Trapnel also became ill when she tried to resist God's call to travel to Cornwall preaching and prophesying (Trapnel 1654b: 3, 5).

For these writers, writing is clearly associated with the negative experience of illness and physical suffering, and the consequent threat to life and safety. This in turn is associated with fears of God's anger and possible punishment, invariably a result of refusing to do God's will as commanded. This nexus of the call to write, illness, fear and threat can be read as constituting a kind of pathologisation of the act of writing, the manifestation of a bodily sickness somehow paralleling or representing the 'sickness' of being a woman writer. This analogy provides more evidence, if any more were necessary, of the reluctance, trepidation and resistance with which these writers greeted the transition to writing and publishing. The overwhelming majority of women writers from the sects, then, work hard to displace themselves from the position of 'author' of their text. Some do this through a metaphorical denial of any agency in relation to their texts ('I am a contemptible instrument'); others do it through biblical self-abnegation ('I am a poor worm') or by more general denials of responsibility for their actions ('there is no self in this thing'); and still others indicate their associations of writing with illness, anger, fear, and life-threatening circumstances.

For a twentieth-century feminist reader, these responses by sectarian women to their newly-found status as writers might seem to be disconcerting and disappointing. Having asserted the significance and the relevance of retaining a notion of authorship which helps to bring these texts under critical scrutiny, it is both chastening and ironic then to discover that, far from proclaiming the joys of authorship, these writers instead lament, circumvent or deny precisely such a role. The desire of the feminist critic to establish the continuity and longevity of a female writing tradition thus appears to be foiled not by the demonic repression of the patriarchs but by precisely the women writers themselves. Whilst such a discrepancy between contemporary agendas and these seventeenth-century authors usefully highlights how texts from the past cannot be adopted wholesale and undigested for current political or critical purposes, it also seems to lead us into something of a critical impasse. Should the contemporary feminist critic join the ranks of the poststructuralists within literary criticism and, prompted by the apparent disclaimers voiced with such ardour by her seventeenth-century sisters, abandon authorship as a valid criterion through which to insert these texts into the seventeenth-century canon, thereby perpetuating the exclusion of these texts from critical scrutiny? At first, second or even third reading, there seems little textual evidence upon which to call in order to counter the rejection of the category 'female author' in these writings, a category upon which so many tenets of contemporary feminist criticism rest.

One resolution of this dilemma might be to introduce the widely adopted distinction between the categories of the 'author' and the 'narrator'; perhaps these writers who so vehemently refuse the privileges and responsibilities of authorship might instead be referred to by the more textually-mediated notion of the narrator. Could their insistence upon their role as mediators of another's (i.e. God's) authority and words mean that the role of 'narrator' might seem a more appropriate term for their role? To adopt such a distinction here might seem to offer a solution to the problem outlined above, in so far as it severs the problematic connection between the historically, socially and culturally situated author and that authoritative voice of the author-in-the-text. Whilst such categorical manoeuvrings might be a tempting conceptual solution, such a shift offers no real satisfactory resolution to this dilemma, since these writers can be seen to be as keen to deny their narratorial role as they are their authorial one. Neither authors, nor narrators, then, these writers insist upon their role as empty vessels, instruments of God and passive mediators of his word.

However, the pitfalls of decontextualised literary analysis could be nowhere more apparent than in an interpretation whose conclusion rested here. For to accept these denials of authorship at face value would be to ignore the interpretations available through a more carefully historicised and contextualised reading. Whilst it *could* be argued that the reclaiming of seventeenth-century female writers under the contemporary banner of authorship exemplifies a misguided plundering of the past motivated by a dubious feminist universalism, such conclusions *themselves* demonstrate the need to contextualise our readings. Once we cease to attempt to adopt these texts wholesale and undigested for our own purposes, and begin to read them not as if they were contributions to contemporary debates, but alongside other texts from the seventeenth century, as part of the struggles of their own time, strikingly different conclusions can be reached. I would argue that if we do this, if we take note of the echoes and nuances within these texts, and read them through seventeenth-century discourses of religion, politics and gender, then these apparently unequivocal statements of self-denial and denigration start to speak in other ways, and we can begin to construct a quite different sense of how 'authorship' might have been negotiated by women writers in the sects of that time.

Any feminist argument for including seventeenth-century women writers from the radical sects in literary studies cannot, then, be made on the basis of a straightforward shared 'celebration of authorship', a reclaiming of the triumphant coming-to-voice of this hitherto silent or silenced group. However, reading these texts in relation to other texts and broader contemporary debates results in a very different set of meanings: what might at first sight seem like a self-effacing and evasive body of writing becomes at the very least productively ambiguous, and, at times, extraordinarily complex and nuanced in its implications. To demonstrate this, I shall look again at the examples I introduced in the preceding section: those texts using the metaphors of the instrument, the worm, and the desired return to the privacy of the closet, but beginning with a return to my concluding discussion of illness. Re-readings of these examples through a variety of discourses and contexts suggest a quite different model of authorship for women writers of the seventeenth century from the twentieth-century one which proved so impossible to graft wholesale onto seventeenth-century writings.

'Miraculously raised from the grave': overcoming illness, becoming an author

Instead of reading the relationship between illness and writing as recorded by Anna Trapnel, Anne Wentworth, Jane Turner and others as indicative of the pathologisation of the act of writing on the part of the troubled author, it is possible to approach the equation differently, and look for other common factors between the two. Rather than seeing them as hysterical responses to the dread duty of writing for publication, if we approach them as metaphors through which the contradictions between femininity and authority are mediated, then we can posit a set of quite different meanings. Both writing and serious illness mark out the sectarian woman as different from her fellows: they both isolate her and threaten her safety and future security; both require explanation, and precipitate a search for a reason or cause. As markers of difference, however, these parallels only become significant when we return to the texts themselves and find the underlying common factor of both phenomena: namely, God. It is God who, we are told, is at work both during and by means of the illnesses, and it is God who, without fail, is responsible for the writings – or, indeed, prophecies – of these women. Both illness and writing then bond the writer with God, and both the illness and the call to write provide vital evidence of that bond, evidence that is necessary to protect the writer from the charges of vainglory or immodesty, writing being an activity at best discouraged and at worst

93

proscribed for women in the seventeenth century as an unseemly entry into the public world. The struggle and the eventual triumph over serious illness acts as a guarantee of the grace experienced by the writer, first tested and then spared by God, whilst the genuinely divine origin of the call to write is, in turn, testified to by the narrative of the struggle with, and overcoming of, illness.

Illness provided crucial substantiating evidence for the writers' claims to the divine origins of, and authorisation for, their activities. As justification for entering the risky world of published writing, it functioned in such a way as to validate the claims that God had singled this woman out to be given faith, to be tested, to be punished or to be saved. Anne Wentworth, in characteristic style, was not slow to spell out the potential for her own case: 'when past the cure of all men, [I] was raised up by the immediate and mighty hand of God. And being thus healed, I was commanded to write, and give glory to him who had so miraculously raised me from the grave' (Wentworth 1677: 7). For Wentworth, her illness did not just explain her writing, it generated and required it; the writing was a consequence of God's having saved her from certain death, a due that she must pay God in order to give praise to her saviour. Similarly, Jane Turner recorded her 'continual converse' with God during her illness in case she were to forget its details, and Anna Trapnel was chosen for public work as a result of the faith she received during her illness. In each case, the illness is constructed and interpreted by the author as evidence of the irrevocable bond between the writer, her text and God, her survival of the illness further testifying to her chosen status, and her acquiescence to the call to write no more than a dutiful obedience as a way to give thanks to God for his grace to her. Moreover, as Diane Purkiss has argued, the linking of the illness with women's prophetic activities helped undermine the usually negative – and feminine – meanings of bodily weakness:

> the attributes used in the dominant discourse to signify feminine inadequacy are privileged as facilitators of verbal empowerment. Illness and physical incapacity stage the body as the passive prey of external forces, hence an authentic site of divine intervention. (Purkiss 1992a: 144)

Far from illness being necessarily a tortured response to the call to write, it can instead be seen as an imperative to authorship, almost unanswerable evidence of the writer's communion with God. Indeed, the very passivity and vulnerability produced by the illness, which initially seemed to pathologise the consequent writing or prophecy, by this reading can instead be seen to validate, authenticate and elevate them, through testifying to their divine origins.

The 'poor worm' turns

Like the instance of illness, the use of the metaphor of the worm to designate the author-figure's place in the order of creation seems at first reading to provide little comfort for the feminist critic: as a statement of self-abnegation, it seems thoroughgoing. Once again, though, if these statements are read through seventeenth-century discourses, then new and quite different meanings can be suggested.

Anne Wentworth used the image of the worm in a section where she was discussing the hindrances to writing, both inner and outer, with which she met:

> I stand to encounter with all discouragements from my own understanding, will, affections, former thoughts and principles within: and with all opposition from difficulties, dangers, temptations of friends, and conspiracies of enemies without; I am sensible any of these things would be too strong for me, a worm of no might or strength; but I have renounced myself, and laid down my own wisdom and will in this work, and am given up to the will of God herein. (Wentworth 1677: 9)

Opposition to Wentworth's actions, then, comes from others, friends and enemies alike; and, more importantly, it comes from herself, her 'own understanding', her 'former thoughts and principles'. The only way to overcome this self-doubt is to overcome the self, thereby destroying 'my own wisdom and will' and allowing the *resulting* self to write, since this is the will of the new controller and legislator of that self, God. The worm, then, is something of no strength or power: as a worm she could not overcome her own doubts and fears about writing. If even the worm ceases to exist, however, then, ironically, its stature is magnified by becoming subject to, and a part of, the almighty will of God; in this form, the new self can achieve whatever she – or, rather, he – desires.

Katherine Chidley, too, is concerned with her status as a writer and her own justifications for writing a controversial and polemical tract. Her text is addressed to Thomas Edwards, and is in answer to his attack on independent churches. This she does coherently and vigorously, attacking his reading of the Scriptures as inaccurate and Edwards himself as 'a bloody minded man, that would have the innocent suffer for the faults of them that are guilty' (Chidley 1641: 61). The relentless and uncompromising nature of her attack is suggested by the biblical quotation with which she prefaces her work (see p. 71 above): 'Then Iael, Heber's wife, took a nail of the tent, and took an hammer in her hand, and went softly unto him, and smote the nail into his temples and fastened it into the ground, (for he was fast asleep and weary) and so he died' [Judges 4:21] (Chidley 1641: title page). Chidley's challenge to Edwards to engage in a 'fair discourse' in order to debate their respective points of view is in line with this combative, competent and confident tone. To be then confronted with her conclusion to the challenge is confusing: 'But if you overcome me, your conquest will not be great, for I am a poor worm, and unmeet to deal with you' (Chidley 1641: 81). The confusion engendered by this statement arises chiefly from its context, the eighty pages of closely argued, point-for-point refutation of Edwards's attack on the Independent churches. The deployment of this image, then, can have a double function: it serves as the necessary self-abnegation and denial of vainglory, whilst at the same time through its immediate context it accretes a kind of power of its own. For is is this very image that denies Edwards any possibility of winning the 'fair discourse': to refuse the challenge would leave eighty pages of argument unanswered, whilst to accept it would be demeaning, for it would mean engaging with the arguments of 'a poor worm', the lowest of the low. Chidley leaves Edwards no way to acquit himself honourably.

Anna Trapnel's autobiographical text, *Anna Trapnel's Report and Plea* (1654), presents, as did Chidley's, a context that argues for the presence of a dynamic, confident and persuasive author. Also like Chidley, Trapnel chose the image of the worm to describe herself. Some people, she wrote 'were sorry to have me go from their quarters, not that I was anything, but the Lord did their souls good though a worm' (Trapnel 1654b: 34–5). Once again, this formulation serves as the standard act of self-abnegation, counterbalancing the potentially vainglorious observation that people regretted her departure. In addition, however, it deflects attention from the 'worm' to the source and effectiveness of the writer's power, and thereby combines in one image a surface impression of powerlessness with a strong undercurrent of power. It is images such as these that both illustrate and reconcile the necessary contradictions of self-abnegation and self-centredness in the texts.

It is Trapnel, too, who makes this identification of weakness with power most explicit. In describing her conversion and God's call to her to prophesy, she stresses that, although initially praying to be spared this 'public-spiritedness', she was persuaded by God with one particular passage from I Corinthians:

> But God hath chosen the foolish things of the world to confound the wise; and God hath chosen the weak things of the world to confound the things which are mighty;
>
> And base things of the world, and things which are despised, hath God chosen, yea, and things which are not, to bring to nought things that are. (I Corinthians 1:27-8)

Trapnel goes on to say that 'I could be contented to be made use of under these terms, as a fool, and base, and despised, and as a thing that is not' (Trapnel 1654b: 17). It is unsurprising that it should be this particular text that reconciled Trapnel to the call to 'public-spiritedness', for it is one that allows her to leave unchallenged the world's view of her as foolish, base, despised, 'a thing that is not'. This last phrase recalls in particular the legal position of seventeenth-century women, where they existed only in relation to their husbands and fathers, not in their own right.[8] Trapnel was not alone to call on this citation to validate her actions: Arise Evans used it in relation to Elinor Channel (see p. 73 above), and it was used too by Anne Wentworth to describe her condition before her call to write (Wentworth 1677: 3, 14), again highlighting the irony of having to deny the self before the self can attain any power or significance.[9] This text further helps to explicate the image of the worm: there too the subject is presented as weak and despised, yet at the same time that picture is subverted by its being invested with the greatest power and authority available, that coming from God. It is this reconciliation of worldly nothingness with divine usefulness that, as Trapnel says, made her 'contented' to enter the public arena, and that surfaces again and again in the tropes used to figure the author in the text, and her relationship to God and to her text.

Instrument as agent: the sects and the Bible

The incidences of illness, together with the trope of the worm, suggest that the connection with God that is established through the accounts and their contexts is of central importance: in one, God saves the author in order that she might do his work, whilst in the other the denigration of the self as a worm allows the emergence of a new self, one without human weakness and with new-found divinely ordained authority. This authority is accorded by God's engagement with the author-figure, and validates both her writing and her accounts of how she came to write. It is this connection with God that is the key to re-reading these texts, and an examination of these images' articulations of this connection opens up wider and more challenging meanings than those hitherto suggested.

Thus the 'instrument' in the hand of God that I initially described as passive, inarticulate, a mere mouthpiece for another's words begins to look rather different when we consider the ways in which the image can be seen to develop a more complex version of the power relationship between author and God. For example, once the statement is read as focusing equally on the author and on God, Mary Cary's apparently characteristic self-effacing protestation of unworthiness begins to seem more double-edged and ambiguous than on the first reading:

> I am a very weak, and unworthy instrument, and have not done this work by any strength of my own, but have been often made sensible that I could do no more herein (wherein any light, or truth could appear) of myself, than a pencil or pen can do, when no hand guides it. (Cary, 1651: 'To the Reader')

The accumulation of assertions of weakness, unworthiness, and incapacity ends with the comparison of the author with a 'pencil or pen' – inert, silent and powerless until deployed by somebody else. As a denial of self, it functions to deny the writer's responsibility for her own writings, and as such acts as protection against charges of immodesty or impropriety. She does not, however, deny the authority or usefulness of her writings (they may offer some 'light, or truth'), but accords responsibility for this with God, the hand that guides and shapes her literary activities. The image of the instrument, then, serves a triple purpose: first, it serves as the standard but necessary expression of self-effacement, removing the responsibility for the writing from the author and placing it with God. Second, it also infuses the writer and her text with power, by emphasising that any 'light, or truth' found in her words comes direct from the omnipotent, the source of all power, so that her words, her truth are isomorphic with God's truth, and as such become themselves divine, authoritative and unassailable. Third, by suggesting the passivity of herself as 'pencil or pen' and the omnipotence of God as author, Cary is also suggesting the controlling power of the author in the writing process: if God is author and she is pen, so she too, as a writer, also wields a pen and of necessity partakes of that control.[10] It is, then, an image that fuses a denial of the power of the author-figure with the relocation and assertion of that power. It both shifts the focus from the unworthy 'instrument' herself on to God, the wielder of the instrument, and at the same time it draws attention to the authority of her words and the power of the figure in the position of the author.

Thus far, a more careful *intra*textual reading has opened up the nuances and ambiguities of Cary's text; however, if we examine the image of the instrument as it appears *inter*textually, then the nuances are multiplied still further, and, indeed, the meanings substantially transformed. The most important text through which to re-read concepts and images deployed by sectarian writers is, unsurprisingly, the Bible. As Christopher Hill has demonstrated (Hill 1993), the Bible was a touchstone for seventeenth-century sectaries. It was the one text that was genuinely widely accessible, and as such writers could rely on their readers' knowledge of it in some detail. As the word of God, its words and precepts carried an authority that could not be questioned without risking the credibility of the challenger.[11] Biblical references and allusions were, then, woven into sectarian writings, by both men and women, as guarantees of the legitimacy of the message being conveyed.[12] These citations are sometimes direct, credited with book and chapter references, but more often they are buried, embedded, helping to form the characteristic tone and style of the texts, but also creating a network of allusion which helps to diffuse and reshape the initial intratextual meanings. Given the extent to which the Bible shaped and textured these writings in general, and in particular the metaphors of authorship under consideration here, it is of crucial importance that the relationship between the two is at the centre of any analysis.

At first, turning to the Bible in order to analyse the meanings of the 'instrument' of God is perplexing, for the evident importance of the image for the sectaries does not seem to be rooted in an appropriation from the Bible. There are certainly many scriptural references to 'instrument' or 'instruments': Cruden's *Concordance* (1930) lists some thirty-four references. Of these, most refer to musical instruments; other references are to instruments used in religious ceremonies, and to weapons as 'instruments of death'. As few as three refer directly to people being used as instruments by somebody else, whether God or another person. There is, however, one rather extended discussion of an 'instrument', and it is this that helps clarify the meanings of the image of the instrument for the sectaries:

> Fear not, thou worm Jacob, and ye men of Israel; I will help thee, saith the Lord, and thy Redeemer, the Holy One of Israel.
>
> Behold, I will make thee a new sharp threshing instrument having teeth: thou shalt thresh the mountains, and beat them small, and shalt make the hills as chaff.
>
> Thou shalt fan them, and the wind shall carry them away, and the whirlwind shall scatter them: and thou shalt rejoice in the Lord, and shalt glory in the Holy One of Israel. (Isaiah 41:14-16)

Here the concept of the instrument structures and gives meaning to the whole passage. Jacob will be made 'a new sharp threshing instrument, having teeth': the sense of newness here would have been significant for the women prophets and writers for, in their own time, if not in biblical times or in dissenting sects of previous centuries, there were few precedents for female religious activists, and novelty, as well as public activity, needed constant justification. The sense of power, too, is central: the instrument is 'sharp' and 'threshing', and has 'teeth'; it will destroy mountains and hills, making them as 'chaff'. The instrument is hereby invested with a power and agency all of its own, quite unlike the other instances noted above. It is certainly created by God, and given its power by God, but it is stressed that it is the instrument that has the teeth and will beat the mountains to chaff; it is the instrument that will fan this chaff, thereby generating the wind that will blow the chaff away.

The instrument, then, is a 'doer', something that was a priority to the sectaries, who consistently criticised those they saw as 'talkers only'.[13] It could not act alone, for it was created and invested with its power by God, but the power it had been given was the power to act. The verbs in the passage are primarily active: 'thou shalt make', 'thou shalt beat', 'thou shalt thresh', 'thou shalt fan'. It is God speaking here, and the power and the authority to act come from him, as does the command, here insistently expressed in the repetition of 'thou shalt'. Yet the command merely serves to highlight in what ways the 'instrument' will become agent. The overall emphasis of the passage is undoubtedly that it is the instrument who is the key actor in this process.

Underlining the relevance of this passage for the women writers in the sects is the phrase occurring in verse 14, 'thou worm Jacob': once again, it is the worm, low, despised and powerless, that is transformed into the active and powerful instrument. The transmutation of the worm into the 'sharp threshing instrument having teeth' is exactly the process identified as being that of their own spiritual development in the work of women such as Anna Trapnel and Anne Wentworth, and suggested by their own use of the image as discussed above.

The image of the instrument, then, constitutes a paradox, for it figures something both active and passive, both in control and controlled. The contradiction posed by this notion of an 'active instrument' is, however, resolved by the figure of God, which functions to hold the terms of the contradiction stable, preventing it from threatening the credibility of the writer. I have written of this already in relation to the biblical references to the instrument: since God is choosing and empowering the instrument, then it is possible for the writer to stress God's role as prime mover, the authority, to the exclusion of her own part. Yet, at the same time, as in Isaiah 41:14–16, the instrument, once created, acts powerfully, even independently, with its own momentum. Thus, both 'I's are present, the passive and the active, the absent and present, with the figure of God as linchpin. His status as both originator and investor of power enables the active to call themselves passive, and thereby maintain their image as modest and decorous, whilst at the same time providing the means for the weak to be powerful, the neutral to be political, and the instrument to be agent. The terms of such contradictions are all authorised by their biblical origin, where 'God hath chosen the foolish things of the world to confound the wise; and ... the weak things of the world to confound the things which are mighty' (I Corinthians 1:27). Not only, then, do these writers seek both to efface themselves from their texts whilst maintaining the importance for their readers of those same texts, but they also effect this Janus-like manoeuvre through recourse to the ultimate and unquestionable authorities: God and his revealed word, the Bible. Even for the Quakers, whose ultimate guide and touchstone was their own consciences, the Bible remained of central importance: for conscience served to ratify and augment the 'truth' of the Bible, or to reconcile its conflicting or contradictory truths; it in no sense supplanted or dispensed with it.

Trapnel, the closet and the Bible

My final example, from Anna Trapnel's *The Cry of a Stone* (1654), demonstrates not only how such a contextualisation can be productive in terms of the kinds of reading that become available, but also how such multiple readings can be seen as integral to the structure and functioning of the text. In the following passage, initially discussed above, Trapnel is describing, in a quite familiar way, how the work she has been called to do by God is antithetical to her own nature, but endurable since it is done in God's name:

> If the body suffer never so much, if it be for thyself, thy saints, thy kingdom, it is better for her than to be in her own habitation, and in pleasant gardens; and when thy servants [*sic*] has done thy work, she shall be willing to lock up herself in her closet again, and not to be seen of men; oh Lord thy servant knows there is no self in this thing. (Trapnel 1654a: 42)

This statement certainly functions as the requisite disclaimer from the author-figure of any personal responsibility for the decision to write, and suggests a longing for a return to a private, domestic space. In addition to this, though, we learn about the process whereby Trapnel became reconciled to the execution of God's work, which, in her case, is prophesying, travelling extensively to do so, and disseminating God's word as widely as possible, even though it takes her into the public domain. She contrasts this public duty with the alternative private domain, her 'own habitation' and 'pleasant gardens', which she has left behind only for the duration of her work for God; once this is completed, she will retire once again to the realm of the private. Now, however, as she contemplates this return, it is no longer described as 'pleasant'; now it is a 'closet'[14] in which she will lock herself, 'not to be seen of men'. Far from being something pleasant and her 'own', her habitation has now become a confined and constricting space in which she is incarcerated and isolated, invisible to 'men', the movers in the public domain. Despite the apparently unwelcome prospect of such a retreat and confinement, Trapnel does, however, in effect preclude the possibility of it ever coming about. She claims she will work only until God's work is complete; this, of course, would not be until the day of judgement, the second coming of King Jesus, and the establishing of the New Jerusalem on earth, when Fifth Monarchists believed the whole social order would change, and all members of society would be equal. As another Fifth Monarchist prophet, Mary Cary put it, this would be a time when 'not only men but women shall prophesy; not only aged men, but young men; not only superiors but inferiors; not only those that have university-learning, but those that have it not; even servants and handmaids' (Cary, 1651: 238). In the future envisioned by Fifth Monarchists, differential access to the public sphere on the basis of gender was clearly not countenanced, and the question of 'retirement' was certainly not at issue.

Another striking feature of this passage is Trapnel's constant referencing of herself in the third person, as 'the body' and 'thy servant'. This results in the separation of the 'I' of the subject of the text from the 'I' of the author-figure, and facilitates such apparently paradoxical statements as her concluding 'thy servant knows there is no self in this thing', where 'thy servant' is referring to Trapnel herself. Here the author-figure, the agent, the 'self' that is active in the writing process, denies not only her own agency and activity, but also her 'selfhood'. On the one hand, this seems no more than an oxymoronic conundrum, a self denying itself; on the other, it hints at a complex construction and understanding of the self, to which I will return later in this chapter.

Thus far, a careful intratextual reading can alert us to the ambiguities and nuances of the text, ambiguities which suggest a much more complicated response to the work of prophesying and writing than my 'first reading' could give. Combining this with a move that re-embeds the text in seventeenth-century discourse by examining the biblical context, though, takes the reading one step further.

There are two significant references to the 'closet' in the Bible. Both concern the division of the public and the private, and both concern hypocrisy. The first is from Matthew:

> And when thou prayest, thou shalt not be as the hypocrites are: for they have to pray standing in the synagogues and in the corners of the streets, that they may be seen of men. Verily I say unto you, They have their reward.
>
> But thou, when thou prayest, enter into thy closet, and when thou hast shut thy door, pray to thy Father which is in secret; and thy Father which seeth in secret shall reward thee openly. (Matthew 6:5-6)

This clearly condemns those that pray (or perhaps prophesy) in public as hypocrites, and contrasts them with those that pray in private, whom God will reward. Since Trapnel's text links the closet with no longer being 'seen of men', it seems probable that this is an allusion to this particular biblical text, thereby suggesting that the move from the public to the private is a desirable one. However, this reading is called into question by the passage from Luke 12: 'Therefore whatsoever ye have spoken in darkness shall be heard in the light; and that which ye have spoken in the ear in closets shall be proclaimed upon the house-tops' (Luke 12:3). The reference to the 'closet' here has rather different implications. Darkness, secrecy and closets are counterposed to light, proclamation and openness, so that the restrictions and isolation of private utterances give way to a public recognition and acceptance of a message proclaimed from 'the house-tops'. These references produce two conflicting understandings of privacy, public utterance and hypocrisy, neither of which can be claimed as definitive or final, for they are dependent on allusion rather than on a clearly cited reference. As such, the two meanings coexist, albeit uncomfortably. What is established is a text pulling in two directions: reluctant yet resolved, private yet public, self-denying yet self-assertive, powerless yet dynamic.

All these examples – illness, the worm, the instrument and the closet – rely on such sets of paradoxes and their resulting ambiguities and shifting meanings. These characteristics, however, testify to more than a late twentieth-century proclivity for a polysemic text; they are crucial to an understanding of the specificities of the author-figure constructed in the texts from women writers in the sects. Each new analytical turn that is taken pushes this construction in a new, often contrary, direction, so that the 'author-figure' slips between the polar positions of passive self-denial and confident assertions of divinely-ordained certainty, never settling on either. What at first, then, seemed like unambiguous metaphors of feminine self-abnegation increasingly seem to produce vehicles for addressing the 'anxieties of authorship' discussed earlier. Each trope, therefore, both demonstrates the particular restraints on women's writing and also exemplifies certain textual strategies whereby the female author-figure can be reworked. It is to a final example of this combination of activity and passivity that I shall now turn.

'A thing that is not in my own eyes': the vindication of Anne Wentworth

Anne Wentworth's second[15] published text, *A Vindication of Anne Wentworth* (1677), is one in which the textual construction of the author-figure depends throughout on the identification of strength with weakness and activity with passivity; indeed, it is not only these polarities which are called into question, but others too, most crucially that between public and private. It is therefore appropriate to conclude the chapter with a detailed discussion of this text, which exemplifies so well the textual mediations of the author-figure in seventeenth-century sectarian women's writing.

Wentworth's text is precisely what the title announces: a forceful, uncompromising and dazzlingly dextrous vindication of certain of her activities, in particular her writings and her decision to leave her husband. She had stayed with him for eighteen years, suffering 'the unspeakable tyrannies of an *hard-hearted yoke-fellow*' (Wentworth 1677: 1);[16] in the end, however, she left him, once Christ, her 'heavenly bridegroom', had called her 'to undertake and finish a work, which my earthly husband in a most cruel manner hindered me from performing, seizing and running away with my writings' (Wentworth 1677: 4–5). Far from her departure marking the end of her troubles, there were more to follow: her fellow Baptists accused her of being 'a *proud, passionate, revengeful, discontented* and *mad* woman, ... one that has unduly published things to the prejudice and scandal of my husband, and that have wickedly left him' (Wentworth 1677: 2). Whilst Wentworth does not question their version of events, she does challenge their interpretation of them. Whilst they attribute her actions to this range of conventionally *feminine* passions, ones which bear witness to her lack of submissiveness and rightful deference to her husband (see Chapter 2), she insists that, on the contrary, she has never acted out of a sense of wilfulness or personal ambition:

> I am not conscious to myself of any *spiritual pride* in this matter, nor in the least
> desirous to have any appearance or to make any noise in this world. Nor durst I for ten

thousand worlds pretend to come in the name of God, or in the pride and forwardness of my own spirit put myself into this work, without his express command concerning it, and his spirit and presence with me in it; having learnt ... how dangerous and desperate an attempt it is, to put the *commission* and *authority* of God upon the dreams and visions of my own heart. (Wentworth 1677: 3)

Far from breaking the bounds of modesty ('pride', 'appearance') or silence ('noise'), she here stresses that she is aware of how 'dangerous' it is to present one's own interests as if they were God's. She has acted, then, only on God's 'express command', in obedience to 'the heavenly vision herein' (Wentworth 1677: 5, 6). Such declarations are by now familiar: like Trapnel, in effect, she asserts that there is 'no self in this thing'; all responsiblity for the writing and for the writer's actions is relocated with God, thereby circumventing any earthly impediments to her fulfilling God's call by means of this justification of them in higher, spriritual terms. But where Wentworth's text differs from many others is in the extent to which she develops this argument, in how integral it is to the overall structure of her vindication, how it is used to justify a number of clearly 'earthly' activities, and how, in this most 'selfless' of texts, the 'self' of the author-figure is strikingly clear.

The self, its dissolution and its reconstitution are at the heart of this text. Having described the initial process whereby she came to write in the familiar terms illustrated above, she goes on to describe how God prepared her to receive and accept his call:

my *God* ... has been so many years *emptying me* from vessel to vessel, *breaking* me all to pieces in myself, and making me to become as *nothing* before him; and who has by many and great tribulations been *bowing* my own will, and fitting me for his service, and who having taught me to tremble at his *word*, has thereby called and commanded me into this work, when I was as a thing that *is not* in my own eyes. (Wentworth 1677: 3)

Far from her chosen status being dependent on who she is, it is contingent instead on the systematic fragmentation of the pre-existing Wentworth. It is the completion of this process of dissolution of the self that marks her out as fit to serve God. This extended detailing of the dismantling – even destruction – of her 'self' is just one instance of how her insistence on her lack of self operates in the text. In relation to her husband, for example, she argues that she will not justify leaving him through any sense of self-preservation, even though he was likely to have killed her: 'he has in his barbarous actions towards me a many times over done such things as not only in the *spirit* of them will be one day judged a murdering of, but had long since *really* proved so, if God had not wonderfully supported and preserved me' (Wentworth 1677: 4). Rather than justifying the saving of this self, the wronged wife of her ungodly and 'barbarous' husband, she instead defends a new self, the self that is constructed consequent to, and by means of, the dissolution of the old one, and therefore one whose existence is unquestionably of divine origin. Given the godly authorisation of this new self, it is one whose preservation can, and must, be ensured at all costs: 'But my natural life, through the springing up of a *better*, not being otherwise considerable, then as it is my duty to preserve it in a subserviency to the will and service of that God, whose I am in *spirit, soul* and *body*' (Wentworth 1677: 4). The call to write comes to Wentworth immediately following the dissolution of her old 'self', when she is 'as a thing that is not'; the new self, then, is constructed by God through the writing itself, in which she is to describe 'my *experiences*, my *great and wonderful deliverances*, my many *answers* of prayers in difficult cases from time to time' (Wentworth 1677: 7). This is to be both a record of God's grace and the means by which the new Wentworth is constructed – in the execution of God's commands. The new self is thus contingent on the old: her raw material is the recording of both God's grace to the old Wentworth, and the systematic divine dissolution of the old Wentworth. Nothing that she writes in this process, she declares, is untrue; anything distasteful, including her 'plain dealing' with a 'relation in the flesh' could not have been omitted without '*prejudice* to the truth' (Wentworth 1677: 7).

Her justification for both leaving her husband and for writing, then, rests on the many facets of her relationship with God. First, she must ensure the peace of her soul, 'a life more precious than this natural one' (Wentworth 1677: 4); second, she must finish the work of writing to which Christ has called her, and which her husband was hindering, and this involves saving the new Wentworth constructed directly by the intervention of God; and third, she must safeguard her new 'self' because of her duties towards others: she must, she writes: 'have my *just* and *necessary* liberty to attend a more than ordinary call and command of God to publish the things which concern the *peace of my own soul*, and *of the whole nation*' (Wentworth 1677: 6). Here, for the first time, is an indication of the broader significance Wentworth attaches to her writings. As well as having a personal importance for the peace of her own soul, they also have a directly public and political importance, since they concern the peace '*of the whole nation*'. She thus insists upon the public dimensions of her 'private' spiritual experiences; they affect not only herself, her husband and her congregation, but they also become a test case whereby the vindication of one woman's breach of the social norms, and her analysis and interpretation of this breach and of the resulting oppression she undergoes, are represented as a model for the understanding of national political issues. 'This matter is now become a *public figure*', she writes. 'I am called to wrestle not only against *flesh and blood, but against principalities, and powers, against the rulers of the darkness of this world, and against spiritual wickedness in high places*' (Wentworth 1677: 11, 10). She emphasises that this broader significance is, once again, something of which she has been assured by God: 'And he afterwards revealed to me what I did not then know, that my *oppressions* and *deliverance* had a *public ministry* and *meaning* wrapped up in them' (Wentworth 1677: 12). In this text, then, the public and the private, Wentworth's personal and spiritual experiences and their implications for the rest of the nation, cannot be separated. The latter are 'wrapped up' in the former; an analysis of her life leads to a critique of '*spiritual wickedness in high places*'. The iniquities of her husband are explicitly identified with 'the *same spirit* throughout the nation, which everywhere oppressess the true seed, as I have been oppressed by it' (Wentworth 1677: 13), and upon which the wrath of God shall fall.

Thus the distinction between private and public, family and state, are under-mined by this text. In this, Wentworth was not exceptional: far from the family being seen as a private and discrete unit, a safe haven from the hierarchies and divisions of a harsh public world, it was frequently discussed as a structure deeply implicated within the social order. As I outlined in Chapter 2, the family was frequently used as a figure and model of the state, with the patriarchal husband ruling his family by virtue of the same authority as the one by which the king ruled the nation. Both theologians and political theorists took, almost as a matter of course, the family as a model of the right ordering of the state. William Gouge, for example, said of the husband in his domestic conduct book *Of Domesticall Duties* (1622) that 'hee is as a king in his owne house' (quoted in Davies 1977: 566), whilst in *Patriarcha* (1680) Sir Robert Filmer argued that the authority a father has over his children 'is the fountain of all regal authority, by the ordination of God himself' (quoted in Amussen 1985: 197); moreover, 'If we compare the natural duties of a Father with those of a King, we find them to be all one, without any difference at all but only in the latitude or extent of them ... all the duties of a King are summed up in an universal fatherly care of his people' (quoted in Malekin 1981: 46). Wentworth was not unusual, then, in having an understanding of the family as a 'public' rather than a 'private' institu-tion. Where she was unusual, however, was in her utilisation of this analogy not with reference to the usual archetypal or idealised family and state, but with reference to her own family, which here is taken as figuring the state and nation in which she herself lived. Whilst the character of the traditional idealised analogy is supportive of the patriarchal status quo, her recasting of it in this way has quite the contrary effect; it relies for its impact on the widespread currency of the terms of the analogy, but shifts these terms from the ideal to the actual in order to argue for the corruption of both component parts: husband and social order. Amussen notes that by the time Locke came to write about the family in the later seventeenth century, he defined it as private, but 'he did so only after it had ceased to play a significant role in the public maintenance of social order' (Amussen 1985: 217). If the execution of Charles I was perhaps one element of major significance in this process – the 'father' of the nation removed by his 'children' from his seat of authority – then we might be witnessing in Wentworth's text another indicator of the same process. In any case, it seems unlikely that the analogy of the family died a natural death, simply 'ceasing' to play such a role; it seems more likely that this role was rendered untenable through the refiguring of the terms and assumptions on which it rested.

What impact, though, do such claims for the public significance of her own experiences have on the authorial 'self' constructed in the text? In sum, they make the author-figure and her experiences both the subject and the meaning of her text. The whole logic and structure of the text depend upon the viability of the analytical and interpretive voice of the 'new' Wentworth, the phoenix who arises from the ashes – or fragments – of the old one. Rather than the dissolution of the old identity, the process whereby God was '*breaking* me all to pieces in myself', signifying the destruction of the author-figure, it signifies its opposite: the construction of a new, divinely ordained voice of authorial authority. This voice is authenticated not only

105

by its divine authorisation, but also by the interreliant 'truths' uttered by that voice concerning the iniquities of husband, detractors and government. Without the 'self' in the text, there would be no text; but nor would there be the commanding voice of this textual 'self' without the preceding textual dismantling of the pretextual, oppressed, and submissive Anne Wentworth.

'Look not at your own weakness, but look at him who is calling you'

And so you, dear babes, that are little and weak in your own eyes, to you is this message
sent, look not at your own weakness, but look at him who is calling you in his eternal
love, who will make the weak strong, and will pull down the mighty from their seat.
(Jones 1650: 2)

This quotation comes from a short Quaker pamphlet written in the early 1650s by Sarah Jones. Whilst in many ways it is a very typical Quaker statement from that time, urging people to turn from carnal manifestations or worldly concerns to the spirit of God appearing as the inner light, it is also a remarkably good summary of the characteristic textual stance of the author-figure in these sectarian writings. At first, quite the contrary to Jones's advice seems to be operating in these texts: many of the author-figures seem to be looking precisely at their 'own weakness', whether as frail and sick women, as passive instruments, as 'poor worms', as reluctant movers in the public world of prophecy, or as the fragmented self who is 'as a thing that is not in my own eyes'. However, this focus on authorial weakness gives way to an altogether different picture when the texts are read more closely both intra- and intertextually. What becomes clear is that this focus on such incapacity and passivity is a means whereby the ultimate authority – God – can fill the space created by the lack of 'self' resulting from assertions of weakness, unworthiness, or even absence. Furthermore, far from author-figures being constituted *in spite of* these protestations, they are constituted *through* them: the passivity and weakness are markers of the presence of God, and thus create the circumstances in which the divinely-originating voice which is driving the text can be heard.

Once again, then, we see the struggle between the 'unequal bodies' and 'equal souls' (see Chapter 2) of women being played out in these representations of the author-figure. Through a series of textual moves, we see the frailty of the feminine body give way to the strength and authority of the spiritual self. On the one hand, there are the denials of any part in the production of the text by the weak and incapable body of the 'carnal' woman, and the contrary assertion that the whole work is the result of the hand of God. On the other hand, there are the interpretations of the weakness and powerlessness of the feminine body precisely as indicators of the presence of God, and also the site for his intervention and action. Just as the negotiation of silences discussed in Chapter 3 can be seen as a manifestation of the clash between the two sets of demands, between loyalty to the husband and loyalty to God, or between the status of the feminine and thus unequal body in relation to the ungendered and therefore equal soul, so here we can understand the characteristic textual constructions of the author-figure in the texts by sectarian women to be in dialogue with the same set of issues. Moreover, just as silence was a gendered phenomenon in that it engaged directly with one of the chief social and religious prescriptions to women, so the issue of authorship is similarly gendered: all the constructions of the author-figure examined in this chapter take as their starting point the frailty and unworthiness of women. They then negotiate or refigure this weakness in a number of different ways, all of them concluding that the direct intervention of the hand and voice of God in their work is its ultimate justification. From the feminine weakness of the initial interpretation of the author-figure offered in this chapter, then, we move to a figure that, on the contrary, is motivated and vindicated by the unanswerable and omnipotent presence of God himself. As Sarah Jones suggested, a focus on the strength of 'him who is calling you', God, will make the weak strong – or, at the very least, will produce an author-figure who can claim a power and authority unavailable by other, earthly, means.

Such an author-figure is undoubtedly confusing to a reader approaching these writings in the expectation of finding at work in the text the controlling omnipotence of the Romantic author, whose creative imagination generates and suffuses the whole text. Such expectations might indeed leave the contemporay reader disappointed by the self-denying author-figures of the sectarian women's texts. However, what I have demonstrated in this chapter is that by reading the texts through contemporary discourses of femininity (with their prescriptions for a passive, compliant and silent female subject) and of religion (which reinforce the notions of women's unequal bodies but, crucially, insist on women's equal inheritance with men of divine grace), we can demonstrate a quite different model of authorship, specific to these writers at this time. Rather than the self of the Romantic author authenticating their texts, we find instead the assertion of the absence of an authorial 'self', whose place is filled in the texts by the authorising presence and voice of God. Rather than dismissing as irrelevant any consideration of the author from these texts, then, what we need to do is take account of the specific textual construction and characterisation of the author-figure in this body of writing, and the context in which they were produced, in order to try to understand precisely how such writing found a passage into print in an unfriendly world.

5

'Look into the written word': language practice, writing and gender in the radical sects

Language has become the *sine qua non* of twentieth-century thought. Tracing the development of disciplinary and theoretical perspectives, particularly over the past twenty-five years or so, we find questions of language moving centre-stage to become the explicit and implicit focus and circumference of their concern. From being seen as the preserve of rather recherché and arcane classicists and linguists, we can discern the cumulative impact of linguistic theories both on a host of increasingly influential epistemological and ontological theorising and on previously stable disciplinary identities. Whether we look at structuralism or poststructuralism, modernism or postmodernism, literary studies, cultural studies, history or geography, we find ourselves returned again and again to the fundamental significance of language for the ways we comprehend ourselves, our world, our pasts and our futures.

In some ways structuralism can be said to have set in motion this linguistic snowball, by proposing that language was a system of signs, whose logic and meaning depended on the differentiation of one sign from another. A sign comprises two elements: the 'signifier' (a word or 'sound-image') and the 'signified' (the concept associated with that word); these two elements are inseparable – to quote a common example, it is not possible to distinguish the word 'dog' from the concept that sound-image elicits – and it therefore seems as if this composite 'sign' refers transparently and straightforwardly to its referent 'in the world': 'We feel as if *dog* is a label for something which exists unproblematically, in some ultimate and incontestable way' (Belsey 1980: 38). Saussure, however, proposed that this association of sign and referent was arbitrary: there was no reason that a 'dog' should not be called something else; nor was there any reason why language should identify a particular class of objects called 'dogs'. Saussure explained this point through examining the different conceptual division of the world in different languages: 'If words stood for pre-existing concepts, they would all have exact equivalents in meaning from one language to the next; but this is not true' (Saussure in Belsey 1980: 39). Rather than language deriving its meanings from any *necessary* or natural association between a sign and a referent, these are instead seen to derive from the differences between signs: 'concepts are purely differential, and ... are determined not by their positive content but by their relations with the other terms of the system' (Belsey 1980: 40). Thus language, in this structuralist (originally Saussurean) model, ceased to be seen as *referential* (deriving its meanings by referring to something in the world) and came to be seen as *relational* (deriving its meanings through the differential relationships between signs). From this theory developed the disciplines of semiology, the study of sign systems, including linguistic ones, and the popularisation of linguistics as a subject, focusing more specifically on the structure and meaning systems of language itself. Structuralism, then, was important for its establishment of the theory of the sign, and for its predicating of signs' meanings on difference rather than on reference.

Later, with developments in poststructuralism, which both elaborated and challenged certain of structuralism's premises, language continued to be of central concern. The poststructuralist work that most directly builds on and modifies Saussure's work on the sign is that of Jacques Derrida, which has challenged Saussure's understanding of the relationship between the signifier and signified. Saussure took the meaning of the sign – the relationship between its two component parts – to be fixed, 'the result of an already existing social contract to which individual speakers are subject' (Weedon 1987: 24). Derrida questioned this assertion of the fixity of meaning: 'For Derrida there can be no fixed signified (concepts)[;] and signifiers (sound or written images), which have identity only in their difference from one another, are subject to an endless process of deferral' (Weedon 1987: 25). Instead of the fixed Saussurean signifieds, Derrida proposes the production of meaning through *différance*: a combination of *difference* and *deferral*. It is the notion of deferral that is new here: the meaning of the signifier is not fixed to a particular signified, but shifts according to the discursive context:

> The meaning of the signifier 'woman' varies from ideal to victim to object of sexual desire, according to its context. Consequently, it is always open to challenge and redefinition with shifts in its discursive context. What it means at any particular moment depends on the discursive relations within which it is located, and it is open to constant rereading and reinterpretation. (Weedon 1987: 25)

It is because of this endless possibility of rereading and reinterpretation that meaning is said to be deferred. Moving beyond the much-critiqued dualisms of structuralisms, then, poststructuralist work on language introduces a more fluid and plural model of meaning production and interpretation.

These developments have had an impact both on studies in the textuality of culture and on analyses of the human subject. Increasingly, all kinds of cultural phenomena (films, advertisements or tourist attractions, as well as literature) have been seen by academics as texts with internal meaning systems which produce a 'language of their own'. As with structuralism, the meanings produced by these systems are not seen as referential, but relational, relying on their relationship with, and difference from, other signs within that particular symbolic system, and, again, their meanings are not seen as fixed but as open and constantly open to rereading. Foucauldian discourse theory, with its rewriting of history as the struggle of discourses over definitions of power–knowledge relations, is just one example of the 'textualisation' of culture, and, despite Foucault's refusal of such categorisations,[1] is thus usually seen as one particular development within poststructuralist theory. With his rewriting of history as a project of mapping genealogies rather than tracing past truths,[2] Foucault's work further reinforced the importance of processes of categorisation, and thus of the politics of language, to the ways in which we make sense of the world.

The other key domain in which poststructuralism has been influential has been psychoanalysis, particularly in the work of Lacan on the production of human subjectivity: 'Following Saussure, Lacan believes that without language, everything must remain not only unobservable but undifferentiated, without structure: and since (as Freud demonstrates) the unconscious is highly structured, it cannot exist before language does' (Cameron 1985: 20). Lacan thus proposes that it is only with the acquisition of language that the child becomes a full subject: 'If it is to participate in the society into which it is born, to be able to act deliberately within the social formation, the child must enter into the symbolic order, the set of signifying systems of culture of which the supreme example is language' (Belsey 1980: 60). With his now famous claim that the unconscious is structured like a language, Lacan shifted previously biological models of the development of gender and sexuality into the linguistic domain. Uniting psychoanalysis and linguistics in this way, Lacan's influential work on how the subject problematically acquires (or fails to acquire) an identity thus continues the privileging of language and its significance in contemporary culture.

Related trajectories could be traced through the theorising of modernism and postmodernism. Literary modernism, for example, was concerned to explore the formal and aesthetic character of language. This paralleled developments in structuralist linguistics from around the same time in that, exploring the implications of non-referential langue and the arbitrariness of meaning, writers experimented with the possibilities of representation in language. If words had meanings only in relation to each other, what relationship had writing with the world which it had previously been taken to represent? If literature no longer could be taken to represent an agreed and unchanging 'reality', what was its new brief to be? Whilst there was a multiplicity of formulations of these kinds of questions, and indeed of answers to them, in general it would be true to say that literary modernism's questions focused on the divergency and fluidity of systems of representation:

> This particular surge of modernism, therefore, had to recognize the impossibility of representing the world in a single language. Understanding had to be constructed through the exploration of multiple persepctives. Modernism, in short, took on multiple perspectivism and relativism as its epistemology for revealing what it still took to be the true nature of a unified, though complex, underlying reality. (Harvey 1990:30)

The shift from modernism to postmodernism so widely debated across the social sciences and the humanities during the last ten to fifteen years has been characterised as one in which language and representation have been key emblems of cultural change. For whereas previous representational practices had been thrown into question within modernist movements, the representability of 'reality' itself has been blown apart within some accounts of postmodern culture. Like the taken-for-granted divisions between 'nature' and 'culture', 'art' and 'real life', that between 'representation' and 'reality' has been seen by many to have dissolved in these postmodern times. The move that postmodernism has made in this respect has been to challenge the fixity and integrity of this 'underlying reality'. Rather than modes of representation fragmenting, better to represent the multiple perspectives on the world, postmodernism has instead extended the notion of fragmentation into 'reality' itself, rejecting the notion of a universally knowable and fixed reality. This in turn calls into question the credibility of the claims of 'grand narratives' (such as history, science, medicine and art) to make sense of the world.[3] The demise of modernism's grand narratives is met with the acceptance of 'the fragmentation, the pluralism, and the authenticity of other voices and other worlds' (Harvey 1990: 49), where no one voice or world holds ultimate authority over any other. With the collapse of a stable and knowable world comes the end of the possibility of representation itself; words are taken to refer only to each other, texts to other texts, signifiers to other signifiers rather than to signifieds. Insted of the world being the original which art or literature then seeks to represent, the notion of originality itself dissolves, and everything, in this great play of intertextuality, becomes a copy or simulacrum of another text. Language itself, by this account, becomes a game of self-referentiality, of mimicry and of surface play.

Postmodernism's impact has been widespread, having been taken up and explored in relation to a range of different fields and disciplines:

> It has been defined as a new aesthetic characterised by pastiche, self-referentiality, fragmentation, hybridization of styles, linguistic multiplicity, and as a movement in Philosophy registering a crisis in the legitimation of Western knowledge through a breakdown of meta-narratives ... Similarly, 'postmodernity' has been variously defined as the Age of the Hyperreal, where all distinctions between truth and appearance, depth and surface, latent and manifest have broken down as representation gives way to simulacrum; ... as a new political age of 'difference' where notions of democracy and consensus have failed under pressure from the emerging voices of those 'others' whose exclusion has facilitated the establishment of the dominants as part of an ostensible regime of truth. (Patricia Waugh, in Wright 1992: 341-2)

More specifically in relations to question of language, if postmodernism posits an age in which the original itself is already a copy, then the issue of how language can best represent the world becomes a redundant question.

In all these diverse theoretical developments, which have made a profound impact on late twentieth-century thinking, therefore, language – as a system, a metaphor, a determining process, a cultural touchstone or a parodic play – has been at the centre of our understandings and conceptualisations of culture. This has been true not only in the most obvious disciplines such as literary studies or linguistics, where one might expect to find a preoccupation with language at the heart of disciplinary debates, or in subjects such as philosophy or film studies where representation and reality have always been key conceptual concerns, but also right across subjects such as anthropology, geography, sociology and history, where the redesignation of theories of language as integral to many broader disciplinary debates might seem rather unexpected or surprising. Furthermore, one might argue that the way in which such theories cross-cut and call into question disciplinary self-definitions and boundaries has contributed in large measure to the growing interdisciplinarity of academic work. If, for example, poststructuralist theories of the subject fundamentally inform the work of psychologists, literary theorists and sociologists, and if postmodernism's theories of fragmentation are significant within work in economics, political theory and film studies, then on what grounds do we maintain disciplinary boundaries, and in what ways might we reconfigure such divisions in order to draw on the strengths of such interdisciplinary theories? It is undoubtedly concerns such as these which have both driven the establishment of interdisciplinary 'centres' within academic institutions and fundamentally reshaped much disciplinary work itself over the past decade.

Feminists working in all these fields have engaged with these heated debates about the meaning of language and its role in relation to social, political and cultural inequality and change. Starting from a common desire to address the gendered and patriarchal character of language, there has been an array of analyses and responses, ranging from the practical reform of sexist terminology to the celebration of the female body and its insciption in a feminine language.

One early response to the 'problem' of a patriarchal language was Casey Miller and Kate Swift's *Words and Women* (1976). Whilst they castigate the misrepresentations and derogation perpetrated by a language biased in favour of men, they none the less see the specifically sexist aspects of language as open to reform, and indeed their book offers a range of non-sexist alternatives to the offending lexical and grammatical forms. 'Purged of its prejudices, our language can indeed in the mouth of a "conscientious" user disseminate "accurate" information' (Cameron 1985: 75). Whilst reformist proposals such as these have had a discernible impact on language-use in the media and academia, and indeed in more general usage, they have been criticised for assuming that sexism in language is limited to certain identifiable aspects of its grammar and terminology: the generic use of 'he', for example, or the habit of calling women 'girls'. Instead, it is argued, sexism is 'silently' manifested in who gets spoken or written about and how they are represented, not just in the labels attached to them. In addition, such reformism is often criticised for its liberal and over-optimistic view of people's goodwill towards feminist change: 'sexist language is an outdated excrescence which everyone but a few reactionaries would dearly love to be rid of; mere force of habit is the only thing that props it up' (Cameron 1985: 74).

More radical analyses of patriarchal language have been made in the work of Dale Spender and Mary Daly. Dale Spender's *Man-Made Language* (1980) has been highly influential, both for the insights it offered and for the debates it sparked off. Spender argues that patriarchal language excludes, denigrates and controls women by virtue of the fact that it is literally 'man-made': formed by men in their own interests, and therefore defining and limiting the meanings available within a given culture at a given time:

it is through their control over meaning that men are able to impose on everyone their own view of the world; women, without the ability to symbolise their exerience in the male language, either internalise male reality (alienation) or find themseles unable to speak at all (silence). (Cameron 1985: 108)

Spender's work was widely taken up by feminists for the analysis it offered of the inherent structural and historical sexism of language. It highlighted the politics of 'naming', in terms both of patriarchal inequalities being inscribed in language and of the importance of inventing new forms of expression to represent women's experiences which had hitherto been excluded from language. Above all, perhaps, it succeeded in moving language centre-stage within feminism, by politicising it, and providing a means to draw attention to the way language constituted and perpetuated inequalities in a wide range of different contexts. Subsequently, however, Spender's work has been critiqued by other feminists. By some, it has been criticised for oversimplifying the relationship between language and meaning, for suggesting that language 'encodes' (or fails to encode) a series of understandings or meanings that originate in experience. Maria Black and Rosalind Coward argue that 'experience and identity cannot be seen as the origin of meaning, but as its outcome' (quoted in Cameron 1985: 117). For them, then, experience and identity are the *product* of language, since language determines the parameters and structures of thought and therefore subjectivity itself. Other critics, however, criticise Spender precisely for being over-deterministic in her view of language. Deborah Cameron, for example, points to a contradiction in Spender's work: on the one hand, she embraces the view that 'a patriarchal reality is constructed primarily through a patriarchal language' (Cameron 1985: 112), in which case language *constitutes* the reality which consequently restricts and distorts women's lives; on the other hand, she argues that women need to encode their own meanings in language in order to dismantle this patriarchal order. How, Cameron asks, can women both be constituted by language and themselves reconstitute language?

> In Spender's work it is always rather unclear whether women are without linguistic resources because they are without power (in which case they cannot change language without changing their status first) or whether they need linguistic resources before they can increase their power. (Cameron 1985: 112)

It is, Cameron concludes, Spender's determinism that causes the problem, for this, she argues, 'confuses[s] the power with the myth that justifies it' (Cameron 1985: 113)

A quite different feminist response to the notion of a fundamentally inegalitarian language came from Mary Daly in *Gyn/Ecology: The Metaethics of Radical Feminism* (1978). Like Spender, she argues that the language we have inherited is deeply implicated in the structures of patriarchy:

> The fact is that the female saying 'I' is alien at every moment to her own speaking and writing. She is broken by the fact that she must enter this language in order to speak or to write. As the 'I' is broken, so also is the Inner Eye, the capacity for integrity of

knowing/sensing. In this way the Inner Voice of the Self's integrity is silenced: the external voice babbles in alien and alienating tongues. (Daly, quoted in Cameron 1985: 92)

Daly's strategy in the face of this is to draw attention to, and to exploit, the lost meanings embedded in language, either through breaking them down into their constituent syllables (re-member, hag-iography, the-rapist), or by reclaiming words' obsolete (and women-friendly) meanings (spinster, crone, hag). Such a radical re-vision of language was welcomed for its nerve and verve, and for the way it conceptually and syllabically took revenge on a violent system of representation, offering ironic and defiant responses to patriarchy's definitions of womanhood. However, its polemical and political impact might be measured more in terms of its imaginative journeyings and its celebration of separatist utopias than in terms of any practical usage in feminist linguistic politics. As Deborah Cameron pragmatically points out, 'Mary Daly's constant parenthetical interrogation of etymology and structure in the words she uses ... would be either tedious or just impossible in talk' (Cameron 1985: 166).

Spender and Daly, then, share a view of language as originating in men's experiences and perpetuating their interests, so that women are excluded from 'meaning', and thus also from power, both in, and by means of, language. Their work might be summed up as arguing that women

> live and speak within the confines of a man-made symbolic universe. They must cope with the disjunction between the linguistically-validated male world view and their own experience, which cannot be expressed in male language. Indeed, since language determines reality, women may be alienated not only from language but also from the female experience it fails to encode. (Cameron 1985: 93)

A similar challenge to the patriarchal character of language, but precipitative of very different strategies and alternatives, can be found in a second body of feminist work on language: namely, that emanating from so-called 'French feminisms', which are in large part in critical dialogue with Lacanian psychoanalysis and poststructuralism. Whilst representative of a number of diverse theories and positions, 'French feminisms' have nevertheless been united (some would argue misleadingly)[4] under this national appellation precisely through their common concern with theorising 'the feminine', which has taken debates about language and subjectivity in a new and radical philosophical direction.[5]

As we have already seen, Lacan proposed that a child only accedes fully to the symbolic order with the acquisition of language; additionally, however, he argued that male and female children are differently inscribed in this process because of their respective relationships to the meanings of sexual difference. The much-debated 'phallus' is used by Lacanians as a trope signifying the sexual character of power relations between the sexes and the key signifier in this symbolic order: 'For both sexes, the crucial fact of which they must become aware in order to perceive and understand sex differentiation is whether they – and their parents – have the phallus or not' (Cameron 1985: 120). Whilst for some the symbolic phallus is preferable to the more biological Freudian model of sexual difference, for many feminists even Lacan's linguistic alternative leads to a kind of implicit determinism:

> the important concept in Lacanian accounts of language acquisition is the idea of *inserting oneself in a pre-existing order*: and it is difficult to see how anyone could do this unless the order, and the meanings it made available, were fixed and stable, produced outside the individual and enjoined on her as the price of entry into human society. (Cameron 1985: 124)

One such theorist whose work has been included within the loose umbrella-term 'French feminism' is Julia Kristeva. A literary and cultural theorist as well as a psychoanalyst, her work modifies Lacan's schema by elaborating the concept of 'the semiotic':

> The semiotic is a set of pre-signifying impulses and drives that chaotically circulate in and through the infant's body; ... The symbolic is the domain of propositions and positions, the site for the creation of unified texts, cultural representations and knowledges; the semiotic is the undirected and uncontrolled input of the repressed impulses, energies and spasms of the infant in the first case, and later, of the subject in moments of crisis and psychic upheaval ... In the broadest terms, the semiotic is the input of the undirected body, while the symbolic is the regulated use and organized operations of that body in social production. It is only through the Symbolic that we can have access to the semiotic; the former provides the latter with a voice and mode of representation. (Grosz, in Wright 1992: 195)

This 'mode of representation' can be discerned in language in 'rhythm, intonation, gaps, meaninglessness and general textual disruption' (Cameron 1985: 125-6). The semiotic is most strongly linked with those who take up a 'feminine subject position', marginal to the symbolic order (the masculine subject position, in contrast, being fully integrated into the symbolic order); this position is not defined by biology, however, but is open to both men and women. 'Anyone taking up a feminine subject position retains strong links with the pre-Oedipal mother figure, and their language shows the influence of the chora [the semiotic] to a marked degree' (Cameron 1985: 126). Kristeva cites French modernist poetry, with its lack of logical construction, as as example of the irruption of the semiotic into the symbolic. Kristeva, then, rejects what she sees as Lacan's deterministic model of identity-formation in relation to language, and indeed challenges the binarism of male vs. female, shifting instead the emphasis on to non-biological and more fluid notions of masculine and feminine.

The work of philosopher and psychoanalyst Luce Irigaray has also contributed enormously to feminist debates about language, subjectivity and representation. Irigaray critiques Freud for his phallocentrism (in which he takes an account of masculine development as the norm against which to measure that of the feminine), and Lacan for his privileging of the phallus and construction of the female body as lacking. Irigaray's work (most importantly *Speculum of the Other Woman* (1985a) and *This Sex Which Is Not One* (1985b)) sets up instead a playful and provocative model of the feminine based on the specificities of the female body not as defective or castrated man, but in relation to itself. Insisting on the importance of challenging patriarchal definitions of the category 'woman', she argues for

> an integral relationship between sexuality and language. In her view, female sexual pleasure is fundamentally autoerotic and plural. While male sexuality is concentrated on the penis, women have a multiplicity of sexual organs ... When freed from their patriarchal definition and the repression of their sexuality, women are assumed to be fundamentally different from men and their use of language is other than the logical language of the symbolic order. (Weedon 1987: 63, 65)

For Irigaray, the inscription of masculine desire in the symbolic systems of language leads her to critique the fundamental categories and epistemologies of Western thought as hopelessly patriarchal. The important task for feminism thus remains to develop new forms of meaning, reciprocity and mutuality, based on the specificity of female sexuality and the metaphors of the female body.

A third and final feminist whose work on language has radically challenged its 'phallogocentrism' is Hélène Cixous. Drawing on Derrida's deconstructionism, she critiques the inscription of binary oppositions (including those of gender and sexuality – male/female, penis/lack) whose 'hierarchization of meaning serves to subordinate the feminine to the masculine order (Weedon 1987: 66). According to Cixous, feminine writing (which is the more likely, though not the exclusive, prerogative of biological women) can undermine the repressive structures of patriarchal language. Drawing on the energies of the feminine libido, the resources of the unconscious and the imperatives of the body, Cixous issues a rallying call to women to bring together representation, subjectivity and sexuality by reinscribing their bodies in their own language.

This brief summary of critical debates about patriarchal language exemplifies the ways in which feminist work has both extended the theoretical frameworks through which language moved centre-stage during the 1970s and 1980s, and yet has also challenged many of their basic conceptualisations and assumptions. In particular, the dualisms of the structuralist heritage and the determinisms of its schema have been seen to have further reinscribed the position of women as 'other' within the patriarchal symbolic order. The extension of such structuralist mappings to the realm of the unconscious has also been thoroughly problematised by those wishing to imagine a space beyond such an order.

Three overarching and interrelated questions central to this chapter can be seen to inform the debates outlined above. First, what is the relationship between representation and reality, culture and nature, language and experience? Does the first term in each pairing describe or represent the second, or in some ways construct it? Are the two terms polar opposites, or does this misrepresent the continuities between the two? This question can be seen to have informed the challenge posed by structuralism to exisiting theories of language; modernism, with its concern better to represent our fractured and contradictory experience of being alive; and much feminist work, with its aim of exposing the extent to which language reflects, perpetuates or constructs patriarchy. A second question might be: what are the internal

116

dynamics, functions and politics of different kinds of language? How do we make sense of language and derive meaning from it? This became a key question for structuralist work, with its positing of meaning as relational, and has since been developed in poststructuralist questioning of structuralism's fixing of the signifer to the signifed. A third and final question might be: is 'life' representable? In other words, is there something in excess of language to be 'captured' by it, or does language fully determine and circumscribe all aspects of what we think of as 'life' or 'experience'? This concern can be found in modernism's experimentation with forms of representation, poststructuralist formulations of the constitution of the human subject in language and the linguistic character of the symbolic order, in post-modernism's emphasis on the signifier over the signified, and in some French feminism's call to inscribe female experience through the female body.

In these poststructuralist and postmodernist times, then, statements such as 'we do not speak language, but language speaks us', 'subjectivity is constituted by language', 'nature itself is a cultural construction' have become commonplace, as there has been a loss of belief in the authenticity of experience and the dismantling of a unified and rational individual to experience it. This shift from a view of language as a tool through which man can describe his world to a view in which language is seen as a symbolic order beyond the grasp of the human subject, indeed which determines his or her very sense of self, is generally seen as a recent and radical development. Indeed, many of these debates assume that this foregrounding of and preoccupation with language is a characteristically twentieth-century phenomenon, figuring our modern and postmodern loss of confidence and certainty about our identities and our world, whilst preceding centuries' ideas about language are implicitly taken to have been stable and static. However, if we turn to the seventeenth century, we find a parallel concern with issues of language, meaning and representation: a preoccupation with a perceived 'crisis' in language, a concern for the ways in which meanings derive from language, shifts in theories of signification, and debates about the politics of language and its reformability. Whether we look at the writings of Anglicans, Puritans or radical sectarians, writers from a scholarly or a less educated background, we find explorations of the signifying capacity and the boundaries of language. Indeed, the seventeenth century rivals the twentieth for its somewhat tortured consciousness of the power and problematics of language. Whether this earlier manifestation of the preoccupation with language was structured around a similar set of questions and answers to the later one, and, much more specifically, how the writings of sectarian women manifested and worked through these preoccupations, are the issues with which the rest of this chapter will be concerned.

In the previous chapter on questions of authorship, it was already apparent that the justifications for writing offered by women writers from the sects had a number of implications for understandings of the character and function of language. The relocation of the responsibility for writing with God, and the consequent denial of any involvement of their worldly and hence immodest 'selves' in the process, resulted in a contradictory manifestation of the author-figure in her texts: whilst asserting her lack of agency in relation to her writing, the author-figure none the less accretes power through her identification with the will and word of God. This clearly has implications for the language of the texts themselves: for if the writer is both absent and present, passive and active, visible and invisible in relation to her own writings, then is the language in which she communicates God's message represented as straightforwardly divine, and therefore inherently truthful and beyond interpretation and questioning; or is it seen as a human and therefore fallible and potentially misleading means of communication, as open to corruption as is humanity itself? The attempted erasure of the author-figure, then, raised a number of questions in relation to the use and perception of language itself, and therefore also to the status and texture of the texts. For if language is seen as complex, corruptible and open to question, then on what authority are readers to take these texts as reliably communicating God's truth? And if it is seen as the revealed word of God, then on what grounds do we accept that God is indeed speaking through these sectarian writers? Already, then, it is apparent that the questions about language preoccupying seventeenth-century writers hinged on concerns alien to those twentieth-century theorists outlined above: for once the notion of a divine language is included in the equation, then quite different conceptions of signification, authenticity and representation are bound to follow. Before attempting to answer these questions through a reading of texts from the sects, however, I want first to explore how the possibility of this contradictory reading of language is rooted not only in the jointly present and absent author-figure, but also in ideas about seventeenth-century language use itself, and in particular the changing conceptualisations of the relationship between language, the truth and the self.

The world, the text and the self: theories of language change in the seventeenth century

Twentieth-century theorists of seventeenth-century language have found that, despite the inclusion of notions of the divine in debates about language, nevertheless a concern with the origin of meaning, the referentiality of language, and the relationship between the individual or subject and the language s/he speaks are all paramount. Through research from diverse disciplines and theoretical positions, from poststructuralists to more traditional historians and literary critics, we can trace a multitude of different manifestations of these issues. Some write specifically of changes in the conceptualisations of language itself, whilst others investigate the construction of the self of the author in language; together, despite their disparate starting-points and conclusions, they demonstrate that concerns about language are at the heart of the seventeenth-century preoccupation with the origin and reliability of linguistic and textual authority, meaning and truth.

One key argument about changing perceptions of language in the seventeenth century was put forward by Michel Foucault in *The Order of Things* (1970). Here, he suggests that there was a major shift in the way the relationship between words and the things or notions that they represented was perceived in the seventeenth century. He argues that, throughout the Renaissance and the sixteenth century, language was seen as something infinitely complex, 'present' in the world in that it communicated *of* itself and not only *by means of* itself. It was not a 'mirror, to reflect things' particular truths' (Foucault, 1970: 34-5), but opaque and mysterious, interwoven with all the other elements of the created world. Every element of the world was a 'mark' or 'sign', that corresponded, through a system of different, though interlocking, forms of similitude,[6] with other elements: the microcosm figured the macrocosm and vice versa, each drawing on, illuminating and helping to untangle and map out the meaning of the other. The whole world formed one great text, composed of inherently, divinely, meaningful signs waiting to be interpreted. Thus events and experiences were painstakingly analysed in order to discern the meanings latent within them: Patricia Crawford notes, for example that 'People examined events as testimonies of the Lord's purposes, and they thought that a civil war was so serious a national calamity that it must be divine retribution for national sins' (Crawford 1977: 44). Crawford goes on to examine in details the 'readings' of the execution of Charles I, and the disparate meanings that were drawn from this event.

Similarly, language itself was seen as a thing of nature, and therefore of God, as much as were the 'signs' of rocks, trees, the stars, political events, or humanity itself, placed by God as part of the fabric of his creation, and therefore inherently of significance and able to communicate its significance or have its meaning drawn from it. Not only did individual words have this material reality in the world, which made them subject to interpretation as much as any other sign; so too did each individual letter:

> As letters acquired the status of things in the Renaissance, they also took on a property commonly attributed to natural objects: they were understood to possess symbolic significance ... For instance, Renaissance Neoplatonists saw ideal mathematical propostions in the physical configurations of letters, and believed these proportions to have symbolic, almost Pythagorean meaning. (Elsky 1983: 248)

This, suggests Elsky, informs the meanings available in readings of George Herbert's hieroglyphic poems (such as 'The Sonne', 'Love-joy', 'Easter Wings' and 'The Altar'), with 'their use of words as physical things, as plastic forms to be shaped through rhyme, line length, and the symbolic, hieroglyphic significance of letters themselves' (Elsky 1983: 252). These, he argues, 'illustrate the way Herbert sees meaning as divinely ordained in the sensible elements of language. ... its physical properties – visiblity and audibility – are tied to the spiritual significance of its referents' (Elsky 1983: 252, 258). At stake here, then, was the relationship between the 'signifier' (the word or sound-image, but also the letters making up the word) and the signified (the concept indicated by the word); the signifier was not fixed to a signified, but slipped, through these relationships of emulation, analogy and so on, between signifieds. Moreover, within this Renaissance framework there was no distinction between the 'sign' and the 'referent'; 'things in the world' were signs too, signifying through the same system that words did. The world was united as a seamless system of signification, then, through the existence of one overriding element: God himself. All signs referred, in infinitely complex ways, to him.

The change that Foucault argues took place in the seventeenth century was the separation of *words* from *things*. No longer of the same order, words came to be seen as having a task, to translate and represent the 'truth' of nature, but no presence or significance of their own; words ceased to be things, and instead came to *refer* to things, to be signs of things. 'Language has withdrawn from the midst of beings themselves and has entered a period of transparency and neutrality' (Foucault, 1970: 56). Whereas previously, when the word was seen as an opaque and ever-shifting sign, its form, composition and characteristics held meaning, now meaning was relocated wholly with the referent, the thing or notion represented by the sign: 'the signifying element has no content, no function, and no determination other than what it represents' (Foucault, 1970: 64). Language was no longer problematic in terms of its layers of meaning or its richness or complexity of suggestion, but only in terms of how accurate a representation of the 'truth' of the referent it was. And this was open to reorganisation and improvement: 'For everyone concerned with language in the middle of the seventeenth century, it seemed possible to organize, recover, or invent a language that represented the order of things in the world' (Cohen 1977: xxiii). Language, then, had ceased to be conceived as a complex, allusive and symbolic set of 'marks', an element in the world, and had instead come to be seen as a way to transcribe, reflect or represent the world.

Joan Webber's work offers a perspective on the manifestations and implications of such concerns and debates by contrasting the Anglican and Puritan styles of self-characterisation in certain seventeenth-century autobiographies. Like Foucault, she suggests that there was a crucial shift in the course of the seventeenth century, though she focuses more narrowly on the linguistic representation of the self rather than on language itself. She suggests that this shift comprised a move from the self being constructed as a complex and interpretable textual – and linguistic – emblem, to the self as transparent, uncomplicated and fixed in its meaning. The former she characterises as the 'Anglican I', the latter as the 'Puritan I'. The conservative Anglican use of the first person singular 'I', she suggests, is meditative, anti-historical, ambiguous, symbolic: John Donne, for example, uses himself as a timeless and generalised symbol, a microcosm of cosmic and divine workings. Everything is artificial, in the sense that it is God's art, and therefore inherently meaningful and open to interpretation. The Puritan 'I', on the other hand, is active, time-bound, and as simple and visible as possible. His (*sic*) life illustrates God's merciful nature, but illustrates it through example rather than through symbolism. He sees himself as a historical character, fixed in time and space (Webber, 1968: chapters 1 and 2).

Although this analysis is indeed descriptive of the stylistic differences between such writers as Donne and Bunyan, it also links with Foucault's theory, for these two writers are divided not only by the forms of their religious beliefs, but also by time, for half a century lies between them, and, in Foucault's terms, a very significant half-century. Just as Foucault charts a change from a perception of language as visible, allusive and interpretable to a view of it as transparent, referential and insignificant, so Webber charts a parallel change in linguistic constructions of the self, from a self that is interpretable, symbolic, a sign to be read to a self that is fixed in meaning, and which signifies only by reference or example, not through allusion or interpretation.

Each, then, posits a shift from the symbolic to the referential, from the opaque to the transparent.

These generalised theories of changes in the conceptualisation of language and the self remain, in these critics' hands, discussed in relation only to canonical seventeenth-century writers and philosophers. Foucault ranges from Descartes, Bacon and Cervantes to Hume, Berkeley and Condillac. Webber focuses her discussion on those seventeenth-century English divines who best illustrate her theory of this change in the textual construction of the self: Donne, Bunyan, Baxter and Traherne. Neither she nor Foucault touch on those writing from outside the mainstream of the intellectual or religious establishments. How, then, do these arguments relate to those outside these categories, to women writers from the sects who, whilst spiritually closer to the Puritans, stylistically are often much closer to the Anglican allusiveness and circularity of argument? Do they construct a first-person textual persona closer to the Anglican, symbolic, allusive one or to the Puritan, timebound, exemplary one, and do they articulate an understanding of language closer to the visible, signifying one of the Renaissance, or the transparent, referential one of the later seventeenth century?

In the textual constructions of the self examined in the previous chapter, there is little sense in which the authorial persona in the radical texts I have been investigating could be called 'time-bound' or 'historical'. As I have argued, the self of the author in these texts is, in general, unstable and shifting, unanchored in the time and space of seventeenth-century England. Thus, many texts mark the dissolution of the corrupt and feeble gendered and material body of the author, in order to open the soul to God:

> Quakers and others recorded their attempts to apply the acid of self-criticism, fasting and incessant prayer to their own bodies and personalities; to dissolve the habits, passions, gestures, and little secret sins that made them who they were; to expose themselves as creatures without status, without intelligence, without gender; to become blank. 'I am as a white paper without any line or sentence,' wrote one Friend. (Mack 1992: 7)

Other texts invest the material body of the author-figure with a very *un*material significance, reading it and its apparently feminine failings (weakness, illness, weeping, fasting and so on) as 'signs' of God's intervention in and appropriation of herself, her life and her significance (Purkiss 1992a). As Hannah Allen put it: 'The soul of man hath a singular affection for its own body, rejoicing in its prosperity, and sympathizing with it in all its maladies, miseries, and necessities. Hence if the body be out of frame and tune, the soul cannot be well at ease' (Allen 1683: sig.D1ʳ). In each case, it is the interrelationship between author-figure and God which problematises the conception and representation of the body and the self, and this relationship is worked through in terms of the language of the text itself:

> God is the transcendental significant and the guarantor of meaning and authority which, in these texts, reside inseparably in the Word with all its many meanings. The word of God ... is an intervention at a super-linguistic level in the symbolic order. To

represent oneself as speaking God's word is theoretically to dissolve the unified subject-position of the speaker – for when is the speaker an 'I' and when God's agent? (Wiseman 1992a: 189)

In order to trace more fully the basis in ideas about language of the ascription of truth, significance and the authority of the authorial self, I shall turn to the writings of Anna Trapnel, of all the women writers in the sects the one who most explicitly anatomises her understandings of the workings and meanings of language. I shall then situate these understandings in relation to the specifically seventeenth-century debates about language, before returning to questions of language and truth in seventeenth-century writings.

Language and truth in the writings of Anna Trapnel

The legitimacy and authority of the texts written by women in the radical sects depend, I have argued, on the texts being accepted as God's words rather than the author's. This did not, however, preclude an interest, even an anxiety, concerning the language in which God transmitted his message through the medium of the author. How would people know that these were indeed God's words, and recognise them as the truth? How reliable was language as a vehicle for God's truth, when it was obviously corrupted and contorted by those not following his path?

Such questions found different expression and different answers in the different sects. For some sects, such as the Baptists, as well as for the more orthodox Puritans, the Bible remained the ultimate, indeed only, manifestation of God's word. For them, the problem of language was primarily one of scriptural interpretation: what was the meaning of a particular text, for example, or did a given sectarian utterance accord with the agreed meaning of such a text? For other sects, however, such as the Fifth Monarchists or the Quakers, the problem was more acute, for whilst the authority of the Scriptures as the authentic word of God was not questioned, they were not the *only* source of the divine word, for these sectaries 'were more prone to accept the transmission of the Word through dreams and visions as an equal or superior authority to the Bible' (Smith 1989: 269). Thus, whilst the Bible remained one touchstone for the authentication of prophetic utterances, it was not the only one, and this created an additional level to the problem of the authentication of language. One dimension of the problem was to identify the spiritual status of an utterance; this involved not only looking for scriptural parallels, but other processes of authentication too. The physical body of the prophet was read as a sign, for example: was a prophet weakened by her fasting, for example (in which case it may not be spiritually induced), or did she, like Trapnel, remain strong and healthy (in which case it was a mark of divine sanction) (Smith 1989: 48-50; Purkiss 1992a: 143-51)? Attention was also paid to the physical character of the written prophecy as well as its overt meaning: 'words, letters and even sentences became for the sectarians hieroglyphs or speaking pictures, where the material, visual and graphic qualities of words signify as much, or in place of, their linguistic sense' (Smith 1989: 284).

Another imperative was to work through the issue of the possible contamination of a genuinely divine utterance by its vehicle, human language:

> The search for divine speech left the radicals in a dilemma. All speech seemed to leave traces of carnality, however reformed or pure. Reason's capacity as a guide for at least some comprehension of divine purpose was not trusted ... Yet no area was more vulnerable to the paradox than the actual organization of spoken and written discourse, which, of course, had to have a 'form', however offensive this was to the radicals. In this respect radical religious language attempted to modify the established forms of [orthodox] Puritan discourse, ultimately to let the spirit speak in full freedom and power, so the radicals maintained. (Smith 1989: 308)

It has been suggested that such concerns with the origin and character of the signifying power of language were at the root of some of the most well-known controversies marking the clash between orthodox Puritanism and sectarian interpretations. Patricia Caldwell, for example, has suggested that the trial and expulsion of Anne Hutchinson from her congregation in New England in 1637 was symptomatic of 'a monumental crisis of language' (Caldwell 1976: 346), where the orthodox Puritan accusers subscribed to a view of language as reliably communicative, something upon which one could absolutely confer and agree a meaning, whilst Hutchinson herself found such agreement impossible, judging words to be ultimately indeterminate in their meanings and hence always secondary to an inner (and inexpressible) spiritual state.[8] Similarly, as I shall detail later in this chapter, the particular language practice of the different sects was often singled out by critics as essential and definitive manifestations of the errors of their beliefs: thus, as Richard Bauman notes, Quakers were criticised both for their 'plain style' (such as their insistence on the use of 'thee' and 'thou' for the second person singular), and for the particularities of their discourse (their incantatory style, their distinctive phraseology used to characterise the individual's apprehension of God). Moreover, the Quakers themselves focused specifically on the language of those to whom they were opposed: their strongest attacks on 'false ministers' were framed in terms of the legitimate and illegitimate uses of speech: 'What is the nature of God's Word in the practice of religion? How does one become a legitimate speaker of God's Word? These were the questions that lay at the heart of the conflict' (Bauman 1983: 35).

In the writings of the Fifth Monarchist prophet Anna Trapnel such questions and concerns generated a quite explicit investigation of the shifting relationship between language, writing and the communication of God's truth. In one of her more straightforward statements on the subject of language, Trapnel describes 'the written word', the Scriptures, as a 'record' of the truth as declared by Christ, and also as a resource through which access to Christ could be gained:

> For it is true says Jesus Christ,
> Look into my record,
> And see whether I have not declared
> What you are unto me; ...

> O look into the written word
> And there drink you of me,
> For I am flagons of wine and
> You shall partake of me. (Trapnel 1654a:34)

The word of God is signalled here as a 'record', implying a simple transcription of God's message, important for *what* it signifies but not for *how* it signifies. It is, however, more than just a transparent medium, for it is also seen to render Christ concrete to the reader ('I am flagons of wine'), representing him as material rather than spiritual, and hence able to be internalised and consumed by the reader ('You shall partake of me'). Experiencing the truth through the written word means ingesting that truth, incorporating it into the bodily self. As Nigel Smith said, 'The radical Puritans ... present themselves as mechanisms which can be affected by the Scriptures, for which they become a repository' (Smith 1989: 33). This helps explicate the emphasis of the body as a sign: for the ingestion of Christ through the written word of God will be transformative of the consuming body, and will mark it a sacred rather than profane:

> The life of the body becomes in effect the allegory (the theatre) of spiritual life ... A
> language written in terms of sicknesses, levitations, visions, odors, etc., in other words
> in corporal terms, replaces the 'spiritual' vocabulary forged by the medieval tradition.
> (de Certeau 1988: 145 n.34)

Trapnel's body, then, is not of a different order from the language she speaks, but part of the same signifying system; together they are communicative or representative of truth or of deception, of God or Satan. Just as problematic as the body, with its carnal and therefore corrupt materiality, however, is language itself, for it too is (since the fall of Babel) fully human, carnal and corrupt, until appropriated by God for his own ends. The communicative powers of language, then, are not transparent, but disturbingly complicated. Whilst language must gain its meaning and its authority from God alone, revealing truth in and of itself, not only by means of itself, it is none the less necessary to demonstrate that a particular linguistic utterance (verbal or textual) is indeed invested with this divine authority: 'let them [her enemies] know that is so too, by the language of it, by the rule through which it comes: how is the written word carried forth in it? Thy spirit takes the scripture all along, and sets the soul a swimming therein' (Trapnel 1654a: 68). The 'written word' is the physical manifestation of God's word: his spirit inhabits and transforms written language to create the Scriptures. It is this combination, God and language, which 'sets the soul a swimming therein'. Whether 'the soul' is the reader who is immersed in the text, or whether it is the 'soul' of the text that brings it to life as a manifestation of God's truth that is set moving in the language, is ambiguous. What is clear, however, is that language functions with God to create an authoritative meaning for the reader. 'The written word', however, is not the same as written language:[9] language is the means, the substance, the 'rule' or structure, the set of marks, whilst 'the written word' is this infused with God. An absence of God would not mean an empty set of marks, communicating in an earthly rather than a spiritual sense, but would create a vacuum that would necessarily be filled by the antithesis of God, Satan. Thus constant vigilance is necessary to distinguish the true works of God from those masquerading as such but in fact emanating from the devil.

Trapnel's concern is thus with language as an authoritative manifestation of divine truth, and with the way the relationship between the two is articulated in the structures of language itself. Writing of Cromwell, for example, she says:

> How can he do any living things among dead men, dead things? Does he not confound himself in his own language? Do not his actions fly in his face? Does not his conscience say, 'Thou tongue, thou sayest not right?' ... I tell you the Lord God will eclipse your glory, he will put a stammering speech into you, you shall not suck from God's wine-cellars. (Trapnel 1654a: 70)

Trapnel is exploring here the contradictions present in one man, contradictions which defy the heavenly order ordained by God. She counterposes 'living things' and 'dead things', which she says cannot coexist within this order, and she uses Cromwell's speech as an illustration of the impossibility of the harmonious existence of such contradictions, for this is the meeting-point of language with truth or deception. The source of the imagery here is biblical, stemming from the account in Genesis of the building of the tower of Babel. Until this moment, 'the earth was of one language and one speech' (Genesis 11:1), but as a punishment for the building of the tower, God decided to 'confound their language, that they may not understand one another's speech' (Genesis 11:17). Cromwell confounds himself, for his actions belie his words; his conscience and his tongue are at odds. God, it is implied, will not permit such a disparity to continue: a departure from the truth will necessarily result in a stammering speech.[10] Language, actions and truth are all interrelated and, ideally, in alignment.[11] If any one element is out of true, then this will ultimately be revealed in the other elements, for truth and God cannot be undermined by having lies appear in a coherent and convincing way: the necessary correspondence between things demands that bad conscience be reflected in a 'stammering speech'.

This perspective on the necessary harmony between language and truth is reiterated in many places in Trapnel's text. She writes that 'many are infected, their language is infected, it was sweet before, but now it is confused, it had an harmony, but now it hath no relish' (Trapnel 1654a: 31), language here reflecting the confusion and disharmony of her opponents' views and actions as they betray Fifth Monarchist hopes for power. Likewise, 'they have cried down the king, the court, and such things, and how are your tongues now tipped with their language, if your hearts had not now turned you aside?' (Trapnel 1654a: 55), where once again the materiality of language for Trapnel is apparent: tongues can be 'tipped' with corrupt language, almost as arrows can be tipped with poison. Again, too, the necessary harmony between language and truth is asserted.

This picture becomes complicated, however, by another passage which apparently identifies 'stammering speech' with the saints, or Trapnel's fellow-sectaries:

Oh this is a time not for a man to reign, but for the Lord Jesus, and this voice sounds out here and there by a son or a daughter; oh but when shall all the sons and all the children cry for King Jesus? The reason is because of the infirmities of the flesh, and because thine are of a stammering speech, and of stuttering tongue, but thou hast promised that the time shall come that there not be a people of a deeper speech than thy people, and they shall not be of a stammering tongue. Come oh all you disputants, monarchs, scribes and rabbis of the world ... oh, you shall be the men that shall be of a stammering lip, and of a stuttering tongue. (Trapnel 1654a: 31)

This seems to contradict directly the previous passage, where disharmony of speech was indicative of carnality and corruption. In the context of the rest of this passage, however, it appears that the 'stammering speech', together with the 'infirmities of the flesh', is symptomatic of the disjointed and disordered state of things, where lies can masquerade as truth, where the strong are still powerless, and where the truth sounds likes falsehood. With the coming of King Jesus, all this will change: the world will be turned upside down – and thereby set the right way up – and God will no longer tolerate a misalignment of truth and language. Lies will sound like lies, confusion will be uttered in a stammering tongue, whilst God's people will be of a 'deep speech'.

Thus far, the references to language have been to spoken language, 'speech'; Trapnel does, however, also explore the relationship that this has with written language. This too is seen as having a direct connection with God, indeed, at times, an independent physical existence that comes to inhabit the body of the reader just as Christ himself does when he is consumed by believers as if he were 'flagons of wine'. Writing of the soldiery, for example, she says, 'oh when the handwriting is come up in their veins, will not their knees smite together?' (Trapnel 1654a: 63). The power of written language, and the physical effect it can have on the reader, is unmistakable. In the light of this, it is important to note how Trapnel describes the process by which language is inscribed on the page, and the bearing that this has on truth:

> though I fail in an orderly penning down these things, yet not in a true relation of as much as I remember, and what is expedient to be written; I could not have related so much from the shallow memory I have naturally, but through often relating these things, they become as a written book, spread open before me, and after which I write. (Trapnel 1654b: 34)

According to Trapnel, a 'true relation' is not dependent on an 'orderly penning down'; 'truth' is not mere chronicle or 'fact'. Memory and expediency play a major part in the selection and ordering of her material. So too does 'often relating these things': repeatedly telling her own story shapes and orders the material, until it turns *itself* into a book. It is through this combination of memory, expediency (whether in the obsolete sense of hastiness, or the more familiar one of fitness or usefulness) and narrativisation that the book is written, and the text takes on a material existence separate from its author. Rather than there being a self-conscious and deliberate act of writing, then, she asserts that the writing (in the sense of the selecting and ordering of her experiences) is done *before* she writes; all she does then is 'read' and copy and cite it, just as she cites that other text, the Bible, in her writings. Once again, she is relocating responsibility for the text away from herself, but instead of placing it directly with God in this instance, she identifies the process of writing as something independent of her, and therefore for which she is not responsible: she could not have done it only from the 'shallow memory I have naturally'. It is only when memory combines with expediency and repetition that she can write, and it is this combination, distinct from an unselective chronological 'penning down', that results in a 'true relation'.

Language, then, is never an unproblematic or transparent signifier of the world to Trapnel; as Foucault suggests of the Renaissance understanding of language, it is always present, allusive, communicating more symbolically than referentially. This is confirmed elsewhere in her writing, where, although not writing directly of language, it is clear that words and things are functioning as signs and marks, as prompts for associations, for the summoning of related words and concepts. On her journey to Cornwall, for example, she writes:

> my thoughts were much upon the rocks I passed by in my journey, the dangerous rocky places I rode over. And whereas I used to be very fearful, when I rode on smooth ground, now I feared not, but was very cheerfully carried on, beholding my rock, Christ, through these emblems of rocks. (Trapnel 1654b: 10)

For Trapnel, rocks are emblems to be read and interpreted. Actual 'dangerous rocky places' become metaphorical, suggesting the difference between the 'smooth ground' of a life without Christ, and the difficulties and dangers of life with him; the rock of Christ renders her fearless of rocks. She explores and exploits every implication of the word. Anything can be an emblem, be it a linguistic association that she makes: 'at Salisbury the judges met in their circuit: and there I was mightily filled with apprehension of Christ's circuit he was taking in the earth' (Trapnel 1654b: 8), or something she sees: 'the fifth day's journey, singing much of creation-excellencies, as trees, grass, and several plants, and corn that grew as I went by' (Trapnel 1654b: 8). The result is a text that is generically diverse: it cannot easily be categorised as religious, personal, autobiographical, political or travel journal. It is all of these things, for all links that are made by suggestion or association of word or idea are valid; all are evidence of the interconnectedness of God's creation as revealed through emblems.

Trapnel's awareness of the power and elasticity of language extends throughout her writing. Her texts suggest her relish of what is represented as the successful manipulation of, and skill with, language, particularly in recounting her exchange with the justices before whom she was sent in Cornwall, where she displays her own wit and expertise in argument:

> I said, 'Why may I not pray with many people in the room, as well as your professing woman that prays before men and women, she knowing them to be there; but I know not that there is anybody in the room when I pray: and if you indict one for praying,

why not another? Why are you so partial in your doings?'

    Justice Lobb. 'But you don't pray so as others.'

    A.T. 'I pray in my chamber.'

    Justice Travel. 'Your chamber!'

    A.T. 'Yea, that it's my chamber while I am there, through the pleasure of my friends.'

                                                  (Trapnel 1654b: 28)

Here language is Trapnel's tool, her 'instrument', which she uses skilfully and without compromise to make her mark and win her argument. She picks up inconsistencies and contradictions in her opponents' arguments and reads them to her own advantage. She denies the justices' words any secure fixity of meaning; instead, she appropriates their terms and reinvests them with her own meanings.

It seems clear that Anna Trapnel's perception of language correlates with Foucault's characterisation of the Renaissance understanding of language. For Trapnel, language is never a neutral, transparent communicator, a simple medium for the transmission of material truths about the world. It is endlessly complicated, interconnecting, allusive and suggestive. Language is present in her texts, not simply as a transparent medium through which to communicate God's message pure and unmediated, but as a symbol, an emblem that needs deciphering and interpreting, its meanings latent and opaque, needing to be teased out, just as the other elements of God's creation, the rocks, stones, trees and grass, need interpreting.

'A natural way of speaking': the search for linguistic transparency

If Trapnel thought of language as complex, symbolic, and inevitably negotiating a relationship with the truth that was fraught with potential snares, then others saw the kind of sectarian language use that her work typifies as equally problematic. Much of the considerable output of the seventeenth century on the subject and nature of language is formulated in terms of the character and function – whether ideal or perceived as actual – of different sorts of religious discourse, and in particular the self-conscious development of a 'plain style' in Puritan and Latitudinarian[12] speaking and writing, and the relationship of perceptions of sectarian language to this.

The Puritan advocacy of a 'plain style' in preaching and writing was developed initially in contradistinction to the intricacies of the kinds of elaborate discourse associated with Anglicanism. The sermons of such clergymen as John Donne and Lancelot Andrewes are often invoked to typify such discourse, and are usually characterised in the way that we found Joan Webber characterising the self-inscription of the Anglican 'I': it is seen as elaborate, cerebral, witty, scholarly and allusive. In contrast, the Puritans, from as early as the 1570s, rejected this linguistic mode along with the spiritual principles and practice associated with it. Fisch quotes the influential early Puritan preacher Lawrence Chaderton on the matter:

Wherfore many doe stuffe their sermons with newe deuised words, and affected
speeches of vanitie ... Many with unnecessary sentences, prouerbes, similitudes, and
stories collected out of the wrytings of prophane men: many with curious affected
figures, with Latine, Greeke and Hebrue sentences, without any iust occasion offered
by their texte. (Chaderton 1578, in Fisch 1952: 231-2)

Instead, Chaderton proposed to speak 'not in the excellencie of wordes, or in the
inticying speach of mans wisdome, but in plaine euidence and demonstration of the
trueth' (Chaderton 1578, in Fisch 1952: 231). This draws directly on Paul's first
epistle to the Corinthians (1 Corinthians 2:1, 4), and is also reiterated in his second
epistle, where he advocates that 'we use great plainness of speech' (2 Corinthians
3:12); these texts were both to become axiomatic to the Puritan advocacy of plainness
in speech, and the principle set out by Chaderton here was to be reiterated many
times by later Puritan writers.

It was not, however, until after the decades following the restoration of Charles II
in 1660 that the 'plain style' gained a wider cultural currency:

From the 1660s particularly in London a remarkable change in preaching style and
method was effected whereby the elaborate witty preaching of earlier Anglicans and
what was regarded as the speculative and enthusiastic preaching of the puritans gave
way to a new plainer, more simple kind of sermon. (Rivers 1991: 49)

The Latitudinarian recommendations concerning preaching style are reminiscent of
Chaderton's a century earlier:

he that would teach men what faith is, he must first acquaint men with the thing, and
describe it in as proper and simple words as can be, and not by figurative and metaphorical phrases. Indeed after a man hath delivered the simple notion of a thing in
proper words, he may afterwards illustrate it by metaphors: but then these are not to be
insisted upon, and strained to the utmost extent of the metaphor, beyond what the true
notion of the thing will bear. (Tillotson 1742-43, in Rivers 1991: 56)

By the end of the century, this 'collective language and rhetorical method' had
succeeded in establishing itself 'as the standard for rational public discourse' (Rivers
1991: 37). Already, then, it is clear that there was no simple, absolute or fixed
Anglican/Puritan split between an elaborate and a plain style. After the Restoration,
the plain style was no longer associated exclusively (and pejoratively) with the
Puritans, but had been annexed by the 'liberal' wing of the Anglican church (the
Latitudinarians, who were increasingly dominant within the Church of England),
whilst an elaborate style was by this point associated with the radical Puritans: the
sects or, as they came to be known after the Restoration, the Nonconformists. Whilst
the serpentine convolutions of the process of this shift of identification need not be
detailed here,[13] I want to outline some of its key manifestations – in relation to the
new science, to universal language schemes and to ideas about preaching – and the
ways in which they had an impact on ideas about the status of the sects themselves.

The Royal Society was the post-Restoration focal point of the drive for a 'plain style'. Its influential members distilled what were to become the definitive statements concerning the desirability of this 'plain style' of speaking and writing for the development of the new science, which was characterised by a reliance on empiricism, experiment and observation.[14] This was part of a developing emphasis on taxonomy and classification,[15] which necessitated, if it were to represent nature accurately, a simple, unproblematic language, incapable of misinterpretation, where the word and its referent corresponded so exactly that all risk of ambiguity and confusion was eliminated. Thomas Sprat, in his *History of the Royal Society* (1667) exemplified this desire when, in what is undoubtedly the most famous statement on the subject, he recommended a prose style free from

> amplifications, digressions, and swellings of style: to return back to the primitive purity, and shortness, when men deliver'd so many *things*, almost in an equal number of *words*. They [the Royal Society] have exacted from all their members, a close, naked, natural way of speaking; positive expressions; clear senses; a native easiness; bringing all things as near the Mathematical plainness, as they can: and preferring the language of Artizans, Countrymen and Merchants, before that, of Wits, or Scholars. (Sprat in Knowlson, 1975: 41)

Here, then, is Sprat's vision of the ideal relationship between 'words' and 'things': each word would correspond precisely with the 'thing' it represented. The passage also demonstrates the urge towards a transparent, inconspicuous language: it should be 'primitive', 'clear', 'naked' and 'natural'. The implication is that in this way language can attain truthfulness and thereby become uncontroversial, for it will then be unable to be manipulated for political ends.

The most systematic practical counterpart to Sprat's suggestions can be found in the many universal language schemes that were devised in the seventeenth century. Many philosophers, from highly educated scholars such as Bishop John Wilkins to schoolmasters such as Cave Beck (Cohen 1977: 1-6), argued that such language schemes, whereby ideographic or numerical symbols would correspond absolutely to things or to notions of things, thereby bypassing words with all their ambiguities and irregularities, were the only way of obtaining an accurate account of the natural world:

> scholars sought to provide a universal character that through the actual compositon of its 'words' would accurately mirror the various qualities of natural things and the relations between them. In this way, language would not only be a means of acquiring knowledge; it would itself be knowledge, since each word would provide an actual description of the thing signified. (Knowlson 1975: 8)

Just as the intermediary of the priest, who was seen as having come between the believer and God, had been decentred or bypassed by the Protestant emphasis on the 'priesthood of all believers', so the intermediary of language, which, similarly, was thought to confuse and mislead the scientist about the elements of nature, would have to be superseded. Such intermediaries were no longer felt to illuminate or explain; instead, they obscured the truth by preventing people from experiencing it directly.

The implications of these schemes were not confined to science, but were also seen to apply directly to religion, for they were believed to be 'likely to remove one of the greatest obstacles to the religious harmony that they had so much at heart' (Knowlson 1975: 10): namely, a metaphorical and therefore misleading language. As Wilkins wrote in the most famous work in English on a universal language scheme, *An Essay towards a Real Character and a Philosophical Language* (1668):

> this design will likewise contribute much to the clearing of some of our Modern differences in Religion, by unmasking many wild errors, that shelter themselves under the disguise of affected phrases; which being Philosophically unfolded and rendered according to the genuine and natural importance of Words, will appear to be inconsistencies and contradictions. And several of those pretended, mysterious, profound notions, expressed in great swelling words, whereby some men set up for reputation, being this way examined, will appear to be, either nonsense, or very flat and jejune. (Wilkins 1668: 'Epistle Dedicatory')

Religious error, then, arose through imprecise and thereby misleading language, and would continue to have influence for as long as these 'affected phrases' remained unchallenged. This, in Wilkins's opinion, could only be effected through bypassing altogether the pitfalls of language as it had hitherto developed, and by introducing a properly precise, uncontradictory and incontrovertible scheme, such as his 'real character'. This would restore the 'genuine and natural importance of Words', by eliminating their metaphorical element and re-establishing an exact relationship between the word and its referent. This, like other schemes, started from the premise that its proposals for language reform 'touch on the most critical issues, on God's word, man's speech, and the book of nature' (Cohen 1977: 6).

The political dimensions of these various debates about the characterisation and referentiality of language were quite explicit, and apparent to contemporary commentators. The drive for the use of the vernacular was one area of importance, for example, summed up in a pamphlet ascribed to the Leveller John Lilburne:

> That considering it a Badg of our Slavery to the Norman Conqueror, to have our Laws in the French Tongue, and it is little lesse than brutish vassalage to be bound to walk by Laws which the People cannot know, that therefore all the Laws and Customes of this Realm be immediately written in our Mothers Tongue. (Lilburne, in Jones 1953: 317)

The vernacular, then, was seen as a democratising or 'levelling' force that would make the law accessible to all. Similarly, the Quaker insistence that 'thee' and 'thou' should be used for the second person singular had overt political overtones, for which it was widely feared: 'such as now introduce Thou and Thee will (if they can) expel Mine and Thine, dissolving all property into confusion' (Fuller 1655, in Hill 1972: 247).

Nowhere, however, were the political implications of language use clearer, and its relationship with contemporary views of the sects more fully explored, than in the debates over the proper style for preaching. There has been debate as to how precisely the language of the sects was characterised after the Restoration: R.F.

131

Jones suggests that, by the time of the Restoration, pedantic and rhetorical preaching was usually associated with the Puritans and sectarians of the revolutionary period. 'Fine preaching' had become the rhetorical counterpart of fanatical religion, for 'enthusiasm' was detected in both, so when Sprat complained of 'amplifications, digressions and swellings of style', he was referring not to the allusive and convoluted prose styles of Anglican preachers such as Donne or Andrewes, but to the writers and preachers from the sects. The conforming clergy claimed the plain style as their opposition to this, a sign of their dedication to religious 'truth'. Rhetoric was seen as obscuring this truth, for it appealed to the emotions and not to reason: 'Sick of the religious controversies that had brought so much woe in their wake, men [sic] were beginning to discover in language the causes of the evil' (Jones 1951:b 123). Taking issue with Jones, Harold Fisch suggests instead that the sectaries or nonconformists were castigated not for their stylistic elaborations, but for 'a lack of all literary grace whatever'. Quoting John Eachard's 1671 treatise, *Observations upon an Answer to an Enquiry*, he writes that 'They did not impart the Scripture to their flock through imaginative exposition, but they hurled it crudely at them with an abundance of "*canting*, insignificant *phrases*, and tedious *tautologies*"' (Fisch 1952: 243). Instead, he suggests that complaints of an elaborate style were directed more against 'non-Puritans of an earlier age', such as Donne or Richard Hooker, or those who still followed in that tradition (Fisch 1952: 244). Whilst such debates are useful in that they highlight the complexity of the debate about the origins and attribution of the 'plain style', more recent critics seem to have decided in favour of Jones's analysis: Isabel Rivers, in her extensive study of the Latitudinarian adoption of the plain style, sums up their attitude towards sectarian language use thus:

> Nonconformist language, conformists were agreed, employed specialised and unnecessary terms and phrases and was metaphorical and allegorical when it should have been plain and explanatory. As a result it obscured instead of clarifying the meaning of religion and formed an impassable barrier between nonconformists and the rest. (Rivers 1991: 124)

She goes on to quote from Samuel Parker's *A Discourse of Ecclesiastical Politie* (1670), which, she suggests, offers a useful summary of conformist objections to nonconformity:

> And herein lies the most material difference between the sober Christians of the Church of *England*, and our modern Sectaries, That we express the Precepts and Duties of the Gospel in plain and intelligible Terms, whilst they trifle them away by childish Metaphors and Allegories, and will not talk of Religion but in barbarous and uncouth Similitudes; and (what is more) the different Subdivisions among the Sects themselves are not so much distinguish'd by any real diversity of Opinions, as by variety of Phrases and forms of Speech, that are the peculiar *Shibboleths* of each Tribe. (Parker 1670, in Rivers 1991: 124)

132

Parker's characterisation is reiterated in the work of one the most famous Latitudinarian exponents of the plain style in preaching, Joseph Glanvill. He explains why preaching should be 'plain, practical, methodical, affectionate':

> Much mischief is fallen on religion by reason of the transgression of this rule: mysterious, notional preaching hath put many conceited people upon meddling with that they can never well understand, and so hath filled them with air and vanity, and made them proud, fantastical, and troublesome; disobedient to their governors, and contemptuous to their betters. (Glanvill 1677: 19-20)

'Notional preaching', preaching concerned with ideas and opinions, encourages people to meddle 'with what they can never well understand', thereby inciting disobedience, even rebellion. With the aim of avoiding this, Glanvill recommends preachers to be wary of 'conceited fashionable phrases' (Glanvill 1677: 26), even though the 'manly unaffectedness and simplicity of speech (Glanvill 1677: 23) which he proposes in their place may displease their congregations:

> Thus if you teach men to believe Christ's doctrines, to obey his laws, to trust to his promises, and to conform to his example, these shall be counted dull, dry and unedifying things, that no-ways affect or move: but if you tell the people, that they must roll upon Christ, close with Christ, get into Christ, get a saving interest in the Lord Christ: oh this is savoury, this precious, this is spiritual indeed; whereas if anything more be meant by those phrases than what the other plain expressions intend, it is either falsehood or nonsense. (Glanvill 1677: 26-7)

This clearly refers to the style developed by some writers in the sects, particularly the Quakers and Ranters. Owen Watkins discusses the particular phraseology used by the Quakers, such as 'breathings or stirrings after God' and the 'motion of the Seed within', as a means by which Quakers could convey the power of the inner light to the sceptical (Watkins 1972: 214). Anna Trapnel was 'gathered up into the visions of God' (Trapnel 1654a: sig.A2^v); Jane Turner, amongst others, wrote of 'precious souls' (Turner 1653: 'Word from the Author to the Reader'), and Elizabeth Hincks employed, if not the words 'a saving interest', other commercial metaphors to describe her faith: the spirit is a 'commodity' with which individual believers have to 'trade' (Hincks 1671: 7, 9). Christopher Hill, too, has noted Bunyan's regular use of commercial metaphors of sureties, creditors, oaths and satisfaction; 'We are redeemed by right of purchase,' wrote Bunyan; 'Christ paid for everything in advance' (Bunyan, in Hill 1988: 180-1). Glanvill suggests that such a style encouraged insurrection and insubordination, because it is metaphorical and elliptical: the words do not correspond closely enough to 'things' and so do not form 'clear and distinct conceptions' (Glanvill 1677: 54).

Yet Glanvill, like other Latitudinarians, is also aware that the 'affections' must to some degree be engaged by the preaching, otherwise religion 'hath no considerable hold' upon those that hear it (Glanvill 1677: 54). A justification for this concession is that 'God himself doth condescend; he speaks in our language, and in such schemes of speech as are apt to excite the affections of the most vulgar, and illiterate' (Glanvill

1677: 56). Once more, it is the style in which this is done that is all important: 'we ought to feed our people with wholesome food, and not with trash, and poison, though they long never so much for them' (Glanvill 1677: 58). Although people's 'affections are raised by figures, and earnestness and passionate representations; by the circumstances of the voice, and gesture, and motion' (Glanvill 1677: 55-6), this is not an excuse to deliver the message in 'jingles and quibbles, in witticisms and flourishes' (Glanvill 1677: 69). Instead:

> The preacher should endeavour to speak sharp and quick thoughts, and to set them out in lively colours; this is proper, grave, and manly wit, but the other, that which consists in inversions of sentences, and playing with words, and the like, is vile and contemptible fooling. (Glanvill 1677: 72)

Here language is seen as being by no means *inherently* transparent or truthful. At worst, it can impress the hearer through the affections only, by 'playing' or 'fooling' with words. The contrast to this is a 'natural', plain language in which 'proper, grave' expression is a fitting form for the 'truths' being communicated. Ironically, this natural way of speaking has been lost and now has to be re-learnt and consciously embraced. Its perceived naturalness and truthfulness correspond to that of 'common sense': it is so ingrained and so widespread within certain social groupings that it comes, usefully, to be seen as natural and normal, rather than a discourse with political implications.

Moreover, Glanvill's use on more than one occasion of the adjective 'manly' to describe the plain style that he is advocating hints at the *gendered* politics of the debate about plain style. The post-Restoration Latitudinarian advocacy of the plain style was part of a wider move to reject the Calvinist tradition which emphasised the depravity of human nature and God's arbitrary exercise of free grace, and to promulgate instead the importance of the capacity of human reason and free will to co-operate with divine grace in order to achieve a holy and happy life (Rivers 1991: 1). Thus, the plain style was associated with rationality, moderation, and the possiblity of human happiness; and it is this style, and thereby these associations, that Glanvill designates as 'manly'. Though unarticulated, this implicitly designates the sectarian style as feminine, and, by association, its beliefs and practices are also thereby feminised. Whilst rationality was a quality that was rejected by radical sectarians as carnal and therefore corrupt, its opposite, irrationality, could be rendered equally problematic through its association with femininity; and feminisation has long been recognised by feminists as a strategy for downgrading a characteristic, quality or skill. Thus, Glanvill's advocacy of a plain and 'manly' style has implications not only for *how* preachers should speak if they are to be accorded respect, but also for *who* should speak: for if the feminised speech of male and female sectarians is unacceptable to Glanvill, so 'manly wit' from women preachers would be equally unsuitable. Gender difference, then, could be mobilised as a justification for exclusionary practices and derogatory ascriptions, not only in terms of the 'sex' of the author, but also in terms of perceived modes of communication and expression.

Absent author, present language?

These characterisations of the language of the sectaries are entirely consistent with what we have seen of Trapnel's particular linguistic/textual practice: far from hers being a 'plain style', it is reflexive, self-conscious and elliptical, investigating itself and its status as authoritative and truthful. To interrogate the status of language, its possibilities and its potential pitfalls, in the way that Trapnel does, testifies to the presence of an author to carry out such an investigation; in turn, such an author-figure necessarily becomes a 'visible', present, ambiguous and interpretable sign or symbol, in need herself of interpretation, explication and justification. This is, however, somewhat at odds with the author-figure whose construction I discussed in the previous chapter, who is at pains to absent herself from her writings, to deny her own agency in relation to her output. For if, as I argued there, there is no author of these texts other than God, with the language of the texts being God's word mediated through passive instruments, then the *language* of the texts themselves is also God's, and is therefore infallible, and perfect; this, in effect, renders the language 'invisible', in that it is not open to dispute in the way that the human language is. There is, then, a contradiction: an investigation of language bespeaks an investigating author, whilst the absence of a human author is matched by the assertion of a divine author and hence a divine and indisputable language. Yet what we have found so far is an absent author articulating and investigating a visible and very much 'present' language. There is, however, another characteristic feature of language use in these texts that complicates the picture still further; for although I have been arguing, through a case-study of Trapnel and with reference to other sectarian writers, that language in these texts was a visible presence, to be worried over, played with, investigated and unravelled, there is a sense in which it is also deployed in these texts so that it becomes *at the same time* absent, unproblematic, transparent and unquestionable. It is to this aspect of these writings that I shall now turn.

Perhaps the first thing to strike a twentieth-century reader of sectarian writings is the extent to which devotional, particularly biblical, imagery and narratives structure these texts, whether autobiography, prophecy, pamphlet or admonitory tract. This is generally true, whatever the status of the Bible within a particular sect: it applies as much to the Quakers, with their more metaphorical or allegorical interpretation of the Bible, as it does to the Baptists, with their literal understanding of the Scriptures as the only source of God's word. This feature of these writings has received considerable attention from critics: Owen Watkins, for example, writes that the language of the followers of all the sects 'came from the Bible, from devotional literature, from the preachers and from common usage among fellow believers' (Watkins 1972: 209). He describes how writers often applied biblical imagery to their own times of spiritual dejection, so that an inward experience would be identified with a historical episode from the Scriptures, and he assesses the importance of this identification:

Since an autobiographer could rely on his readers to recognise any Biblical allusion, he had at his disposal an immense range of materials from which to find an image, an episode, or a situation which could embody an otherwise elusive and perhaps incommunicable experience. (Watkins 1972: 21)

More recently, Christopher Hill has extended this analysis, noting how the use of biblical allusions not only provided a kind of shorthand, a common language of recognisable implications and associations for the reader, but it also allowed them to be pragmatically elliptical: 'The advantage of quoting the Bible was that the preacher or writer could rely on a name to remind his audience of parts of the story that he did not think it prudent to emphasize' (Hill 1993: 68). Moreover, the translation of the Bible into the vernacular had made it available to many more people than before, 'including artisans and women, and they read their own problems and solutions into the sacred text' (Hill 1993: 4). Whilst many deplored this outcome,[16] it none the less meant that 'the Bible was the source of virtually all ideas; it supplied the idiom in which men and women discussed them' (Hill 1993: 34). So, for example, in the first twelve lines of *Herein is Held Forth the Gift* (1659), written by the Quaker Sarah Blackborow, there are references to 'death's dominion', 'everyone in your own vessels', 'the bread which comes down from heaven' and 'the water of life', all of which allude to biblical texts; the rest of her pamphlet is similarly saturated with scriptural paraphrases and references. Sometimes the assumptions made by the author about the reader's ability to identify such allusions can be confusing to a modern reader. At first sight, Anne Audland seems to be letting her enemies off lightly when she says that 'liars must be cast into the lake' (Audland, 1655: 2). This is, however, a contracted reference to a punishment detailed five times in just three chapters of Revelation, whereby sinners would be cast alive into a lake of fire burning with brimstone (Revelation 19:20; 20:10, 14, 15; 21:8). The reference was evidently so well known that it was not necessary to quote it in full; the reader could be trusted to make the necessary amplification and associations.

Biblical imagery was, then, an important means of communicating and condensing a common set of emotions, references and associations, a way to draw on and reinforce a tradition by quoting from it, in the same way that Anglican writers such as Donne or Andrewes were able to draw on their tradition of classical learning to bolster the authority of their sermons: citation of established and authoritative texts was a key mode of authentication in all kinds of literary production of the time (Purkiss 1992b: 72-4). The use of biblical imagery by the writers in the sects was, however, more than just a reliable way of signalling a common heritage to the reader, but was also connected with the locus of authority and power in relation to the author, the text and the reader. By identifying herself, her fellow sectaries or her nation with biblical characters or situations, the subject effectively deflects the textual focus from her 'carnal' self, her life and her experiences, thereby avoiding any charge of immodesty or impropriety. Moreover, she simultaneously decentres the language in which she is communicating: by identifying her own life with biblical narratives, the language of the text ceases to be 'visible' in that it ceases to be human and becomes divine, authoritative and self-evidently truthful. As with the author-figure in the previous chapter, the decentring of the language does not lessen its authority; instead, it augments it, by ascribing its origin to the omnipotent author of all. The use of biblical narratives and imagery, then, at once deproblematises language, removes it from the realm of speculation, and, through its relocation with God, lends it a reliability, a truthfulness, that could not otherwise be claimed for it.

This process is particularly clear in a number of passages from the Quaker Joan Vokins's autobiography. Writing of the time of her conversion to the Quakers, she says:

> And I was even as Israel at the Red Sea, compassed all round on every hand; great was the strait that I was then in, much hardship; the sea was before, and the enemy presenting so much impossibility, that his proud waves of temptations, buffetings, and false accusations had almost sunk me under ... and he [God] did arise and rebuke the enemy, and made way for me to travel on in my heavenly progress, and overturned mountains that were on each hand, and dismayed Pharaoh and his host (which I may compare my relations and the professors[17] unto) ...
>
> ... the enemy ceased not, but night and day, as a roaring lion, and a cunning hunter, seeking for the precious life, and chased my poor soul as a partridge on the mountains. (Vokins 1691: 20, 22)

Here, undoubtedly, the biblical imagery is an integral part of Vokins's account of her conversion and the opposition she experienced during that period. By identifying herself with Israel and her enemies with 'Pharaoh and his host', she is able to suggest the importance of this time in her own 'heavenly progress', the special nature of her relationship with God, the doubts she was experiencing about that relationship, and the magnitude of the opposition she felt she was facing, opposition that was all the more significant because it came from her 'relations' and 'professors', or fellow-worshippers. The imagery suggests an individual being attacked from all sides, and dramatises the picture by externalising the inward struggle and presenting it in the panoramic terms of an archetypal religious episode.

The significance of this passage does not end here, however, for *through* communicating all this, Vokins is able to create an image of herself of dignity and depth, supremely important, yet without running the risk of charges of immodesty, vainglory or egotism. All the power and significance of her struggle derive from the image she uses to describe it, so that attention is shifted away from the seventeenth-century writer to the terms and context in which she sets herself. Whilst Quakers, and other sectaries, would not have denied the central importance of the individual's experience and struggles, there remained the problem of how to represent this experience without appearing immodest. This problem was to a large degree resolved by identifying oneself with a scriptural character or one's situation with a scriptural episode, thereby achieving a kind of grandeur and a significance for oneself, by deflecting attention away from the self in its seventeenth-century manifestation.

This aspect of the significance of biblical allusions becomes clearer when Vokins's account of herself is compared with another account where such allusions are not used. In *Choice Experiences* (1653), for example, Jane Turner is also concerned with describing and defending her understanding of her experiences, even in the face of all opposition asserting its validity. Like Vokins, her self and her experience are central to the text, but, without the deployment of biblical narratives, the image of the self she is able to construct is quite different. Instead of seeing the individual soul as the beleaguered Israel struggling against 'Pharaoh and his host', Turner presents herself and her apprehension of the nature of her adversaries in this way:

> First, for my experience to myself in particular, I confess through the mercy of God it was far short of that which many precious ones in those days fell into, yet I can truly say it was so much as did truly discover to me the nature and tendency of them all, to be so vile. (Turner 1653: 175)

Because she is dealing directly with herself and her experience here, she tempers this account by adding a rider to it, to the effect that what happened to her was nothing compared with what happened to other 'precious ones', counterbalancing any possible imputation of self-centredness. This difference does not arise from a different concept of the individual's relationship with God and his or her struggle with evil. Despite Vokins being a Quaker and Turner a Baptist, they both saw this relationship in quite intimate and personalised terms: Turner wrote of her 'sweet communion' and 'continual converse' (Turner 1653: 2) with God over a period of seven or eight weeks when she was ill, and Vokins, as in the passages above, often referred to God's direct intervention in her life. The differences, then, seem to arise from the modes of description these writers deployed, the use of a powerful biblical reference allowing Vokins to produce an autobiographical persona of greater status and dynamism than Turner could.

Many other texts derive a similar resonance and authority by referencing the Bible. Dorothy White, for example, adopts the first person to speak God's words directly, in her exhortation to 'the heads and rulers of this nation' to repent: 'I will overturn all the powers of the earth, both heads and rulers, that are now ruling and governing in this nation, by the force of cruelty, and by the unrighteous power are striving to rule and govern over the nations' (White 1659: 1). This recalls a passage from Ezekiel, in which appears another very common biblical figure which is also alluded to by writers such as Margaret Fell, Mary Cary and Anne Wentworth, foreseeing a time when the rich and the poor, the strong and the weak, would change places:

> Thus saith the Lord God; Remove the diadem and take off the crown: this shall not be the same: exalt him that is low, and abase him that is high.
>
> I will overturn, overturn, overturn it: and it shall be no more, until he come whose right it is, and I will give it him. (Ezekiel 21:26-7)

Once again, the use of the phrase 'I will overturn' adds authority to White's message, addressing the 'heads and rulers' of England in the same terms as God addressed the 'profane, wicked prince of Israel' in Ezekiel 21:25.

In each of these instances, then, the deployment of biblical narratives and imagery to delineate the spiritual progress and beliefs of the author serves to remove the language, and hence the self, from the realm of the problematic; if the language is

God's, then the self constructed in that language is, likewise, of divine origin, defined and safeguarded by the word of God.

The self, however, was not the only beneficiary of this use of the Bible: more directly political pronouncements, too, were expressed in these same terms. Again, it is not that spiritual and biblical allusions were simply a disguise for the political, or a strategy to approach the political, for this constructs the relationship between the two as conscious and contrived. The relationship was, rather, one where the religious, the political and the personal were all part of one mutually allusive and interconnecting system. Thus an element from one domain could suggest another from a different one with no sense of uneasiness or disparity; the texts betray no sense of uneasiness or need to justify these links or parallels; as Christopher Hill put it: 'in the forties uneducated men and women read back into the Bible themselves and their problems, and the problems of their communities, and found Biblical answers there, which they could discuss with others who shared the same problems' (Hill 1993: 199). The Bible, then, provided more than a common idiom for the seventeenth-century radicals; it also provided analyses of and strategies for their own times.

Thus for Mary Cary, for example, the temporal and the spiritual were not mutually exclusive areas of activity: the ideas, ideals and pronouncements of the latter were quite specifically related to those of the former. For Cary, Charles I *was* 'the little horn' that would precede the second coming, referred to in the prophecy in Daniel and Revelation; he was the fulfilment of the prophecy and therefore an integral part of it (see Appendix A). The comparison is not a comparison between two distinct but similar things, but is the recognition of an affinity, a 'truth'. Similarly, for Trapnel, Cromwell was at first 'Gideon, going before Israel, blowing the trumpet of courage and valour' (Trapnel 1654a: 6); later, when she lost trust in him, she had a vision 'of the deadness of Gideon's spirit to the work of the Lord, shewing me that he was laid aside, as to any great matters, the Lord having finished the greatest business that he would employ him in' (Trapnel 1654a: 10). The soldiers were saints, England was Israel, God was the 'colonel', Christ was general, king, protector and 'conservator'. The identifications were complete, and nowhere more apparent than in this passage from Trapnel, where the two statements are presented together as almost synonymous; no conjunction, no justification or explanation of the juxtaposition was deemed necessary: 'The kingdom of Lord Jesus is at hand, all the monarchies of the world are going down the hill' (Trapnel 1654a: 20). For Trapnel, the arrival of the kingdom of Lord Jesus necessarily involved the demise of the world's monarchies. One could not happen without the other, each depended on the other. The two events did not belong to separate 'spheres', since they were both part of God's overall scheme for the world.

Both Cary and Trapnel were Fifth Monarchists, for whom the identification of the spiritual and the political might be expected to be more overt and explicit than for others, but in fact for writers in other sects this identification was just as central. Grace Barwick, a Quaker, for example, makes these two statements within a page of each other:

is it not high time to remove the oppression of tithes, is not that oppression yet finished in the nation ...

> For it is truth and freedom and just judgement and mercy, that good men seeks after, and its these things will please the nation. It is not the changings of governments into new titles and names, but it is truth and perfect freedom that the best of men delights in ... Forget not to recompense the interest of oppressing laws and priests. (Barwick 1659: 3, 4)

The establishing of the new Jerusalem relies not only on the concept of truth and freedom, but also on the abolition of tithes and the end of oppressive laws and priests. These coexist in the Quaker perception of Christ's kingdom, which will still, in this pre-Restoration atmosphere, exist on this earth and not, as Quakers asserted in later years, in the heart only. Elizabeth Hooton and her co-authors, also Quakers, equate spiritual understanding with action, as did many of the sectaries, saying that 'it is not the hearers but the doers shall be justified' (Hooton *et al.* 1652: 4). Here they identify 'Cambridge or Oxford scholars' and priests that are 'scribes and Pharisees' as the perpetrators of the false learning that they are condemning (Hooton *et al.* 1652: 3). Once again, no distinction is drawn between 'scholars' of the seventeenth century and the scribes and Pharisees of scriptural times: they all represent, and are part of, the same ungodly forces.

In these instances, then, the deployment of biblical narratives and identifications serves to universalise the quite overt political arguments being offered by these writers. By framing these arguments outside the temporal and contested terms of their own day, and expressing them instead as elements within the timeless and incontestable truths of biblical prophecy, once again the texts move towards the incontrovertible, their language 'invisible' in its incontestability, and the authority thereby attained divine and infallible rather than questionably human.

Syntax and authorial status

The specifically seventeenth-century politics of the arguments discussed above are constructed through familiar biblical narratives that invited acceptance of their truths rather than contestation of their meanings. If truth resided in God and was revealed through the Scriptures, then reliance on the Bible for imagery and vocabulary by these writers, and the resulting deflection of attention from their human frailty to the divine origins of their messages, lent their writings an authority and validity unattainable in purely human terms. It is not only the imagery and vocabulary, however, that show this concern to locate their own justifications for writing with the source of truth, God. This characteristic is also embedded in the fabric of the texts themselves, in the characteristic syntactic formations, and even in the prevalent verb forms.

The concern to locate responsibility for writing with God, and thereby to become the objects rather than the subjects of their texts, often resulted in extraordinarily convoluted and complicated sentence structures, every statement, request or exhortation being filtered through God before being directed at a particular person or group of people. In *The Cry of a Stone* (1654), for example, in a prayer concerning 'thy servant that is now upon the throne', Trapnel writes: 'Oh but blessed Lord, let thy handmaid entreat thee to persuade him' (Trapnel 1654a: 19). Here the action of the sentence passes from Trapnel to God to Trapnel to God to 'thy servant ... upon the throne' (presumably, in 1654, Cromwell). Thus all the responsibility for the persuasion lies with God, not with the writer. Similarly, in the lines 'give thy handmaid leave to tell thee, thy children are like dead bones now in the valley' (Trapnel 1654a: 21), God is ultimately responsible for the information Trapnel gives him, by giving her leave to tell him. Mary Cary takes similar pains to locate the responsibility for her message with God, saying that she is publishing her works in order 'to expose them to the public view of all men'. She continues:

> And having so done, shall leave it to the eternal Jehovah to make it effectual, to those ends to which he hath appointed it, which may be first, to convince those of their folly, that persist in ways contradictory to, (or crossing of) his present designs. (Cary 1651: 'To the Reader')

Lacking authority herself, as a 'weak and unworthy instrument', her own opinions as to why her work may be useful are of no value. To invest them with significance she has to present them as the possible 'ends' to which God has appointed it. Only in this way can she be justified in communicating them to the reader.

Similar instances can be found in other texts. Jane Turner, having lamented the fact that the greatest discouragement she received came from 'the saints themselves', asks God to exhort them to 'encourage one another in all good things' (Turner 1653: 5). She herself cannot ask such a thing at the risk of being thought immodest in categorising her writing amongst 'good things'. Elizabeth Hooton *et al.* take care to locate their warning as emanating from God, not themselves, albeit in what might seem a rather hastily appended attribution of authorship: 'O foolish people, that have eyes to see and cannot see, ears to hear and cannot hear, hearts and cannot understand; but what will you do in the end, saith the Lord?' (Hooton *et al.* 1652: 1). Again and again, the syntax demands that attention be focused on the origin of the message and the message itself, not on the writer who is communicating it. In this way, the writer's own lack of spiritual authority is never foregrounded.

The same shift of attention from the writer to the origin and content of the message can be detected in another often-noted feature of seventeenth-century religious writing: the habitual use of the passive voice. Watkins has assessed the importance of the passive, suggesting that through it: 'we are made aware of that sense of contact with something other which is the essence of religious experience, and the device itself helps to suggest the user's perception of himself [*sic*] as a lonely soul at the mercy of mighty spiritual forces' (Watkins 1972: 209). It is undoubtedly the case that the use of the passive voice implies an 'otherness', something outside the writer that is acting on her, and it is this aspect that initially seemed at odds with, particularly, the Quaker message, with its explicit internalisation of God as the 'inner light'. When Joan Vokins, for example, wrote that 'it was with me to go to Long Island'

(Vokins 1691: 33), or 'still it was upon me to go to Boston' (Vokins 1691: 35), there is a suggestion of otherness, but the mundanity of the context rather precludes the possibility of inferring from it 'a lonely soul at the mercy of mighty spiritual forces', although in other contexts this would certainly be possible. Instead, it serves once again to remove the responsibility for the action of the individual and locate it firmly with God, thereby denying any personal interest or 'will' in it.

Barbara Blaugdone, therefore, writes, 'And then I was made to go and call the people forth from among the dumb idols, and suffered much imprisonment for it', and 'I was made to speak in a market place' (Blaugdone 1691: 9-10, 27). In each case the responsibility for her actions lies elsewhere. In Mary Howgill's case, she stresses not that it is she who is warning Cromwell, but simply the fact that he has been warned: 'and when the day comes upon thee, thou shalt me remember, that thou was warned of all thy evil' (Howgill 1657: 4). In one of Sarah Blackborow's tracts, both these elements are apparent: the origin of the message and the message itself; even the title indicates this emphasis: *Herein is Held Forth the Gift and Good-Will of God to the World*. The text too demonstrates this process:

> *be ye warned* (who *are* before *mentioned*) how you seek by your power or authority to hinder the testimony by suppressing the meetings of the Lord's people, his sons and daughters, who *are made* in Christ's spirit *to declare* to all people how they came to witness Christ Jesus the saviour. (Blackborow 1659: 8; my emphasis)

The 'power and authority' of the 'rulers, justices of peace, constables and other officers' to whom this is addressed are nothing compared with those who speak – or are made to speak – 'in Christ's spirit'. Once again, the use of the passive has deflected attention from the fact that it is Blackborow who is communicating the warning and instead focused on the authority of those that speak their testimonies, coming from 'Christ's spirit'. Grace Barwick, even in the fairly standard conclusion to her epistle 'To John Lambert, and the rest of the officers', focuses on the origin of her message and on her own mere instrumentality in the process: 'for the Lord God will surely bring to pass all that he hath spoken unto you by his handmaid who is known by the name of Grace Barwick' (Barwick 1659: 2). Dorothy White, who has through much of her text related much of God's message in the first person, takes care in the conclusion to stress where the authority for the message came from, and her own mediatory role in transcribing it: 'This is to you that are ruling and govern-ing the nation, for a warning and a message, as received by the spirit of the living God, as it was given to me to be delivered to you, for you to read in the fear of God' (White 1659: 1). The message emanates from God and is intended for the rulers of the nation: this, above all, is what this conclusion conveys. The role of White herself is understated. She casts herself as no more than a mouthpiece, an instrument of God; and this, in the end, rather than the 'lonely soul at the mercy of mighty spiritual forces', is what characterises the constant use of the passive in these texts.

Returning to Foucault's argument concerning the shift in seventeenth-century perceptions of language, my reading of this aspect of these texts would seem to confirm his findings. The characteristic early seventeenth-century understanding of language as consisting in a tertiary structure of God, speaker/writer and text appears indeed to have been conflated and simplified into the binary one of God and text, the one absolutely corresponding to the other without need of an intermediary or inter-preter. In this way the message of the text can be focused on, without any considera-tion of the conveyor of that message – its earthly author. As I argued in Chapter 4, the significance of the writer lies in demonstrating convincingly that she is indeed God's instrument, an empty vessel, and not the originator of her own text. By ensuring her disappearance from the text, she eludes an engagement with her prob-lematic status as a woman writer. This erasure of the *act* of writing, and with it a potentially corrupt language, then, suggests that the 'word' of the text could be wholly parallel or isomorphic with the 'thing' of God's message, without the inter-vention of a significant third party in the figure of the author.

This suggests that, in the sects too, this new perception of language was making its mark: the written word could be seen less as a sign to be interpreted, and more as a representative of a thing or notion. This in itself could be seen to have significance for access to authorship: this perception could be argued to legitimate authorship for those claiming to represent God's dealings with them (with the emphasis on God and his works) rather than on the writer herself.

The godly resolution

If, as I have been suggesting, the language of the texts is rendered unproblematic through the erasure of any earthly associations by its habitual references and allu-sions to the Bible, how does this relate to the characterisation of sectarian language offered earlier in this chapter, in which I suggested that it was typically closer to Anglican language use – allusive, circular and witty – than to the Puritan 'plain style'? How is it possible to see language as at once visible and invisible, human and divine, corrupt and infallible? Are these contradictions embedded in the texts, unre-solved and thus suggestive of some of the linguistic gymnastics executed in the negotiations for this textual space? Or are they instead tensions rather than contra-dictions, held together and yet kept apart by some third force?

There is a sense in which the texts produced by women writers in the sects could be said to dwell on the cusp of the change in language practice argued by Foucault to have taken place in the course of the seventeenth century, these writings moving between the two (apparently contradictory) understandings of the character and function of language. Trapnel, for example, as we have seen, wrote of language as complex, opaque, and fraught with meanings to be delivered by means of her own divinely-originating insight; language, by this account, is a dense, difficult and potentially deceptive cipher. Conversely, the habitual and systematic deployment of biblical allusions and references in sectarian writings, to the extent that texts can come to seem at times almost like collages of scriptural gleanings, renders the mean-ings and authority of the texts incontrovertible through their divine authentication. This dual identification extends from the language of the texts to the designations of their author-figures: as well as being bodies marked out as divinely authorised by their trances, visions, dreams, tears or fastings, they were also instruments and empty vessels, mediums void of signifying capability in themselves, communicating only through themselves rather than of themselves. At the same time, then, as asserting the complexities of the signifying capabilities of words and bodies – asserting the textuality of the prophesying figure as well as the prophetic linguistic utterance – there can be found the counter-assertion of the emptiness of the prophesying body and the transparency of prophetic discourse. This latter move is effected through the naming of God as the author, the originator of the words that are produced, the earthly authors being no more than conduits for the language that is produced though them. In this account, the speaker or writer, the 'instrument' or 'vessel', is unimportant, functional but not actually present in the text in any significant sense.

The tension between these two apparently contradictory understandings is stabilised by reference to the divine; it is recourse to a sense of godly authentication that maintains the equilibrium of the texts. Just as the meanings of the prophesying body and the prophetic utterance are deciphered and guaranteed through the successful establishing of their divine origin, so the denial of any earthly taint to either the utterances or the bodies of the prophets vouchsafes the authenticity and reliability of the ensuing discourse. Both positions, then, are dependent on the emptying of the sign (linguistic or bodily) of its human, corrupt component; it might either be colonised by God, or erased by God. The figure of God thus serves as the third force: the linchpin holding in place the terms of the contradiction and authenticating its disparate meanings. This third force provides the terms and the rationale for the yoking of opposites: the passive and the active, the absent and present, the transparent and the significant. Moreover, the reliability of such contradictions is also assured by scriptural reference. Time and time again, sectarian writers cite passages from the Bible that depend on paradox and opposites for their meanings. One of the most frequently referenced examples of these is the one discussed in Chapter 4:

> God hath chosen the foolish things of the world to confound the wise; and God hath chosen the weak things of the world to confound the things which are mighty:
> And base things of the world, and things which are despised hath God chosen, yea, and things which are not, to bring to nought things that are. (I Corinthians 1:27-28)

In this case, as in the linguistic paradox under consideration here, the reconciliation of opposites is effected by God's action.

Sectarian language is thus not rendered transparent in the sense suggested by Foucault, whereby it becomes isomorphic with its referent, but it is instead rendered reliable through the assertion of its identification with the divine; in other words, the emphasis shifts away from the word's referent and onto its author and origin. Once this can be guaranteed – and it is this that the texts seek so eagerly to do – then the referent, which may indeed be elusive, difficult or debatable, can be both secure and unstable. Language and the author-figure can be both present and absent, empty and significant: in each case, its divine origin assures its authenticity.

For women writing in the context of the radical sects, the centrality of this divine intervention is especially significant. In each instance, it is the intervention of the divine that legitimates their discourse; without it, both their arguments and their language practice remain deeply problematic on account of the gendered character of their status. As women writers, the authority of their language is vulnerable to criticism in each case; with the godly sanction, however, their language is buttressed against attack. Thus, the complexities, the difficulties, the shifting meanings of language and its deployment, as exemplified by Trapnel, are saved from any attack that relied on the flawed status of its female progenitor either by reading a divine significance to the lowly status of its earthly author or by shifting attention to the ultimate author of those complexities. Similarly, the notion of a transparent or unproblematic language can be deployed by women writers only if the language is identified with God; if an earthly language were transparent, all that could shine through would be the relationship between the subject/speaker/writer and the object/referent – a relationship in which a woman speaker/writer would necessarily, in this context, be an unequal partner. A language and a speaker/writer emptied of their human elements, however, would not be open to criticism for usurping God's role – for all that would remain would be the divine element. In each case, then, women writers in the sects construct themselves as the objects of language, rather than claiming the the privileges of being its subject, creator or speaker, with all its attendant pitfalls. The assertion of the divine intervention of God here thus enables them to negotiate the anticipated criticisms of others and to participate in the spreading of God's word through the combination of these linguistic manoeuvres.

6

'Who may bind where God hath loosed?': responses to sectarian women's writing

This question – 'who may bind where God hath loosed?' – appears in the preface to to the Fifth Monarchist prophet Anna Trapnel's *The Cry of a Stone*, published in 1654. This apparently rhetorical question has an air of expansiveness and confidence, emanating from the assurance that God is at work in the expanding production of these texts and spoken prophecies; and, a reader might infer, the unspoken question behind this articulated one might be to ask who could oppose a project motivated by the power of God and hope to succeed in this opposition. As I have already discussed, this was indeed an argument often used by women writers in their texts: they suggest that, since it is not with them that their works originate, but with God, they can be neither praised nor blamed for their writings. As Trapnel put it in her *Report and Plea*: 'I was nothing, the Lord put all in my mouth, and told me what I should say, and that from the written word, he put it in my memory and mouth: so that I will have nothing ascribed to me, but all honour and praise given to him whose right it is' (Trapnel 1654b: 28). However, as well as suggesting this confidence, Trapnel's question also hints at a certain anxiety. Despite the emphasis placed by women writers on the spiritual origins of their work, their texts constantly testify to an awareness that they were being published in an environment hostile to any activity that was seen to break the bounds of modesty and silence; and this becomes particularly apparent when the question is read in its textual context. The author, just before asking 'who may bind?', begs people not to reject the ensuing prophetic text, not to 'bind up the goings forth of the most free and eternal spirit' in any 'law, custom, order, or qualification of man, how ancient or accustomed soever' (Trapnel 1654a: sig.A2ʳ). Here, the possibility that God's word *could* be successfully 'bound up' or silenced by any number of man-made impediments is quite clearly countenanced and feared. In other words, the plea against interference in God's work as expressed by these women writers demonstrates precisely their fragility as writers at this time.

The question prefacing Trapnel's text therefore pulls simultaneously in two different and contradictory directions: on the one hand, it demonstrates an unusually confident celebration of women's right to write; on the other hand, its rather anxious tone articulates the precariousness of such audacity. Not surprisingly, perhaps, experience justified this anxiety: there are records of reactions to women writing which are

146

largely hostile, and often vehemently so. As I shall discuss later in this chapter, the hostility of men's reaction to women's religious activities (whether preaching, prophesying or writing) at times took the form of physical violence as well as verbal and written abuse.

So far in this book, I have considered the different textual manifestations of the (potentially) conflicting duties emanating from the perception of the 'unequal bodies' but 'equal souls' of women. I have suggested that the negotiations of silence, authorship and language (see Chapters 3, 4 and 5) are, in different ways, negotiations of issues implicated in the conflict between duties owed to men and duties owed to God, all of which stem from the differing perceptions of the status of men's and women's bodies and souls. In this chapter, I want to consider a final manifestation of these negotiations: that between the writer and her readership. In many ways, this is the issue that underpins all the others: for, as I have argued throughout, all the issues discussed so far hinge on the texts' production and reception in a climate hostile to female authorship. In this chapter, then, I will examine more closely the grounds for such a claim: why was it that these texts excited such hostility? Was it their subject-matter, their concern with current religious and political issues? Or did they enact some kind of generic transgression, whereby their formal characteristics – prophecy, or spiritual autobiography, for example – offended? Moreover, what kinds of responses were envisaged by and enacted upon these authors and their writings?

Such questions have exercised other feminist critics who have studied the phenomenon of sectarian women's writing, and indeed a central question for such investigations has been whether there is a relationship between the proliferation of writing by women during this period and the apparently increasing hostility which met its publication. One explanation is offered by Dorothy Ludlow (1978) in her work on English preaching women between 1640 and 1660; here she suggests that this hostility was reserved especially for women who wrote, preached or prophesied any kind of political message. The divine calling in itself, she argues, was not generally feared by men. It was only when women overstepped the boundary between the private and the public sphere that men felt that they had to register their opposition, for it showed a concern for current affairs in which women supposedly had no part to play. Phyllis Mack has put forward a broadly similar argument:

> I would speculate that women were perceived as prophets when they reinforced challenges to authority which had already been made by others, and dismissed as insane or accused of witchcraft when their statements went too far according to the political preconceptions of their audience. (Mack 1982: 32)

If Ludlow and Mack are correct, then the texts most likely to be met with such hostility would be the tracts, pamphlets and prophecies dealing with contentious contemporary issues such as tithes, the status of the clergy and the limits of a husband's authority, whilst 'personal' texts such as spiritual autobiographies should escape such censure. It is this issue that I will focus on first: on what did this hostile reception rest? Was it, as Ludlow suggests, the public and political texts alone that were criticised; or was it all of them? Was it the content of the writings, the subjects about which women chose to write, that determined the response? Was it the genres which they adopted and adapted? Or was it simply the audacity of female authorship which offended and challenged?

Before considering the details of the responses to these writings, I shall characterise the various forms of sectarian writing: first, the more overtly 'public' and 'political' texts, and then the more 'personal' or 'spiritual' ones. I shall then investigate the kinds of reactions the writing actually received and the reactions predicted by the writers, and proceed to offer an analysis of how the insights offered by dialogic theory might be fruitful. Next, I shall offer some explanations for this hostility of response by exploring the challenges offered by the so-called 'private texts' and by assessing any common ground between these generically disparate writings. Finally I shall discuss the limitations of the public/private distinction in relation to these writings.

'Public' and 'political' interventions: tracts, pamphlets, prophecies

Some of the most overtly 'political' of the literature produced by the sects were the prophetic[1] tracts and pamphlets that appeared in such numbers in the 1640s and 1650s, during the time of the Civil War, the Commonwealth and Cromwell's Protectorate. As I outlined in Chapter 1, these were predominantly of Quaker origin, generally very short, usually had an overwhelming sense of urgency and imminence. Titles such as Grace Barwick's *To All Present Rulers, Whether Parliament, or Whom Soever of England* (1659), Hester Biddle's *Wo to Thee City of Oxford* (1655), and Dorothy White's *Upon the 22 Day of the 8th Month, 1659* (1659) give some indication of the highly topical and varied nature of the material.

Although their material was heterogeneous, the authors were united in their attributions of the inspiration of their work. Usually, they claimed, the command to write came directly from God. Whilst for many writers from other sects, and indeed for Quakers writing after the Restoration of 1660, this call was a source of anxiety and reluctance, for early Quakers such as Dorothy White it was, apparently, a spur to unproblematic authorship: 'The word of the Lord came unto me, saying, "Write, and again I say, write with speed, to the heads and rulers of this nation"; oh! earth, earth, earth, hear the word of the Lord' (White 1659: 1). In the same year, Grace Barwick, another Quaker, had a message from God instructing her to travel 150 miles to deliver the word of God direct to 'all present rulers' (Barwick 1659: 1). Very often, authors addressed their writings to a specific and named person or persons (generally the rulers of the nation, as here) or to a local audience. Jeane Bettris, for instance, addressed the inhabitants of Aylesbury in these words: 'Saith the Lord, "For I have measured thee as I measured Sodom in the day of her highness, and the same sin that I found in her is found in thee"' (Bettris 1657: 1). Bettris's tone of warning and admonition is common to many Quaker tracts of the period: Anne Audland warned a Justice of the Peace who tried and sentenced her for disrupting a service at a church in Banbury that God 'will visit you for these things, and plead with you for all your hard speeches, and all your ungodly deeds: and give you your portion with hypocrites, except you speedily repent' (Audland 1655: 3). Similarly, Sarah Blackborow urged people to leave 'adultery and transgression' and to 'hearken diligently to hear the voice of God' (Blackborow 1659: 3).

The concern with the present and the immediate future, the imminence of God's judgement, and the necessity of speedy repentance are all characteristic of these pre-Restoration Quaker writings, and preclude the apologies or justifications for writing and publishing that customarily accompany the work of other women writers in the radical sects. No mention is made here of their unfitness to write: they have a message to convey, and there is no room for inappropriate reticence. Anne Audland writes: 'when the book of conscience is opened, thou mayst remember that thou wast forewarned in thy life-time ... And so your false blasphemy I do deny, and the living God will judge between me and you' (Audland 1655: 2,3). Here she insists both on the importance of her own role in God's scheme and on the need for others to recognise this. Mary Howgill's opinions are just as unequivocally expressed. She condemns Cromwell, telling him: 'thou hast chosen the glory of the world, and art as a stinking dunghill in the sight of God ... and when the day comes upon thee, thou shalt me remember, that thou wast warned of all thy evil' (Howgill 1657: 1,4). Typically, the imminence of Christ's second coming is intimately connected with the current political situation, the 'present rulers', and the attitudes and activities of individuals and communities familiar to the writer.

This preoccupation with the public and political world which characterises early Quaker writings becomes all the more striking when compared with the writings of Quakers after the Restoration. By this time, the attitude towards political affairs was quite different and Quakers seemed determined to distance themselves from any such controversial matters. The title of Mary Mollineux's collection of poems, *Fruits of Retirement* (1702), itself suggests this more quietist spirit, and her poems suggest that the status quo, however inequitable, is there to be transcended rather than challenged. One poem in particular, 'Of a Happy Life', confirms this emphasis on the inner life to the exclusion of the outer. Its subject is 'The honest man, that lives in health / enjoying still sufficient wealth':

> That hath an equal loyal spouse,
> An handsome, habitable house;
> Inherited, or purchased, that
> He need not fear the sullen threat
> Of griping landlord; but if not,
> Finds true content in any lot;
> Since in the closet of his mind
> Dwells solace not to be defined. (Mollineux 1702: 141)

Compared with the earlier Quaker tracts of the 1650s or early 1660s, which were resonant with warnings and exhortations, attacks on tithes and 'hireling priests', this tone of acceptance is markedly different. It illustrates the change of political climate after the Restoration, when the passing of the Conventicle Acts in 1664 and 1670 forbade all religious meetings except those where the liturgy of the Church of England was used; the penalties for disobedience ranged from fines to imprisonment or deportation.

As explicitly concerned with contemporary political issues as the earlier Quaker texts were the prophecies of the Fifth Monarchists, written by women such as Anna Trapnel and Mary Cary. Like the Quaker tracts and pamphlets, these texts also exemplify the integration of spiritual aspirations and expectations with political and material ones. This conjunction was chiefly effected through a very particular understanding of prophecy, not as a foretelling of the future, but as an apprehension and interpretation of God's intentions for the future through a reading of signs, including scriptural prophetic texts. 'Prophecy' thus had a broad definition:

> scholars had, since the Reformation, been interpreting biblical prophecies which involved dreams or visions ... in terms of the events in recent history, so that, in effect, they were able to give precise dates for the Second Coming of Christ. But it was as important, if not more important, for the sectarians to feel the Second Coming as a *spiritual immanence* within themselves. Consequently, just as some of the sectarians expressed their sense of inspiration by adopting Biblical prophetic styles, so the radical prophets relive the archetypes of biblical dreams and visions. (Smith 1989: 85)

Mary Cary exemplified the breadth of contemporary understandings of 'the prophetic' when she wrote that 'all might prophesy, that is (in the lowest sense) be able to speak to edification, exhortation and comfort' (Cary 1651: 237). Elsewhere, she wrote: 'the things that are here spoken of, being now in a great measure accomplished: for all prophecies are best understood in the fulfilling of them' (Cary 1651: 36). The 'prophecies' referred to here are, more specifically, biblical prophecies, in particular those of the books of Daniel and Revelation, the key scriptural prophetic texts for the sects.[2] This commentary gives a clear indication of the topicality and immediate relevance of biblical texts for sectaries: their interpretation, sphere of application, and realisation belong neither to the distant past nor to the distant future, but are a crucial component in the working through, and the making sense, of contemporary issues.

Another example of this conjunction between scriptural prophecy and contemporary events is the Fifth Monarchist perception of Christ's second coming and the establishment of the New Jerusalem in very material terms. King Jesus's arrival was thought to be imminent, and would entail the downfall of all earthly monarchies. This, though inevitable, none the less had to be worked and fought for, and consequently Trapnel's prophecies include both spiritual and political visions that together fulfil God's promise to his people. God communicated with her, for example, about the army: 'I conversed with God by prayer, and reading of the scriptures, which were excellently opened to me touching the proceedings of the army' (Trapnel 1654a: 4); and he also communicated with her about the ministry of the Church of England: he 'filled me that day with prayer, and singing, and discovering the tottering, shaking condition of clergy-function' (Trapnel 1654b: 9). Through her prophecies, then, Trapnel criticises any institution or person perceived as standing in the way of the preparations for Christ's second coming, and this includes a detailed criticism of Cromwell's career. Initially, she suggests, he had been 'Gideon,[3] going before Israel, blowing the trumpet of courage and valour' (Trapnel 1654a: 6). Later, once he was seen by Fifth Monarchists as having betrayed their cause, she had a different vision, one 'of the deadness of Gideon's spirit to the work of the Lord, shewing me that he was laid aside, as to any great matters, the Lord having finished the greatest business that he would employ him in' (Trapnel 1654a: 10). She also described another, even less equivocal, vision in which Cromwell appeared at the head of herd of cattle, and ran 'at many precious saints that stood in the way of him' (Trapnel 1654a: 13). Since the saints were to take power until the arrival of King Jesus, here was a clear case where God's plan needed assistance in its fulfilment from the saints themselves.

Despite the sense of betrayal and frustration experienced by the Fifth Monarchists in the early 1650s, of which their disappointment in Cromwell was just a part, they continued to believe in the imminence of Christ's second coming. The manner in which they anticipated preparing the way for the arrival of King Jesus, and the portions of the Bible on which they concentrated to justify these actions, indicate just how threatening such an integration of the spiritual and political could be. Christopher Hill has made clear the importance for the sectaries of the period of the biblical image of 'the world turned upside down'.[4] The phrase indicated that not only would those currently in power be toppled, but also that they would be replaced by those hitherto powerless in society, 'the saints' or God's chosen people. The people to be toppled from power were those that

> do covet to treasure up most riches for themselves, and to poll, and rob, and cheat the people, to enhance their own estates, and make themselves great in the world, and their children gay and splendid amongst men; as do kings, princes, and evil governors, (not to mention some sorts of committee-men). (Cary 1651: 56-7)

Instead, these 'kings, and nobles, and mighty men, are to be subjected to his saints', who will seek 'the public weal, and safety, and happiness, and salvation of all' (Cary 1651: 62, 56). Similarly, Trapnel suggests that the saints would be drawn primarily from those that 'before were poor and mean' (Trapnel 1654a: 33), and whose ambitions are for spiritual, not material, gain:

> you seek not great things for yourselves, but for the Lord's anointed ones; you cry to the Lord, and not for earthly palaces, nor Whitehall garden-walks, nor kitchen-belly-cheer, nor lardery-dainties, nor banquet-sweetmeats, nor council-robes, nor parliament tithes, nor emperor advancement, nor great attendance, nor for colonels' and captains' silken buss, and garnished spangled coats, and gilded cloaks, and brave London and country houses; I say, fellow-prisoners and sufferers for Christ, seeing we have none of this in our eye nor desires, let us bid defiance to all reproaches and vilifying and derisions against us.[5] (Trapnel 1654b: 50)

Elsewhere, she distinguishes further between the saints and the socially advantaged: 'there are many fleshly, national religious ones, but the poor, fatherless and widow are the companions of the pure religious ones' (Trapnel 1654a: 30). The people

Trapnel cites are those without a voice, or at least a public voice: the poor, and the 'fatherless and widow', women without men and therefore not 'owned' by anyone, and so without a mouthpiece or spokesman.[6] But with the coming of Christ, she implies, they will find their voices.

Mary Cary echoed Trapnel's vision of an egalitarian spiritual future: 'the time is coming ... when not only men but women shall prophesy; not only aged men, but young men; not only superiors but inferiors; not only those that have university learning, but those that have it not; even servants and handmaids (Cary 1651: 238). Again, the world was to be turned upside down, the usual hierarchies upended: women, the young, 'inferiors', the uneducated, servants and handmaids were to be equal to (or, the implication is, above) their social superiors. Her reference to the prophesying of servants and handmaids is an allusion to Acts 2:17-18, part of which was used by the Quaker Anne Audland as an epigraph to her pamphlet *A True Declaration of the Suffering of the Innocent* (1655):

> And on my servants, and on my handmaidens, I will pour out in those days of my spirit, and they shall prophesy.

This passage from Acts (together with 1 Corinthians 1:27-8, discussed above, p. 96) was often referred to, and used as a justification of activities that were readily condemned by those opposed to the sects. In a sense, these verses epitomise the political and spiritual aspirations of the sectaries.

It is easy to see why such prophecies should have provoked fear and hostility in their audiences: they challenge directly most of the contemporary social hierarchies and institutions, and propose to replace those in power with those currently disadvantaged or disempowered by their rule. Indeed, it would have been much more surprising if there had been no outcry against such subversive writings.

'For my own private use': women's spiritual autobiography

These warning tracts and prophecies are in many ways in sharp contrast to the spiritual autobiographies. Whilst the prophetic literature is characterised by its all-inclusiveness, its integration of the spiritual and prophetic with the political, the spiritual autobiography's emphasis is on the work of God in its narrowest manifestation: his role in the journey through sin, conversion, doubt and faith of an individual.[7] The life was written about chronologically, following an almost formulaic pattern which detailed stages of spiritual awareness and grace. This generally began with an account of the unregenerate childhood of the subject, who was later troubled by a conviction that she or he was leading a life of sin, which was accompanied by a dissatisfaction with the religious consolation on offer, together with a search for the truth. This search was underscored by a diligent attendance to sermons, prayer, Bible reading (the period of being 'under the Law'), and a general reformation of outward behaviour, all of which proved to be insufficient. The next stage was a strong conversion experience, when the power of the Gospel was experienced in the heart rather than just in the understanding; this was accompanied by a feeling of reconciliation and consolation, a time under 'the Gospel' rather than 'the Law'. The rest of the autobiography was generally an account of the attacks made by Satan on this state of grace, the doubts that assailed the heart, the prayer and self-examination that followed, and the subsequent reconciliation, until the pattern had repeated itself. It was a record, then, of a constant movement of conviction of sinfulness followed by the experience of forgiveness, not just once in a lifetime, but continually.

This structure meant that the form the autobiographies took was fairly constant: there was a 'tendency to select for the record those episodes which could be seen to belong to a recognisable sequence' (Watkins 1972: 228). There was relatively little variation in the narrative of events, and indeed little of what we might now expect from an autobiography: namely, details of the subject's particular circumstances or experiences. 'Anything uniquely personal has been left unnoticed, or unexpressed, or subsumed into a standard form of words' (Watkins 1972: 228). Rather than the autobiography functioning to individuate the author through stressing his or her difference from the mass of his or her fellow-creatures, it instead served to identify him or her with a particular spiritual community, by demonstrating how the mercy of God, which had been extended to such a sinner as he or she, was, if not universal, at least universal for his elect. 'He [*sic*] was the bearer of a message which exactly confirmed the experience of others, but which had nevertheless come as a personal revelation' (Watkins 1972: 235). The emphasis was on how she or he had fulfilled the role of God's instrument, rather than on why she or he had been chosen in the first place. Because of this generic focus on the doubts and hopes of an individual Christian, then, spiritual autobiography appears to have a much more circumscribed and 'private' perspective, in contrast with the more expansive concern of prophecy with the state of grace or sin of the whole Christian community.

This contrasting characterisation, although a very broad generalisation, is a useful starting-point when comparing these two genres of sectarian writing. The address of Jane Turner's spiritual autobiography *Choice Experiences* (1653), for example, is very different from the address of Trapnel's prophecies. Trapnel's *The Cry of a Stone* is dedicated to 'all the wise Virgins of Sion', but it also has a much wider application: 'it is not for you only, but for all' (Trapnel 1654a: sig. A2ᵛ). Turner's work, on the other hand, is addressed to 'the churches of Christ who worship God in spirit and truth ... especially those my dear brethren at Newcastle, Berwick, and Scotland' (Turner 1653: 'Epistle Dedicatory' by John Turner). This sense of restriction or limitation is reinforced in the ensuing prefatory letter, written by Turner's husband: 'I know it would seem very strange to you, if this following treatise should come to your hands without my public owning of it, as indeed well it might, considering my near relation with the author' (Turner 1653: 'Epistle Dedicatory' by John Turner'). From the outset the gender boundaries of writing and publishing are articulated. Not only does John Turner circumscribe his wife's activities by owning them, but Turner herself excuses the act of writing by saying it was done 'at several times in my husband's absence, which may be some satisfaction as to my spending that time. I did intend them only for my own private use' (Turner 1653: 'A word from the Author to the Reader'). To write when her husband was at home would have broken one of the rules of propriety; to intend the writing for anything other than 'my own private use' would have broken another. Modesty and respectability can thus here be seen to be predicated on a notion of 'private' femininity.

Whilst Trapnel and Cary were themselves 'pressed in spirit' to publish their prophecies in order to communicate them to as many people as possible, in Turner's text it is her husband who is 'pressed in spirit' to publish, 'judging it might be profitable to some precious souls ... though it be written but in a broken scuttering way' (Turner 1653: 'Epistle Dedicatory'; 'A word from the Author to the Reader). Trapnel and Cary aimed to communicate their message of the imminence of the realisation of God's kingdom on earth. Turner wrote 'as a remembrancer of the old loving kindness of the Lord towards me, and 'twas not in the least in my thoughts that ever it should have been presented to a public view' (Turner 1653: 'A word from the Author to the Reader').

Turner's text highlights clearly the contrast between spiritual autobiographies and the 'public' writings of Trapnel and Cary. Typically, they do not have the urgency of Trapnel's, Cary's, or some of the early Quaker prophets' work, nor an intimate and immediate concern with the directly political issues of Parliament or the leadership of the country. They tend instead to be calm, reflective and personal, interspersing 'experiences' with 'observations', drawing religious precepts from personal events.

'Let her mouth be stopped': men's reactions to women's religious authorship

Thus far, distinguishing the 'political' from the 'spiritual' is useful in characterising differences between the writings of Turner and other spiritual autobiographers, and those of prophets such as Trapnel and Cary. This, however, then raises the question as to whether this distinction between 'public' and 'private' texts made any difference to the kinds of responses which met this literature.

Perhaps surprisingly, it did not: distinctions betwen 'public' and 'private' texts figured little in the reception of these writings. Whether prophecy or spiritual autobiography, these texts received condemnation and castigation from male critics, both outside and inside the sects. Before beginning to explore the reason for this hostility, I want first to detail more fully the kind of reactions received by sectarian women, whether preachers, autobiographers, or prophets.

Quaker women preachers and prophets were particularly vulnerable to direct retaliation from their audiences because of their frequent interventions in public places: in the 1650s this tended to take the form of challenging priests in churches, addressing crowds in market places, or refusing to show deference to those of higher social rank, whilst after the Restoration it was more likely to be in the form of a refusal to take an oath in court. All these actions were liable to result in imprisonment. In 1655, for example, Dorothy Waugh, a Quaker, spoke in a market-place in Carlisle. For this she was seized and put in prison, where an iron bridle was brought:

> that which they called so was like a steel cap and my hat being violently plucked off which was pinned to my head, whereby they tare[8] my clothes to put on their bridle as

they called it, which was a stone weight of iron by the relation of their own generation, and three bars of iron to come over my face, and a piece of it was put in my mouth, which was so unreasonable big a thing for that place as cannot be well related, which was locked to my head, and so I stood their time with my hands bound behind me with the stone weight of iron upon my head and the bit in my mouth to keep me from speaking. (Waugh 1656: 30; see Appendix D)

Whilst brutal punishments were not confined to the women in the sects – the branding and flogging suffered by James Nayler after his Christ-like entry into Bristol riding on a donkey in 1656 is only the best-known example[9] – the use of the bridle in Waugh's case suggests there was a gender dimension to the perception of her transgression. The bridle was the favoured punishment in the north of England for the scold (her southern counterpart was more likely to be sentenced to the cucking-stool) (Underdown 1985a: 123); and scolding 'was overwhelmingly a female offence, and equally overwhelmingly one committed by women of low status against equals or superiors' (Underdown 1985a: 120). The imposition of the scold's bridle as a punishment in Waugh's case, then, suggests that her offence was perceived as a transgression of the proper orders both of social rank – Waugh had been a servant in the household of the Camms (a prominent Quaker family) – and of gender. Moreover, as I discussed in Chapter 2, the bridle was a frequent trope for the necessary curbs to be put on a wife in order to fit her to her duties as a wife. Waugh's punishment, then, was somewhat overdetermined both socially and symbolically.

Constraints upon women's activities were, then, much more than verbal or written disapproval and discouragement. Women faced not only iron bridles, but also imprisonment (Channel 1654: 6; Trapnel 1654b: 38–47; Cotton and Cole 1655; Evans and Chevers 1662) and violent assaults from those they addressed. The Quaker Barbara Blaugdone wrote:

And as Mary Prince and I was coming arm in arm from a meeting, that was at George Bishop's house, there was a rude man came and abused us, and struck off Mary Prince her hat, and ran some sharp knife or instrument through all my clothes, into the side of my belly, which if it had gone but a little farther, it might have killed me. (Blaugdone 1691: 10)

Elsewhere in her account she records that, during the course of her travels, she was imprisoned wherever she went, whipped at Exeter 'till the blood ran down my back', and threatened by a butcher who 'swore he would cleave my head in twain; and had his cleaver up ready to do it' when he was restrained by a woman in the crowd (Blaugdone 1691: 15, 27).

The number and diversity of the reactions to women's religious activities were striking. As well as the physical violence encountered by women preachers, their actions also met with written condemnations. David Brown published *The Naked Woman* in 1652, outraged both at a woman's stripping naked in Whitehall in mockery of a sermon and at the minister's failure to retaliate. Many of his concerns, it seems, revolved around the gendered question of who was behind her action: she should have been asked 'With what company she walketh?', 'If she hath a husband? ... And if he and she live together?' (Brown 1652, quoted in Hobby 1988: 28). A similar concern with gendered propriety can be seen in a pamphlet written by Edward Burrough, a leading Quaker, in response to Jane Turner's *Choice Experiences* (1653). He castigated her book as 'nothing but airy imagination and confusion'. Her language, he wrote, 'is the language of Babylon wholly; and she is yet a servant in bondage in Babylon unto the mistress of witchcraft'. Most tellingly, he suggested that she had broken the feminine bounds of both silence and modesty by writing in this way: 'let her mouth be stopped, and let shame strike her in the face, who professes her self to know the Lord' (Burrough 1654: 3, 7, 12). His association of her with witchcraft, untimely language and shamelessness once again locate her transgression firmly within a gendered context.

This catalogue of accusations was by no means unusual. Elizabeth Poole, who recorded her visions and their connections with contemporary events, was condemned in a royalist pamphlet as a 'monstrous witch full of deceiptful craft' (quoted in Yoshioka 1977: 384) Anna Trapnel, too, was habitually the subject of such abuse: 'England's rulers and clergy do judge the Lord's handmaid to be mad, and under the administration of evil angels, and a witch, and many other evil terms they raise up to make me odious, and abhorred in the hearts of good and bad, that do not know me' (Trapnel 1654b: 'To the Reader'). She recorded the surprise of those who came to hear her preach: 'as some have said, they thought I had been a monster, or some ill-shaped creature, before they came and saw, who then said they must change their thoughts, for I was a woman like others, that were modest and civil' (Trapnel 1654b: 49). A woman preaching was evidently felt to be so much 'out of order' that her body must reflect this state and be 'ill-shaped'.[10] To see that this was not so, to find her 'modest and civil', within accepted social boundaries, necessitated a re-evaluation of established ideas, for this challenged all social preconceptions.

Accusations and recriminations came from within as well as from outside the radical sects. As we have seen, Jane Turner, a Baptist who had for a time attended Quaker meetings, was castigated by the Quaker Edward Burrough. The Quakers and the Muggletonians accused each other of witchcraft. Anne Wentworth was accused by her detractors, who were her fellow-Baptists, of being 'a *proud, passionate, revengeful, discontented*, and *mad* woman ... that has unduly published things to the prejudice and scandal of my husband; and that hath wickedly left him' (Wentworth 1677: 2; original emphasis). Once again, the sins of pride, passion, revenge, discontent and madness are linked with the activities of publishing her writing and rebelling against the natural order by usurping the authority of her husband.

Whilst there are many accounts confirming that these kinds of criticism and retribution were indeed meted out to women sectaries – they were not, in other words, simply fabricating fictions in order to enhance their own credentials as God's elect persecuted by the unregenerate – there are none the less a number of issues that need to be addressed in relation to these representations of the responses these writers both expected and received. First, it is worth reiterating that, however undoubted the likelihood of these kinds of incident occurring, we cannot assume that these are, as it were, transparent records of events, that these instances happened precisely in this way or were received in exactly this manner. As discussed in Chapter 2, these are literary representations, constructed within and through their own contexts and conventions, and attention to which may lead us to rather different conclusions from those elicited by an dehistoricised reading. Whilst, then, there is no reason – quite the contrary – to read these as simple fabrications, there is an important sense in which they are drawing on biblical and other cultural precedents in order to confirm their status as authentic and divinely originating spiritual experiences, for there was always a danger that these events and actions might be, or might be perceived to be, the work not of God but of Satan, or of the self-will of the prophet, preacher or writer. Constant self-surveillance and self-verification needed to be presented as evidence to convince both sympathisers and opponents of the presence of God in this work.

In relation to this process of authentication, Diane Purkiss has demonstrated the ways in which seventeenth-century prophetic trances and their attendant physical states were understood in relation to such scriptural and spiritual precedents. Fasting, for example, such as that undertaken by Anna Trapnel, Purkiss argues, was not primarily associated with weakness and self-destructiveness; instead, 'fasting in Puritan discourse represented not just an act of personal self-denial but an act of quasi-magical efficacy' (Purkiss 1992a: 145). The same was the case for other bodily signs, such as 'trembling, weeping and fainting' (Purkiss 1992a: 149), and, most strikingly, the Quaker practice of 'going naked as a sign':

> This involved appearing in a public place – the streets or market of a town, or a religious gathering – unclothed, though it is not always clear just how unclothed; some were stark naked, some wore modest coverings about their loins, others wore certain essential undergarments or sackcloth; but by the standards of the period all were naked. (Bauman 1983: 88)

The motivating impulse behind this, as Bauman says, was 'the desire to proclaim an ideological message' (Bauman 1983: 88) through the metaphorical enactment of this message; this 'sign' was variously glossed as an indicator of how the powerful would be stripped of their worldly coverings, a sign of the future spiritual condition of the Church of England, or a trope of the spiritual condition of the Quaker enacting the sign (Bauman 1983: 88-9). Equally important, however, was the origin of these signs:

> The charter for these semiotic enactments was biblical; the Quakers saw themselves in the image of the apostles and prophets of the primitive Christian church and thus found themselves called upon to carry God's message – the Truth – to the world in similar ways ... In an age saturated with verbal religious discourse, striking nonverbal enactments represented a ready means of attracting attention to the Quaker message ... the performance of 'signs' was seen by the early Quakers as an appropriate and efficacious means of delivering reproofs and prophecies to the sinful world. (Bauman 1983: 84-5)

If, as for Quakers and other radicals, language was unreliable and fraught with the dangers of carnal infiltration and corruption (see Chapters 3 and 5 above), then the enactment upon the body of these various signs could be a means of communicating God's message more powerfully. In the same way, it would be possible to read the women sectaries' accounts of recriminations and persecutions as records of non-verbal signs of their chosen status – for there were countless biblical precedents for the persecution of the godly, from the Israelites in Egypt (see Vokins 1691: 20-1) to the sufferings of Christ himself (see Trapnel 1654b: 23; Waugh 1656). Such accounts in themselves, then, can be seen as authentications and guarantees of the godliness of the subject.

'And so you, dear babes': dialogics and textual address

As well as paying attention to the function of these representations of opposition to and persecution of the 'self' of the author-figure in terms of their authentication of her godly status, it is also important to consider how such representations function to shape the texts themselves: for the texts do not exist separate from the responses they anticipate, but are structured in relation to, and therefore through, them. The implications for a text of such an observation have been most widely debated within dialogic theory, and it is to this that I shall now turn in order to explore some of the the issues for the texts and their authors of their anticipated readerships.

As recent work on Bakhtinian dialogic theory has amply demonstrated, neither spoken utterances nor written texts are articulated in a vacuum, but are produced in relation to the (anticipated) receiver of that utterance. This 'recognition of the im-possibility of saying, meaning or, indeed, *being*, without the reciprocating presence of an addressee' (Pearce 1994: 2; original emphasis) is the founding observation on which all dialogic philosophy is based. Two implications of this principle need to be further drawn out: first, that there are no exceptions to this analysis of the utterance: even the most apparently private text, such as the personal diary, for example, is 'a discourse informed by the cultural codes, values and interests of the social group to which we belong' (Pearce 1994: 41). Second, the addressee may be actual or imag-ined, specific or general:

> Utterance, as we know, is constructed between two socially organised people, and in the absence of a real addressee, an addressee is presupposed in the person, so to speak, of a normal representative of the social group to which the speaker belongs ... we assume as our addressee a contemporary of our literature, our science, our moral and legal code.
> (Voloshinov, *Marxism and the Philosophy of Language* (1929), quoted in Pearce 1994: 40)

Pearce goes on to quote what she calls 'one of the most eloquent expressions of dialogism', which indeed gestures towards many of the implications of this initial observation:

> Orientation of the word toward the addressee has an extremely high significance. In point of fact, *word is a two-sided act*. It is determined equally by *whose* word it is and *for whom* it is meant. As word, it is precisely *the product of the reciprocal relationship between*

speaker and listener, addresser and addressee. Each and every word expresses the 'one' in relation to the 'other'. I give myself verbal shape from another's point of view of the community to which I belong. A word is a bridge thrown between myself and another. If one end of the bridge depends on me, then the other depends on my addressee. A word is a territory shared by both addresser and addressee, by the speaker and his interlocutor. (Voloshinov, *Marxism and the Philosophy of Language* (1929), quoted in Pearce 1994: 43; original emphasis)

This quotation itself is suggestive of many of the insights of dialogic analysis that are most pertinent to the seventeenth-century writings discussed in this book. First, the idea that all utterances are produced for a real or imagined addressee is borne out in significant ways in these texts: I have, for example, already cited a number of sectarian texts specifically addressed to named individuals or communities, such as Hester Biddle's *Wo to Thee City of Oxford* (1655), Grace Barwick's *To All Present Rulers, Whether Parliament, or Whom Soever of England* (1659), Jeane Bettris's address (1657) to the inhabitants of Aylesbury, or the dedication of Jane Turner's autobiography to her 'dear brethren at Newcastle, Berwick and Scotland' (Turner 1653). Second, the determining effect of the addressee on the text is clear in any number of examples: the very title of *Anna Trapnel's Report and Plea* (1654) suggests not only that there is an addressee, but also that the subject matter needs to be articulated as a plea to that addressee: it must convince him (probably) of the justness of Trapnel's account. The title of *A Vindication of Anne Wentworth* (1677) tells a similar story of a text constructed not only for someone else, but in relation to their attitudes and expectations: a vindication is both necessarily addressed to someone else, and constructed in such a way as will be most likely to effect such a vindication. Katherine Chidley's *The Justification of the Independent Churches of Christ* (1641) is produced in answer to Thomas Edwards's attack on Independency, and is structured as a point-for-point refutation of his arguments. Indeed, it is worth noting to what extent the dialogic character of the texts is announced, in a compressed but unmistakable form, in the titles alone of these texts: the words 'report', 'plea', 'vindication' and 'justification' proclaim from the outset that these texts are written to perform a particular function, from information-giving to persuasion, in relation to a particular audience. Lastly, the textual production of the author-figure through the addressee's 'view of the community to which I belong' suggests particularly clearly the process that I identified in particular in Chapter 4, whereby the representation of the author-figure as weak, passive, an instrument in the hand of God, and obedient to his will rather than to their own, drew on current ideas about the nature of the godly and, in particular, the nature of the individual who might be chosen by God to prophesy. In each of these instances, then, the addressee can be seen to have a key function in the production of the text – so that, indeed, the text can be said to be 'dialogic', in dialogue with this addressee.

Even more pertinent for this study, however, are the propositions made in dialogic theory in relation to the complexities of the addressee-figure, and consequently of the text itself. The suggestion is that texts rarely address a single, unified addressee, but are likely to address any number of different addressee-positions:

> This addressee can be an immediate participant-interlocutor in an everyday dialogue, a
> differentiated collective of specialists in some particular area of cultural comunication,
> a more or less differentiated public, ethnic group, contemporaries, like-minded people,
> opponents and enemies, a subordinate, a superior, someone who is lower, higher, famil-
> iar, foreign, and so forth. And it can also be an indefinite, unconcretized *other* ... Both
> the composition and, particularly, the style of the utterance depend on those to whom
> the utterance is addressed, how the speaker (or writer) senses and imagines his address-
> ees, and the force of their effect on the utterance. (Bakhtin, *Speech Genres and Other
> Late Essays* (1952-53), quoted in Pearce 1994: 73-4)

Thus, a text may address two or more of these addressees *sequentially* (which Pearce
identifies as 'shifting' or 'split' address'), or *simultaneously* ('multiple address'); both
of these (amongst others) are indicated by the term 'double-voiced discourse' (Pearce
1994; 21-2, 50-2). This helps account for texts which might seem to exhibit a contradictory range of positions: considering again the title of Anna Trapnel's *Report and
Plea*, we can see even here an example of split address: the 'report' might be addressed to one kind of addressee – perhaps somebody looking for a clearly documented account of her travels in Cornwall, her prophesying there, and her subsequent imprisonment – whilst the 'plea' might address either those antagonistic,
hostile or cynical towards her experiences and her prophecies, or those who have
power over her and need convincing of her version of events and their meanings.
Similarly, Katherine Chidley's text (1641) can be read as an example of split address:
in its prefatory quotation of the biblical account of Jael's destruction of Sisera (see p.
71 above), it at first addresses those sympathetic to her challenge to, and defeat of, a
more powerful male figure in defence of Independency, whilst later it identifies the
author-figure as a 'poor worm, and unmeet to deal with you [Thomas Edwards, her
disputant]' (Chidley 1641: 81), in which she addresses not only Edwards himself but
also those who identify weakness and deference in women as signifiers of worthiness and
modesty. Single texts, then, typically address a wide range of different constituencies.

I want to focus now on the specific discursive formation of two particular
constituencies of addressee for sectarian writers: the 'opponents and enemies' and
the 'like-minded people' identified in my last quotation from Bakhtin. As we have
already seen, sectarian texts often aroused strong feelings of both antagonism (from
religious, political or other sectarian opponents) and sympathy (from like-minded co-
sectaries). Edward Burrough, for example, (a Quaker) published his hostile reply to
the Baptist Jane Turner's *Choice Experiences* (1653) within a year of the latter's
appearance; whilst Anna Trapnel was able to publish four texts in a single year
(1654), a prodigality which testifies to there being a market for her prophecies
(particularly since two of them were slightly reworked versions of the same narrative). According to dialogic terminology, a specific textual address to an antagonistic
addressee is designated 'hidden polemic', and to a sympathetic addressee 'hidden
dialogue'; again, these may exist sequentially or simultaneously within a text. Clearly, for
texts produced within the context of spiritual communities that provoked equally

vehement opposition and loyalty, these two aspects of dialogic thinking are particularly apposite. For texts directed towards these constituencies of addressee, however, the modification enacted by the adjective 'hidden' seems over-cautious and inappropriate; the 'dialogue' and the 'polemic' in these texts, far from being hidden, are overt, direct, and unmistakable.

> In a hidden polemic the author's discourse is directed toward its own referential object, as in any other discourse, but at the same time every statement about the object is constructed in such a way that, apart from its referential meaning, a polemical blow is struck at the other's discourse on the same theme, at the other's statement about the same object ... The other's discourse is not itself reproduced, it is merely implied, but the entire structure of the speech would be completely different if there were not this reaction to another person's implied words ... In hidden polemic ... the other's words are treated antagonistically, and this antagonism, no less than the very topic being discussed, is what determines the author's discourse. (Bakhtin, *Problems of Dostoevsky's Poetics* (1929), quoted in Pearce 1994: 53)

Chidley's text, just referred to, would be a perfect example of this not-so-hidden polemic; Anne Wentworth's *Vindication* (1677) of herself is structured throughout in relation to the designations of herself by her opponents as self-willed, passionate, revengeful and, above all, mad (see in particular Wentworth 1677: 8–9). Anna Trapnel's apparent longing to return to the privacy of the closet (see Chapter 4 above, pp. 100–2) is clearly engaging with a particular dominant understanding of women's proper place; the focus on illness also discussed in Chapter 4 offers both a justification for writing and a model for others to follow. In these, then, we can see the text in polemic 'with censorious "answer words" not present in the text itself' (Pearce 1994: 185). We see a textual anticipation of hostility to their accounts of their authors' actions on the grounds that they were women refusing the confines of the domestic and the familial, instead engaging in the immodest act of public utterance, and particularly on the grounds that the sects, particularly the Fifth Monarchists and Quakers, represented a spiritual and political agenda that was anathema to the dominant religious and political groupings. As women members of the sects, these writers were clearly vulnerable to these more powerful groups, and needed to justify their activities to them in order to shield themselves from their criticisms, condemnations or attacks.

These texts speak not only to critics, however, but also to fellow-believers, so that we can trace 'dialogue' as well as 'polemic' through them. To these addressees, in particular, messages of encouragement, of strength even in adversity, would be seen to be paramount, as would evidence that would reassure sympathisers that these prophecies were indeed the work of God. The Quaker Elizabeth Hincks's *The Poor Widow's Mite* (1671) is dedicated to: 'such bees as suck their honey from the flowers and blossoms that God makes to spring; that they may have to keep themselve alive in the dark stormy winter 1671' (Hincks 1671: 1). Throughout, the text is in dialogue, sometime explicitly, sometimes implicitly, with particular issues for Quakers at this time. In a time of concern about 'backsliding' amongst Friends, she writes:

> So those that true experience have, pray tell it to each other
> What for their souls the Lord hath done, be it sister or brother
>
> (Hincks 1671: 6)

Here Hincks is addressing the need for Quakers to reinforce each other's faith through dialogue with each other. Later, she confirms the post-Restoration shift in Quaker practice towards quietism, pacificism, and non-engagement with contemporary politics:

> And therefore are our meetings now, not kept in any spite
> Of king, or law, or parliament, but purely in God's sight.
>
> (Hincks 1671: 16)

Subsequent sections of the text are headed 'Something about Speaking, Who is to Speak, or What to be Spoken?' (in which she condemns the no-longer-acceptable practice of prophesying on the basis of dreams: such 'dreaming prophets', she says, 'do fawn and lie and flatter' (Hincks 1671: 18)); 'Something about Silence', 'Something about the Cause of Darkness, Ignorance and Persecution', and 'Something as to the Order in our Meetings, wherein we do not Respect Persons, for which the Spirit stirs up to Persecution' (Hincks 1671: 20, 27, 35). Throughout, then, Hincks's text is in dialogue with the principal Quaker debates of the time, concerning the status of prophecy, speaking, silence, persecution, and the organisation of meetings. Similarly, Sarah Jones's exhortation to her readers is a clear example of an explicit address to a sympathetic addressee: 'And so you, dear babes, that are little and weak in your own eyes, to you is this message sent, look not at your own weakness, but look at him who is calling you in his eternal love, who will make the weak strong, and will pull down the mighty from their seat' (Jones 1650: 2). It can also, however, be seen to be in polemic with a hostile audience, in its warning of the inevitability of the divine overturning of current rank and hierarchies. Likewise, the sectaries' accounts of hostile responses from critics cited above can be seen as instances of dialogue, in that they offer confirmation of the author/prophet's status through suffering at the hands of the ungodly, but also of polemic, as they demonstrate the inevitable failure of the persecution and its power merely to strengthen their resolve. Evans and Chevers's account (1662) of their imprisonment by the Inquisition in Malta is an example of precisely this: their narrative of their persecutions in prison both addresses and denigrates their oppressors, and confirms their own strength and righteousness.

This recognition of the multiplicity of address within a given text, and its capacity to anticipate at once a sympathetic and an antagonistic audience brings me to the final element of dialogic theory that I want to mention here: a consideration of the importance of the extraverbal (or extratextual) context for the production of meaning. Whilst an emphasis on *dialogue* inevitably foregrounds the verbal or linguistic construction of meaning, the Bakhtin school also included a consideration of the *nonspoken*, extra-linguistic constituents of dialogue. Voloshinov, for example, urged

> the study of the connection between concrete verbal interaction and the extraverbal
> situation – both the immediate situation and, through it, the broader situation ... *Verbal*

communication can never be understood and explained outside of this connection with a concrete situation. Verbal intercourse is inextricably interwoven with communication of other types, all stemming from the common ground of production. It goes without saying that the word cannot be divorced from this eternally generative, unified process of communication. In its concrete connection with a situation, verbal communication is always accompanied by social acts of a nonverbal character (the performance of labor, the symbolic acts of a ritual, a ceremony etc.), and it is often only an accessory to these acts, merely carrying out an auxiliary role. (Voloshinov, *Marxism and the Philosophy of Language* (1929), quoted in Pearce 1994: 42; original emphasis.)

Pearce goes on to give precise examples of just how this extraverbal context functions in relation to particular utterances (see Pearce 1994: 77–8) but, crucially for this study, notes how this observation relates not only to the 'unified purview' shared by two interlocutors, but can broaden to include 'family, kinsmen, nation, class, days, years and whole epochs' (Voloshinov, 'Discourse in Life and Discourse in Poetry', *The Bakhtin School Papers* (1924–28), quoted in Pearce 1994: 77). In considering the writings of women from the sects this is important, for it allows us to take account of the specific extratextual circumstances in which texts were produced: the way that conversion narratives, for example, were written as part of the process whereby a new member was admitted to a congregation, or the way that Anna Trapnel's *The Cry of a Stone* (1654) was transcribed from her utterances whilst she was in a trance that lasted twelve days.

Moreover, this inclusion of the extraverbal context also facilitates the recognition of the operation of power dynamics within the dialogic process: for necessarily there will be power differentials between author and particular addressee-positions. By recognising the multiplicity of addressee-positions, we are reminded of 'the power dynamics that operate in each and every act of communication' (Pearce 1994: 74):

By naming relationships between friends and family, between persons of 'higher or lower social standing', [Voloshinov] alerts us to the power dynamic that is present in every verbal (spoken or textual) exchange. Every utterance is determined fundamentally by the degree of intimacy, formality or social hierarchy that informs our relationship with our addressee. (Pearce 1994: 40)

Pearce welcomes this '*power-inscribed* version of the dialogic' (Pearce 1994: 101) in particular; as she says, 'As feminists we can never forget that our dialogues rarely exist between equal parties' (Pearce 1994: 102). This, then, is an essential coda to all discussions of dialogicality, for these can, at times, conflate notions of the *reciprocity* of dialogue with a 'utopian tendency' to see this reciprocity as conciliatory and democratising, rather than as a struggle over utterances and their meanings. As previous discussions in this book have stressed, an understanding of the extratextual circumstances of writing – in particular, the position of the sects *vis-à-vis* the prevailing social and political circumstances (the relative openness of the 1650s contrasted with the repression and persecution of the post-Restoration years, for example), and the prevailing definitions of femininity and their relationship to writing and publishing

– are an indispensable element in the reading of these texts. Not the least reason for its importance is precisely the way in which this reading necessitates a consideration of the power dynamics in the production and construction of these texts.

'Reader, whosoever thou beest': Anna Trapnel's *Report and Plea* (1654)

Having established the range of possible applications of dialogic theory for sectarian women's writing in general, I want now to offer a more detailed reading of one text in relation to this body of theory: Anna Trapnel's *Report and Plea* (1654). This text is, as I have suggested is indicated by its title, a sustained piece of both dialogue and polemic: the text is, from the outset and throughout, overtly and directly structured around an engagement with both a sympathetic and an antagonistic addressee. The title-page announces it as not only a 'report and plea', but also offers an alternative title, naming the text as 'a narrative' and 'a defiance'. This double title, in which each alternative title is itself split into two parts, serves as an initial marker of the 'double-voiced discourse' of the ensuing text.

Trapnel wrote and published the text in 1654, hard on the heels of two other accounts of her words: *The Cry of a Stone* and *Strange and Wonderful Newes from White-Hall* had already appeared that year, both giving accounts of the trance she fell into at the examination of the Fifth Monarchist preacher and writer Vavasor Powell by the Council of State at Whitehall. This episode had brought her into the public eye, and consequently she was invited to go on a mission to broadcast her prophecies to sympathisers in Cornwall. As a result of her politically contentious prophesying on this visit, she was arrested, tried, returned to London and imprisoned in Bridewell. The *Report and Plea* is an account of this journey and its consequences.

The text opens with a prefatory epistle, addressed 'To the Reader'; however, the 'reader' thus addressed shifts back and forth through this epistle from occupying an antagonistic position to a sympathetic one. It opens, for example, with the words:

> The Lord, and my Father (courteous reader) having put me upon this work and employment, I pray don't call it idleness, lest you would be likened to those 'who call good evil, and evil good; and put darkness for light, and light for darkness'; against whom there is a woe pronounced from the Lord (Isaiah 5:20). (Trapnel 1654b: sig. A2^r)

Whilst the projected reader may be 'courteous', there is no expectation that s/he will be friendly; indeed, on the contrary, the first 'reader' to be addressed by the text is quite clearly a hostile one. From here, however, the text moves on to incorporate an address to Trapnel's supporters. It offers both a direct address to them, urging them to draw from the text a greater understanding of how ill-treated she has been: 'Pray, Christian reader, well observe the ensuing discourse, whereby you may understand the voice of malice and envy uttered and acted by the clergy and rulers against me (Trapnel 1654b: sig. A3^r) and an *indirect* address, offering biblical precedents and justifications for the suffering they endure:

> Power and spear is drawn against the Lord and his anointed; for the holy unction that

the holy one hath given his, they suffer, and who can be sad, whatsoever is laid upon them by men or devils, when thereby they are not losers, but great gainers from the Lord, though losers from men? And therefore men may give losers leave to speak to them, which have offered them so much injury. (Trapnel 1654b: sig. A2ᵛ)

This shifting engagement with the concerns of her opponents, warning them of divine retribution, and with the concerns of her sympathisers, with reassurance that their suffering is a sign of their righteousness and ultimate salvation, characterises the double address of the text, a duality that is maintained, in one form or another, throughout the whole piece.

The conclusion to the prefatory epistle makes clear just how central this multiple address is to the structure and aim of the whole text:

Reader, I beseech this of thee, whosoever thou beest; under forms,[11] or without forms; obedient to ordinances for the Lord's sake, or yet in the dark concerning them: I beseech all sorts of people, high and low, to weigh in the balance of the sanctuary,[12] the true relation which followeth. (Trapnel 1654b: sig. A4ʳ)

This speculation on the variations in spiritual grace and social rank amongst her potential readership highlights the unpredictability of just who will read the text, why they will read it, and what they will make of it. It also indicates the necessity of addressing it to her two main potential constituencies, her opponents and her sympathisers. It is this, I would suggest, that accounts for the two principal sections of the ensuing text: first, 'The Narrative or Relation' (Trapnel 1654b: 1), and, secondly, a much shorter section entitled:

A defiance to all reproachful, scandalous, base, horrid, defaming speeches, which have been vented by rulers, clergy, and their auditors, and published in scurrilous pamphlets up and down in cities and countries, against Anna Trapnel, late prisoner in Bridewell for the testimony of Jesus the Lord. (Trapnel 1654b: 49)

Overall, it is possible to read the 'Narrative' as an exercise in 'dialogue', addressed principally to a sympathetic audience, and the 'Defiance' as in 'polemic' with her detractors, answering in turn each of the many accusations that has been made against her. Thus, the 'Narrative' begins with eleven pages of 'dialogue' with sectarian concerns with the authenticity of Trapnel's call to travel to Cornwall to prophesy. This addresses the persistent sectarian anxiety that such calls may, instead of being of divine origin, emanate either from the devil or from the will of the individual believer herself. Most texts, to a greater or lesser extent, offer evidence of divine involvement in an action; here, Trapnel offers six pages of detailed narrative relating to her call, her reluctance to go, her temptations from the devil to refuse God's call or to incapacitate herself to prevent her going, and her final conviction that the call is indeed from God and must therefore be followed. Similarly, her narrative of her journey to Cornwall, her sympathetic reception from both previous sympathisers and from the hitherto unsympathetic, her accounts of the converse she has with God at key moments, her outwitting of the Justices at her arrest and committal for trial, and her survival of and release from imprisonment in Bridewell are written in such a way as together to testify to the lack of 'self' in the narrative and, conversely, to the palpable presence of God in the proceedings. In the 'Defiance', Trapnel expressly addresses her opponents in the title, and then in the text answers their accusations that she is a witch, impostor, vagabond, whore, and 'dangerous seditious person'. She counters each of these accusations quite explicitly, offering evidence that will both confirm her own self-interpretation and undermine theirs.

However, because of the instability and unknowability of the composition of the readership, and the resulting 'double-voiced discourse' of the text's multiple address, each of these sections can also be said to be *simultaneously* dialogue and polemic, addressing at once (rather than sequentially) both constituencies. This is the case not only of the textual addressee – the still notional readers of her text – but also of the addressees in the text – those people who come to witness her prophesying during her visit to Cornwall: 'And after dinner, there came many to see me, some out of good-will, and love to what they had heard was of God in me, and others came to gaze, and others to catch at my words, so as to reproach me; but the Lord taught me how to speak before them all' (Trapnel 1654b: 15). When prophesying, Trapnel could not differentiate between the different constituents of her audience: one utterance must serve all, and the utterance that does so is, of course, the one from God, for it is he that 'taught me to speak before them *all*' (my emphasis). A similar problem is addressed by her writing. Again, she cannot match specific utterance to specific reader; instead, a simultaneous multiple address needs to 'speak' to 'them all'.

The 'Narrative', which comprises the main section of the text and is the account of the journey, arrest, trial and imprisonment of Trapnel, is, I have suggested, principally addressing a sympathetic addressee. This addressee is offered extensive evidence of the divine origins of Trapnel's actions, through accounts of her visions, through her interpretations of them, and through her citations of biblical texts that act as precedents for these visions and interpretations. Thus, early in the narrative, Trapnel writes:

> And when I came to my friends' house at Hillington, I lay all next day silent, but exceedingly filled with the presence of the Lord, who shewed me a vision of my Cornwall journey: I beheld high rocky hills, and variety of places and towns, and how I should be as I rode in the coach, much melody I should have; this I saw, and heard this saying, that as sure as Paul in Acts 16:9 'had a vision appeared in the night: There stood a man of Macedonia and prayed Paul, saying, Come over into Macedonia and help us'; and the Lord said, 'As truly do I thy Lord call thee to Cornwall by this vision'. Then I answered, and said, 'Paul was to preach there; what is that word to me?', then reply was, 'But as sure as his was a vision from the Lord to go to Macedonia, so as sure had I a call and true vision to go to Cornwall.' (Trapnel 1654b: 2-3)

Whilst this account of the author's vision, its interpretation and the authentication of these through reference to specific biblical texts offers evidence to the sympathetic addressee of Trapnel's status as prophet, it also can be seen to be in polemic with an antagonistic addressee, in that it counters, through these same means, any mis-

166

interpretations by her antagonists of her actions. Misinterpretation is something expressly anticipated in the text on a number of occasions: Trapnel records, for example, how she was reluctant to speak in front of certain people:

> I seeing many come into the room, and Mr Powel, a teacher in those parts, came in with his wife, and another woman, so that being there, I thought to be silent; but some desiring to have me speak, I said I was loth to speak before that critical-pated man, who would take my words and put his own sense upon them, and so ensnare me; and it proved according as I said. (Trapnel 1654b: 16)

Elsewhere, she notes how she had the 'courage to look my accusers in the face: which was no carnal boldness, though they called it so' (Trapnel 1654b: 24), and, later, how one of her guards 'endeavoured to catch my words, and to ensnare me, putting his own sense upon them' (Trapnel 1654b: 33). Words, Trapnel discovers, are indeed a 'bridge' thrown between (at least) two people, in which only 'one end of the bridge' depends on her, the other depending on her addressee (see Voloshinov, quoted on p. 159 above); over this latter element, she finds she has no control. Thus, 'misunderstanding' – in other words, an interpretation at odds with the author's own – is something which is explicitly acknowledged and addressed by this text.

The misappropriation and misconstruction of her actions and words, then, was a danger that Trapnel anticipated. It is also, though, something that the particular construction of this text itself goes some way to mitigate, precisely through its combination of polemic and dialogue. On several occasions, at key moments in the narrative, the text records a hostile response to Trapnel from a particular audience which is then transformed – through the kind of process of vision, interpretation and citation discussed above – into a sympathetic one. When she first arrives at the house of Captain Langdon, for example, a Fifth Monarchist sympathiser with whom she stayed in Cornwall, she records how many people came to see her:

> and most of them gave me but a sour greeting, they having been informed before concerning my spirit, as it was reported to me afterwards; but they frowningly and dissemblingly saluted me, though their hearts were against me, as many of them made it appear largely afterwards; and some became loving friends among them, that loved me not when I first came. (Trapnel 1654b: 11)

Here we see the tranformation of anatagonism to sympathy effected through the physical presence of Trapnel herself; former impressions had been based on (mis)information about her, which were then dispelled (in some cases) through witnessing the prophet for themselves.

The same process is recorded in relation to Trapnel's committal proceedings. As she is taken to the court, she tells how:

> I had followed me abundance of all manner of people, men and women, boys and girls, which crowded after me; and some pulled me by the arm, and stared me in the face, making wry faces at me, and saying, 'How do you now? How is it with you now?' And thus they mocked and derided at me, as I went to sessions. (Trapnel 1654b: 23)

Again, the text establishes the antagonism of Trapnel's audience as they contemplate her for the first time. Following on from this is an account of Trapnel's performance in court, the dramatic qualities of the scene underlined by the way that the exchanges between Trapnel and the magistrates are at times set out as in a play, with the characters' names set next to their words, rather than the two being integrated into continuous prose. This not only stages Trapnel's triumph over the (consistently and persistently hostile) Justices, but also provides the means for the transformation of the initially hostile spectating crowd into a supportive and sympathetic band of disciples:

> And as I went in the crowd, many strangers were very loving and careful to help me out
> of the crowd: and the rude multitude said, 'Sure this woman is no witch, for she speaks
> many good words, which the witches could not.' And thus the Lord made the rude
> rabble to justify his appearance. (Trapnel 1654b: 28)

Trapnel's appearance in court is thus framed by her encounters with crowds who, when they witness her for themselves, change their view of her. This framing device both gives an account of the transformation of response from hostility to sympathy, and also enacts this transformation through denying the need to address the hostile and the sympathetic with different arguments and different evidence. Presentation of the truth, she asserts, will be sufficient to erase the distinction between the two constituencies. This truth is God's truth rather than a chronological or narrative accuracy: 'I shall relate the truth without addition: though I cannot (it may be) remember all the passages in order, yet as many as the Lord brings to my mind, I shall relate' (Trapnel 1654b: sig. A4ʳ). The truth is figured in the body of Trapnel and the word of God, which are unified through the process of prophesying. Witnessing either of these phenomena can be transformative: 'As some have said, they thought I had been a monster, or some ill-shaped creature, before they came and saw, who then said they must change their thoughts, for I was a woman like others, that were modest and civil, and many commending words they uttered' (Trapnel 1654b: 49). Witnessing God's truth, whether in the 'modest and civil' shape of Trapnel herself or in the divinely originating words she spoke when prophesying, was enough to change antagonism to sympathy, and (in dialogic terms) to turn polemic to dialogue. For once the transformation has been effected, the text's task will no longer be to convince a hostile addressee of the injustice of their response, but instead to demonstrate and share the author's certainty of the justice of her actions and words with a sympathiser. Her 'report' of the 'truth' thus constitutes her plea to her oppressors; and yet through enacting the plea and convincing her detractors, the plea once again becomes a report. Such a refusal of opposition, and a recasting of it as sympathy, is demonstrated in one part of her account of her time in Bridewell:

> And truly the Lord made this and many more annoyances, received in Bridewell prison,
> to be very pleasantly embraced by divine love appearing in the midst of all trials; my
> God made this smarting scourge (as from man it was so) but God I say made it easy; for
> his tenderness was much, he made foes become friends, and the harsh to be kind, and

overcame the rough and hasty spirits ... and all things that were afflictive, the Lord quickly broke such fetters. (Trapnel 1654b: 44–5)

The polarities between hostility and sympathy, persecution and divine reward, are thus denied in the narrative. It becomes impossible to distinguish absolutely between the two constituencies of addressee, for to do so would be to fix them in these two contrary positions and deny the transformative power of her experiences and her words on her antagonists. It is therefore fundamental that the two be merged, and be addressed simultaneously through a 'report' of the 'truth'. She writes at the conclusion to her 'defence' (in which a similar merging of hostile and sympathetic addressees is enacted):

And now in this defiance let all take their share; enemies take yours, and don't be offended at true speaking, but be humbled and repent that your evil words, and unjust actions, and thoughts of your heart may be forgiven you, and for you I shall pray.

And to friends, I have this word, do not you find fault with oppressions, but labour to amend them with candid and charitable constructions, and spiritual application of those scripture observations which are your due. (Trapnel 1654b: 58–9)

Although enemies and friends are separated in this conclusion to the 'defiance', suggesting a split or shifting address, it also makes clear that the defiance itself has addressed both: 'let all take their share'. Moreover, it anticipates a process whereby those who remain her enemies may find mercy – through their own prayers and through hers – and thereby, the inference is, become her friends. Thus these apparently polarised categorisations of 'enemies' and 'friends', and also therefore of dialogue and polemic, are *necessarily* called into question and re-addressed as unfixed and fluctuating, for it is on the possiblity of such a process of transformation that Trapnel's work is predicated.

The transformative capacity of Trapnel and her words, however, are not total; there is a limit to the changes she expects to bring about, and these limits are set most clearly in relation to the social rank and power of her audience. Those who are untransformed by her presence or her words and remain hostile to her are those of higher social rank and who have institutional power over her: the 'rulers and clergy' whom she consistently brackets together (see Trapnel 1654b: sig. A3[r], 21, 49). From these, she expects no conversion to sympathy, for these are the people who will be toppled from power when her prophecies are fulfilled; her constituency of potential supporters comprises those of lower rank, those who make up the crowds who come to gaze at her, those who stand to benefit from the upending of hierarchies which the Fifth Monarchists expected with the coming of King Jesus and the establishing of the New Jerusalem. This is made explicit at the time the Justices first try to arrest her; as her supporters refuse to assist in the process, 'one of my friends told them that they must fetch their silk gowns to do it then, for the poor would not do it' (Trapnel 1654b: 21). Trapnel's dialogue is quite explicitly one between unequal parties, then: it is the site of struggle between institutional power and its absence, between godliness and ungodliness, between belief and unbelief. These disparate elements are at stake, in one form or another, whether the addressee is antagonistic or sympathetic. Whether the text is addressing a sympathiser requiring authenticating evidence of Trapnel's divine call or an opponent whose interpretations must be countered, there is never a simply reciprocal, let alone conciliatory, series of dialogic exchanges; indeed, there is little temptation to read Trapnel's text as anything other than a dialogics of struggle, perhaps even of battle (see Bauer in Pearce 1994: 101).

A dialogic reading of Trapnel's *Report and Plea* demonstrates unmistakably the extent to which the text is predicated on, and structured through, an anticipated response. That response incorporates both the hostile and the sympathetic and, whilst the address at times quite clearly differentiates between these two addressee-positions and addresses their concerns sequentially, the text as a whole can be seen to address both constituencies simultaneously, constituting a double-voiced address that incorporates the possibility of transformation, of the hostile becoming sympathetic, within this mode of address. Thus dialogics can usefully highlight not only the structure of a text, but also, through this, become an interpretive tool for the working through of the text's possible meanings.

Responses, both actual and anticipated, were, then, highly significant for the production of this writing. The texts are structured by and predicated upon their projected readerships and their responses, and are thus resolutely and passionately products of their time: they are written from within particular political and religious groupings, to whom they write in order to belong,[13] rather than to set themselves outside. They are in dialogue with these groups, just as they are in polemic with their critics. However, the anticipation and construction of these different addressee-positions, sympathetic and antagonistic, does not seem to depend on the genre of the writing, in the same way that the actual responses discussed above are not generically determined. Whether women were preaching, prophesying or writing their spiritual autobiographies, male critics, from both within and outside the sects, were united in their hostile responses to these activities. The puzzling question still remains, then, as to why autobiography should meet the same level of hostility as prophecy. What were the particular characteristics of spiritual autobiographies that meant they were greeted with such intense hostility? And furthermore, might the hostility be explained by what they had in common with the more obviously political texts?

'Despising the service of women': the threat of female authorship

In order to answer these questions and make sense of the hostile reaction to the publication of spiritual autobiography, it is necessary to place it within the context of its generic history. The increase in the numbers of spiritual autobiographies written after 1640 is generally taken to be associated with the increasing influence of Puritanism and the later radical sects at this time. Despite their many differences, these sects had in common the belief that all of God's elect were equal in grace in the sight of God, and were required to take an active part in their own spiritual well-being. This had particular implications for women. This spiritual equality allowed women a sphere of activity in which to articulate their faith, instead of having to be receptacles of received religious ideas. Such liberty manifested itself with increasing force in many areas, in preaching and parish protest as well as in prophesying, tract-writing, and spiritual autobiography; but it was especially in the area of spiritual autobiography that women could, and did, claim equality with men. Indeed, the genre itself testified to this claim, for its focus on the individual believer, whether male or female, proclaimed the primacy of that individual in God's scheme.

This tendency towards individualism[14] encouraged, amongst other things, a belief in the necessity of action: since the fundamental and all-embracing aim was to fulfil God's will on earth, then no effort and no sacrifice would be too great.[15] Judging by some of the texts under consideration here, it seems that men were threatened by the idea that any form of spiritual action would deflect women from their ordained position as subordinate to men. Jane Turner's stress on the fact that she wrote in her husband's absence is one indication of this; other women's reluctance to publish is another. The Quaker Elizabeth Stirredge, for example, wrote of her fear concerning the reaction her writings would receive: 'Lord, look upon my affliction, and lay no more upon me than I am able to bear. They will not hear me that am a contemptible instrument. And seeing they despise the service of women so much, oh Lord make use of them that are more worthy' (Stirredge 1711: 70). Women, despite being equal with men in the sight of God, equal to the point that he called upon them to undertake his work and convey his message to his people, were by no means received in the same way in the fulfilment of this work as the men with whom they were purportedly equal.

If men feared that spiritual activity would deflect women from their proper position within the family and household, then closer examination of spiritual autobiographies suggests that they were quite right to be fearful: the threat posed by these texts becomes much clearer once we look at the actual subject matter on which these women writers concentrate, and at what they omit from their accounts. Joan Vokins, for example, a Quaker writing her autobiography in the 1690s, said: 'I could take no comfort in husband or children, house, or land, or any visibles, for want of the marriage union with the lamb of God' (Vokins 1691: 35). Here she directly addresses the spiritual, but also compares it with her material circumstances: her earthly marriage is compared with her spiritual union with Christ. There is no doubt which liaison is more important to her. As Cynthia Pomerleau wrote, this perhaps illustrates part of the function of religion in Vokins's life: 'In effect, she could admit that she was not satisfied with her domestic lot without actually rebelling against it' (Pomerleau 1980: 29). For Vokins, then, husbands and children of necessity come second:

> if I had disobeyed the Lord, to please them, I might have provoked him to have withholden his mercies from us all, and to bring his judgements upon us ... Then husbands, and wives, and parents, and children, and servants, shall receive according to their doings; and none that disobeys the Lord can be excused. (Vokins 1691: 23-4)

What is also clear, however, is how much Vokins's own peace of mind depends upon following her divinely-initiated course: 'The feeling of his sweet refreshing life that he communicates to my soul, is a hundred-fold better than husband or children, or any other outward mercies that he hath made me a partaker of, though very near and dear to me' (Vokins 1691: 70). Significantly, it is almost only in the comparisons between God's demands and her family's that her family is mentioned; otherwise, the focus is exclusively on Vokins and her own spiritual progress.

It was perhaps this emphasis on the spiritual, to the exclusion of the material, that disturbed many male readers of women's early spiritual autobiographies. It is, in fact, one of the characteristics most often noted by critics in relation to spiritual autobiographies of this time: most interpret it as an indication that the sole interest of these writers was the spiritual, so that all things material were of no consequence. This assumes, however, that this 'impersonal' tendency has the same meaning for all the sectaries, irrespective of gender. But for women these familial details presented very particular problems. To include details of their homes, families and selves in any material sense would have laid them open to the charge of vainglory and immodesty, for it would have implied the singularity and inherent interest of their own circumstances. And yet to ignore these aspects was to imply that women's 'proper' areas of concern, their homes, husbands and children, were of secondary or even peripheral importance. This presented a paradoxical situation for these women writers; but, given that a choice had to be made, in almost all cases women chose finally to omit all references to their outward circumstances. Given the prescriptions concerning women's proper spheres of activity (the family and the household), the omission of such details by women writers would present a threat to male critics in a way that their omission by male sectaries would not.

The spiritual autobiography itself, then, presented particular problems for male critics, both generically, in that it was a place where women actively claimed equality with men, and also in terms of its denial of the primacy of the family in women's lives. This suggests that Ludlow's argument that it was only *public* religious activity by women that was met with hostility by men is untenable. Moreover, the distinction between private and public religious activity itself is hard to sustain after an investigation of the reception of the so-called private texts such as spiritual autobiographies. It is to the commonalities between these generically disparate 'public' and 'private' texts that I want now to turn, in order to assess what part these might have played in men's responses to them.

'The bridle of all subjection': condemnation and constraint

Before considering the general status of sectarian women's writing in the seventeenth century, I want first to outline what one seventeenth-century commentator said on the subject of women's religious activity. Daniel Rogers, a Puritan divine, gives a clear indication in his marriage manual *Matrimoniall Honour* (1642) that it was not the *subjects* of women's writing or preaching to which he objected, but its context and implications. He wrote that women who preach, prophesy or write have 'shaken off the bridle of all subjection to their husbands, ... not blushing one whit' (Daniel Rogers, *Matrimoniall Honour* (1642), quoted in Yoshioka 1977: 425). He argues that, even if what they say is unobjectionable or even spiritually sound, they are still of the devil's ranks, because they are usurping authority: 'Such immodesties and insolencies of women, not able to containe themselves within the boundes of silence and subjection, I am so farre from warranting, that I here openly defie them as ungrounded, and ungodly' (Daniel Rogers, *Matrimoniall Honour* (1642), quoted in Yoshioka 1977: 427). To Rogers, then, Trapnel's question as to 'who may bind where God hath loosed?' would have seemed irrelevant, for it stood in contradiction to the position of 'silence and subjection' that God had ordained for women in relation to their husbands.[16] *Any* spirit provoking women to preach or write, thereby breaking these 'boundes', was thought therefore to be the work of the devil. Women, Rogers's words imply, are unruly; they need a 'bridle' in order to keep them subject to their husbands.[17] Immodesties and insolencies are never far below the surface and so have to be 'contained' within certain bounds. The images that Rogers uses suggest constraint, restriction and the containment of forces that threaten to disrupt.

Rogers's reference to the 'boundes' of silence recalls the discussion in Chapter 2 of the contemporary seventeenth-century discourses of containment and feminine disorder. In Rogers's terms, women had to be 'contained' within the 'boundes' of silence and subjection to ensure that their intrinsic disorderliness was kept on a tight rein. The resulting humility and modesty were thus not 'natural', but had to be achieved or enforced. Rogers's train of thought goes some way towards explaining the kind of responses women writers received, and also men's fear and vehement hostility, as disorderliness threatened to break out.

Rogers's (and others') disquiet was well founded, in that women's writing, as well as preaching and travelling, was often a direct challenge to the authority of the husband over the wife. As we have already seen, Anne Wentworth defended her decision to leave her husband as necessary to save herself from his 'cruel usage', and also as crucial if she were to continue the work to which God had called her: namely, her writing, which, she tells us, her 'earthly husband in a most cruel manner hindered me from performing, seizing, and running away with my writings' (Wentworth 1677: 2, 4-5). Wentworth plainly sets limits on the authority ascribed to her husband, just as Katherine Chidley had done when she asked: 'what authority [the] unbelieving husband hath over the conscience of his believing wife. It is true he hath authority over her in bodily and civil respects, but not to be a Lord over her conscience; and the like may be said of fathers and masters' (Chidley 1641: 26). This forthright statement from Chidley gives substance to Rogers's fears: she and Wentworth (and, indeed, Vokins) are, doubtless, breaking the bounds of silence and subjection to their husbands by insisting both on the limits of their husband's authority, and on their duty to defy them if their consciences demand it. Likewise, the Quaker Thomas Curwen, writing of his wife Alice Curwen's response to God's call, invokes a notion of 'containment' (or its absence) directly reminiscent of Rogers's own use of the word: 'the Lord's presence was with her, wherein she could not contain herself, but she breathed forth praises to the Lord' (Curwen 1680: 'Thomas Curwen's Testimony'). Doing God's work, then, was conceived of precisely in terms of the breaching of boundaries, provided those boundaries were clearly 'carnal' rather than God-given.

Another clue to the hostility that met these texts by sectarian women is provided by the justifications for writing offered by these authors. Despite the repeated assertion that 'there is no self in this thing' (Trapnel 1654a: 42) ('this thing' referring to her prophesying), the central reference-point within these writings none the less remains the self: individual perceptions of truth and godliness. As Jane Turner put it, 'True Christian experience ... is truth brought home to the heart with life and power, by the spirit of God' (Turner 1653: 202). The decisive factor in deciding how to act is internal and personal, an individual apprehension of the 'spirit of God'. While this assertion of the primacy of the individual conscience and consciousness does not necessarily challenge the dominant social ideology, it did not balk at doing so if that was what this apprehension demanded. The precedent, the authority, for spiritual activity therefore was not fixed, formalised, or institutionalised, but was as fluid as the consciousness of the individual concerned.

Consequently, it was difficult, if not impossible, to define boundaries beyond which writers should not go; for if God called, a writer could not refuse to follow. The texts of a writer such as Anna Trapnel, for example, are open-ended in the sense that no area of her life, of her thoughts or of her experiences was out of bounds. The possibilities were limitless, provided that they were prefaced with a call from God to enact them. The openness of these writers to the hitherto unacceptable is one important element in the threat that women writers of spiritual treatises posed to male commentators of the time.

The final common element to these disparate texts that I want to consider is their didacticism: it was not only the public and political texts that aimed actively to instruct the reader, but also the most private of spiritual autobiographies.

Whilst the autobiography was concerned with the working-out of God's grace through the life and experiences of one individual, and therefore had a much more restricted or 'private' focus than the prophecies of the early Quakers or of Fifth Monarchists such as Mary Cary or Anna Trapnel, the genre none the less presented particular problems for sectarian writers. Both author and addressee needed reassurance that the actions being recounted were indeed actions for God and not for the individual, who was no more than God's instrument on earth. Whilst perpetual self-examination was necessary to ensure that it was God's will being done, and not either an act of self-glorification on the part of the believer or the work of Satan masquerading as God's will, the 'self', however, should not intrude. This had a particular relevance for the writers of spiritual autobiographies. On the one hand, this was a form appropriate to someone who saw their life as a pilgrimage, a working-out day by day of God's plan for one of his elect, delineating the times of doubt and certainty, alienation and reconciliation, in the life of the individual. On the other hand, it was a form of writing that laid its author open to charges of vainglory and immodesty, because of this necessary concentration on the life of that individual. This was countered by often very vigorous self-denials on the part of the author: in publishing his or her record, s/he would

repudiate the idea that it should be read because he [*sic*] was an exceptionally interesting person, a unique personality; no one in the seventeenth century could have done this without having to admit to the most monstrous egotism. Even the vulgar prophets [such as the Ranters Coppe or Foster] claimed a hearing because they had an urgent message for the world or because they found themselves being used as instruments of a mighty power: it was not ostensibly a matter of their personality, except when they had to reply to attacks which discredited their message and work. But, of course, whether the writer's concern was pastoral or evangelical or prophetic, he found himself involved in presenting a 'self' to the reader, if only because he was the main subject of the story. (Watkins 1972: 226-7)

The autobiography, then, was necessarily constructing a version of the author's self, and, moreover, it was doing so in the cause of didacticism. The 'self' was intended to teach by example, to engage the reader in such a way that he or she would then regard his or her life in a similar manner. This meant that the autobiography was not only a straightforward narration of events, but also provided a commentary and analysis of those events, to draw the reader towards the author's interpretation of his or her life. 'He tried to re-create his experiences so as to convey both the impact they had on him at the time and their meaning in the light of subsequent experience and knowledge' (Watkins 1972: 237). The self was at once irrelevant (there was nothing in that individual that accounted for God choosing her) and the focus of the text (in that the individual's experiences exemplified the work of God).

These 'private' texts, then, all have a public function. Despite Jane Turner's claims that her writing was intended as no more than 'a remembrancer of the old loving kindness of the Lord towards me', and thus only for 'my own private use', she then belies these words with a contradictory claim concerning the relationship between the private and the public in her writing. She recommends to the reader:

a close walking with God in all spiritual duties, meditations, self-examination, self-watching, self-judging, self-humbling and prayer ... not that these private duties are above public but that they prepare for public, and by these we are acquainted with our own hearts. (Turner 1653: 'A word from the Author to the Reader')

Examination of the self and the resulting self-knowledge are not therefore ends in themselves, but are preparations for public duties; and the words Turner has written are intended to facilitate this self-knowledge. As John Gardner wrote in his preface to Turner's work, 'These inward experiences are not intended to limit others, but to provoke self-examination and spiritual quickening' (Turner 1653: John Gardner, 'To the reader'). Even this most private of texts, then, has overtly didactic and public ends: they are, according to Turner, intended to promote the fulfilment of active, public duties in the reader.

The public implications of writing on such apparently private subjects as outlined above are still clearer in Anne Wentworth's *Vindication* of 1677. She defends all that she has written, including that which was 'to the prejudice and scandal' of her husband, on the grounds that she was commanded by God to write and publish. Her writings, she says, are both private and public: they concern 'the *peace of my own soul,* and *of the whole nation*' (Wentworth 1677: 6; original emphasis). When fellow Baptists from her own congregation rebuked her for what she was doing, she was confident that God would make the significance of their hostility clear. He 'will search out this matter, and make a true and manifest judgement of it, for there is nothing *hid* from him, and this matter is now become a *public figure*' (Wentworth 1677: 11). That her personal and private experiences have importance and relevance in a wider and more public sense is something that God has made clear to her:

> he afterwards revealed to me, (what I did not then know) that my *oppressions* and *deliverance* had a *public ministry* and *meaning* wrapped up in them ... and he has also revealed to me what wrath shall fall upon the *same spirit* throughout the nation, which everywhere oppresses the true seed, as I have been oppressed by it. (Wentworth 1677: 12, 13)

The private and public implications of her experiences and her writings are inseparable and interdependent. Events happening to an individual do not occur in isolation, but are connected with 'the same spirit throughout the nation', so that their meaning is both personal, spiritual, and private, and also political and public.

This interdependence is central to an understanding of why 'personal', spiritual texts like spiritual autobiographies were perceived as so subversive and threatening. As Owen Watkins suggested in *The Puritan Experience* (1972), all these works had a 'palpable design' on the reader: 'They were written to persuade, to cause reading to issue forth in action' (Watkins 1972: 233). Action, as opposed to mere reflection, was the desired end: as the Quaker Elizabeth Hooton wrote: 'it is not the hearers but the doers that shall be justified' (Hooton *et al.* 1652: 4). The refusal to recognise that the private was distinct from the public, and the resulting breaking of the accepted bounds of the private, then, is reinforced by the refusal of passivity embodied in these forceful attempts to teach, persuade, admonish, cajole, warn and convince the reader.

In conclusion, then, I am suggesting that the collapsing or refusal of the distinction between the private and the public in these texts, whether autobiographical or prophetic, enabled women's active engagement in the so-called masculine world of public and political affairs. The didactic significance of all the writing I have discussed thus confirms the problematic nature of the public/private distinction in this context, as, indeed, it has been shown to be in others.[18] Not only is it important to realise that this public/private distinction is misleading in relation to the kinds of women's writing being produced in the seventeenth century; it is also important to realise that the denial of this distinction by these writers themselves formed a crucial component of their justification of their own participation in political life. Transgressing the contemporary prescriptions of, or exhortations to, feminine modesty and silence, these seventeenth-century women writers refused to be bridled and constrained, justifying their intervention in contemporary politics through their appeal to God's authority. Such a refusal of their previous exclusion from political life constituted a threat to the established hierarchy of gender privilege and to women's position in relation to their domestic obligations. These domestic concerns are marginalised within these writings, where family matters are only rarely considered, and then generally only in an unfavourable comparison with the importance of their spiritual obligations. Furthermore, when there was real competition between these two sets of demands, the spiritual invariably triumphed. Reference to God's will justified a set of hitherto unjustifable actions for women: some used it to justify their independent movement around the country, and indeed around the world, and the consequent abandonment of their domestic duties; others used God's authority to set limits to their husbands' attempts to control their writing, and in the case of Anne Wentworth this led to the abandonment of her husband in order to fulfil God's command to write.

This combination – the rejection of the bounds of modesty by writing and publishing, and an engagement with the public sphere, necessitating the abandonment of domestic duties – was enough to incur the wrath or dismay of many men at this time. This makes clear why all these texts were met with such uniform hostility from men both outside and inside the radical sects. In the face of such hostility, these women's writings demonstrate an awareness of the precariousness of their position as writers: a precariousness which was precisely manifested in the quotation with which I began this paper: 'who may bind where God hath loosed?'.

Indeed, precariousness could be said to characterise sectarian women's position in relation to writing for publication. Whilst the 1640s and 1650s saw an unparalleled increase in published texts by women writers,[19] the vast majority of them from the sects, the 1660s and later decades saw a rapid decline in the production of all but the Quaker texts. If the discourse of the 'disorderly woman' (see Chapter 2) offered a licence for women to act outside the boundaries of femininity – its ambiguity allowing women to exploit their own putative lack of rationality and responsibility for their actions – it did not do so by challenging those definitions of disorderliness, but by exploiting them. And it is this, argues Phyllis Mack, that opened the way for the subsequent silencing of sectarian women's voices. She suggests that women's right to exercise 'public authority' by preaching, prophesying and publishing was based not on the recognition of any previously unnoticed qualities of leadership or spiritual authority, but, on the contrary, on traditional beliefs in women's greater receptivity to the prophetic or spiritual message because of their irrationality and passivity:

> Within that narrow sphere she could range very high – all the way to a union with God and an identification with cosmic Wisdom – and very low – all the way to an invasion by Demons. The combination of her despised status, and her ecstatic, yet authoritative behaviour, made the female prophet a perfect symbol of a world turned upside down. (Mack 1982: 25)

However, the symbol of the world turned upside down could easily be reinterpreted as the symbol of a monstrous inversion of the natural and God-given order, so that precisely those beliefs and conceptions of femininity that had allowed women to prophesy in the 1640s and 1650s were later to restrain them. Thus the justification for repression and silencing had never been countered; it had merely been appropriated and reinterpreted in the context of very particular social and political circumstances. This, Mack suggests, is why after the Restoration sectarian women were so successfully returned to their 'silent' status once more.

In the light of this argument, it is important to return once more to the notion of the 'ungendered soul' (Riley 1988: 42) that I discussed in Chapter 2. I have suggested that ideas about women's 'unequal bodies' and 'equal souls' help explain many of the apparent contradictions within and between these texts, from the disclaiming of the status of 'author' to the celebration of the dissolution of the self by God. Whilst this denial of earthly agency and the subsequent claiming of divine instrumentality indeed functioned to facilitate the production of these texts in such numbers, it is possible, with Mack, to speculate that the adoption of these dominant discourses of body and soul, albeit deployed in far from conventional ways, left open the door for the refusal and rejection of their reinterpretations. With the increasing separation of the spiritual from the political in the post-Restoration years,[20] spiritual arguments for engaging in contemporary debate would no longer have such purchase. In addition, Denise Riley argues that the conception of the soul itself began to change, losing its 'ungendered' status until, by the time of Rousseau, the soul itself had become sexed (Riley 1988: 36-7):

> In this long process, those appeals to the ungendered soul which had provided such useful platforms for seventeenth-century feminists, religious radicals and reformers, Quakers and members of Civil War sects, became anachronisms ... That the soul before God had no sex was not an argument available for feminist deployment after the eighteenth century's revisions of Nature and Reason. (Riley 1988: 42-3)

This 'slow loss of the sexually democratic soul' (Riley 1988: 18) undermined the foundations of the arguments that generated and justified the production of these texts from the sects. Those that continued to be produced were either increasingly isolated voices (such as Anne Wentworth's), or else produced in the context of a sect – the Quakers – that consciously ensured its own survival by redefining the activities of its members that were deemed acceptable.[21] However, the changes beginning with the Restoration did not amount to the complete catastrophe for women's published writings that such an analysis might suggest. Whilst the 1660s and beyond saw a marked decline in women's publications from within the sects, other women writers began to engage in print with matters of public and social concern. By 1700, Aphra Behn had written some incisive exposés of the sexual double standard resulting from unequal opportunities, educational and otherwise, afforded men and women; Anne Finch had observed that a woman writer would be ridiculed, ignored or dismissed as 'an intruder on the rights of men' (Finch, in Goulianos 1974); and Mary Astell had denied that the differences between men and women were divinely ordained or 'natural', arguing instead that they were the result of socialisation: 'Women are from their very infancy debarred those advantages, with the want of which they are afterwards reproached, and nursed up in those vices which will hereafter be upbraided in them' (Astell in Spender 1983: 56). The site and terms of resistance to the status quo had changed, but resistance none the less remained. If the discourses of body and soul and of religion and politics altered in the post-Restoration years, thereby undermining the arguments made by sectarian women, then new resistances were mounted on new foundations. The emphasis shifted from the radical challenge represented by women in the sects, which was, after all, a challenge of background and of social rank as well as of the controversies in which they engaged. It was principally women of higher rank who made their mark in these later debates, often arguing for the education of women of their own class alone. There were, then, undoubtedly substantial losses, as well as some gains, in the years following the Restoration. Nevertheless, the sectarian women writers successfully instigated the yoking together of two hitherto contradictory, if not incompatible, categories: that of 'woman' and that of 'writer'. Whatever the fluctuations in fortune of this newly forged entity, it was one that was never again to be divided as it had been before the radical experiment of the middle years of the century.

7

'It's weakness that is the woman': readings of Priscilla Cotton and Mary Cole's *To the Priests and People of England* (1655)

Conclusions are indeterminate creatures. Grouped under this rather misleadingly solid and definite name we can find pieces of writing taking a multitude of forms and performing a variety of functions, with little in common other than their position after the penultimate chapter and before the bibliography. Some conclusions condense, recapitulate and restate the main arguments of the book, rehearsing again in brief the themes and findings on which these depend; others step back from the main body of the book in order to achieve a critical distance from which to reflect on the whole project, highlighting its problems and limits as a way of anticipating and countering others' verdicts before they are voiced; others still barely reflect on the completed project, instead using the conclusion as a place to raise all the questions generated by the current book in order to set the agenda for the next.

In this conclusion, I am opting for yet another version of the final chapter. Since this book has surveyed such a broad sweep of theoretical terrain, from the debates emerging from feminist historiography's encounter with poststructuralism to the possibilities offered by dialogic theory for a reading of seventeenth-century radical sectarian women's writings, and since it has explored the relevance and limits of these through the analysis of such a wide range of texts from a number of sects produced in very different religious and political circumstances during the latter part of the century, I shall not attempt to summarise all the theoretical and textual debates introduced in the course of the book. Rather, I shall offer a case study which focuses in detail on one text, thereby juxtaposing all the key issues from the book in relation to one textual instance. This detailed textual analysis offers the reader two things: first, the chance to see the connections between the different approaches detailed in each chapter so far; and secondly, the opportunity to bring together the general theoretical claims pursued in this book in a synthesising reading of one particular text not widely available to twentieth-century readers.

The text under scrutiny was written by the Quakers Priscilla Cotton and Mary Cole, entitled *To the Priests and People of England*, published in 1655. I have chosen this example for two main reasons. The first is scholarly: the themes, structure and language of *To the Priests and People of England* quite neatly bring together many of the principal ideas and analyses which I have been concerned to set out in the rest of the book. The second reason is more pragmatic: in order to allow readers to assess my interpretations for themselves, I wanted to be able to reproduce the text in its entirety here; and this piece by Cotton and Cole is short enough to allow me to do this (it is reproduced here in Appendix C), but also suggestive of many of the questions and paradoxes which such texts raise for the twentieth-century feminist critic.

In the rest of this conclusion, then, I shall analyse this text by considering it in relation to each to the topics raised in the preceding chapters of the book. First, I shall consider how a 'contextualisation' of this piece of writing might contribute to its analysis: is it just a way to make sense of a time-bound and alien piece of ephemera, or does it allow us to see the text as embedded and implicated in wider issues of gender, religion and writing? Secondly, I shall investigate the place of 'silence' both in, and in relation to, the text: what does a consideration of 'silence' have to offer us in relation to such a determinedly assertive and iconoclastic piece of writing? Thirdly, I shall link the question of silence to that of authorship: what position do the textual constructions of the author-figures take in relation to their outpourings, both textual and verbal? Who has the right to write and speak, and who does not, and why? Next, I shall turn to the question of the language of the text: what features could be said to characterise its linguistic practices, and how do these relate to the preceding arguments about silence and authorship? Finally, I shall consider the ways in which the text is predicated on the anticipation of a hostile reception: in what ways do the projected audience and its response structure and determine the text itself? Does the text simultaneously address a sympathetic reader-ship, and if so, how does this relate to the hostile audience addressed so explicitly in the title? Throughout, I shall investigate the relevance of gender for understanding these processes and issues: in what ways might the text be said to be gendered, and what does that mean for a text produced at a time when gender meant something so radically different from its current late twentieth-century meanings?

'All the church may prophesy': contextualisations

To the Priests and People of England (1655) is a short, declamatory, and pugnacious pamphlet, written by two Quaker women imprisoned in Exeter gaol from 1655 to 1656. The importance of the text lies in its engagement in the debate about women speaking, and particularly in its reworking of the terms and meanings of that debate. The text begins by condemning the malice, hypocrisy and evil of the priests and their followers who persecute and imprison the 'just and pure seed of God', the Quakers. Cotton and Cole trace the precedents for such evil-doing back to its biblical origins, and argue that the priests' inverted and corrupt understandings disqualify them from any kind of spiritual authority – an authority which, through a series of interpretive moves on scriptural texts, they then appropriate for themselves. Throughout the piece, their arguments about the grounds of spiritual authority and about who has the right to 'prophesy' are fundamentally informed by notions of gender and by a reliance on the incontrovertibility of the Scriptures. Both 'gender' and the meanings of the Scriptures, however, have radically different connotations from those that might be expected by a twentieth-century reader.

Radical sectarian texts by women, such as this one by Cotton and Cole, were produced at the intersection of several powerful, and interconnected, contemporary discourses: those of gender, and those of religion and spirituality. Discourses of gender, founded in the work of classical writers such as Aristotle and Galen as well as in the epistles of St Paul and the theological works of Aquinas, Luther and Calvin, and manifested in a host of contemporary seventeenth-century locations, from the popular plays and pamphlets debating the true nature of women, to medical theories, to the domestic conduct books produced by (mostly) Puritan divines,[1] proposed that men and women were of a quite different physiological order, which resulted in mutually distinct temperaments. According to these accounts, men were rational, dispassionate, intellectual, ruled by their heads; women were irrational, emotional, sensual, ruled by their bodies. Just as the head took precedence over, guided, and safeguarded the well-being of the body, so men should take precedence over women. Women, in turn, should learn to subject themselves to men, curb their lustful natures, and cultivate a demeanour consistent with the regard for 'honour' required by a husband of his wife: respectful, modest, silent, chaste, deferent. It followed from this that men and women were to accept different areas of responsibility: men, by and large, were the movers in the public world; women's domain was the domestic and the familial. Writing, particularly writing for publication, involved (to different degrees, depending on the circumstances) a negotiation of the public world, and thus did not sit easily with what was deemed appropriate for women. Thus from a notion of women's and men's 'unequal bodies' came a set of discourses ascribing an almost wholly distinct set of social duties, responsibilities and activities for women and men.

Discourses of religion clearly coincide with these ideas in a number of ways. As I have already suggested, many of the above ideas were specifically founded in religious writings, and these were regularly cited as justifications for the differential positioning of men and women within the social order. However, religion offered an additional dimension that pulled against these gendered designations: for women and men were equal before God. Equal in sin and death, they were also equal in grace and in their inheritance of salvation. Whilst women's bodily inequality justified their subjection to their husbands, this subjugation was restricted to earthly matters; their spiritual equality with men ensured that, if there was a conflict between loyalty and duty to God and loyalty and duty to a husband, the former should take precedence. If God, for example, called a woman to testify to her faith or to prophesy in public, and her husband opposed it, she should (with due reflection and prayer) follow God's command. Here, then, contingent upon the notion of the 'ungendered soul' (Riley 1988: 42), was a domain in which women could act more autonomously, relatively unfettered by the restrictions generally imposed by discourses of femininity.

The intersection of the discourses of gender and spirituality was a key site for the justification of their activities by women sectaries. This is as true for Cotton and Cole as for others. Considerations of gender, as they impacted upon the appropriate behaviours of men and women, clearly structure the text, particularly the concluding section, which is the culmination of an argument constructed against the priests who have visited them in gaol. In this section, the authors are concerned to justify women's 'prophesying' or speaking in church, and thus they take as their unavoidable reference-point the Pauline prescriptions concerning this matter. They thus cite (either by allusion or by quotation) all the main scriptural texts that were used to prescribe women's silence: the first is Paul's interdiction of women's speaking in church from 1 Corinthians:

> Let your women keep silence in the churches: for it is not permitted unto them to speak; but they are commanded to be under obedience, as also saith the Law.
>
> And if they will learn any thing, let them ask their husbands at home; for it is a shame for women to speak in the church. (1 Corinthians 14:34-5)

Implicitly alluded to here, and a text usually coupled with the above one, is that from Paul's first epistle to Timothy:

> Let the women learn in silence, with all subjection.
>
> But I suffer not a woman to teach, nor to usurp authority over the man, but to be in silence. (1 Timothy 2:11-2)

The second reference with which Cotton and Cole directly take issue is also concerned to define appropriate gendered behaviour:

> Every man praying or prophesying, having his head covered, dishonoureth his head.
>
> But every women that prayeth or prophesieth with her head uncovered, dishonoureth her head: for that is even all one as if she were shaven. (1 Corinthians 11:4-5)

These are the scriptural texts of which Cotton and Cole need to take account in constructing their argument. Whilst their prescriptions might seem unequivocal and thus unanswerable, Cotton and Cole undermine the authority of these statements in three main ways. First, they counter Scripture with Scripture, citing other verses from the Bible which contradict these ones; second, they question the apparently gendered basis of these prescriptions; and, lastly, they replace the apparently unshakeable binary opposition of 'men' and 'women' as the criterion for speaking, and replace it with another, ungendered, binarism.

Cotton and Cole undermine the authority of the Pauline directives by citing other scriptural texts that seem to contradict them. The most important of these is also from Paul's First Epistle to the Corinthians: 'For ye all may prophesy one by one, that all may learn, and all may be comforted' (1 Corinthians 14:31). This, they argued, is significant, for scriptural inconsistency is inconceivable; it is thus the *interpretations* of these texts that need to be reworked in order to reconcile each of these texts with the others: 'for else thou puttest the Scriptures at a difference in themselves, as still it's thy practice out of thy ignorance; for the Scriptures do say that all the church may prophesy one by one, and that women were in the church, as well as men, do thou judge' (Cotton and Cole 1655: 6). Once this discrepancy has been established, then the source of the discrepancy can be located and countered: in this instance, this means challenging the notion that the 'women' to whom Paul referred corresponded to the category 'female', based in biology. This argument, too, is routed back to the Scriptures, in an allusion to Paul's Epistle to the Galatians: 'There is neither Jew nor Greek, there is neither bond nor free, there is neither male nor female: for ye are all one in Christ Jesus' (Galatians 3:28). Here we are faced with both the contradiction – the scriptural decree that women should keep silent in church, and the scriptural declaration that all may prophesy – and the possibility of its resolution: the distinction between male and female is irrelevant to Christ, and hence the 'women' who were to keep silent in church were a category distinct from the category 'female'.

This brings us to the second means whereby Cotton and Cole rewrite the meanings of the Pauline prescriptions: the questioning of their apparently gendered foundation. If the biological categories 'male' and 'female' are irrelevant to Christ, then for the category 'women' to retain any meaning in Paul's decrees it must connote something other than female; what it connotes, say Cotton and Cole, is weakness: 'thou tellest the people women must not speak in a church, whereas it is not spoke only of a female, for we are all one both male and female in Christ Jesus, but it's weakness that is the woman by Scriptures forbidden' (Cotton and Cole 1655: 6). This idea is further developed through reference to the text from 1 Corinthians 11 quoted above, concerning the necessity for men and women to speak in church with their heads respectively uncovered and covered. Again, Cotton and Cole dislodge this prescription from its gendered connotations, and again they do it by invoking the Scriptures. The 'head' to be covered or uncovered, they say, is Christ: 'now thou wouldst know the meaning of that head, let the Scripture answer, 1 Corinthians 11: 3, "The head of every man is Christ."' (Cotton and Cole 1655: 7). Since 'man' is 'vanity, weakness, a lie', when he (or she) speaks, Christ, who is the 'true head' must be uncovered in that speaking. When the 'woman' – who is weakness – speaks, she (or he) 'must be covered with the covering of the spirit, a garment of righteousness, that its nakedness may not appear' (Cotton and Cole 1655: 7). Whilst the terms 'male' and 'female' retain their gendered connotations, 'man' and 'woman' are ungendered and attain a purely symbolic or metaphorical signification.

With the unseating of gender as the key criterion of the right to speak in church, it might seem that what remains is an undifferentiated and liberal acceptance of *anyone*'s right to speak in church. This is, however, far from the case, for before this peroration on gender, several pages have been spent establishing another binary opposition as the criterion by which to judge the authority of a speaker; this is the opposition between 'the seed of the woman, and the seed of the serpent', 'the generation of Cain and [of] righteous Abel' (Cotton and Cole 1655: 1), or the elect and the unregenerate. It is only the elect, 'the seed of the woman', the descendants of Abel, who speak righteously and truthfully; it is the others who denied Christ, put him to death, 'burnt and butchered' the martyrs, and now persecute the just. This, then, is the binarism which determines the right to speak; having established this in the early part of the text, Cotton and Cole then move on to undermine the scripturally-based gendered dimensions of speaking.

For this piece of writing, then, a consideration of 'context' has had two distinct meanings. First, it has meant taking account of the two principal discourses – those of gender and religion – through which the text is constituted. For women writers in the sects, the bringing together of these two discourses produced a very particular configuration of femininity, as carnal, sensual, irrational and therefore inferior to men, but also as *spiritually* equal with men in their inheritance of grace and everlasting life, and (for Quakers) in their apprehension of the inner light. It is in the space opened up by the possibility of contradiction in this formulation that the arguments in *To the Priests and People of England* are constructed. Second, a consideration of 'context' has meant that a careful intertextual reading, between the seventeenth-century text and the Scriptures, has been undertaken. The former cannot be read in isolation from the latter without both misrepresenting the forces that produced and structured the text, and missing out on layers of allusive meaning generated by the interaction between the two. I shall return to both these issues in subsequent sections.

'Your whole religion is but a noise': gender, silence and writing

It is not only to the subtle rhetoric of citation within this text that we need to pay analytical attention, but also to the silences and absences it manifests. Questions of silence can be seen to be at once both marginal and central to Cotton and Cole's polemic. On the one hand, the text articulates its argument without apology or justification; there is little sense that the authors are struggling with an internalised and feminine sense of unease with public proclamation or a desire to retreat to a more appropriately modest state of silence. On the other hand, the whole text is a refutation of scriptural (and priestly) prescriptions to just such a feminine silence. However, when we consider the text in the light of the debates about silence outlined in Chapter 3, this contradiction becomes all the more important for an analysis of the text.

As I detailed in that chapter, 'silence' has come to signify different things for critics writing from different perspectives. Feminist work on silence has tended to chart the patriarchal forces that prevent women from writing in the first place, or else that ignore, belittle or condemn their work when it is produced. It is possible to trace the stated reluctance to publish, or the many apologies for writing, found in the sectarian women's texts to this patriarchal condemnation of women's voices. In contrast to what might be called this 'repressive' view of the operation of silence in relation to women's writing is Macherey and Foucault's recasting of silence as *productive* of both texts and their meanings. In this respect, Macherey urges readers to take account of what is necessarily left unsaid by a text – its 'reverse side' – and the ways this might produce or structure what is said by the text. Foucault, rather differently, suggests that discourses of silence in themselves have been productive of texts or utterances that engage with, negotiate, concur with, counter or circumvent different kinds of silence. Following these theorisations, it is possible both to detect textual silences in these writings – 'absent centres' to the texts which structure the ideas that are articulated there – and to see how many of the texts written by sectarian women are indeed structured through an engagement, direct or otherwise, with prescriptions of silence. All three of these approaches can be useful for an understanding of Cotton and Cole's text.

Of all three perspectives, it may at first seem most difficult to relate the feminist one to Cotton and Cole's text. Here, after all, is a text that has none of the prefatory epistles that so often in sectarian women's writings justified the existence of the text, apologised for the forwardness of the writer for bringing it to the public's attention, or expressed a longing to return to a life of retirement. Instead, we have a direct, forceful and confrontational text that in its first sentence warns the 'priests and people' of their impending 'everlasting woe and torment' unless they cease their persecution of the truth. This tone, whilst distinct from many other texts both from the 1650s and later, is characteristic of the early Quaker pamphlets, which typically address a specific audience and warn or exhort them to repent and turn from their evil ways. Also typical is the fact that this text is written from prison: again, many Quaker texts both from the 1650s and after the Restoration were written during periods of imprisonment. This detail offers one sense in which the text relates to silence, or at least to silencing: for imprisonment was often a response to the Quaker practice of speaking out in public places, such as interrupting church services, admonishing local officials or clergymen, prophesying in market places or town squares, or 'going naked as a sign'.[2] Whilst there was in some instances clearly a gendered dimension to the punishments undergone by women engaging in such activities – the imposition of the scold's bridle on Dorothy Waugh discussed in Chapter 6 is one outstanding example of this, though there are many others[3] – imprisonment such as that of Cotton and Cole was something to which both male and female Friends were subjected, and so cannot easily be interpreted as a patri-archal silencing of transgressive women's speech.

However, if we consider the relationship of Quakers to silence more generally, then there is a sense in which all attempts to silence Quakers can be seen to have a gendered dimension. For the Quakers, silence was at the heart of their spiritual beliefs and practice, embodied most clearly in the largely silent meeting for worship. As Bauman has demonstrated, for Quakers silence was the ideal spiritual condition, out of which any speech must come and towards which all speech must strive. It was in a state of silence that one would be most likely to apprehend the 'still, small voice' of God within, and any speech should aim to make the hearer more alert to that voice in the ensuing quiet. However, a state of silence did not transcend concerns of gender in a seventeenth-century context: it was an important component of accept-able femininity, the condition recommended as properly modest and respectful for a woman. Quakers were, therefore, adopting as a central part of their religious code a specifically feminine practice. For Quaker men, it is possible that this was under-stood as part of their refusal of generally accepted good order, of a piece with their refusal of hat-honour and deferential titles, their unwillingness to greet passers-by, and so on (Bauman 1983: 43-52); in other words, it was part of the Quaker aim to 'turn the world upside down'. For Quaker women, it is unlikely that any manifesta-tion of silence on their part would cause consternation, but more that their refusal to be silent would be seen to be problematic. Quaker women had to be doubly sure that their speech was appropriate: like all Quakers, male and female, they had to be sure that the impulse to speak did indeed originate with God, but they had also to deal with a more general social antipathy to women's speaking. Thus, all responses to the adoption of the principle and practice of silence has a gendered dimension: for male Friends in that it was part of a general rejection of social or 'carnal' hierarchies, and for female Friends in that their silence was provisional and impermanent, matched by speech sanctioned by sectarian doctrine.

In Cotton and Cole's text, a concern with the instability and precariousness of silence could be said to be an 'absent centre' structuring the discourse of the text. This is perhaps the 'reverse side' of their concern with locating the scriptural justification for their own speaking, and for ungendering, in the ways described above, the criteria whereby speaking might be justified. For Quakers, their speech was not in opposition to silence, but had to be perceived to be on a continuum with it; what it had therefore to be distinguished from was the speech of 'Cain's generation'. It is for this reason that part of the argument by which they establish the 'priests and people' to whom the text is addressed as unregenerate is by an identification of their speech – indeed their whole religion – as 'but a noise' (Cotton and Cole 1655: 5). In the middle of the text, in a section in which they ask the question 'what good doth all your preaching and hearing do you?', they conclude that their opponents' religious assemblies, with their over-reliance on speaking, become a 'place where you set forth your pride and vanity to the utmost'; moreover, there is such a preponderance of 'injustice, violence, falsehood and deceit … that scarce can a man tell what men mean by what they say any longer'. Unregenerate speech, then, misleads and confuses, and results in 'but a noise, the life, power and substance is not in it' (Cotton and Cole 1655: 5). Noise is the polar opposite to both silence and the speech that issues from it. Thus yet another binary opposition – that between speech and silence – is called into question by the text.

The Quaker emphasis on the godliness of silence is thus one way in which silence could be said to be productive of this text. More obvious, however, is the overall concern to return the priests who have been persecuting them to a state of silence. The following passage forms the culmination of the final stage of the argument, and concludes the very lengthy paragraph which focuses on undermining conventional categories of gender, and rewrites the meanings of 'men' and 'woman' in ungendered terms:

> Indeed, you yourselves are the women, that are forbidden to speak in the church, that are become women; for two of your priests came to speak with us; and when they could not bear sound reproof and wholesome doctrine, that did concern them, they railed on us with filthy speeches, as no other they can give to us, that deal plainly and singly with them, and so ran from us. (Cotton and Cole 1655: 7-8)

By ungendering the criteria for godly speaking, and making it dependent instead on the state of regeneracy of the (potential) believer, the priests can in turn, since they are demonstrably unregenerate, be identified with weakness, and thereby with 'womanliness', and thus become the category of person who should refrain from speaking. The text, then, has a double focus: its explicit subject concerns who has the right to speak, and who does not. Through identifying themselves with the former and the priests with the latter, however, we can discern the 'reverse side' of this focus: as well as making a strong case for their own speech, they are making an equally strong one for the priests' silence, a desire that breaks through into the main argument of the text only in this concluding moment.

This, in turn, brings us to the Foucauldian designation of discourses of silence as productive rather than repressive of utterance. We have already seen one way in which this is quite clearly the case with this text: the entire argument of this piece of writing is an elaborate, forceful and polemical engagement with the attempt to silence women in a religious context. By taking issue both with the scriptural justifications for those proscriptions and with the priests' endeavours to use them to silence Quaker women, this text can be said to be dependent on discourses of silence for its genesis and its argument. Without these, this text could not have been written. Moreover, because of the particular meanings and importance of silence in a Quaker context, silence can also be said to be productive of this text in a more general sense: for, if all Quakers had to be convinced of the godly origin of, and sanction for, an utterance, and if all such utterances were understood to emanate from within, and tend towards, a state of quiet, then silence itself can again be seen as the driving force behind this piece of writing. Lastly, because of the specifically gendered meaning of silence at this time, texts such as Cotton and Cole's are rooted in and engage with silence in yet another way: the demands for a silent, passive and deferent femininity require a still more vigorous and thoroughgoing justification of speaking. This combines with the centrality of feminine silence to the Christian religion in general, and the very particular significance of silence within Quakerism specifically, to produce a text with multiple dependences on, and relationships with, differing manifestations of silence.

The text, then, for all its bold and vociferous assertiveness, is implicated in these definitions and understandings of silence in a wide variety of ways. It demonstrates the lengths that were gone to, including imprisonment and other kinds of persecution, to silence groups such as the Quakers who spoke out in such unconventional and confrontational ways. Moreover, its overt concern with speaking is matched by its largely implicit (until the end) concern to reduce their oppressors to a state of silence. Finally, the various discourses – of femininity, of Christianity, of Quaker spirituality – that had investments in the silence of women are engaged with here to the extent that they can be said to be productive of the text as a whole. Far from 'silence' being indicative of a lack or an absence, here it can quite clearly be seen as an active presence at work in many ways within and around the text itself.

'It's weakness that is the woman by the Scriptures forbidden': authorship and self-denial

Cotton and Cole's text brings into sharp focus a key issue for feminist critics approaching seventeenth-century sectarian women's writing. Whilst we may initially eagerly seek out these writings, perhaps as examples of the suppressed tradition of women's writing, or as early instances of women's negotiations of their entry into the 'public' world, we find, on closer inspection, texts that signally fail to celebrate the coming to voice of their female authors. This is compounded in the case of Cotton and Cole's text by a rejection of the category 'women' as having any value at all; instead, the concept is castigated and condemned as signifying weakness and worthlessness. Faced with statements such as these, so antithetical to her own starting-point, does the feminist critic skirt round their apparently implacably negative interpretations, instead focusing on the fact of the writing's existence rather than on its terms and arguments? Or does she read these rejections as conscious and deliberate strategies of infiltration, a way of colluding with the oppressor in order to gain a degree of toleration for her own work? Both these arguments rely heavily on an anachronistic twentieth-century perspective, and suggest instead that the category 'women' – and indeed the category 'author' – need to have their meanings reworked by means of an examination of the contemporary seventeenth-century connotations and parameters of those terms.

These issues, relating as they do to the significance of the authorship of a text for its interpretation, and to the gender of that author for the text that is produced, are at the heart of some of the most absorbing and enduring debates in literary criticism of the last twenty years. As I outlined in Chapter 4, Barthes's dismissal of the significance of the author for the 'meaning' of a text, claiming that it is language that speaks, not an author, and that a text is no more than 'a tissue of quotations' of indeterminate and shifting meaning, culminated in his celebrated pronouncement of 'the death of the author' as a valid or useful critical construct (Barthes 1977). This was paralleled by a move by Foucault, who was similarly critical of the deployment of what he called the 'author-function' – the notion of a unified and consistent author-figure, by reference to whom all the contradictions, inconsistencies or un-evenness of a text could be explained and resolved, and its meaning fixed and determined. Instead, like Barthes, Foucault suggested that this notion of the author simply served to set an artificial and unsustainable limit to the polysemous character of writing, whose meanings could actually never be fixed or finalised; but he also suggested that it served to establish the character and boundaries of 'true art', and thereby to distinguish this from popular or mass culture. The notion of the author, was, according to Foucault, a demarcating and exclusionary device: by defining the character and function of an 'author', it effectively excluded certain kinds of groups from the category. It was on these grounds that he too argued for the abandonment of 'the author' as of any significance for the analysis of a text (Foucault 1977).

For feminist literary critics, this proclamation of the 'death of the author' proved to be double-edged.[4] Whilst it fundamentally undermined the criteria of individual authorial genius by which the 'great men of literature' had for so long dominated the literary curriculum, it at the same time disallowed the terms of the arguments by which feminist critics had been arguing for the inclusion of women writers in the canon: for how could the gender of an author be important when authorship itself had been demonstrated to be a redundant bourgeois construct? This problem has elicited a variety of responses. Some feminist critics have questioned the whole impetus behind 'the death of the author' move, remarking on the coincidence of the development of this theory with the moment that hitherto marginalised groups (such as women, black people, or lesbian and gay writers) were beginning to argue for the inclusion of their work within the canon and curriculum. Others have begun to reappraise the notion of 'women's writing', retaining it as a category but shifting the criteria by which the category is constituted from women authors to women readers. Others still have argued for a modified retention of the author-figure within literary studies, not as the all-controlling and authoritative genius, but as a historically specific and therefore changing construct which functions differently at different times both for the production and reception of texts.

In this book, I have opted for this final model of authorship as offering the most appropriate way to begin to make sense of the body of sectarian writing by women, since it allows a critical interest both in the gendered production of these texts and in the ways in which this gendered authorship itself was productive of particular patterns and structures within the texts themselves. However, this model's focus on the historical specificities of texts does render unavoidable a confrontation with the problem that I identified at the outset of this section: the denial, rejection or castigation of the category 'women' and the category 'author' by women authors. What were the implications of those categories, and how were they deployed and rewritten by sectarian women writers?

In this respect, it is undoubtedly disconcerting and confusing for a feminist critic to find herself dealing with a text such as Cotton and Cole's, the force of whose argument rests on such contrary premises from those we might predict. As I argued earlier in this conclusion, the argument developed by this text moves inexorably towards the conclusion that 'woman' signifies 'weakness', finally using the term 'women' pejoratively to denigrate the priests who have been opposing the authors. The identification of the priests as women forms the polemical high-point of the text, the conclusion towards which all the rest of the argument has been leading: 'Indeed, you yourselves are the women, that are forbidden to speak in the church, that are become women' (Cotton and Cole 1655: 7-8). However, as I have suggested, this argument involves the recognition and negotiation of a number of versions of femininity and its contemporary meanings which are not reducible to the equation in this text of 'women' equals 'weakness' equals 'negative construction of femininity', as might at first seem the case to a twentieth-century reader. The text's case, as it relates to the gender of its authors, rests on two rhetorical devices. First, the text carefully constructs its author-figures as 'the just and pure seed of God', regenerate, and therefore permitted to speak in church, and thus not women; conversely, their opponents are established as of the generation of Cain, unregenerate, therefore not permitted to speak. Secondly, the weakness and vanity of the priests is argued to identify them as women, and this provides an additional argument for their keeping silent.

Since the spiritual condition of the authors permits them to speak, which in turn means that they are not 'women', the idea of constructing the kind of apologies and justifications for writing that I identified in other texts (see Chapter 4) becomes redundant. Dissociated from weakness, vanity and other carnal or human failings, the authors become ungendered examples of righteous speakers, movers in the spiritual plane. In so doing, they do not deny the existence or the social significance of gender: they write of 'a son or a daughter' being moved of the Lord to go to speak in an assembly of people (Cotton and Cole 1655: 6), and recognise that weakness and therefore womanliness is something to which both sexes may fall prey: 'Here mayst thou see from the Scriptures, that the woman or weakness *whether male or female*, is forbidden to speak in the church' (Cotton and Cole 1655: 7; my emphasis). Gender, therefore, has no significance in relation to regeneracy or to speaking. Moreover, both because gender has no meaning in relation to spiritual matters, and because the authors refuse the categorisation of themselves as women, the idea of apologising or justifying the authoring of this text becomes anomalous. By disavowing the significance of the gender of a speaker, and instead establishing spiritual regeneracy as the definitive criterion for judging an utterance godly or otherwise, any reinvestment of the authors with a significantly gendered identity through introducing an apology or justification would undermine the credibility of the text's argument. Conviction of membership of God's elect was sufficient justification in itself; and this, untypically, remained an area in which the importance of gender could authoritatively be denied.

By these means, the identification of 'women' with 'weakness' becomes less a problematic female rejection of women's worth and more a highly imaginative and nimble negotiation of contemporary social and spiritual designations of appropriate femininity, whereby the question of authoritative authorship is circumvented through an elaborate argument justifying (certain) female speaking and (certain) male silence. Whilst this does not sit easily with a feminist desire to reclaim these early instances of women's coming to voice, it does strike a familiar chord in relation to certain poststructuralist conceptualisations of identity. For them, as for Cotton and Cole, identity is not fixed, stable and unalterable, grounded in certain immovable facts such as gender. Instead, it is provisional and unstable, its meaning never finalised but constantly deferred. To be female, according to Cotton and Cole's text, did not necessarily entail a fixed range of meanings associated with femininity; instead these meanings – weakness, vanity, unworthiness – were open to both sexes. Thus, at certain times and under certain conditions, men could be women, and vice versa. As Phyllis Mack so concisely suggests, this feature of Cotton and Cole's text hints at a more widespread lack of fixity in matters of identity:

> seventeenth-century men and women lived in a more formalized and public cultural environment. For them, the decision whether to stand or sit, to become a farmer or a minister, to marry or to remain celibate, to nurse and caress an infant or to send it away, all were seen to depend more on family position, social convention, or public policy – on an almost intangible web of social and political relationships – than on individual impulse. For those men and women, a phrase like 'gender roles' would have meant precisely what it said; the adoption of the social roles or conventions of masculine or feminine behaviour. And the existence of those fixed conventions, whose character was trumpeted from pulpits, thrones, and parliaments, not only gave a kind of theatricality to the actions of men and women; it implied that roles could be switched.

Hence the rituals of reversal and the practice of cross-dressing in the theater, on the street, and in the village square, all of which were central to the festive life of contemporaries and were invested with a meaning very different from similar practices in our own culture. (Mack 1992: 6-7)

For Quakers such as Cotton and Cole the fluidity of such a notion of identity meant that the significations associated with a gendered identity could be deployed to denigrate or silence one's opponents. Thus the newly-figured meanings of 'women' can be deployed to inscribe the priests as women: 'indeed, you yourselves are the women, that are forbidden to speak in the church, that are become women'. Here, both the current condition of the priests (they are women) and the instability and changeableness of this state (they are become women) are suggested, thereby including the notion both that they cannot justifiably speak out now, but also that the instability of this identity can allow for the transformation of identity and a change of behaviour, such as the cessation of persecution. At the same time, the sex of the author or speaker could, through a series of scripturally-based rhetorical moves, be made immaterial or even insubstantial. By annexing the authentic and (in this case at least) ungendered voice of prophecy to themselves, the question – and, in a seventeenth-century context, problem – of female authorship ceases to require a textual acknowledgement. Female authorship thereby has a spiritual justification that dissolves the significance of the social meanings of femininity. At least, it does so in the text: for after the rhetorical flourish of the ascription of femininity to the priests, we are rapidly returned to the material conditions of these women speakers/authors: 'So leaving you to the light in all your consciences to judge of what we have writ, we remain prisoners in Exeter gaol for the word of God' (Cotton and Cole 1655: 8). For all the negotiation and rewriting of the category 'women', and for all the refusal of its limits, the authors, as they say, 'remain' in jail, subject to the 'consciences' of their opponents. Those social meanings so deftly undermined by the moves and turns of the textual polemic return with an inevitable actuality, their power to constrain and define recognised by those who have hitherto been denying them, as the text comes – as it must – to a close.

'Thou puttest the Scriptures at a difference in themselves': textual authority and language

The redefinitions and reascriptions of meaning effected by Cotton and Cole's text are made possible by a very particular conception of the possibilities of language and how its meanings are constructed. In this text, as I have already demonstrated, rather than the linguistic meanings of certain key concepts, such as 'women', being construed as fixed and unchanging, they are understood to be unstable and unfixed, and open to reworking and transformation. This raises a fundamentally important question concerning the use of language in these writings: if meanings are so unstable and open to change, from where does the language within texts such as that of Cotton and Cole derive its authority? In other words, if these authors can remake the meanings of language in order to justify their understandings, what is to stop these in turn being reworked and discredited by their opponents?

This assertion of the importance of questions of language is substantiated by reference to the intense debates concerning the character and function of seventeenth-century language. First, then, I want to outline these in order to situate Cotton and Cole's text in relation to them. As I discussed in Chapter 5, it has been suggested[5] that there was a fundamental shift in the course of the seventeenth century in the way that language was perceived and in the way that its meanings were thought to be made. Earlier in the century, it is suggested, language was seen as a dense, opaque, allusive system of signification, in which words constituted a set of signs that referred, in a number of circuitous and ultimately indefinable ways, to other, equally significant and indefinable, signs; all these (whether words, or animals, or human beings, or the stars, or 'nature', or political events) were conceived of primarily as elements in God's created order. By this account, the meanings of words, like the meanings of the stars or of political events, needed untangling, analysing and interpreting; they were thus open to contestation. By the latter part of the century, it is argued, language was thought of more as a system of reference than a system of signification: each word referred to (or should refer to) an element in the natural world; by this account, language would cease to have meaning in itself; it would lose its opacity and become a transparent and incontrovertible way of referring to, ordering and classifying the objective world. This change brought with it a general change in style, or in the values placed on particular styles, from an allusive, metaphorical, ahistorical, circular style (with Donne and Andrewes the key exemplars) to one that was simple, referential, clear, direct, time-bound and historical – the famous 'plain style', with its origins located variously in Puritanism, the new science, and the post-Restoration Latitudinarianism (with apologists in Sprat, Wilkins and Glanvill).

Given this paradigm, we might expect to associate Quaker language use with this latter conceptualisation: after all, Quaker 'plain style' is one of the most often noted – and earliest noted – features of Quaker language practice. This 'plain style' included a refusal of common greetings such as 'good day' or 'farewell', a rejection of deferential titles of address such as 'master' or 'your grace' or the self-referential 'your obedient servant', and an insistence on using 'thou' and 'thee' in the second person singular. One argument that Quakers advanced to explain and justify these breaches of social convention was that language should at all times be an expression of absolute truth; consequently, the Quaker demand for truthfulness resulted in

> a resort to extreme literalness, that is, a refusal to accept any verbal usage, no matter how conventional or no matter how sanctioned by the canons of etiquette, if it violated the standard of Truth at any level. Indeed, … the Quakers viewed custom and the use of what they saw as empty ceremonial forms as fundamentally incompatible with spiritual rigor. Thus if they identified a particular kind of customary behaviour as contrary to the Truth, it was to be shunned as a lie. (Bauman 1983: 45)

Commonplace greetings, deferential titles, the use of 'you' instead of 'thou': all these, in some sense, breached the requirement of absolute truthfulness. This, then, betokens a view that language should be as referentially accurate as possible, corresponding as completely and incontrovertibly as possible to the 'truth' of a situation, and thus aligns it with the more general move towards a plain style in the latter part of the century.

As well as justifying their 'plain style' through a commitment to truthfulness in all things, there were more specific justifications for the particular focuses of their attention identified in the Scriptures. To show deference to someone on the grounds of social rank, by addressing them as 'master', calling them 'you' instead of 'thou' as well as by doffing the hat, was to show respect to their 'persons', their position within the world. This was alien to the way of God, as is made clear in a verse much quoted by sectaries: 'Then Peter opened his mouth, and said, Of a truth I perceive that God is no respecter of persons' (Acts 10:34). God's people should thus follow suit: 'But if ye have respect to persons, ye commit sin, and are convinced of the law as transgressors' (James 2:9). It is to this notion that Cotton and Cole are referring when they write of the priests: 'Now thou dost respect persons I know, and art partial in all things, and so judgest wickedly, but there is no respect of persons with God' (Cotton and Cole 1655: 7). Similarly, the use of idle, and therefore untruthful, words, such as commonplace greetings, was forbidden by the Bible (Matthew 12:36-7), as, indeed, was the swearing of oaths (Matthew 5:34-7), another characteristic example of a Quaker refusal to transgress biblical injunctions.[6] In all these cases, then, a very literal understanding of the function of language was matched by, and indeed based in, a very literal interpretation of the Scriptures.

As with so many other Quaker, and indeed sectarian, writings, Cotton and Cole's text certainly manifests a marked reliance on the Scriptures for the formation and development of its arguments. The categorisations which are used to designate the priests and the Quakers as, respectively, unregenerate and godly were biblical: 'there is the seed of the woman, and the seed of the serpent'[7] (Genesis 3:15; Cotton and Cole 1655: 1); 'there is the generation of Cain and righteous Abel' (Genesis 4; Cotton and Cole 1655: 1); Christ is quoted to identify the need for recompense for the blood of Abel (Matthew 23:35; Luke 11:51; Cotton and Cole 1655: 1); a range of scriptural examples are cited where 'Cain's generation' 'persecuted the just under some false colour' (Cotton and Cole 1655: 2), and this is brought forward into more contemporary times: 'so in the days of the bishops, martyrs were burnt and butchered under the name of heretics' (Cotton and Cole 1655: 2). Later in the text, it is in part through straightforward biblical citation that Cotton and Cole justify the equal role of women in spiritual matters:

> it's very plain, Paul, nor Apollos, nor the true church of Christ, were not of that proud envious spirit that thou art of, for they owned Christ Jesus in man or woman; for Paul bid Timothy to help those women that laboured with him in the gospel, and Apollos hearkened to a woman, and was instructed by her, and Christ Jesus appeared to the women first, and sent them to preach the resurrection to the apostles, and Philip had four virgins that did prophesy. (Cotton and Cole 1655: 7)

A biblical reference-point, then, was an indispensable anchor for each of the arguments made in the text.

However, this kind of straightforward reliance on citation or reference to authorise an argument is by no means characteristic of this text: for despite the fact that
apparent scriptural literalism plays its part in the Quaker adoption of a 'plain style',
the text also articulates the idea that the Scriptures are not the unproblematically
authoritative body of work that this characterisation might seem to suggest. First, the
priests, like the scribes and the Pharisees before them, are themselves highly conver-
sant with, and reliant on, the Scriptures, and this, for them, has proved to be no
guarantee of godliness: 'Is it not strange, ... that they that read the Gospel every
Sabbath day, that spake of Christ, should murder and put him to death' (Cotton and
Cole 1655: 1). This calls into question the whole notion of the reliability and
referentiality of language: 'the scribes and Pharisees spake good words, they spake of
the messiah, yet they killed the substance of what they spake: so the priests speak
true words, good words, and yet kill, and persecute, pursue, and imprison the substance and life of what they speak' (Cotton and Cole 1655: 2) Speaking 'good words'
is no guarantee of godliness of spirit. There can, it seems, be a fundamental and
misleading discrepancy between language and the truth, arising in this instance from
a disparity between the 'form' of the words, with their apparent godliness, and their
underlying lack of 'substance'. Similarly, Cotton and Cole set down the errors that
can result from a knowledge of the Scriptures that is not accompanied by a personal
knowledge or experience of the light of Christ within:

> if you did abide in the light, you should come to witness the life and power of what you
> profess, and so come to that life that gave forth the Scriptures, and not wrest them to
> your own opinions and lusts: one saying, 'Lo!' here in Presbytery; another, 'Lo!' there
> in Independency; and another, in Prelacy; and another in Baptism. (Cotton and Cole
> 1655: 3)

Language itself is not to be trusted if it is not imbued with the 'life and power' of
God; without this, it is nothing but a manifestation of faulty human understanding
or 'carnal reasoning'. Even the Scriptures are open to abuse if they are not ap-
proached with this same spirit: they can be 'wrested' to fit in with and justify a wide
range of untenable and ungodly opinions – and here Cotton and Cole explicitly
include other sects, such as the Independents and the Baptists, in their criticisms, as
well as the clergy of the Church of England. For language to be invested with a godly
authority, and for biblical interpretations to be imbued with that same authority,
then, they need to be accompanied by an inner conviction and experience of the
'inner light', the manifestation of God within each believer.

This brings me to the second principal way in which Cotton and Cole's text
diverges from the 'literalist' characterisation of the Quaker attitude to the Scriptures
that I set out as the foundation of their 'plain style'. Whilst their insistence that texts
should not be 'wrested' to fit in with particular sectarian opinions or interests indicates a literalist approach to biblical texts, their approach to the interpretation of the
Scriptures cannot, in any simple sense, be said to be 'literalist', but rather tends
towards the highly metaphorical or allegorical. As we have seen already, the climax
of their argument relies on figurative readings: the identification of the priests as

'women' in the final lines of the piece is dependent on a series of boldly metaphorical interpretations of key biblical texts. First, the 'woman' forbidden by Paul to speak in the church (1 Corinthians 14:34–5) is interpreted not as a 'female' but as 'weakness'. Secondly, the 'head' that must be uncovered when a 'man' speaks and must be covered when a 'woman' speaks (1 Corinthians 11:4–5) is not a literal, physical 'head', but is interpreted as 'Christ':

> Man in his best estate is altogether vanity, weakness, a lie. If therefore any speak in the church, whether man or woman, and nothing appear in it but the wisdom of man, and Christ, who is the true head, be not uncovered, do not fully appear, Christ the head is then dishonoured. Now the woman or weakness, that is man, which in his best estate or greatest wisdom is altogether vanity, that must be covered with the covering of the spirit, a garment of righteousness, that its nakedness may not appear, and dishonour thereby come. Here mayst thou see from the Scriptures, that the woman or weakness whether male or female, is forbidden to speak in the church. (Cotton and Cole 1655: 7)

The reference-point and source of justification is clearly still scriptural; and yet it is purely the metaphoricity of the interpretation that confers the kind of flexibility and fluidity of meaning to language that permits them to make their arguments and to conclude that the priests are 'women' and should therefore keep silent.

However, the interpretation is so metaphorical, so contrary to the 'literal' meaning of the biblical text, that it begs the question of what distinguishes this kind of interpretation from precisely the 'wresting' of meanings by other sectaries and priests so decried by Cotton and Cole themselves. The text offers two possible counter-arguments to this accusation. First, the authors stress the central necessity of 'conscience' as a touchstone of godliness: the individual apprehension of the 'truth' or the inner light that guides the believer's judgement. It is to this that Cotton and Cole are appealing when they close their text with the words: 'so leaving you to the light in all your consciences to judge of what we have writ' (Cotton and Cole 1655: 8); it is this that the erring priests are failing to recognise in themselves: 'if you would hearken to the light of Jesus Christ in your consciences, it would lead you from your own wisdom, learning and self-conceitedness, into the simplicity of Jesus Christ, which is a mystery of faith hid in a pure conscience' (Cotton and Cole 1655: 4). The conscience, then, offers a capacity for understanding that is indefinable, mysterious, and unquantifiable in 'carnal' terms; and it is this that lies behind the well-known Quaker hostility to university-learning:

> So you now, would you hearken to Jesus Christ, and obey his light in your consciences, you would come down to humility and the fear of the Lord, to the true wisdom and understanding, that you would not need so many authors, and books, you would not need to rent your heads with studying, but you would come to see your teacher in you, which now is removed into a corner. (Cotton and Cole 1655: 4)

Conscience, then, is one key justificatory mechanism for this kind of metaphorical interpretation of the Scriptures. Unlike for other sects, such as the Baptists and some Independents, for whom 'revelation was a closed account', for the Quakers:

the Scriptures were rather the tangible reports of the Word of God that was in those who spoke and recorded them ... an important record of God's earlier messages to men, and thus serviceable as a guide and a standard, but no more intrinsically valid than the Word of God within themselves, continuously revealed. (Bauman 1983: 25-6)

Such an understanding of the role of 'conscience', the 'inner light', or the 'Word of God within themselves' helps make sense of the interpretive leaps that are made with the aid of metaphor in this text, and that give the meanings of linguistic concepts the astonishing variability or flexibility that I have noted throughout this conclusion.

Additionally, however, there is another justification offered in the text for these metaphorical interpretive leaps: and this is an assertion that the Scriptures them-selves *require* such metaphorical readings in order to make certain texts agree with other texts from the Bible. Any inconsistency that appears in the Bible is not God-given, but a result of faulty human understanding and ignorance of the light within: 'the Scriptures are not divided, they agree, and hold out one thing; but you divide them, because you live not in that life that gave them forth' (Cotton and Cole 1655: 3). It is this point, Cotton and Cole argue, that leads them to interpret the 'woman' forbidden to speak in church as weakness; for to do otherwise would be to set the Bible against itself: 'it's weakness that is the woman by the Scriptures forbidden, *for else* thou puttest the Scriptures at a difference in themselves, as still it's thy practice out of thy ignorance' (Cotton and Cole 1655: 6; my emphasis). If scriptural texts contradict each other, then they do so because of the error of the reader, not out of any inherent contradiction within the Bible itself. Thus, if the Scriptures say both that women must keep silence in church and that all may prophesy, some way must be found to draw these two texts into line with each other, so that the Scriptures are not 'at a difference in themselves'. The way that this is done is by reference to yet other biblical texts: first, the one that denies the significance of gender for spiritual-ity ('we are all one both male and female in Christ Jesus' (Galatians 3:28; Cotton and Cole 1655: 6)), thereby legitimating a metaphorical interpretation of 'women' as weakness; and, secondly, the identification of the 'head' to be covered or uncovered when speaking in church as Christ, by reference to 1 Corinthians 11:3. This is a very different kind of justification from that of 'conscience': whilst that was individual, indefinable, and intangible, this is text-based, referential, and, to a degree at least, verifiable. And this, in turn, returns us to a much more literalist deployment of the Bible, away from which the metaphorical character of the interpretation of the Scrip-tures seemed so clearly to have moved us.

What remains is a text whose conceptualisation and deployment of language is richly contradictory. On the one hand, the Quaker 'plain style' is manifested in Cotton and Cole's blunt and uncompromising address to their opponents: 'We have no envy nor malice to any creature, priest or people, but are to mind you of your conditions, without any partiality or hypocrisy, and wish your eternal good: and what we contend against is your greatest enemy, and will be your everlasting woe and torment' (Cotton and Cole 1655: 1). Allied to this is an (at times) literalist reliance on the Scriptures to provide the basic terms ('the generation of Cain', 'the seed of the woman') and arguments ('all may prophesy one by one') of the text. Both these features – the 'plain style' and the reliance on the Scriptures – is rooted in a distrust of human language with its reliance on 'carnal' reasoning and understanding, which can only serve to confuse and corrupt:

> what good doth all your preaching and hearing do you? Break your sleep, rent your brains, and as it were, speak out your lungs, and alas who is bettered by it! ... scarce can a man tell what men mean by what they say any longer ... your whole religion is but a noise, the life, power and substance is not in it. (Cotton and Cole 1655: 5)

Instead, the believer is urged to turn to a language imbued with the 'truth' of God and emanating from the conscience or inner light; for, as Bauman says, 'God's words did not suffer from the communicational defects of natural language' (Bauman 1983: 27). What is at stake here, then, is the desire to equate language with the 'truth' in a variety of ways: through refusing the 'lies' inherent in everyday circumlocutionary linguistic etiquette; to root all utterances in the demonstrable truths of the Scriptures; and to trust to the 'truth' of the individual apprehension of the inner light.

On the other hand, the use of language in the text is far from the referential ideal of the 'plain style' in its substantial reliance on metaphor, and the consequent unconventional and unstable interpretations that follow from this. What sets the boundaries to this instability and flux of meaning, however, and prevents (at least rhetorically) the tables being turned on their interpretations, are precisely the reliance on both the authority of the Scriptures and on the light of conscience detailed above. For these each, in their different ways, impose the authority of God – God in the Scriptures, and God speaking through the conscience – on the interpretations arrived at by the authors, and thereby render them ungainsayable, incontrovertible and unanswerable.

In this way, Quaker writings such as Cotton and Cole's combine elements of both language styles said to characterise the seventeenth century: the highly metaphorical, allusive, interpretive and ahistorical style associated both with Anglicanism in the earlier part of the century and, in a different form, with sectaries of the middle years of the century;[8] and the 'plain style', more referential, more literal, less rhetorical, and associated variously with more orthodox Puritanism and, later, with the new science and Latitudinarianism. *To the Priests and People of England* is both interrogative of the meanings and limits of language, and referential, in the sense that language can (in its divine manifestation) be equated with 'truth', and in the sense of the Scriptures themselves being seen as a source of that truth. The retention of the Scriptures as a source of authentication for interpretations is important here, for it suggests that, despite the fluidity and indeterminacy of meanings, agreement can *none the less* be reached on the just interpretation of the Scriptures, and hence on the meanings of language itself:

> God is gathering his people out from idol-shepherds into his own fold, to make them one flock and to give them one shepherd, that they may serve him with one consent, for he hath fulfilled this Scripture in thousands this day whom he hath gathered out of

Antichrist's opinions to worship one God in one way, in spirit and truth, speaking all the same things: if you speak with ten thousand of them, they all agree, having one king, one law giver. (Cotton and Cole 1655: 4–5)

For Cotton and Cole, godliness, the 'spirit and truth', will result in unity of speech and understanding, his people 'speaking all the same things; ... they all agree'. Optimistically, they argue that the apprehension of the 'truth' through the individual conscience, far from resulting in schism and dissent, will result in unity and harmony.

Rather than there being any absolute chronological or denominational split in the adherence to a metaphorical or a plain style, we can see in these writings a cross-fertilisation or interaction of the two, resulting in a peculiarly potent deployment of language: its meanings are rendered flexible enough through its metaphorical character, but are also fixed sufficiently through reference both to the Scriptures and the divinely-originating inner light. It is through a combination of these two conceptions of language that Cotton and Cole are able both to deconstruct the everyday 'carnal' associations of gender and yet also to ground their arguments in the Bible itself.

'Now to you all I speak': anticipated responses and dialogic theory

To the Priests and People of England announces itself, from the title onwards, as a text with a clearly defined audience. Paragraphs frequently begin with an indication of their specific address, to 'Friends', 'people', 'you all', 'Friends and people', and 'apostate England' (Cotton and Cole 1655: 1, 2, 3, 5). Within those paragraphs, there are frequent reminders that the text is speaking directly to its anticipated readership: 'you' and 'thou' recur frequently through the text. Moreover, the title indicates precisely what kind of text is being produced for this audience: a 'warning', in which the authors will 'discharge' their consciences. Having said this, though, to what extent does this explicit identification of an addressee (or addressees) determine the form of the text and the direction of the argument? Does the textual address distinguish between the 'priests' and the 'people' of the title, or address them as a homogeneously hostile group, all equally in need of 'warning'? In either case, how is this manifested in the text itelf? More generally, how significant was the culture of opposition suggested by, and anticipated in, this text for the specificities of textually-articulated sectarian aims and expectations?

In order to begin to assess the significance of the addressee in the text, and this more general culture of opposition, I want to turn again to dialogic theory as one of the places in which the importance of address both in and for a text has been most systematically theorised. As I suggested in Chapter 6, according to dialogics, all utterances, verbal or textual, need to be considered as participating in a dialogue with an explicitly or implicitly imagined addressee. To reiterate a much-quoted point of Voloshinov's:

> *word is a two-sided act.* It is determined equally by *whose* word it is and *for whom* it is meant ... I give myself verbal shape from another's point of view of the community to which I belong. A word is a bridge thrown beween myself and another. If one end of

the bridge depends on me, then the other depends on my addressee. (Voloshinov, *Marxism and the Philosophy of Language* (1929), quoted in Pearce 1994: 43; original emphasis.)

The emphasis here is on the reciprocity of any utterance, its equal dependence on both the speaker (or writer) and the addressee, actual or imagined. Moreover, it is recognised that the 'addressee' anticipated in this formulation is unlikely to be a stable construct, a single or unified subject position, but might, within the course of a piece of writing, shift to include 'a more or less differentiated public, ethnic group, contemporaries, like-minded people, opponents and enemies, a subordinate, a superior' (Bakhtin, *Speech Genres and Other Late Essays* (1952-53), quoted in Pearce 1994: 73-4). Sometimes these addressee-positions may be addressed sequentially, in separate parts of a text, and at other times they may be addressed simultaneously; in all such instances of multiple address, the resulting text is seen as an example of 'double-voiced discourse'. Additionally, those sections of a text that project a sympathetic audience are designated, within dialogic theory, as engaging in 'hidden dialogue' with this addressee-position, whilst those projecting an antagonistic audience are said to be in 'hidden polemic' with them. For the purposes of texts such as Cotton and Cole's, with their highly explicit modes of textual address, the modifier 'hidden' seems redundant or perhaps even misleading; I have therefore dispensed with it, and shall talk simply of 'dialogue' and 'polemic'.

Dialogic theory is significant in relation to texts such as Cotton and Cole's in the first instance for its insistence that we recognise the reciprocity of utterance. Whilst in a text such as this one, so overtly predicated on an anticipated audience, we are unlikely to forget this presence, the notion of the *productive* power of this reciprocal relationship, the way in which the dialogic character of the text actively constructs the text in very particular ways, is undoubtedly worth underlining. In the case of Cotton and Cole's work, without a highly specific interlocutor, or set of interlocutors, there would be no text; the whole *raison d'être* of the text is an engagement with a specific set of antagonists, the 'priests and people of England'. Both responding to prior hostility, and anticipating the objections they expect to receive to their writing, the authors construct a series of arguments designed first to fix their opponents firmly within the category of the ungodly, the 'generation of Cain', and secondly to use this designation as part of the justification for their argument that the priests, because of their weakness and vanity, should keep silent.

If this is the case, is the text then constructed as one seamless piece of undifferentiated polemic, engaging with and disabling any projected counter-arguments before they can be deployed against the authors? In some senses, this is certainly the case: the whole text can be read as a sustained polemic, locked in battle 'with censorious "answer words" not present in the text itself' (Pearce 1994: 185). That this is the case is brought to the fore by the one moment in the text when these censorious 'answer words' are present in the text itself: in a move that formally owes a debt to orthodox Puritan rhetoric (Smith 1989: 323), but in dialogic terms demonstrates just how dependent the structure and argument of the text are on anticipated hostile responses, the regular format of the text in paragraphs is interrupted by the following lines:

> Objection: 'But do not the priests declare against evil works?'
> Answer: Yes, they do so. (Cotton and Cole 1655: 2)

Here, the anticipated objection to be raised by the addressee is voiced in advance by the authors, explicitly integrated into the argument of the text, and thus defused before it can damage the case that is being made. Whilst, however, the text is certainly characterised by the anticipation and deflection of hostile reactions through its polemic, this polemic is far from being undifferentiated: the anticipated readership is undoubtedly conceptualised as overwhelmingly hostile, but there are significant differences in the ways that the 'priests' and the 'people' are addressed; the projected hostility of the two groups is not of the same order or character.

The text opens with the general term of address, 'Friends', a word not just reserved for fellow-Quakers, as one might suspect, but used more generally for supporters and opponents alike (Bauman 1983: 47), and immediately moves on to suggest that it is the intention of the authors 'to mind you of your conditions, ... and wish your eternal good'. This, they say, will entail self-reflection and self-recognition on the part of their audience: 'it lieth upon you all to know what generation you are of' (Cotton and Cole 1655: 1). This is reiterated later in the text, when the reader is reminded that: 'Now to you all I speak, sin not against the light in your own consciences, be not wilfully blind, but hearken to the light of Jesus Christ in your consciences, that you may come to see what generation you are of, whether of Cain or Abel' (Cotton and Cole 1655: 3). Thus far, then, the address is explicitly inclusive of both constituencies of opponent identified in the title; they emphasise that 'to you all I speak (Cotton and Cole 1655: 3), and urge both constituencies to turn to the inner light and abandon their evil ways.

More characteristic of the text, however, are the moments when the priests are separated out from 'the people' who currently support them, and each group addressed differently. In the second paragraph of the text, for example, the address is specifically to the 'people', where they are informed of the persecuting priests' pedigree:

> Now people, this was the same generation of Cain in them after Christ's death, that persecuted the apostles and put them to death; and it was the same spirit in them that put the martyrs to death, and of that generation were the bishops that persecuted, and so it continueth still to this day in the world; for Cain's generation is now still envying, hating, and persecuting the righteous Abel. (Cotton and Cole 1655: 1)

The process of tracing the descent of 'Cain's generation' through from those who crucified Christ and persecuted the apostles to the bishops who put the martyrs to death and thence to the present day, where 'now Cain's generation hates the just and pure seed of God, because it declares that their works are evil' (Cotton and Cole 1655: 2), identifies the priests quite unequivocally with this ungodly Cainish generation. The 'people', however, are not so readily categorised: outlining the priests' lineage in this way offers them a chance to differentiate themselves from this evil line and to associate

201

themselves instead with the 'just and pure seed of God'. True, the people are undoubtedly currently antagonistic, and in need of an uncompromising warning:

> priests and people that live in Cain's race do pursue and persecute even to the very death, the life and power of what they do preach. And know you of a truth, that all the blood since Abel shall be required of this generation; for, as it groweth to the end, it heighteneth and ripeneth its malice and wickedness, and so shall its judgement be, for double plagues shall be poured out upon her. (Cotton and Cole 1655: 3)

However, there is also the possiblity of change for these people; they are capable of transferring their allegiance from the priests to the 'just and pure seed', of taking heed of the inner light that shines within them:

> This I warn you in love, for I cannot but think that there are some among you that ponder on this day, and if you would hearken to the light of Jesus Christ in your consciences, it would lead you from your own wisdom, learning, and self-conceitedness, into the simplicity of Jesus Christ, which is a mystery of faith hid in a pure conscience. (Cotton and Cole 1655: 4)

Whilst the text remains in polemic with the sinfulness of their ways, it none the less inscribes the possibility of transformation, hope and salvation within the warnings themselves. It even urges people to recognise their own power, and to turn it against the sins of the oppressors: 'Now fret not at this, you that live in Babylon in confusion, in divisions: for the little stone cut out of the mountain without hands, shall break Babylon's idols' (Cotton and Cole 1655: 5).

Those sections of the text explicitly in polemic with the priests are altogether less sanguine of their chances of transformation. All reference to biblical priests quite unequivocally identifies them with Cain, and hence ascribes to the seventeenth-century priests an unremittingly evil and hypocritical heritage (Cotton and Cole 1655: 1, 2). They are said to take pride in their learning – a favourite target of Quaker pamphleteers – and this is another source of their unregeneracy: 'you boast of your learning, that you have the Hebrew and Greek, and know the original:[9] but you see Pilate and the Jews had the Hebrew, Greek and Latin, yet knew not the original, for had they known it, they would not have crucified the Lord of life and glory' (Cotton and Cole 1655: 3). The priests are not explicitly excluded from the possibility of benefiting from the transformative powers of conscience – they are included, after all, in the address 'to you all I speak, sin not against the light in your own consciences' – but none the less it is clear that the priests must be held responsible for the evil done at their instigation, and that the differentiation between evil 'shepherds' and the 'flock' that has been led astray is one that derives from God: 'he [God] will tear his flock out of the mouth of the greedy devouring shepherds, that have made a prey upon them, and the idol-shepherds shall have their arm dried up, and their right eye darkened' (Cotton and Cole 1655: 5).

The final two paragraphs continue in polemic with an antagonistic addressee, identified as 'apostate England' (Cotton and Cole 1655: 5), but clearly continuing to address the corrupt influence of the unregenerate clergy, whom Cotton and Cole see as abusing their power. They are warned of the limits of this power, and blamed for turning people against the Quakers:

> having a guilty conscience, and fearing they would declare against thy wickedness, thou incensest the people, telling them that they are dangerous people, Quakers, so making the people afraid of us: and incensest the magistrates, telling them that they must lay hold on us, as troublers of the people, and disturbers of the peace, and so makes them thy drudges to act thy malice, that thy filthiness may not be discovered, and thy shame appear; but God will make them in one day to forsake thee, and leave and fly from thee, though for the present thou lordest it over magistrates, people, meeting-house, and all, as though all were thine. (Cotton and Cole 1655: 6)

Whilst Cotton and Cole set clear limits on the power currently exercised by the priest – 'God will make them in one day to forsake thee' – this passage above all emphasises the social and institutional power the priest was perceived to have: he influences not only 'the people', but also the magistrates; moreover, and worst of all, he is a pretender to the throne of God:

> [thou] hast got into the seat of God, the consciences of the people, and what thou sayest must not be contradicted: if thou bid them fight and war, they obey it; if thou bid them persecute and imprison, they do it; so that they venture their bodies and souls to fulfil thy lusts of envy and pride. (Cotton and Cole 1655: 6)

The paragraph then moves away from the specific address to 'apostate England', and undertakes the ungendering of the category 'woman' and its association instead with general human weakness. Finally, the direct, second-person mode of address returns, but this time in the plural, 'you', confronting two priests who had visited Cotton and Cole in prison: 'Indeed, you yourselves are the women, that are forbidden to speak in the church, that are become women' (Cotton and Cole 1655: 7-8). Having established the *general* identification of 'women' with 'weakness', this shift now effects the *specific* identification of these two priests, and through them all the clergy, with weakness and femininity, as the culmination of the whole polemical direction of the piece.

Within this piece of polemic, it is thus possible to distinguish two quite distinct oppositional addressees: the priests and the people. Whilst the warning announced by the title is addressed to both groups, and the general exhortation is made to both groups to look to their consciences and establish of which 'generation' they are, none the less the text distinguishes quite clearly between the addresses to the two, urging a shift in allegiance by the people from the 'priests', or indeed from other sects, to the Quakers. In contrast, the address to the priests is more condemnatory, identifying them unequivocally with 'Cain's generation' and, in the final paragraph, with the weakness of 'women', thereby condemning them to silence. For a text coming from a religious group in its very early years, its members actively working to convince people of the justness of their cause, such a distinction between potential converts and out-and-out opponents might be expected; however, this text demonstrates it to be one that, in terms of its dialogic address, it carries into the formation of the argument itself.

The text is certainly predominantly characterised by this extended, if multiply-addressed, polemic; what though, of the question of dialogue? Can the text in any sense be said to posit a sympathetic addressee? Perhaps not surprisingly for a text written in gaol, the answer is that it barely acknowledges the possibility of a supportive reader. The dextrous anticipation of opposition and rebuke at every stage of the argument is really what characterises this text. There is one moment, though, which might perhaps be said to address just such a sympathetic interlocutor. In the first paragraph, having commented on the failure of the scribes, Pharisees and priests of biblical times to recognise Christ as the true messiah, instead putting him to death, Cotton and Cole comment on how this can have come to pass: 'Now Christ Jesus himself gives the reason, and thanks his Father, that he had hid it from the wise, and prudent, and revealed it to babes, because it was the Father's good pleasure, and the Scriptures declare them to be ignorant, that had the Hebrew, Greek and Latin' (Cotton and Cole 1655: 1–2). Just as Christ had cause to thank God for revealing his plans to 'babes' rather than to the 'wise and prudent', so the Quakers have cause to do likewise. They are the 'babes' chosen by God, and a reminder of this, embedded in the text as it is here, is a salutary reminder of the new order – the 'world turned upside down' – that such choices herald, and thus serves as a source of encouragement to those already convinced of the justness of the Quakers' beliefs.

There is one final element of dialogic theory which is of fundamental importance to this text, and that is the notion of the 'extraverbal situation' and its contribution to dialogic exchange:

> *Verbal communication can never be understood and explained outside of this connection with a concrete situation* ... In its concrete connection with a situation, verbal communication is always accompanied by social acts of a nonverbal character (the performance of labor, the symbolic acts of a ritual, a ceremony etc.), and it is often only an accessory to these acts, merely carrying out an auxiliary role. (Voloshinov, *Marxism and the Philosophy of Language* (1929), quoted in Pearce 1994: 42; original emphasis.)

In relation to a piece of writing such as *To the Priests and People of England*, what we might call the extratextual situation is clearly of paramount importance. In 1655, the Quaker movement was still in its infancy, originating in the north only in the early 1650s, and moving south only in 1654. Cotton and Cole would have been amongst the first Quakers to prophesy in Exeter, where they were arrested and imprisoned, and from where they wrote this text. It is the extratextual situation – the newness of this sect, and the context of the prison – that undoubtedly determines the sense of isolation in the text, the two authors pitted against a hostile world. The immediate context of the prison, indeed, is written into the text in the concluding sentence: 'So leaving you to the light in all your consciences to judge of what we have writ, we remain prisoners in Exeter goal for the word of God' (Cotton and Cole 1655: 8). Not only does this remind us of the determining power of the situation in which the text was written, it also confronts us with 'the power dynamics that operate in each and every act of communication' (Pearce 1994: 74). The reciprocity of dialogue does not necessarily bring with it a mutuality or equality: as Pearce says, 'our dialogues rarely exist between equal parties' (Pearce 1994: 102). Despite the sophisticated intricacies of the polemic enacted by the text, this concluding sentence reminds us that the dialogue is indeed profoundly unequal: whatever the power or persuasiveness of the argument constructed by the authors, they none the less have no power to change their immediate situation: they must, as they say, 'remain prisoners', hoping (though not expecting) that the consciences of their opponents will be touched by their writing. There can be few sharper reminders of the 'power-inscribed' (Pearce 1994: 101) character of dialogic exchanges, nor of the significance of the extratextual situation for the production and character of the text.

Dialogic theory is, then, a highly suggestive way both to chart, and to assess the impact of, an anticipated audience on the structure and argument of a piece of writing such as Cotton and Cole's. The text explicitly posits two specific constituencies of antagonistic addressees, and shapes particular stages of its argument differently in relation to each of these groups. As well as recognising the inscription of these addressee-positions within the text, dialogic theory also underlines the importance of the extraverbal or extratextual context in which the utterance is produced, and of the power differential inherent in the different speaker/addressee positions. The combination of these two factors – the anticipation of a hostile audience, and the recognition of the impact of the socially-produced extratextual situation – brings us forcefully back to the material conditions in which texts such as these were produced, and the impact these inevitably have on the kinds of texts that have been left to us.

'Christ Jesus in man or woman': gender and spirituality in sectarian women's writing

Throughout, Cotton and Cole's text is constructed at the intersection of discourses of gender and sexuality. It is not, of course, that there was anything new in this intersection: an imagery of femininity has always been central to Christian doctrine,[10] and the discourse of femininity in the seventeenth century relied heavily on the religious, specifically scriptural, genealogy of its tenets. What proved to be so significant, though, for writings such as Cotton and Cole's but also for sectarian women's writing more generally, were the particular interpretations of gender and of spirituality that were generated within the context of the radical sects.

In these two discourses, the potentially contradictory designations of femininity were brought sharply into focus, and interpreted in such a way that a new kind of spiritual activity for women was, for a time at least, articulated and legitimated. Whilst women were generally exhorted to recognise their bodily inferiority, to keep its carnal disorderliness in check, and consequently to subject themselves to the superiorly constituted male, this ultimately extended only to earthly matters. In spiritual matters, women's responsibility for the salvation of their own souls, and their equal inheritance with men of the possibility of this salvation, marked out a space in which gender had no dominion and in which, therefore, women could act – write, prophesy, preach – on a more equal footing with men, at least hypothetically.

This, at least, was the case with the more radical of the sects, such as the Quakers and the Fifth Monarchists: their reliance on the Bible, with its injunctions to women to submit themselves to men, was mediated by their insistence on the importance on the immediate revelation of God to the individual, a revelation which might prompt a re-evaluation of the received meanings of a scriptural text, as indeed we have seen with Cotton and Cole's text. Other sects, such as the Baptists and some Independent congregations, were bound by a much more rigorously literal understanding of the Bible, which consequently limited the activities they tolerated of women.

In all the sects, though, there was a markedly greater acceptance of women's public activities, including writing and publishing, than was the case in orthodox Anglicanism. And in all cases, the way that this was justified, either overtly or covertly, was through reference to divine authorisation. Whether by disclaiming their own authorship, and attributing it instead to God, or by citing a range of biblical precedents for women's religious activities, or by aligning their own practices and beliefs with true godliness and their opponents' with the contrary, the arguments developed to vindicate and fortify the writings and prophesying by women during this time were all firmly grounded in a set of religious explanations and justifications. It is not the case, then, that these texts were linked to religion, but still identifiable separate from it, but rather that they were produced within, and as a part of, religious discourse, that fundamental shaper of mid-seventeenth-century history. For this reason, if for no other, these writings need to be seen not as marginal to mainstream political events of the 1640s and 1650s, but as centrally productive of, as well as produced by and implicated in, the circumstances of this historical moment. After 1660, the configuration of spirituality and politics shifted, with the two increasingly separated from each other, and with this shift sectarian writers found themselves more in opposition than in the mainstream from then onwards. From this point, the focus of the texts was increasingly on sectarian rather than on national politics, although in the context of the sects there continued to be no absolute distinction between the two. Whether we are looking at pre- or post-Restoration writings, however, we need to begin from the basis of the centrality of God, and his power to sanction practices contrary to those sanctioned by the social order, and then to chart the particular manifestations and configurations of this pre-eminence through these changing political circumstances.

This emphasis on the spiritual, and on the authorising capacity of the ungendered soul in relation to its divine progenitor, however, did not preclude a consideration of the meanings of the female body, either spiritually or socially, in these writings. As we saw earlier,[11] the female body was read as a complex and ambiguous sign, potentially indicative both of social disorderliness and spiritual election. The physical bodies of women prophets, specifically, were carefully interpreted; their tears, fasting, weakness or illness could signify either the divine presence or human – specifically feminine – frailty. Typically, then, her own bodily signs were interpreted by the female prophet herself, as well as by her audience, cited as evidence of the godly authority for her prophecies.

Moreover, the body of the writer or prophet signified in another sense: when not occupied by the divine presence, as it was in the cases of the women who prophesied, it was seen as the inhabitant of the social domain, and as such its social meanings of weakness and potential unruliness, and the consequent need for subservience, were affirmed. Whilst arguments were predicated on the equal *souls* of men and women, women's *bodies* were always seen as signifying something different from men's, whether the exceptional spiritual superiority of the woman prophet consumed by the divine presence, or, more characteristically, the proper social inferiority of women. Thus, whilst the spritual equality of women with men took precedence over their social inequality, it never replaced or neutralised it, never challenged the foundations on which that social inequality rested. The body remained as a profoundly important sign of difference, and whilst that sign was reinterpreted, its sphere of influence restricted to the earthly, it none the less retained a set of meanings for sectarian women writers that were fundamental to their conception of the place of women in the spiritual and material worlds.

Cotton and Cole were untypical in the way that they negotiated the contradiction between the equal soul and the unequal body. Most sectarian women writers addressing this issue challenged the significance of the unequal body on the grounds of spiritual authority: God choosing them to undertake his work, to convey his message, is the means whereby they transcend the limitations of gender; this is generally justified through recourse to the Christian reliance on paradox, whereby God chooses the weak to take precedence over the strong (often with reference to 1 Corinthians 1:27). In this way, they acknowledge women's weakness, and use this as the basis on which to argue their being chosen by God to do his work. Cotton and Cole, however, whilst retaining the association of 'women' with 'weakness', redesignate 'women' as a concept separate from that of 'female', arguing instead that it is a general signifier of human frailty and vanity. Thus, by their account 'women' (that is, any males or females who manifest these carnal frailties) have no right to speak; only those ungendered by their experience of God have this right. Thus, rather than accepting that women (females) are weak and are therefore chosen by God to speak, they argue that women (females) are no more likely to be weak than men, and that 'strength' and 'weakness', 'women' and 'men' are not gendered categories. It is ungendered weakness that precludes the right to speak, rather than gendered weakness that prompts God's choosing them to speak.

In both these arguments, however, gender is constructed as a centrally important source of meaning, something that has to be negotiated, acknowledged, challenged, redefined, or fought over. Cotton and Cole are exceptional in refusing the social designation of 'women' as necessarily indicative of weakness and vanity; they nevertheless engage with, even struggle with, this designation. Indeed, the vehemence with which they struggle with it testifies to its potency and centrality for their position as sectarian prophets and writers. This, then, serves as a reminder that, despite the reliance of these writers' arguments on spiritual justifications, they also of necessity engage with the interpretations of gender constructed within a society profoundly convinced of fundamental, highly meaningful and unchangeable differences between men and women, differences that prescribed quite distinct codes,

207

conventions and practices for each sex. Whilst, in any analysis of these texts, we trace the discursive negotiations of these definitions, it is also important to situate these within the context of their material manifestations: to remember, for example, that because of the social meanings ascribed to femininity, women's religious discourse would be read differently from men's, would have different meanings, and elicit different responses and, very often, as in the case of Cotton and Cole, different penalties.

'It's weakness that is the woman': Cotton and Cole's rhetorical ungendering of the concept of 'weakness' and of the persecuting priests (to which the title of this chapter refers) is suggestive of many of the paradoxes and fascinations of these writings by women from the radical sects. The disarming and apparently contradictory refusal of conventionally gendered categories (such as 'woman') reminds us of the centrality of paradox – something beloved of seventeenth-century and twentieth-century critics and commentators alike – to Christian doctrine. It reminds us, too, of the appropriations and redefinitions of these paradoxes with the writings from the sects: a move which legitimates the hitherto unjustifiable production of a body of writing that was often rhetorically ingenious, and which helps account for their interest for the contemporary feminist literary critic. Nevertheless, however compelling these paradoxes may be for such critics, we cannot afford to ignore the repeated assertion of the equation between femininity and weakness. The continued presence of the notion of 'weakness' meant that the writings and the arguments which they constructed continued to be vulnerable to reinterpretation and redesignation as having been generated precisely by the weak and vain carnal bodies of women, rather than by their ungendered souls, as the writers themselves would have it. For a feminist critic approaching these writings in the late twentieth century, then, there are several reasons for caution. As I have argued throughout, whilst some of these texts might at first appear perfect vehicles for appropriation into the feminist project of challenging conventional critical wisdoms about the absence of women's writing, they are none the less never straightforwardly 'proto-feminist' works. The skill and wit of their textual manoeuvres should not tempt us into extracting the moments of 'resistance' (as we may perceive them), either from those of 'constraint', or from their more general historical and religious circumstances of production. To do so would be to privilege the desires of the critic over the evidence of the text. Furthermore, I have suggested that even where the linguistic dexterity might seem impressively strategic, the punishments and sanctions against these women writers somewhat relativise their textual triumphs. Rather than attempting to absorb these writings into a synthesising contemporary feminist literary history, my argument in this book suggests that their value for us lies in their difference and their specificity, as much as in our 'moments of recognition'. It is precisely their strangeness, their particular integration with, and distinction from, other configurations of religion and femininity at this time, as well as their striking resonances with contemporary feminist concerns, that accounts for the increasing critical attention to these texts, and to the reappraisal of their significance to literary studies.

Appendices

Editorial note

These appendices comprise a selection of those texts discussed most fully in the book. If short enough, the complete text is reproduced, whilst the longer text is represented by a substantial extract. I have included only such texts as are not available in other modern editions* (so that although I discuss Trapnel's work at length in the book, none of her writing is included here) and I have tried to select texts and passages that relate, either broadly or precisely, to the themes and focus of this book. The texts are arranged in chronological order.

In editing the texts, I have tried to maintain a balance between modernising the text and leaving it in its original form. Any alteration of spelling or punctuation necessarily changes the text's meanings, more or less subtly; yet to leave these entirely as they stand in the original can drive a wedge between the contemporary reader and the writing, either by making the texts seem odd and colourfully eccentric, or (because of different punctuation practices) by rendering particular passages unintelligible. I have therefore worked with a not altogether comfortable compromise. I have made minimal changes to punctuation. This has not been changed if it is simply unfamiliar or would be deemed incorrect by current standards, but only if it hinders ready comprehension by a contemporary reader. Thus, colons and semi-colons have usually been retained where we might expect to find full stops. Spelling has been modernised, except when the word-sound would be significantly changed by modernisation (as in 'murther' or 'burthen'). Italics have been removed when they signify proper nouns, quotations or reported speech (and replaced by the modern conventions), and have been retained only when they signify emphasis. Capitals have been retained only for proper nouns. Abbreviations of words, names, titles, and books of the Bible have all been expanded and given in full. I have silently corrected any obvious printing errors, but footnoted any instances whose meaning might be in doubt, and silently changed certain dates in the form of '17' or '29' in the original to the more familiar '17th' or '29th'. Biblical allusions unreferenced in the original are supplied in square brackets. Marginal notes in the original have been transferred to the relevant point in the text and also appear in square brackets.

Notes are used to clarify particular points, whether historical, biblical or linguistic, in the original texts, and to give brief introductory glosses to the texts and their authors.

* Other seventeenth-century texts referred to in the book, or extracts from them, can be found in the following places:

Editorial note

Trapnel 1654b, Evans and Chevers 1662, Wentworth 1677, Allen 1683 and Vokins 1691: in Elspeth Graham, Hilary Hinds, Elaine Hobby and Helen Wilcox (eds) (1989) *Her Own Life: Autobiographical Writings by Seventeenth-Century Englishwomen*, London: Routledge.

Trapnel 1654a: to be reproduced in full in Anna Trapnel (1997, forthcoming) *The Cry of a Stone*, ed. and intro. by Hilary Hinds.

The Women Writers Project at Brown University, USA, aims to make available on the Internet by the year 2000 hundreds of texts written by women which have been out of print since their original publication.

Appendix A:
Mary Cary:
from *The Little Horn's Doom and Downfall* (1651)

The Little Horn's Doom and Downfall; or a Scripture prophecy of King James
and King Charles and of this present Parliament unfolded.

Wherein it appears that the late tragedies that have been acted upon the scene of these three
nations, and particularly the late king's doom and death, was so long ago as by Daniel pre-
declared. And what the issue of all will be is also discovered, which follows in the second part.

By M. Cary, a servant of Jesus Christ.

Amos 3:7,8. 'Surely the Lord God will do nothing but he revealeth his secrets unto his
servants the prophets. The lion hath roared, who will not fear? The Lord God hath
spoken, who can but prophesy?'

London, printed for the author, and are to be sold at the sign of the Black-spread Eagle, at
the west end of Paul's, 1651.[1]

To the Reader.

Courteous Reader,

I had written the first of these treatises, entitled *The Little Horn's Doom*[2] *and Downfall*, above
seven years since, but have been withheld from publishing of it until now (for ends best
known unto divine majesty; but (if may so guess), it may be it was because that men would
then generally have been more uncapable of receiving of such things than now they are,
because now these things are fulfilled; and prophecies are then best understood when they are
fulfilled). But now am I so pressed to publish both this first treatise, and this other which I
have but lately written, upon this 27th verse of this seventh of Daniel [having finished it but
since the beginning of the month of August, this present year, 1651], as that I cannot, I dare
not, withhold neither of them from public view any longer; but by publishing of them in print,
I shall expose them to the public view of all men as far as in me lies.

And having so done, shall leave it to the eternal Jehovah to make it effectual, to those ends
to which he hath appointed it, which may be, first, to convince those of their folly, that persist
in ways contradictory to (or crossing of) his present designs, to the disturbing of their own

souls (though they cannot hinder his work, for 'who can let it?' [Isaiah 43:13]), for if he do not convince them, none can. Or:

Secondly it may be to confirm others; for there are some that are already so far enlightened in their understandings, about the present proceedings of God in the world, as they do in some competent measure already discern the footsteps of God, in these great present providences; and do discern also what his designs are in these things.

Who yet are not fully persuaded that the saints'[3] suffering times are expired, and that the 'time, times and half a time' [Daniel 12:7, Revelation 12:14] is come to a period; who possibly may hereby be further enlightened, and satisfied, and further encouraged to rejoice in God, and in his present proceedings in the world.

And now first, if any shall slight these things, because hereby is discovered any delusions, in which they are; or any folly, in the ways they have taken; wherein they do any way support the enemies, and oppose the very real servants of God; or for any other by-end whatsoever: let them know, that their so doing, shall not trouble me at all, if it hurt not them.

And secondly, if any shall hereby receive any light, or any refreshment, let them bless the Lord for it, from whom alone it came: for I am a very weak, and unworthy instrument, and have not done this work by any strength of my own, but have been often made sensible, that I could do no more herein (wherein any light, or truth could appear) of myself, than a pencil or pen can do, when no hand guides it: being daily made sensible of my own insufficiency to do anything as of myself; that to use the apostle's expression, and to speak it feelingly (for I find it daily true), I must profess, 'I am not sufficient to think a good thought, but my sufficiency is of God' [2 Corinthians 3:5], to whom be glory, and honour, and praise for evermore, Amen.

I have only one thing more, which I judge necessary to acquaint the reader with, and that is this: in my former book which I published in April, 1648, I subscribed my name Cary, for that was then my name; for which reason I have thought good to subscribe the same name in the title page of this book also, that the reader may not be put to any doubt, by finding different names in the titles (since I have in this book, so often referred the reader to that); but let the reader know that (having since changed my name) I am now known by the name of,

Mary Rande.

* * *

They that have any knowledge of myself, how worthless a worm I am, do also know how unfit I am either to write books, or to judge of others' writings: yet owing respect to this author, I could not deny a word, being desired to read and say something.

And this I must say (though not concurring in all things touching the personal reign[4] [which I ever accounted a harmless error, if an error]),[5] that this author hath these things commendable in the ensuing treatise.

First, that she hath taught her sex that there are more ways than one to avoid idleness (the devil's cushion)[6] on which so many sit and sleep their last. They that will not use the distaff may improve[7] a pen.

Secondly, a holy, modest, and painful[8] spirit, runs through her endeavours; which I desire may not be slighted by any, nor thrown by: for good wine may be found in this cluster:[9] in this

214

dress you shall neither see naked breasts, black patches, nor long trains; but an heart breathing after the coming of Christ, and the comfort of saints.

Thirdly, Scriptures clearly opened, and properly applied; yea, so well, that you might easily think she ploughed with another's heifer[10] [Judges 14:18], were not the contrary well known.

Upon the whole matter, I believe that it will be acceptable to all those that desire to see Christ as he is; who will not be offended at this treatise, or rather the spouse's wish and longing, 'Make haste, my beloved, and be thou like a young roe, or a hart, upon the mountains of spices,' Canticles[11] 8:14.

Two of this sex I have met with, very famous for more than their mother-tongue, and for that we call learning, yet living. The one an unhappy branch of that tree which is cut off, and pulling up by the roots; of whom I could say much, to whom I owe much. The other of deserved note in Utrecht, the glory of her sex in Holland.[12] But this my countrywoman speaks the best language; yea, I will add: other 'daughters have done virtuously, but thou surmountest them', Proverbs 31:29.

More would I say; but my feeble thoughts or words will add but little to her labours. Doubtless she had good help from above in her travel[13] for this birth: I will bequeath her Solomon's last words of his good houswife:

'Favour is deceitful, and beauty is vain: but a woman that feareth the Lord, she shall be praised. Give her of the fruit of her hands, and let her own works praise her in the gates', Proverbs 31:30, 31.

Hugh Peter

[Further prefatory material follows, after which the prophecy itself begins. Cary argues that the vision of the prophet Daniel, recounted in Daniel chapter 7, relates specifically to contemporary events in England, and in particular to the demise of Charles I.]

Verse 25
And he shall speak great words against the most high, and shall wear out the saints of the most high, etc. [Daniel 7:25]

Our lord and saviour Jesus Christ, John 15. [18-24], tells his disciples, that whosoever despised them, despised him, and whosoever despised him, despised him that sent him. Whereby it's clear, that that person that speaks great words against the saints of the most high, doth therein speak great words against the most high. That this king did speak great words against the saints of the most high, threatening the ruin and destruction of all Puritans and Roundheads as he termed the saints of God, is so well known, as there needs nothing to be further spoken to make it appear; nor need I mention the persons which long before the wars, which merely for their being servants of God were persecuted, imprisoned, fined, banished, and otherwise threatened. And as he spake great words against the most high in his saints, so he spake great words against the laws and ordinances[14] of God, prohibiting of them, requiring godly and faithful ministers to refrain from the worshipping of God, from public praying, and preaching of the word of God, upon the first day of the week.[15] Whereas many a poor soul might have been converted to and confirmed in the ways of God in those ordinances; but he constrained (as it were) the people of the kingdom to a profane and loose life, to dishonour God, by inviting and requiring of them to practice profane and wicked sports upon that day, which was appointed for a holy worshipping of God.[16] Whereas many poor souls needed rather to have been encouraged, and called upon to have more frequently attended upon the ordinances of God, for they perished for want of knowledge. And as he thus spake great words against the ordinances of the most high, so he nourished and supported many wicked and abominable priests (when many holy and faithful ministers of Christ were rejected), who did most profanely abuse the scriptures, and despise the very spirit of God, and that publicly; of which sort there were many among those centuries of scandalous ministers, that were in the beginning of this parliament sequestered for their delinquencies.[17]

Thus in that this king spake great words against the saints, and ordinances, and spirit of God, and had pleasure in such as so did; he therein did as here is said of him, speak great words against the most high.

And shall wear out the saints of the most high.

Was it not long before the sitting of this parliament given out by this king, that he would not leave until he had left no more Puritans in England than there were Protestants in Rome? And is it not generally known what means and ways were used to wear them out, and to make them weary of living in the kingdom? Insomuch as many godly and faithful people being weary of the impositions upon their consciences, of those things which were evil, and the prohibitions of them from that which was good (as their meetings to call upon the name of the Lord, and to confer one with another of the things of God, and the repetitions of sermons) did, being thus wearied, leave their native kingdom,[18] though in all outward respects to their great disadvantage; and those that remained how did they groan under their burthens, and complain to heaven day and night, against the insufferable and wearying proceedings of that unworthy king? Thus did he wear out the saints of the most high.

And shall think to change times and laws, and they shall be given into his hand until, etc.

Therein also, he is more exactly characterized and described: for it is well known, that he did think and intend to change times, and laws. He thought to have made sad times for all circumspect and holy Christians, whom he called Puritans; and times of joy, and rejoicing for all popish[19] and profane persons. And he thought to have changed those laws, which had been by preceding princes made for the privileges of the people, in civil and spiritual respects; and to have imposed laws destructive to the people's freedom and liberty, and to have ruled all by his own will, and made the people slaves thereunto.

And they shall be given into his hand until, etc.

As he thought to change laws, and times, so he did; they were given into his hand for a while, he had times and laws in his hand to change them at his pleasure, and he thought to have done so always. And to this end, consulted with wicked bishops, popish lords, and profane judges;

and to this end also he raised armies, first against the Scots, and afterward against all well-affected people in Ireland, and also in England.[20] Thus this horn that came up in the room of three, did in all things answer this description of him, which is given in these 24th and 25th verses, and he comes in no tittle[21] short of it.

[pp. 8-12]

[Cary continues to detail the ways in which current political and religious events constitute the fulfilment of Daniel's prophetic vision by concluding her exegesis of Daniel 7:25; she then moves on to verse 26. In the closing pages of *The Little Horn's Doom and Downfall*, Cary anticipates and answers objections to her interpretations.]

And thus this part of this prophecy being thus opened and explained, it is made evident that the late king of these three nations, that is by some called the Nonesuch[22] Charles, for his desperate impiety and hypocrisy, was long ago prophesied of as well as (he that was by him styled) his holy father the pope; to whom he was as firm a son, as any king ever was; though he played the greatest hypocrite in professing the contrary, as ever any king did.

I say it is evident, that the late king was long ago prophesied of, as well as the pope; and that as the pope was fore-prophesied of, as being the beast that should be desperately wicked and maliciously cruel against the saints, so is this king fore-prophesied of, as being of the ten horns of the beast, and more stout than his fellows: as exceeding them for wretched wicked dealing with the saints and cruelty to them.

Whereby the proceedings of the parliament with and against him, is cleared from having the least stain or spot of injustice or unrighteousness in it, which some would fasten upon them.[23]

For it is here evident, that as the afflicted condition of the church for twelve hundred years and more under the pope was long ago prophesied of, so this parliament, which were to be the instruments of the church's deliverance in their measure, were also long ago prophesied of. In which prophecy, it was so long ago declared, that to them judgement should be given, and that they should do justice upon that wicked king; take away his dominion, and destroy him unto the end [Daniel 7:26]: and what the issue of all this will be, is discovered in the following verse; but of that in its place.[24]

But now it may be some may slight this interpretation, saying that it is not to be regarded, seeing several have given several interpretations of Scriptures, and most of them have been besides the truth; and so may this will they say.

But to those, I have but this to say; first, that upon this account they may continually slight all that shall be said in opening the Scriptures, though it be never so consonant unto the truth and mind of the spirit of God, the author of the Scriptures. And so God (with such slight spirits) will not have the glory of his pre-decreeing of the things he will have to come to pass many hundred years after; and of his exact bringing things to pass according to the counsels of his own will so many hundred years before resolved upon.

And secondly, they in so doing do give less honour to God than the heathens did to their devilish oracles, which would pretend to foreshew things to come: and less than they do to astronomers,[25] who from the stars do pretend to foretell things: whereas God oftentimes frustrateth the tokens of those liars, and maketh those diviners mad (Isaiah 44:25), and they cannot foreshew anything infallibly (though possibly from the stars, they may give some uncertain hints of things); but it is that which is proper to God alone, infallibly to foretell things to come (as appears, Isaiah 48:3, 4, 5, and Isaiah 46:9, 10) and which he doth from time to time do by his servants the prophets; and therefore what they have declared from God, hath been done for our observation; Romans 15:4, Psalms 107:43, Deuteronomy 29:29. Wherein we may see that what God hath done from age to age hath all along been the fulfilling of his word, of which we are to give him the glory.

And thirdly, though some interpreters have failed of truth, which it may be hath been the hardening of the hearts of some: yet this will not be a sufficient discharge for any from their duty of observing these things; that when the truth appears, God may have the glory.

But fourthly, it is true things have often been uncertainly hit at by some men, before they came to pass: but these things are come to pass, and all prophecies are best understood when they are fulfilled, or near to be fulfilled: not but that oftentimes prophecies have been clearly understood long beforehand by many precious saints.

But fifthly, this is certain, that when the very mind of God in prophecies is unerringly laid open, being clearly and convincingly discovered to his saints and servants, that desire to pry into and observe these things according to their duty; that even then some will not receive them: neither the wise of the world, nor the wicked of the world; as appears, Matthew 11:25. and Daniel 12:10. But though the worldly-wise do not, yet they that have wisdom from above shall have these things revealed to them, and shall understand them, as appears in the same scriptures; for when truth is revealed, the children of truth, having one and the same spirit, shall see it with the same eye, and rejoice with the same joy, in seeing of it: 'My sheep know my voice', John 10:27. They know that it is my voice, and not another's voice: and indeed it is chiefly for their sakes, who know his voice, who have his spirit, that all truths are revealed.

[pp. 41–5]

[After *The Little Horn's Doom and Downfall* concludes, there follows Cary's prophecy based on Daniel 7:27, appearing on the title-page at the beginning of the book as *A New and More Exact Mappe or Description of New Jerusalem's Glory, when Jesus Christ and his Saints with him shall Reign on Earth a Thousand Years, and Possess all Kingdoms.*]

Appendix B:
Elinor Channel:
from *A Message from God, By a Dumb Woman* (1654)

A Message from God, By a Dumb Woman, to his Highness the Lord Protector. Together with a Word of Advice to the Commons of England and Wales, for the Electing of a Parliament.[1] By Elinor Channel. Published according to her desire, by Arise Evans.[2]

Proverbs 31:8. 'Open thy mouth for the dumb in the cause[3] of all such as are appointed to destruction.'

Printed in the year 1653. Or as the vulgar think 1654.[4]

To his Highness the Lord Protector Oliver Cromwell.

The Humble Petition of Elinor Channel.

May it please your highness to understand that your petitioner is an inhabitant at Cranley in Surrey, who upon a Sabbath-day about two months agone, at night, as she was in bed in a slumber, had a blow given her upon her heart, which blow awaked her. And immediately with that, the thoughts of her heart were changed, and all the corruption thereof taken away, that from that day to this, she could think of no evil. And then she heard an audible voice, which said unto her, 'Come away, I will send thee on my message to London, fear not to go, for I thy Lord am with thee.' And the thoughts of your petitioner's heart was so directed that she was given to understand how that the spirit of the Lord had called her; to the end that she should be sent to your highness: and by the same Holy Spirit, inwardly though she be but a weak woman in expression, she was taught in brief how to express her message from God to your highness. And your petitioner being three times hindered by her husband, who is a very poor man, and hath many small children, three of them very young ones, her mind was sore troubled that her sleep went from her; and at some times she was speechless: whereupon your petitioner's husband, seeing her restless condition, consented to let her come to London that she might express her mind to your highness and have rest in her spirit. The premises[5] being considered, and further to give your highness to understand the petitioner's message to you, which she hopes will not only be accepted of you, but will be also effected by you.

219

Appendix B

The Words of her Message are these
that Follow.

1. She is to say upon her coming to you, 'Peace be to this house, and peace be to the whole kingdom, and the peace of God be with us for evermore. Amen.'

2. She is to say to you, 'The God of Abraham, the God of Isaac, and the God of Jacob hath opened the mouth of the dumb[6] to speak for peace. The sword must be stayed. The world draweth toward an end, and the knots of peace and love must be made in all Christian lands.' [By the 'dumb' she meaneth herself, 'cause she had been dumb.]

3. She is to say to you, 'Sir, you have taken upon you to be a protector of your Lord's vineyard, but he requireth that you should make the hedges and the walls of it; which is peace and love, and the true Gospel. And that you should protect the steward to plant his vineyard.' [By the 'vineyard' she meaneth the church and kingdom. By the 'true Gospel' she meaneth that worship we had once. By the 'steward' she means the king.]

4. She is to say unto you, 'If a man fall into the hands of a creditor, if his creditor be one of God's servants, he will not take body and goods; if his body pays the debt, his heir shall have the inheritance.' [By the 'body that paid the debt', she means the late king that died. By the 'heir', his son.]

Be it known to your highness that your petitioner is a true member of the Catholic and apostolic faith,[7] as it was reformed and established in the Church of England, by King Edward VI and continued by Queen Elisabeth, King James, and King Charles. And though the petitioner can say or dispute but little for it, yet she believeth that to be the true and only way of salvation, which in due time shall prevail over all the earth. Amen.

Elinor Channel.

April 19, 1654.

This poor woman came to the court upon the 17th day of last April, and thought immediately to have spoken with his highness the Lord Protector, and to return again the same day: but alas she found it other ways. And some of the guard about the court told her if she had but five pounds to give them, they would help her to the presence of the Lord Protector. Whereupon, after two days waiting in vain at court, being much troubled that she would not come before his highness to discharge her conscience, she came to the city of London, and wandered up and down to see if she could get anybody to take it from her mouth, and publish it in print, that she might get some ease that way: but of a long while, she being a stranger, she could get none to hear or regard her. At last she met with some compassionate body that talked with her, and sent her with a note to me, who took all the report from her mouth, as you have it above, and then sent her away, promising to get it printed, if she could not get the copy delivered to his highness which she had to give him, and have seen her no more since.

But hearing now that such a like woman is about the city, and that she is dumb, and that she was in Fleet Street on Sunday June 18, where she stood mute for a long while, and as it is said, the cruel beadles[8] dragged her to Bridewell,[9] and wounded the poor soul for nothing, but because she stood harmlessly in the street: and that they refused her at Bridewell, and turned her out again among the wanton mad crew, who flocked about her and abused her; when indeed, if there had been any charity in them at Bridewell (as some pretend the house is for that use) there was for them a fair object to shew their charity upon: but she stayed thereabouts until night; and what is become of her since God knows, we hear nothing more of her.

Now this woman was very sensible and profound in what she spake to me, but as she said, when she is dumb, all her senses are taken up, and then the matter which troubles her mind, is dictated and made plain to her by the spirit of God; so that when she comes to herself, she has it by heart. And though it be but short, yet you shall find more truth and substance in it, than in all Hana Trampenel's[10] songs or sayings, whom some account of as the Diana[11] of the English, Acts 19:34, as may appear by this that was written for her.

[*A Message from God*, pp. 1-7]

Appendix C:
Priscilla Cotton and Mary Cole:
To the Priests and People of England (1655)

To the Priests and People of England, We Discharge Our Consciences, and Give Them Warning[1]

Friends,

We have no envy nor malice to any creature, priest or people, but are to mind you of your conditions, without any partiality or hypocrisy, and wish your eternal good: and what we contend against is your greatest enemy, and will be your everlasting woe and torment, if it be not destroyed in you. For know, there is the seed of the woman, and the seed of the serpent in the world [Genesis 3:15; Revelation 12:17], there is the generation of Cain and righteous Abel.[2] Now it lieth upon you all to know what generation you are of: for little did the false prophets and that generation that put to death the true prophets of the Lord think they were of Cain's race; nor did the scribes and Pharisees,[3] that with their priests put Christ to death, think they were of Cain's generation, for they garnished the sepulchres of the righteous, and said if they had been in the days of their fathers, they would not have slain them [Matthew 23:29-30]; yet Christ Jesus told them that all the blood spilt since righteous Abel, should be required of that generation [Matthew 23:35; Luke 11:51]; and that they were the children of them that murthered the prophets [Matthew 23:31].[4] Is it not strange, that the learned priests and scribes, and Pilate that had the Hebrew and Greek besides Latin, should not find out by all their high learning the original[5] of the Scriptures of the prophets, concerning Christ Jesus, that he was the true Messiah: but that they that read the Gospel every Sabbath day, that spake of Christ, should murder and put him to death? Now Christ Jesus himself gives the reason, and thanks his Father, that he had hid it from the wise, and prudent, and revealed it to babes [Matthew 11:25], because it was the Father's good pleasure, and the Scriptures declare them to be ignorant, that had the Hebrew, Greek and Latin, for had they known it, they would not have crucified the Lord of life and glory [1 Corinthians 2:7-8].[6]

Now people, this was the same generation of Cain in them after Christ's death, that persecuted the apostles and put them to death; and it was the same spirit in them that put the martyrs to death, and of that generation were the bishops that persecuted, and so it continueth still to this day in the world;[7] for Cain's generation is now still envying, hating, and persecuting the righteous Abel. Now the persecuting Cainish generation would never acknowledge they were such, but in all ages persecuted the just under some false colour, as they of old said the true prophets were troublers of Israel [1 Chronicles 2:7]; and Amaziah[8] the priest of Bethel said of Amos, that the land was not able to bear his words [Amos 7:10]; and Haman said that the laws of the people of God were contrary to the laws and customs of all nations [Esther 3:8]; and of Christ they said he was a deceiver [Matthew 27:63] and had a devil [John 7:20; 8:48, 52; 10:20]; and of Stephen, that he spake against the holy place and the law [Acts 6:13]; and, that Paul was a pestilent fellow, and a mover of sedition [Acts 24:5]. So that all along it was on a false account the just were persecuted: so in the days of the bishops, the martyrs were burnt and butchered under the name of heretics; so now the seed of the serpent is subtle, and will not persecute the truth, as it is the truth, but under some false pretence or other, else all would see their deceit. But the truth is, it's from the first rise,[9] because their own works are evil, and their brothers' good: they hated Christ Jesus, because he testified that their works were evil. So now Cain's generation hates the just and pure seed of God, because[10] it declares that their works are evil.

Objection:[11] 'But do not the priests declare against evil works?'

Answer: Yes, they do so: the scribes and Pharisees spake good words, they spake of the Messiah, yet they killed the substance[12] of what they spake: so the priests speak true words, good words, and yet kill, and persecute, pursue, and imprison the substance and life of what they speak, for he that departs from evil makes himself a prey to priest and people; and sometimes when the light in their consciences[13] tells them, when they are persecuting the just seed, that they are innocent, yet they wilfully run on against the very light of their own consciences, as did Stephen's persecutors [Acts 7:57].

And is it not so? I speak to that in your consciences, that though the priests speak true words, yet priests and people that live in Cain's race do pursue and persecute even to the very death, the life and power of what they do preach. And know you of a truth, that all the blood since Abel shall be required of this generation [Luke 12:51]; for, as it groweth to the end, it heighteneth and ripeneth its malice and wickedness, and so shall its judgement be, for double plagues shall be poured out upon her.

Now to you all I speak, sin not against the light in your own consciences, be not wilfully blind, but hearken to the light of Jesus Christ in your consciences, that you may come to see what generation you are of, whether of Cain or Abel: and if you did abide in the light, you should come to witness the life and power of what you profess, and so come to that life that gave forth the Scriptures, and not wrest them to your own opinions and lusts [Psalms 56:5; 2 Peter 3:16], one saying 'Lo!' here in Presbytery; another 'Lo!' there in Independency; and another in Prelacy; and another in Baptism.[14] But the Scriptures are not divided,[15] they agree, and hold out one thing; but you divide them, because you live not in that life that gave them forth, yet you boast of your learning, that you have the Hebrew and Greek, and know the original: but you see Pilate and the Jews had the Hebrew, Greek and Latin, yet knew not the original, for had they known it, they would not have crucified the Lord of life and glory [1 Corinthians 2:8].[16]

Therefore know you, that you may be, and are ignorant, though you think yourselves wise.[17] Silly men and women may see more into the mystery of Christ Jesus, than you: for the apostles, that the scribes called illiterate, and Mary and Susanna[18] (silly women [2 Timothy 3:6], as you would be ready to call them, if they were here now) these know more of the Messiah, than all the learned priests and rabbis; for it is the spirit that searcheth all things, yea, the deep things of God, you may know, and yet murther the just, and think you do God good service.

This I warn you in love, for I cannot but think that there are some among you that ponder on this day, and if you would hearken to the light of Jesus Christ in your consciences, it would lead you from your own wisdom, learning, and self-conceitedness, into the simplicity of Jesus Christ, which is a mystery of faith hid in a pure conscience [1 Timothy 3:9]: for your own wisdom must be denied, if ever you will come to witness the life and power of true wisdom, which the fear of the Lord is the beginning of; for so did they of old.

Paul and Apollos[19] were very learned and eloquent, saith the Scriptures, yet Paul counted all his learning dung for the excellency of the knowledge of Christ [Philippians 3:8], let his second chapter of his first Epistle to the Corinthians[20] be a full witness of this: and Apollos was willing to be instructed of his hearers Aquila and Priscilla that were tent-makers [Acts 18:26], and the learned that studied curious arts burnt their books that were of great price, when they came to the knowledge of Jesus Christ [Acts 19:19]. So you now, would you hearken to Jesus Christ,[21] and obey his light in your consciences, you would come down to humility and the fear of the Lord, to the true wisdom and understanding, that you would not need so many authors, and books, you would not need to rent[22] your heads with studying, but you would come to see your teacher in you,[23] which now is removed into a corner, you would come to live a preaching life, and witness that faith you talk of, to purify your hearts [James 4:8] from envy, pride and malice, and to get the victory over the world's glory and honour that is so highly esteemed by you; and coming to see yourselves in the light of Jesus Christ, you will not lord it over God's heritage [1 Peter 5:3], nor lift yourselves up above your brethren in pride [1 Timothy 3:6] and arrogancy, but be a servant to all in love.

Therefore, come now to the light, sin no longer against that in your conscience; for Antichrist must be destroyed by the brightness of his coming [2 Thessalonians 2:8], and God is gathering his people out from idol-shepherds [Zechariah 11:17] into his own fold, to make them one flock and to give them one shepherd [John 10:16], that they may serve him with one consent [Zephaniah 3:9], for he hath fulfilled this Scripture in thousands this day whom he hath gathered out of Antichrist's opinions to worship one God in one way, in spirit and truth, speaking all the same things: if you speak with ten thousand of them, they all agree, having one king, one law giver.

Now fret not at this, you that live at Babylon[24] in confusion, in divisions: for the little stone cut out of the mountain without hands, shall break Babylon's idols.[25]

Now consider, Friends and people, your conditions, for what good doth all your preaching and hearing do you? Break your sleep, rent your brains, and as it were, speak out your lungs, and alas who is bettered by it! Was there ever more pride, lightness, vanity, and wantonness, manifested in your assemblies,[26] than now? You make it the place where you set forth your pride, and vanity to the utmost: was there ever the like injustice, violence, falsehood and deceit in any age, that scarce can a man tell what men mean by what they say any longer?

Men say in effect that God hath forsaken the earth by their wicked practices: the people cry out upon the priests, and say that their opinions have made them so wicked; and the priests cry out upon the people, and say that the fault is theirs: so that the Lord beheld, and instead of righteousness, equity and judgement [Proverbs 2:9], there is a cry.[27] So your whole religion is but a noise, the life, power and substance is not in it.

Oh apostate England, what shall the God of mercies do for thee? What shall he do unto thee? He hath tried thee with mercies, and with the sword, and then with peace again, and yet thou repentest not; he hath given thee his witness, his just one to reprove thee, to convince thee of sin in thy conscience, but thou hast slain the witness, murthered and slain the just: he will not always strive with man, he will now roar from Sion,[28] and the children of the west shall tremble [Hosea 11:10], those that worship their idols; he will redeem Sion with judgement, and he will tear his flock out of the mouth of the greedy devouring shepherds, that have made a prey upon them, and the idol-shepherds shall have their arm dried up, and their right eye darkened [Zechariah 11:17].

Come down thou therefore that hast built among the stars [Obadiah 4] by thy arts and learning; for it's thy pride and thy wisdom, that hath perverted thee; thou hast gone in the way of Cain, in envy and malice, and ran greedily after the reward of Balaam, in covetousness, and if thou repent not, shalt perish in the gainsaying of Kore [Jude 11]:[29] for if a son or a daughter be moved from the Lord, to go into the assembly of the people, in a message from the Lord God, thou canst not endure to hear them speak sound doctrine [2 Timothy 4:3], having a guilty conscience, and fearing they would declare against thy wickedness, thou incensest the people, telling them that they are dangerous people, Quakers, so making the people afraid of us: and incensest the magistrates, telling them that they must lay hold on us, as troublers of the people, and disturbers of the peace, and so makes them thy drudges to act thy malice, that thy filthiness may not be discovered, and thy shame appear; but God will make them in one day to forsake thee, and leave and fly from thee, though for the present thou lordest it over magistrates, people, meeting-house,[30] and all, as though all were thine: and thou sittest as a queen and lady[31] over all, and wilt have the pre-eminence, and hast got into the seat of God, the consciences of the people, and what thou sayest must not be contradicted: if thou bid them fight and war, they obey it; if thou bid them persecute and imprison, they do it; so that they venture their bodies and souls to fulfil thy lusts of envy and pride, and in thy pride thou contemnest all others, thou tellest the people women must not speak in a church [1 Corinthians 14:34-5], whereas it is not spoke only of a female, for we are all one both male and female in Christ Jesus [Galatians 3:28], but it's weakness that is the woman by the Scriptures forbidden, for else thou puttest the Scriptures at a difference in themselves,[32] as still it's thy practice out of thy ignorance; for the Scriptures do say that all the church may prophesy one by one [1 Corinthians 14:31], and that women were in the church, as well as men, do thou judge; and the Scripture saith that a woman may not prophesy with her head uncovered, lest she dishonour her head [1 Corinthians 11:5]: now thou wouldst know the meaning of that head, let the Scripture answer, 1 Corinthians 11:3, 'The head of every man is Christ'. Man in his best estate[33] is altogether vanity[34] [Psalms 39:5], weakness, a lie. If therefore any speak in the church, whether man or woman, and nothing appear in it but the wisdom of man [1 Corinthians 2:4-5, 13], and Christ, who is the true head, be not uncovered, do not fully appear, Christ the head is then dishonoured. Now the woman or weakness, that is man, which in his best estate or greatest wisdom is altogether vanity, that must be covered with the covering of the spirit, a garment of righteousness [Isaiah 61:10], that its nakedness may not appear, and dishonour thereby come. Here mayst thou see from the Scriptures, that the woman or weakness whether male or female, is forbidden to speak in the church [1 Corinthians 14:34]; but it's very plain, Paul, nor Apollos, nor the true church of Christ, were not of that proud envious spirit that thou art of, for they owned Christ Jesus in man or woman; for Paul bid Timothy to help those women that laboured with him in the Gospel

[Philippians 4:3], and Apollos hearkened to a woman, and was instructed by her [Acts 18:26], and Christ Jesus appeared to the women first, and sent them to preach the resurrection to the apostles [Matthew 28:9-10; John 20:14-18], and Philip had four virgins that did prophesy [Acts 21:9]. Now thou dost respect persons I know, and art partial in all things, and so judgest wickedly, but there is no respect of persons with God [Acts 10:34]. Indeed, you yourselves are the women, that are forbidden to speak in the church, that are become women; for two of your priests came to speak with us; and when they could not bear sound reproof and wholesome doctrine [2 Timothy 4:2-3], that did concern them, they railed on us with filthy speeches, as no other they can give to us, that deal plainly and singly with them, and so ran from us. So leaving you to the light in all your consciences to judge of what we have writ, we remain prisoners in Exeter gaol for the word of God.

Priscilla Cotton,
Mary Cole.

FINIS

Printed at London for Giles Calvert at the Black-spread Eagle, near the west end of Paul's, 1655.

Appendix D:
Dorothy Waugh:
'A relation concerning Dorothy Waugh's cruel usage by the Mayor of Carlisle' (1655)

A Relation Concerning Dorothy Waugh's Cruel Usage by the Mayor of Carlisle.[1]

Upon the 7th day about the time called Michaelmas in the year of the world's account 1655, I was moved of the Lord to go into the market of Carlisle, to speak against all deceit and ungodly practices,[2] and the mayor's officer came and violently haled me off the cross,[3] and put me in prison, not having anything to lay to my charge, and presently the mayor came up where I was, and asked me from whence I came; and I said out of Egypt[4] where thou lodgest. But after these words, he was so violent and full of passion he scarce asked me any more questions, but called to one of his followers to bring the bridle,[5] as he called it, to put upon me, and was to be on three hours, and that which they called so was like a steel cap and my hat being violently plucked off which was pinned to my head, whereby they tare[6] my clothes to put on their bridle as they called it, which was a stone weight of iron by the relation of their own generation, and three bars of iron to come over my face, and a piece of it was put in my mouth, which was so unreasonable big a thing for that place as cannot be well related, which was locked to my head, and so I stood their time with my hands bound behind me with the stone weight of iron upon my head, and the bit in my mouth to keep me from speaking. And the mayor said he would make me an example to all that should ever come in that name. And the people to see me so violently abused were broken into tears, but he cried out on them and said, 'For foolish pity, one may spoil a whole city.'[7] And the man that kept the prison-door demanded twopence of every one that came to see me while their bridle remained upon me. Afterwards it was taken off and they kept me in prison for a little season, and after a while the mayor came up again and caused it to be put on again, and sent me out of the city with it on, and gave me very vile and unsavoury words, which were not fit to proceed out of any man's mouth, and charged the officer to whip me out of the town,[8] from constable to constable to send me, till I came to my own home, when as[9] they had not anything to lay to my charge.

D.W.

And all these things are but a taste of the whole,[10] inflicted upon the body of Christ in this nation, whom he hath made conformable to himself[11] to undergo the envy of the wicked till death, and after their death they are not satisfied, neither was they upon him, who gave large money to raise lies upon him, when their envy could reach no further, and it is enough that his servants be as their Lord; for which of all the members of Christ have not suffered by this generation of men that live in their lusts? Yet herein we rejoice that his peace is with us, and that we are justified in his sight not to suffer as evil doers, though in the sight of men we be so accounted.

FINIS.

[*The Lamb's Defence Against Lies*, pp. 29-30]

Notes

Chapter 1

1 Such a critique can be found in (amongst many others) Woolf 1928; de Beauvoir 1953; Millett 1970; Moers 1978; Spacks 1976; Showalter 1978 and 1986; Jacobus 1979; Gilbert and Gubar 1979; Olsen 1980; Russ 1984; Greene and Kahn 1985; Moi 1985; Eagleton 1986; Belsey and Moore 1989; Mills *et al.* 1989; Jay and Glasgow 1992; Wall 1990; Wisker 1992.

2 This takes place most notably in New Historicist and cultural materialist work. See for example Greenblatt 1980 and 1988, Goldberg 1982 and 1986, Dollimore 1984, Dollimore and Sinfield 1985, Belsey 1985, Stallybrass and White 1986, and Veeser 1989.

3 Such as, for example, Smith 1982; Woodbridge 1984; Ezell 1987; Greer *et al.* 1988; Hobby 1988; Graham *et al.* 1989; Cerasano and Wynne-Davies 1992; Brant and Purkiss 1992; Grundy and Wiseman 1992; Lewalski 1993.

4 For overviews of critiques that have been made of the canon, see Widdowson 1982, Eagleton 1983, Batsleer *et al.* 1985 and Doyle 1989.

5 See Battersby 1989 for an extended exploration of this point.

6 See Chapter 7 in Battersby 1989.

7 Although the term 'sectarian' is generally used to refer to these groupings pre-Restoration, and 'non-conformist' for them post-Restoration, these uses remain somewhat controversial. Hill, for example, argues that 'the word "sect" should be prohibited for the period before 1660' (Hill 1993: 35), on the grounds that it suggests too fixed and formalised a set of group identities for those early years. Members of these groupings, however, referred to themselves as 'sectaries', and, until such time as a widely recognised alternative is established, I follow this usage in my own work.

8 The characterisation of the sects that follows draws on a version included in the introduction to Graham *et al.* 1989.

9 'Hat honour' refers to the customary doffing of hats by men when in the presence of a social superior. Male Friends' refusal of this custom was often focused on as an indicator of Quakers' dangerous 'levelling' tendencies. See Hill 1972: 246-8; Bauman 1983: 46-7.

10 For more detailed historical studies of the sects see Braithwaite 1912 and 1919; Underwood 1947; Hill 1972; Capp 1972; Watts 1978; McGregor and Reay 1984; Reay 1985b; Mack 1992.

11 Mack (1982) argues that contemporary ideas about femininity - seen as emotional, irrational and particularly receptive to outside influences - made it more likely that women would be accepted as prophets during these years.

12 In addition to those titles indicated in note 3 above, see Smith 1989, Todd 1989, Hobby 1991, Wiseman 1992a, Ferguson 1992, Mack 1992.

Chapter 2

1 Examples of such historians whose work has included discussions of seventeenth-century women's history include Brailsford 1915, Clark 1919, Bacon 1969 and 1986, Higgins 1973, Rowbotham 1973, Latt 1978, Smith 1982, London Feminist History Group 1983, Fraser 1984, George 1988.

2 For more extended discussions of the importance of analogy for seventeenth-century systems of meaning, see Foucault 1970, Amussen 1985, Goldberg 1986; see also Chapter 5 of this book.

3 The prospect of a disharmonious marriage is also suggested by another instance of the use of the trope of the river. In Philip Massinger's *A New Way to Pay Old Debts* (1633), Lady Allworth warns Lovell against marrying Margaret, the daughter of the *nouveau-riche* Overreach, with these words:

> ... all wealth
> (I mean if ill-acquir'd) cemented to honour
> By virtuous ways achiev'd, and bravely purchas'd,
> Is but as rubbage pour'd into a river
> (Howe'er intended to make good the bank)
> Rend'ring the water that was pure before
> Polluted and unwholesome. (Massinger 1633: 380)

The purity of his family identity would be sullied by the corruption of hers in such a match; importantly, though, it is her *father*'s identity that is the source of the problem here, rather than anything distinctly her own.

4 This quotation is taken from Baxter 1673: 531.

5 There is a good deal of material now available concerning the controversy about women. See, for example, Wright 1935, Kelly 1984, Woodbridge 1984, Shepherd 1985, Henderson and McManus 1985, Purkiss 1992b, and Lewalski 1993: Chapter 6.

6 For further discussion of this, see Thomas 1971, Chapters 14-18.

7 Examples of such conduct books are Heinrich Bullinger, *The Golden Boke of Christen Matrimonye*, trans. Thomas Becon (1543); Henrie Smith, *A Preparative to Marriage* (1591); Robert Snawsel, *A Looking Glasse for Married Folkes* (1610); Gervase Markham, *The English Huswife* (1615); William Whateley, *A Bride-Bush, or a Wedding Sermon* (1617); Thomas Gateker, *Marriage Duties Briefly Couch'd Together* (1620), John Dod and Robert Cleaver, *A Godly Forme of Householde Government* (1621); William Gouge, *Of Domesticall Duties* (1622), Richard Brathwait, *The English Gentlewoman* (1631), Daniel Rogers, *Matrimoniall Honour* (1642). For discussions of these, see Wright 1935, Davies 1977, Hull 1982, Jones 1987.

8 There is a continuing debate about the changing significance (or otherwise) of women's role in the marriage relationship. See, for example, Haller and Haller 1941-42, Haller 1946, Stone 1977, Davies 1977. For a comprehensive list of responses to Stone's thesis of the 'companionate marriage' (1977), see Hobby 1988: 208, n.4.

9 For a discussion of the limits of this distinction, see Ingram 1987: 303.

10 Purkiss, however, notes instances where cross-dressing (men to women) was attributed where there was none, and suggests that this was a way for men 'to dismiss the political activities of women as theatrical stagings of femininity by men ... This way of reading female activity sought to limit its disorderly consequences' (Purkiss 1992b: 82-3). On female-to-male cross-dressing, see Dekker and van de Pol 1989.

11 For discussions of the origins and character of Puritanism, see Tawney 1926, Haller 1955, Manning 1973, Lamont 1970, Hill 1961, 1964 and 1972, Collinson 1967 and 1989, Watkins 1972, Watts 1978, Fletcher 1981, Finlayson 1983, Underdown 1985b, Russell 1990.

12 See Chapter 1 for the specific origins and characteristics of those sects discussed in this book.

13 See also pp.102–61.

Chapter 3

1 See, for example, Goulianos 1974, Bernikow 1979, Spender and Todd 1989. Early second-wave feminist studies of women's writing that have eighteenth- or nineteenth-century starting-points include Moers 1978 and Showalter 1979.

2 One important exception to this is Rowbotham 1973, in which she throws down a gauntlet that was not to be picked up by other feminist historians and literary critics for some years.

3 See, for example, Moers 1978, Showalter 1979, Spender 1986, Spencer 1986, Todd 1989.

4 They also, of course, serve to mediate the authorship of the text. For a full discussion of this issue, see Chapter 4.

5 Examples of texts with several prefatory letters include (amongst others) Cary 1651, Turner 1653, Curwen 1680, Vokins 1691, Mollineux 1702 and Stirredge 1711.

6 For further discussion of this aspect of the text, see Wiseman 1992a.

7 I have borrowed this phrase from Deborah Cameron's article '"Released into language": the study of language outside and inside academic institutions', in Thompson and Wilcox (eds) 1989.

8 Diana was the Latin name of the Greek Artemis, the goddess of the moon and of the chase, who lived in perpetual celibacy. She was the chief goddess of the Ephesians (see Acts 19), but here her characteristics were those of an Eastern nature goddess. See p. 237, note 11, for further comment on this passage.

9 Interestingly, this is the same text that reconciled Trapnel to her public/prophetic duties. See p. 96 below.

10 Hasty or hurried.

Notes

Chapter 4

1 For a discussion of changing ideas about literacy and authorship, see Lury 1992: 367-80.

2 Gilbert and Gubar (1979) show how identified masculinity and authorship have become, in the Western literary tradition, through their own investigation of the impossibility for women to identify themselves within that masculine category 'the author', an inhibition which they named (after Bloom's 'the anxiety of influence') 'the anxiety of authorship'. See Mills *et al.* 1989: 122-53 for an assessment of this theory.

3 Matthew Arnold included this formulation of his definition of culture in 'The Function of Criticism at the Present Time' (1865); a similar definition is to be found in the preface to his 1873 edition of *Literature and Dogma*; see p. 4, above.

4 Medhurst's sources are as follows: Nancy K. Miller (1986), 'Changing the Subject: Authorship, writing and the reader', in Teresa de Lauretis (ed.) *Feminist Studies/Critical Studies*, London: Macmillan, p.106; bell hooks (1991) 'Postmodern Blackness', in *Yearning*, London: Turnaround, p. 28; Paul Hallam and Ronald L. Peck (1977) 'Images of Homosexuality', *Gay Left Review* 5, p. 25.

5 Other discussions and critiques of authorship include: Caughie 1981, Cook 1981, Miller 1989, Mayne 1990, Dyer 1991, Lewis 1992.

6 The Quaker reliance on the inner light is of significance here, as it made the call to write less problematic than it was for other sectaries who relied more exclusively on scriptural justifications. Whilst, then, relatively few Quakers apologise for their coming to authorship, especially in the 1650s, neither do they tend to detail the *process* as clearly as White does here. For a discussion of the inner light, see Bauman 1983: 24-8.

7 Sectaries used the word 'saints' to refer to God's elect: those divinely pre-ordained for salvation.

8 For a discussion of the legal position of women, see Chapter 2, pp. 38–42, above.

9 For a fuller discussion of this point as it relates to the writing of Anne Wentworth, see pp. 102–6 below.

10 I am grateful to Elaine Hobby for suggesting this final point to me.

11 Although in the case of the Quakers this was modified by their reliance on the inner light, their texts are none the less saturated with biblical allusion and reference; it is in the *interpretation* of the significance of certain aspects of the Scriptures that the inner light was most significant, for it allowed, at times, unconventional readings of the Bible to be posited. See Cotton and Cole's *To the Priests and People of England* (1655) (Appendix C below), and my discussion of it in Chapter 7.

12 See Chapter 5 below for a fuller discussion of the significance of the Bible in sectarian women's writings.

13 Hooton *et al.*, for example, wrote that 'it is not the hearers but the doers that shall be justified' (Hooton *et al.* 1652: 4), and Hill quotes Thomas Taylor: 'We teach that only Doers shall be saved, and by their doing though not for their doing' (Hill 1961: 69). Watkins comments on the importance of this in relation to sectarian writing: it was, he says, 'written to persuade, to cause reading to issue forth in action' (Watkins 1972: 233). For the biblical source of this idea, see James 1:22, 23, 25.

14 A 'closet' was a small private room, often a place of retirement, private devotion, or

private study.

15 Wentworth's first published text was *A true account of Anne Wentworth* (1676), to be found in the Folger Library. This title is not included in Wing's *Short Title Catalogue*.

16 All emphasis in the quotations from Wentworth's text is hers.

Chapter 5

1 Examples of Foucault's refusals of particular theoretical and political positions can be found in Foucault 1970: xiv, and Rabinow 1986: 383-6.

2 For an exposition of the difference between history and genealogy, see Foucault's 'Nietzsche, Genealogy, History', in Rabinow 1986: 76-100.

3 For Lyotard on the 'grand narratives', see Lyotard 1984, and Bürger 1992: 77-8.

4 Whilst the term '(new) French feminisms' provided a useful gloss following the publication of Marks and de Courtivron 1981, more recent publications have emphasised the specificity of writers such as de Beauvoir (Evans 1995), Irigaray (Whitford 1991), Cixous (Sellers 1994), and Kristeva (Moi 1986).

5 For a clear and concise introduction to the ways in which these interventions fit into more general debates about gender and language, see Cameron (1985).

6 Foucault explains the differences between the four main kinds of similitude: 'convenientia' or convenience denotes adjacency of place, 'so that in this hinge between two things a resemblance occurs'; 'aemulatio' or emulation 'enables things to imitate one another from one end of the universe to the other without connection or proximity'; 'analogy' is a combination of the two, making possible 'the confrontation of resemblance across space', but also speaking of the 'bonds and joints' of adjacency; the final resemblance is 'sympathy', which follows no predetermined paths, but 'plays through the universe in a free state', finding sameness in spatially and constitutionally disparate elements (Foucault 1970: 17-25). For a critique of Foucault's discussion, see Kibbey 1986: 170, n.21.

7 A similar case could be made concerning some of the poetry of Elizabeth Major, in particular her self-inscription in 'The Author's Prayer'; see Hobby 1988: 65.

8 See also Kibbey 1986 for a discussion of the social values common to the Hutchinson case and the Pequot massacres of the same time, and the relationship of both these to Puritan beliefs and practices of signification.

9 See Caldwell 1976: 354 on the complexities of contemporary meanings of 'the Word'.

10 In Isaiah 28:11, 32:4 and 33:19, stammering is associated with difference, the incomprehensible and the deceptive.

11 Nor are these the only things ideally in alignment: so too were the body and soul: see the quotation from Hannah Allen, p. 121 above.

12 'Latitudinarian' is the name given to a group of theologians who wanted 'to reduce the Christian religion to a few plain essentially moral fundamentals, easily apprehended and put into practice by the ordinary man, and in terms of discipline were prepared to accommodate themselves to the church government of the day' (Rivers 1991: 25-6); they were in a minority in the 1660s, but by the 1690s they were the dominant party within the Church of England.

13 See Jones 1951b, Fisch 1952, and Rivers 1991 for a fuller discussion of this process.

14 On the new science, see Bush 1961 and Hill 1965.

15 See Foucault 1970: 125-65 on the new taxonomies.

16 Christopher Hill notes some of these criticisms: Hill 1993: 15.

17 'Professors' were those who professed to a particular faith, or fellow-believers.

Chapter 6

1 See Chapter 1, pp. 10-12, for a discussion of contemporary seventeenth-century definitions of prophecy.

2 See, for example, Cary's interpretation of Daniel in *The Little Horn's Doom and Downfall* (1651), part of which is reproduced in Appendix A.

3 Gideon was the 'man of valour' chosen by God to lead the army which would deliver the Israelites from the Midianites. See Judges 6, 7 and 8.

4 Hill prefaces his book of that title (1972) with three biblical references to 'the world turned upside down': Psalms 146:9, Isaiah 24:1-2, 20-1, and Acts 17:1-6.

5 'Belly-cheer' meant feasting or luxurious eating; 'lardery-dainties' probably meant dainty foods from the larder; 'buss' or 'busk' meant attire, dress or decoration.

6 See Chapter 2 for a discussion of the legal situation of women.

7 See, though, Purkiss's comment on such generic distinctions, quoted on p. 10 above.

8 'Tare' is an archaic form of the past tense of the verb 'to tear'.

9 On Nayler's entry into Bristol, see Hill 1972: 248-52, Mack 1992: 197-211.

10 For a discussion of contemporary ideals concerning the sympathy of body and soul, see Chapter 5, pp. 121 and 125.

11 'Under forms' meant obedient to the law of the Old Testament.

12 'To weigh in the balance of the sanctuary' meant to test by the standard of divine revelation.

13 Trapnel, for example, repeatedly addresses her own congregation in her *Report and Plea* (1654b), and conversion narratives were professions of faith by individuals wishing to be accepted into an Independent or Baptist congregation (see p. 121 above).

14 See Chapter 2, pp. 45-6 above, for a discussion of Puritan individualism.

15 I discuss the distinction between 'doers' and 'talkers only' on p. 99 above.

16 For a discussion of the significance of silence in a sectarian context, see Chapter 3.

17 The bridle clearly figures significantly as both a trope and method of constraint: see Chapter 2, pp. 28-9, and Dorothy Waugh's description of her punishment, pp. 154-5 above, and Appendix D.

18 Helen Wilcox reaches similar conclusions in her discussions of non-sectarian English-women's autobiographies of the seventeenth century; see Wilcox 1992.

19 I discuss this increase in Chapter 3, pp. 55-6.

20 This is discussed in Hill 1961: 208-16, and Rivers 1991.

21 After the Restoration, the Quakers changed their policy regarding prophecy:

> In 1672, the London Yearly Meeting of Friends issued the following advice to the ministry ...: 'And avoid all imagined, unseasonable and untimely prophesyings; which

tend not only to stir up persecution, but also to the begetting airy and uncertain
expectations, and to the amusing and affrighting simple people from receiving the
Truth ...' (Bauman 1983: 94)

Bauman comments on this, that

though Quaker doctrine and practice continued to demand prophetic inspiration, the
voice of the Holy Spirit speaking through his ministers, the ideal of an unfettered
prophetic ministry accountable only to direct divine guidance was routinized and
brought under corporate control. (Bauman 1983: 147)

It was in this same period that Quaker ministers began to be required to carry certificates
from their local monthly meetings licensing them to preach more widely - a restriction, as
Bauman notes, that would have been unthinkable in the early years of Quakerism
(Bauman 1983: 147). See also Mack 1992: 351-402.

Chapter 7

1 A full discussion of seventeenth-century discourses of gender is included in Chapter 2.
2 See Bauman 1983: 84-94 for a fascinating analysis of 'going naked as a sign' and other
Quaker 'semiotic enactments'.
3 Phyllis Mack identifies a range of different punishments meted out to Quaker women; see
Mack 1992: 168, 196, 248-50, 259.
4 See Chapter 4, p. 84, above, for feminist interventions in debates about authorship.
5 See Jones 1951b, Foucault 1977, Cohen 1977, and Rivers 1991.
6 I am indebted to Bauman 1983: 43-62 for the details of this summary.
7 See Smith 1989: 240-2 for an analysis of the metaphor of 'the seed'.
8 For a detailed analysis of radical sectarian style, see Smith 1989: 308-39.
9 The 'original' language for Quakers was not a human language accessible to human
learning, but the word of God, accessible only by attention to the light within each
believer. See Bauman 1983: 38.
10 See Mack 1992: 18-24, and Crawford 1993: 1-17 and *passim*.
11 See pp. 93-4 and 122-6 above.

Appendix A

1 Cary was a Fifth-Monarchist prophet, who had already published *The Glorious Excellency
of the Spirit* (1645), *A Word in Season* (1647) and *The Resurrection of the Witnesses* (1648).
This prophecy, *The Little Horn's Doom and Downfall*, published in 1651, two years after
the execution of Charles I, is concerned with relating recent events, particularly those
concerning the (mis)rule of Charles I and his (just) overthrow at the hands of Parliament,
with the vision recounted by the biblical prophet Daniel. The 'second part' alluded to in
the title refers to another prophecy published by Cary in the same volume, entitled *A New
and More Exact Mappe or Description of New Jerusalem's Glory*. Cary's first dedicatory
epistle, addressed to Elizabeth Cromwell, Bridget Ireton and Margaret Rolle, is omitted

here, and her second included, in which her own marginal note is included in square brackets. Hugh Peter, whose prefatory epistle is included here after Cary's own, had been chaplain to Cromwell's army, and by 1651 was a prominent Fifth Monarchist writer and preacher.

2 *doom*: judgement.

3 *saints*: God's elect; those pre-ordained by him for salvation.

4 *though not concurring ... personal reign*: though not agreeing with all her conclusions relating to the reigns of particular kings.

5 *which ... error*: Peter's own marginal note.

6 *idleness (the devil's cushion)*: idleness, by means of which the devil gains influence. See Wiseman 1992a: 183-4).

7 *improve*: make good use of.

8 *painful*: laborious, painstaking.

9 *cluster*: collection.

10 *ploughed with another's heifer*: a common seventeenth-century proverb, derived from the story of Samson in Judges 14:18.

11 *Canticles*: the Song of Solomon.

12 *The one ... Holland*: the first woman referred to by Peter is Elizabeth of Bohemia, sister of Charles I (see Greer *et al.* 1988: 39-40); the second is Anna Maria van Schurman (see Hobby 1988: 198-9). Both women were noted for this learning. Many thanks to Elaine Hobby for her help with this reference.

13 *travel*: travail, labour.

14 *ordinances*: sacraments.

15 *requiring godly and faithful ministers ... of the week*: in the 1630s, Laud had confiscated the assets of the twelve Feoffees (the group endowing Puritan ministers' livings), ordered ministers not to preach on controversial topics, and had suppressed 'lecturers' or lay preachers, who were often forced to emigrate as a result.

16 *inviting and requiring ... holy worshipping of God*: both James I and Charles I had authorised the traditional Sunday sports, thereby flying in the face of Puritan opinion. The Laudian Bishop Pierce defended such sports on the grounds that they discouraged people from meeting for illegal religious discussion (Hill 1961: 71).

17 *scandalous ministers ... sequestered for their delinquencies*: in the early 1640s, Parliament established the Committee for Scandalous Ministers, which ejected royalist clergy from their livings, and a Sequestration Committee was appointed to confiscate and administer the estates of 'delinquents' (royalists and Catholics).

18 *leave their native kingdom*: through the reign of Charles I, many religious radicals and separatists continued to go into exile to avoid persecution.

19 *popish*: both Charles I's personal sympathies and his policies seemed, to contemporaries, to be approaching popery. Indeed, Parliament's Grand Remonstrance of 1641 saw England's government being subverted by 'the Jesuited Papists'.

20 *raised armies ... England*: Charles raised an army against the Scots in 1639, and against the Irish in 1642; the first battle of the English Civil War took place at Edgehill on 23 October 1642.

21 *tittle*: a minute amount.

22 *Nonesuch*: unparalleled.

23 *proceedings of the parliament ... fasten upon them*: debate about, and defences of, the rectitude of the execution of Charles I continued amongst radical sectarians through the 1650s and beyond.

24 *of that in its place*: Cary undertakes this in *A New and More Exact Map*, which follows *The Little Horn's Doom and Downfall*.

25 *astronomers*: astrologers. Astrology retained widespread credibility amongst all ranks of society until the late seventeenth century.

Appendix B

1 *Together ... Parliament*: This part of the text, written entirely by Arise Evans, is not included here.

2 *Arise Evans*: a Welsh royalist prophet, who published several pamphlets of his own, here acts as Channel's amanuensis and editor. The first part of Channel's text, then, is represented as a transcription of her own words, with Evans's editorial comments, appearing as marginal notes in the original, here included in the main body of the text in square brackets. The final section of the text, which discusses Channel in the third person, is Evans's.

3 *cause*: misprinted as 'case' in the original.

4 *1653 ... 1654*: according to the Julian calendar, in legal and official use in England until the Gregorian calendar was adopted in 1751, the New Year fell on 25 March. Popularly, however, it was taken as falling on 1 January. Hence the double date given here.

5 *premises*: aforementioned circumstances.

6 *the dumb to speak for peace*: in the Bible, 'the dumb' was used both as a literal and a metaphorical reference, as here. See, for example, Exodus 4:11, Isaiah 56:10, Daniel 10:15, Luke 11:14.

7 *Catholic and apostolic faith*: a reference not to the Roman Catholic faith, but to any church claiming historical continuity with the early, pre-schismatic church: in this instance, the Anglican church.

8 *beadles*: parish officers with the power to punish petty offenders.

9 *Bridewell*: house of correction on the bank of the Thames at the mouth of the River Fleet.

10 *Hana Trampenel's*: the Fifth Monarchist prophet Anna Trapnel.

11 *Diana*: the Roman goddess of hunting, chastity and the moon. There was a famous temple to her at Ephesus, but here her characteristics were those of a nature-goddess. It is Diana of the Ephesians who is referred to in Acts 19:34. Elaine Hobby has suggested to me that this allusion has the following meaning: 'Opposition to Paul (see Acts 19:23-41) is orchestrated on the grounds that to follow Christ would be to abandon the goddess Diana. Trapnel is being aspersed as "Diana", that is, as standing for non-Christian religious values, with a particular implication of sexual as well as religious wrongdoing' (Hobby 1995: private correspondence; I'm grateful for her help with this point).

Notes

Appendix C

1 Thomason has added the date 'October 16, 1655' beneath the title. The authors, the Quakers Priscilla Cotton and Mary Cole, wrote this pamphlet from Exeter gaol.

2 *seed ... Abel*: the words 'seed' and 'generation' are used thoughout the text to signify genealogies or traditions of godliness and ungodliness, 'the seed of the woman' and Abel being associated with the former, and 'the seed of the serpent' and Cain with the latter. Examples of contemporary godly or ungodly behaviour could thus have their origins traced and their character defined by reference to, and through their continuity with, their earliest biblical counterparts. On the metaphor of the seed, see Smith 1989: 240-2.

3 *scribes and Pharisees*: in biblical times, the scribes sought to interpret the Mosaic Law and the traditional law in terms of people's everyday lives; the Pharisees were a group of influential religious leaders characterised by their strict adherence to the Law. Both groups' focus on the minutiae of 'the Law' led to them being denounced by Christ for sanctimonious hypocrisy. For example, see Matthew 5:20; 23:13; Luke 11:39.

4 *children ... murthered the prophets*: here, Cotton and Cole develop the notion of godly and ungodly 'generations', and provide further scriptural evidence for their existence.

5 *the original*: the original language, for Quakers, was not a human language accessible to human learning, but the word of God, accessible only by attention to the light within each believer. See Bauman 1983: 38.

6 *Hebrew, Greek and Latin*: when Christ was on the cross, 'a superscription also was written over him in letters of Greek, and Latin, and Hebrew, THIS IS THE KING OF THE JEWS' (Luke 13:38). (See also John 19:19-20.)

7 *martyrs ... world*: the establishment of an ungodly genealogy continues, here by reference to the persecution and martyring of Protestants during the reign of Mary I (1553-58) by her Catholic bishops.

8 *Amaziah*: 'Amaziel' in original text.

9 *rise*: an origin or source, a beginning; a start (*OED* IV 17 a). Here, the sense is 'so it has been since the beginning'.

10 *because*: 'so' instead of 'because' would make the sense clearer here.

11 *Objection ... Answer*: this rhetorical pattern of 'objection' and 'answer', by which a dialogue is constructed between the argument of the text and its projected opponents, derived from the mainstream Puritan tradition, but was continued in some radical writings. See Smith 1989: 316-17.

12 *substance*: the word 'substance' is used throughout to signify somebody or something's spiritual reality, and is used in opposition to the deceptiveness or unreliability of appearances. This, for Quakers, is the ultimate authority, above that of the external 'Law'. Compare Hebrews 11:1: 'Now faith is the substance of things hoped for, the evidence of things not seen.'

13 *light in their consciences*: drawing on New Testament imagery of Christ as 'the true Light, that lighteth every man that cometh into the world' (John 1:9), Quakers relied on the individual spiritual apprehension of Christ's voice within them above all other - including biblical - authority.

14 *'Lo!' ... Baptism*: 'Lo!' is a biblical exclamation meaning 'look!' or 'behold!'. The refer-

ences to Presbytery, Independency, Prelacy and Baptism – some of the different religious groupings of the time – here serve as examples of the Scriptures being 'wrested' to fit in with factional opinions and interests.

15 *the Scriptures are not divided*: the argument that there can be no contradictions within the Bible, and that any apparent biblical contradictions can be reconciled through searching out its 'truth', is a cornerstone on which the polemic of this text depends.

16 *Hebrew … life and glory*: this point is repeated from the end of the first paragraph.

17 *ignorant … wise*: the rejection of worldly learning in favour of godly or spiritual wisdom is a foundation of early Quaker thinking. See 1 Corinthians 2:3-4: 'And my speech and my preaching was not with enticing words of man's wisdom, but in demonstration of the Spirit and of power: That your faith should not stand in the wisdom of men, but in the power of God.' See also Bauman 1983: 37-40.

18 *Mary and Susanna*: whilst Christ was travelling and preaching, Mary Magdalene and Susanna were two of the 'certain women' who 'ministered unto him of their substance'. See Luke 8:1-3.

19 *Apollos*: 'Apollo' in the original text.

20 *second chapter of his first Epistle to the Corinthians*: in 1 Corinthians 2, Paul declares himself uninterested in anything 'save Jesus Christ, and him crucified'. See note 17.

21 *would you hearken*: the sense of this phrase is 'if you would hearken'.

22 *rent*: rend or hurt.

23 *your teacher in you*: that is, the inward light of conscience; the internal apprehension of Christ.

24 *Babylon*: the chief city of the Empire of Babylonia, in which the Jews were held captive (*c.* 603-536 BC), and the mystical city of the Apocalypse (see Revelation 17). Used symbolically to signify a place of corruption and ungodliness.

25 *little stone … idols*: a reference to Daniel 2:31-45. Daniel had a dream concerning 'a great image' that is destroyed by a stone, which subsequently becomes 'a great mountain and filled the whole earth'. The dream is interpreted as signifying a kingdom that will be conquered and superseded by a kingdom set up by 'the God of heaven' which 'shall stand for ever'.

26 *assemblies*: congregations.

27 *Proverbs 2:9*: Proverbs 2 is concerned with true wisdom, as opposed to 'the ways of darkness'. Note also the verse preceding the one alluded to here: 'He keepeth the paths of judgement and preserveth the way of his saints.'

28 *Sion*: Jerusalem, the holy city.

29 *Balaam … Kore*: both Balaam and Kore (or Korah) were punished for disobedience: the former to God, and the latter to Moses.

30 *meeting-house*: the place (unconsecrated) in which Quakers held their meetings for worship.

31 *queen and lady*: the reference here is multi-layered: 1) it alludes to the Whore of Babylon (see Revelation 17); 2) it echoes Isaiah, in which the 'virgin daughter of Babylon' is urged to 'come down, and sit in the dust', because she has been perverted by her 'wisdom and knowledge' (Isaiah, 47:1, 10); and 3) it may be a criticism of the privileges and power conferred by the social rank of the addressee of this section of the text. Moreover, this

reference begins the process whereby the priests are identified with 'women', a move which is crucial to the development of the argument in the remainder of the text. I am grateful to Elaine Hobby for her help with these allusions and interpretations. See Hobby 1995a and Hobby 1995b for more discussion of these points.

32 *thou puttest the Scriptures at a difference in themselves*: see note 15.

33 *estate*: state, condition.

34 *vanity*: associated biblically not with conceit, but with emptiness, fruitlessness and worthlessness.

Appendix D

1 This short account by Dorothy Waugh, published in 1656, is included in a collection of many such accounts entitled *The Lamb's Defence Against Lies, and a True Testimony given concerning the Sufferings and Death of James Parnell. By such hands as were eye-witnesses, and have subscribed their names thereto*. Waugh, an itinerant Quaker prophet, was a servant woman from Westmorland.

2 *I was moved ... ungodly practices*: it was common Quaker practice to prophesy in public places, whether squares, market-places or during church services.

3 *cross*: whilst this is a direct reference to the market-cross, the monument at the centre of the town acting as a location for meetings and proclamations as well as markets, it also serves as an allusion to Christ's crucifixion.

4 *Egypt*: the country in which the Israelites were exiled, and thus symbolically a place of suffering and persecution; see Exodus 10:22.

5 *the bridle*: the bridle was typically a punishment used in the north of England for scolds; here it is used against another kind of woman whose speaking was deemed disorderly. In each case, then, it was a gendered form of punishment. See Underdown 1985a: 123.

6 *tare*: an archaic form of the past tense of the verb 'to tear'.

7 *'For foolish pity, one may spoil a whole city'*: a seventeenth-century proverb.

8 *whip me out of the town*: this was done so that any costs incurred in charging or imprisoning her would be borne by her own parish.

9 *when as*: an archaic alternative to 'when'.

10 This concluding paragraph, probably added by Waugh's editor, draws out for readers the wider spiritual significance of her experiences by comparing them with those of Christ himself.

11 *conformable to himself*: corresponding to his own life and experiences.

Bibliography

Seventeenth-century texts

This section includes all seventeenth-century texts consulted for this study, and includes: contemporary seventeenth-century publications; texts written in the seventeenth century but published in later centuries; and recent editions of texts originally published in the seventeenth century.

The original spelling has been retained for all contemporary seventeenth-century texts consulted, in order to aid their location.

All the contemporary seventeenth-century texts were published in London unless otherwise stated. Full publication details are given for all later publications.

Adams, Mary (1676) *A Warning To The Inhabitants of England.*
Allen, Hannah (1683) *Satan his Methods and Malice Baffled.*
Andrewes, Lancelot (1967) *Sermons*, ed. G. M. Story, Oxford: Clarendon.
Anon. (1652) *Eliza's Babes: or the virgins-offering.*
Audland, Anne (afterwards Camm) (1655) *A true Declaration of the suffering of the innocent.*
Barker, Jane (1688) *Poetical Recreations: consisting of Original Poems, songs, odes &c.*
Barwick, Grace (1659) *To all present Rulers, whether Parliament, or whom soever of England.*
Bathurst, Elizabeth (1683) *The Sayings of Women, which were spoken upon sundry occasions, in several places of the Scriptures.*
Baxter, Richard (1673; this ed. 1678) *A Christian Directory.*
Beaumont, Agnes (1929) *The Narrative of the Persecution of Agnes Beaumont in 1674*, ed. G. H. Harrison, London: Constable.
Beckwith, Elizabeth and Beckwith, Marmaduke (1692) *A True Relation of the Life and Death of Sarah Beckwith.*
Bettris, Jeane (1657) *A Lamentation for the Deceived People of the World.*
Biddle, Hester (1655) *Wo to thee City of Oxford.*
—— (1660) *A Warning from the Lord God of Life and Power, unto thee O City of London.*
Blackborow, Sarah (1659) *Herein is held forth the Gift and Good-will of God to the World.*
—— (1660) *The Just and Equal Ballance Discovered.*
Blaugdone, Barbara (1691) *An Account of the Travels, Sufferings and Persecution of Barbara Blaugdone.*
Brown, David (1652) *The Naked Woman.*
Burrough, Edward (1654) *Something in Answer to a Book called Choice Experiences.*
Cary, Mary (1651) *The Little Horns Doom and Downfall*, followed by *A new and more Exact Mappe or Description of New Ierusalems Glory.*

—— (1653) *The Resurrection of the Witnesses*.

Cavendish, Margaret (1667; this ed. 1906) 'The True Relation of my Birth, Breeding and Life', in ed. C. H. Firth, *Memoirs of William Cavendish, Duke of Newcastle and Margaret his Wife*, London.

Channel, Elinor (1653) *A Message from God (By a Dumb Woman)*.

Chidley, Katherine (1641) *The Justification of the Independent Churches of Christ*.

Cleaver, Robert and Dod, John (1621) *A godlie forme of housholde government*.

Cotton, Priscilla (1656) *As I was in the Prison-House*.

Cotton, Priscilla and Cole, Mary (1655) *To the Priests and People of England*.

Curwen, Alice (1680) *A Relation of the Labour, Travail and Suffering*.

Douglas, Eleanor (1643) *Amend, Amend: Gods kingdome is at hand: Amen, Amen*.

—— (1649) *The Blasphemous Charge Against Her*.

E., T. (1632) *The Lawes Resolutions of Womens Rights*.

Evans, Katharine and Chevers, Sarah (1662) *This is a short Relation of some of the Cruel Sufferings*.

Fanshawe, Anne (1676; this ed. 1830) *Memoirs of Lady Fanshawe*, ed. N. H. Nicolas, London.

Fell, Margaret (afterwards Fox) (1666; this ed. 1667) *Womens speaking Justified, Proved and Allowed of by the Scriptures*.

—— (1710) *A Brief Collection of Remarkable Passages and Occurrences*.

Forster, Mary (1659) *These several Papers was sent to Parliament the twentieth day of the fifth month, 1659*.

Fox, George (1911) *Journal*, vols. 1 and 2, ed. Norman Penney, Cambridge: Cambridge University Press.

Fox, George, Stubs, John and Furly, Benjamin (1660) *A Battle-Door for Teachers and Professors to learn Plural and Singular*.

Gargill, Ann (1656a) *A brief Discovery of that which is called the Popish Religion*.

—— (1656b) *A Warning to all the World*.

Glanvill, Joseph (1677) *An Essay Concerning Preaching*.

Gouge, William (1622) *Of Domesticall Duties*.

Hacket, John (1692) *Scrinia Reserata*.

Hincks, Elizabeth (1671) *The Poor Widows Mite*.

Hooton, Elizabeth (with Aldam, Thomas, Pears, William, Nicholson, Benjamin, Holmes, Jane and Fisher, Mary) (1652) *False Prophets and false Teachers described*.

Howgill, Mary (1657) *A remarkable Letter of Mary Howgill to Oliver Cromwell called Protector*.

Hutchinson, Lucy (1973) 'The Life of Mrs Lucy Hutchinson, Written by Herself', in *Memoirs of the Life of Colonel Hutchinson*, ed. James Sutherland, London: Oxford University Press.

Jones, Sarah (1650) *This is Lights appearance in the Truth*.

Leade, Jane (1681) *The Heavenly Cloud Now Breaking*.

Massinger, Philip (1633; this ed. 1975) *A New Way To Pay Old Debts*, in Gamini Salgado (ed.) *Four Jacobean City Comedies*, Harmondsworth: Penguin.

Milton, John (1677; this ed. 1968) 'Paradise Lost', in John Carey and Alastair Fowler (eds) *The Poems of John Milton*, London: Longman.

Mollineux, Mary (1702; this ed. 1772) *Fruits of Retirement: or, Miscellaneous Poems, Moral and Divine*.

Parr, Susannah (1659) *Susanna's Apologie against the Elders*.

Peters, Hugh (1641) *Milke for Babes, And Meat for Men*.

Poole, Elizabeth (1649) *An Alarum of War, Given to the Army*.

Powell, Vavasor (1649) *God the Father Glorified*.

Rogers, John (1653) *Ohel or beth-shemesh*.

—— (1657) *Jegar-Sahadutha: An Oyled Pillar.*

Simpson, Mary (1649) *Faith and Experience.*

Stirredge, Elizabeth (1711) *Strength in Weakness Manifest.*

Swetnam, Joseph (1615; this ed. 1807) *The Araignment of Lewde, idle, froward and unconstant women*, London.

Trapnel, Anna (1654a) *The Cry of a Stone, or a Relation of Something Spoken in Whitehall, by Anna Trapnel, being in the Visions of God.*

—— (1654b) *Anna Trapnel's Report and Plea.*

—— (1654c) *A Legacy for Saints.*

—— (1654d) *Strange and Wonderful Newes from White-hall.*

—— (1658a) *A Voice for the Kings of Saints.*

—— (1658b) [Untitled volume in the Bodleian library.]

Turner, Jane (1653) *Choice Experiences of the Kind dealings of God before, in, and after Conversion.*

Venn, Anne (1658) *A Wise Virgins Lamp Burning.*

Vokins, Joan (1691) *God's Mighty Power Magnified.*

Walker, Henry (1653) *Spirituall experiences of sundry believers.*

Waugh, Dorothy (1656) 'A relation concerning Dorothy Waughs cruell usage by the Mayor of Carlile', in *The Lambs Defence Aginst Lyes.*

Wentworth, Anne (1677) *A Vindication of Anne Wentworth.*

—— (1679) *The Revelation of Jesus Christ.*

Whateley, William (1617) *A Bride-Bush or A Wedding Sermon.*

White, Dorothy (1659) *Upon the 22 day of the 8th Month, 1659.*

—— (1662) *An Alarum Sounded Forth.*

Wilkins, John (1668; this ed. 1968) in *An Essay towards a Real Character and a Philosophical Language*, ed. R. C. Alston, Menston: The Scholar Press.

Secondary sources

Alexander, Gill (1982) 'Politics of the Pronoun in the Literature of the English Revolution', in Ronald Carter (ed.) *Language and Literature*, London: Allen and Unwin.

Amussen, Susan Dwyer (1985) 'Gender, Family and the Social Order, 1560-1725', in A. Fletcher and J. Stevenson (eds) *Order and Disorder in Early Modern England*, Cambridge: Cambridge University Press.

Archbishop of Canterbury's Commission on Urban Priority Areas (1985) *Faith in the City: A Call for Action by Church and Nation*, London: Church House.

Armstrong, Nancy and Tennenhouse, Leonard (eds) (1987) *The Ideology of Conduct: Essays in Literature and the History of Sexuality*, London: Methuen.

Arnold, Matthew (1865; this ed. 1953) 'The Function of Criticism at the Present Time', in Frederick L. Mulhauser (ed.) *Matthew Arnold: Selected Poetry and Prose*, New York: Holt, Rinehart and Winston.

—— (1873; this ed. 1968) 'Preface' to 'Literature and Dogma', in R. H. Super (ed.) *Dissent and Dogma*, Ann Arbor: University of Michigan Press.

Bacon, Margaret Hope (1969) *The Quiet Rebels*, New York: Basic Books.

—— (1986) *Mothers of Feminism: The Story of Quaker Women in America*, San Francisco: Harper and Row.

Baker, J. H. (1971) *An Introduction to English Legal History*, London: Butterworth.

Bakhtin, Mikhail (1965; this ed. 1984) *Rabelais and His World*, trans. Helene Iswolsky, Bloomington: Indiana University Press.

—— (1981) *The Dialogic Imagination: Four Essays by M. M. Bakhtin*, ed. and trans. Caryl Emerson and Michael Holquist, Austin: University of Texas Press.

Barbour, Hugh (1964) *The Quakers in Puritan England*, New Haven and London: Yale University Press.

Barbour, Hugh and Roberts, Arthur O. (eds) (1973) *Early Quaker Writings, 1650-1700*, Grand Rapids, Michigan: William B. Eerdmans Publishing Co.

Barrell, John (1983) *English Literature in History 1730-1780*, London: Hutchinson.

Barthes, Roland (1977; this ed. 1981) 'The Death of the Author', in John Caughie (ed.) *Theories of Authorship: A Reader*, London: Routledge and Kegan Paul, in association with the British Film Institute.

Bartkowski, Frances (1988) 'Epistemic Drift in Foucault', in Irene Diamond and Lee Quinby (eds) *Feminism and Foucault: Reflections on Resistance*, Boston: Northeastern University Press.

Bartky, Sandra Lee (1988) 'Foucault, Femininity, and the Modernization of Patriarchal Power', in Irene Diamond and Lee Quinby (eds) *Feminism and Foucault*, Boston: Northeastern University Press.

Batsleer, Janet, Davies, Tony, O'Rourke, Rebecca and Weedon, Chris (1985) *Rewriting English: Cultural Politics of Gender and Class*, London: Methuen.

Battersby, Christine (1989) *Gender and Genius*, London: Women's Press.

Bauman, R. F. (1983) *Let Your Words Be Few: Symbolism of Speaking and Silence among Seventeenth-Century Quakers*, Cambridge: Cambridge University Press.

de Beauvoir, Simone (1953; this ed. 1972) *The Second Sex*, first pub. in French 1949; trans. and ed. H. M. Parshley, Harmondsworth: Penguin.

Beier, Lucinda McCray (1985) 'In Sickness and in Health: A Seventeenth-Century Family's Experience', in Roy Porter (ed.) *Patients and Practitioners: Lay Perceptions of Medicine in Pre-Industrial Society*, Cambridge: Cambridge University Press.

—— (1987) *Sufferers and Healers: The Experience of Illness in Seventeenth-Century England*, London: Routledge and Kegan Paul.

Bell, Maureen, Parfitt, George and Shepherd, Simon (eds) (1990) *A Biographical Dictionary of English Women Writers 1580-1720*, London: Harvester Wheatsheaf.

Bellamy, J. G. (1970) *The Law of Treason in England in the Later Middle Ages*, Cambridge: Cambridge Unversity Press.

Belsey, Catherine (1980) *Critical Practice*, London: Methuen.

—— (1985) *The Subject of Tragedy: Identity and Difference in Renaissance Drama*, London: Methuen.

Belsey, Catherine and Moore, Jane (eds) (1989) *The Feminist Reader: Essays in Gender and the Politics of Literary Criticism*, Oxford: Blackwell.

Bennett, Tony (1983) 'Text and History', in Peter Widdowson (ed.) *Re-Reading English*, London: Methuen.

Berg, Christine and Berry, Philippa (1981) 'Spiritual Whoredom: An Essay on Female Prophets in the Seventeenth Century', in Francis Barker, Jay Bernstein, John Coombes, Peter Hulme, Jennifer Stone and Jon Stratton (eds) *1642: Literature and Power in the Seventeenth Century. Proceedings of the Essex Conference on the Sociology of Literature*, Colchester: University of Essex Press.

Bernikow, Louise (ed.) (1979) *The World Split Open: Women Poets 1552-1950*, London: Women's Press.

Berry, Philippa and Wernick, Andrew (eds) (1993) *Shadow of Spirit: Postmodernism and Religion*, London: Routledge.

Bordo, Susan (1993) 'Feminism, Foucault, and the Politics of the Body', in Caroline

Ramazanoglu (ed.) *Up Against Foucault: Explorations of Some Tensions between Foucault and Feminism*, London: Routledge.

Bottrall, Margaret (1958) *Every Man a Phoenix*, London: John Murray.

Brailsford, Mabel Richmond (1915) *Quaker Women 1650-1690*, London: Duckworth and Co.

Braithwaite, William C. (1912; this ed. 1955) *The Beginnings of Quakerism*, Cambridge: Cambridge University Press.

—— (1919) *The Second Period of Quakerism*, London: Macmillan.

Brant, Clare and Purkiss, Diane (eds) (1992) *Women, Texts and Histories 1575-1760*, London: Routledge.

Browne, Alice (1981) 'Dreams and Picture-Writing: Some Examples of this Comparison from the Sixteenth to the Eighteenth Centuries', *Journal of the Warburg and Courtauld Institutes* 44: 90-100.

Bürger, Christa (1992) 'Modernity as Postmodernity: Lyotard', in Scott Lash and Jonathan Friedman (eds) *Modernity and Identity*, Oxford: Blackwell.

Burrage, Champlin (1911) 'Anna Trapnel's Prophecies', *English Historical Review* 26: 526-35.

Bush, Douglas (1961) 'Science and Literature', in H. H. Rhys (ed.) *Seventeenth-Century Science and the Arts*, Princeton: Princeton University Press.

Caldwell, Patricia (1976) 'The Antinomian Language Controversy', *Harvard Theological Review* 69: 345-67.

—— (1983) *The Puritan Conversion Narrative: The Beginnings of American Expression*, Cambridge: Cambridge University Press.

Cameron, Deborah (1985) *Feminism and Linguistic Theory*, Basingstoke: Macmillan.

—— (1989) '"Released into Language": The Study of Language Outside and Inside Academic Institutions', in Ann Thompson and Helen Wilcox (eds) *Teaching Women: Feminism and English Studies*, Manchester: Manchester University Press.

Cameron, Euan (1984) *The Reformation of the Heretics: The Waldenses of the Alps 1480-1580*, Oxford: Clarendon.

Capp, B. S. (1972) *The Fifth-Monarchy Men: A Study in Seventeenth-Century English Millenarianism*, London: Faber and Faber.

—— (1984) 'The Fifth Monarchists and Popular Millenarianism', in J. F. McGregor and B. Reay (eds) *Radical Religion in the English Revolution*, Oxford: Oxford University Press.

Carr, E. H. (1961) *What is History?*, London: Macmillan.

Carter, Angela (1983) 'Alison's Giggle', in Eileen Phillips (ed.) *The Left and the Erotic*, London: Lawrence and Wishart.

Caughie, John (ed.) (1981) *Theories of Authorship: A Reader*, London: Routledge and Kegan Paul, in association with the British Film Institute.

Cerasano, S. P. and Wynne-Davies, Marion (eds) (1992) *Gloriana's Face: Women, Public and Private, in the English Renaissance*, London: Harvester Wheatsheaf.

de Certeau, Michel (1988) *The Writing of History*, trans. Tom Conley, New York, and Chichester, West Sussex: Columbia University Press.

Chalmers, Hero (1992) '"The Person I Am, Or What They Made Me To Be": The Construction of the Feminine Subject in the Autobiographies of Mary Carleton', in Clare Brant and Diane Purkiss (eds) (1992) *Women, Texts and Histories 1575-1760*, London: Routledge.

Charles, Lindsey and Duffin, Lorna (eds) (1985) *Women and Work in Pre-Industrial England*, London: Croom Helm.

Cixous, Hélène (1976; this ed. 1981) 'The Laugh of the Medusa', in Elaine Marks and Isabelle de Courtivron (eds) *New French Feminisms*, Brighton: Harvester.

Clark, Alice (1919; this ed. 1972) *Working Life of Women in the Seventeenth Century*, London: Routledge and Kegan Paul.

Clow, W. M. (1962) *The Bible-Reader's Encyclopaedia and Concordance*, London: Collins.

Coate, Mary (1933) *Cornwall in the Great Civil War and Interregnum 1642-1660: A Social and Political Study*, Oxford: Clarendon Press.

Cohen, Alfred (1964) 'The Fifth-Monarchy Mind: Mary Cary and the Origins of Totalitarianism', *Social Research* 31: 195-213.

Cohen, Charles Lloyd (1986) *God's Caress: The Psychology of Puritan Religious Experience*, Oxford: Oxford University Press.

Cohen, Murray (1977) *Sensible Words: Linguistic Practice in England, 1640-1785*, Baltimore, London: Johns Hopkins University Press.

Cohn, Norman (1957; this ed. 1970) *The Pursuit of the Millennium*, London: Paladin.

Cole, Alan (1957) 'The Social Origins of the Early Friends', *Journal of the Friends Historical Society* 48, 3: 99-118.

Collinson, Patrick (1967) *The Elizabethan Puritan Movement*, London: Cape.

—— (1984) 'The Religion of Protestants: the Church in English Society 1559-1625', in J. F. McGregor and B. Reay (eds) *Radical Religion in the English Revolution*, Oxford: Oxford University Press.

—— (1989) *The Puritan Character: Polemics and Polarities in Early Seventeenth-Century English Culture*, Los Angeles: University of California.

Cook, Pam (1981) 'The Point of Self-Expression in Avant-Garde Films', in John Caughie (ed.) *Theories of Authorship: A Reader*, London: Routledge and Kegan Paul, in association with the British Film Institute.

Cope, Jackson I. (1956) 'Seventeenth-Century Quaker Style', *PMLA* 71: 725-54.

Crawford, Patricia (1977) 'Charles Stuart, That Man of Blood', *Journal of British Studies* 16: 41-61.

—— (1985) 'Women's Published Writings 1600-1700', in Mary Prior (ed.) *Women in English Society 1500-1800*, London: Methuen.

—— (1993) *Women and Religion in England 1500-1720*, London: Routledge.

Cressy, David (1980) *Literacy and the Social Order: Reading and writing in Tudor and Stuart England*, Cambridge: Cambridge University Press.

Cruden, Alexander (1930; this ed. 1977) *Cruden's Complete Concordance to the Bible*, eds C. H. Irwin and A. D. Adams, Cambridge: Lutterworth Press.

Cust, Richard and Hughes, Ann (eds) (1989) *Conflict in Early Stuart England: Studies in Religion and Politics*, London: Longman.

Dailey, Barbara Ritter (1986) 'The Visitation of Sarah Wight: Holy Carnival and the Revolution of the Saints in Civil War London', *Studies in Church History* 55: 438-55.

Daly, Mary (1978) *Gyn/Ecology: The Metaethics of Radical Feminism*, London: Women's Press.

Davies, Kathleen M. (1977) 'The Sacred Condition of Equality - How Original Were Puritan Doctrines of Marriage?', *Social History* 2, 5: 563-80.

Davis, J. C. (1973) 'The Levellers and Christianity', in B. Manning (ed.) *Politics, Religion and the English Civil War*, London: Edward Arnold.

Davis, Natalie Zemon (1975a) 'Women on Top', in *Society and Culture in Early Modern France*, London: Duckworth.

—— (1975b) 'The Reasons of Misrule', in *Society and Culture in Early Modern France*, London: Duckworth.

—— (1986) 'Boundaries and the Sense of Self in Sixteenth-Century France', in Thomas C.

Heller (ed.) *Reconstructing Individualism: Autonomy, Individuality, and the Self in Western Thought*, Stanford: Stanford University Press.

Davis, Natalie Zemon and Farge, Arlette (eds) (1993) *A History of Women in the West: Volume 3: Renaissance and Enlightenment Paradoxes*, Harvard: Belknap Press.

Dekker, Rudolf M. and van de Pol, Lotte (1989) *The Tradition of Female Transvestism in Early Modern Europe*, Basingstoke: Macmillan.

Delany, Paul (1969) *British Autobiography in the Seventeenth Century*, London: Routledge and Kegan Paul.

Diamond, Irene and Quinby, Lee (eds) (1988) *Feminism and Foucault: Reflections on Resistance*, Boston: Northeastern University Press.

Dollimore, Jonathan (1984) *Radical Tragedy: Religion, Ideology and Power in the Drama of Shakespeare and his Contemporaries*, Brighton: Harvester.

Dollimore, Jonathan and Sinfield, Alan (eds) (1985) *Political Shakespeare: New Essays in Cultural Materialism*, Manchester: Manchester University Press.

Doyle, Brian (1989) *English and Englishness*, London: Routledge.

Duberman, Martin Bauml, Vicinus, Martha and Chauncey Jr, George (eds) (1989) *Hidden From History: Reclaiming the Gay and Lesbian Past*, London: Penguin.

Dyer, Richard (1991) 'Believing in Fairies', in Diana Fuss (ed.) *Inside/Out: Lesbian Theories, Gay Theories*, London: Routledge.

Eagleton, Mary (ed.) (1986) *Feminist Literary Theory: A Reader*, Oxford: Blackwell.

Eagleton, Terry (1983) *Literary Theory: An Introduction*, Oxford: Basil Blackwell.

Ebner, Dean (1971) *Autobiography in Seventeenth-Century England: Theology and the Self*, Paris and The Hague: Mouton.

Edkins, Carol (1980) 'Quest for Community: Spiritual Autobiographies of Eighteenth-Century Quaker and Puritan Women in America', in Estelle C. Jelinek (ed.) *Women's Autobiography*, Bloomington: Indiana University Press.

Ehrenreich, Barbara and English, Deirdre (1979) *For Her Own Good: 150 Years of the Experts' Advice to Women*, London: Pluto Press.

Elsky, Martin (1983) 'George Herbert's Pattern Poems and the Materiality of Language: A New Approach to Renaissance Hieroglyphics', *Journal of English Literary History* 50: 245-60.

Evans, Mary (1995) *Simone de Beauvoir*, London: Sage.

Ezell, Margaret (1987) *The Patriarch's Wife: Literary Evidence and the History of the Family*, Chapel Hill: University of California Press.

Faderman, Lillian (1980) *Surpassing the Love of Men: Romantic Friendship and Love between Women from the Renaissance to the Present*, London: Junction Books.

Feder, Lillian (1980) *Madness in Literature*, Princeton and Guildford: Princeton University Press.

Ferguson, Margaret W., Quilligan, Maureen and Vickers, Nancy J. (eds) (1986) *Rewriting the Renaissance: The Discourses of Sexual Difference in Early Modern Europe*, Chicago and London: University of Chicago Press.

Ferguson, Moira (ed.) (1985) *First Feminists: British Women Writers 1578-1799*, Bloomington: Indiana University Press.

—— (1992) *Subject to Others: British Women Writers and Colonial Slavery, 1670-1834*, London: Routledge.

Findley, Sandra and Hobby, Elaine (1981) 'Seventeenth-Century Women's Autobiography', in Francis Barker, Jay Bernstein, John Coombes, Peter Hulme, Jennifer Stone and Jon Stratton (eds) *1642: Literature and Power in the Seventeenth Century. Proceedings of the Essex Conference on the Sociology of Literature*, Colchester: University of Essex Press.

Finlayson, Michael G. (1983) *Historians, Puritanism, and the English Revolution: The Religious Factor in English Politics Before and After the Interregnum*, Toronto, Buffalo and London: University of Toronto Press.

Fisch, Harold (1952) 'The Puritans and the Reform of Prose Style', *Journal of English Literary History* 19: 229-48.

Fitz, Linda (1980) '"What Says the Married Woman?" Marriage Theory and Feminism in the English Renaissance', *Mosaic* 13: 1-22.

Flandrin, Jean-Louis (1972) 'Mariage tardif et vie sexuelle: discussions et hypothèses de recherche', *Annales: Economies, Sociétés, Civilisations*, 27: 1351-78.

Fletcher, A. and Stevenson, J. (eds) (1985) *Order and Disorder in Early Modern England*, Cambridge: Cambridge University Press.

Fletcher, A. J. (1981) *The Outbreak of the English Civil War*, London: Edward Arnold.

—— (1985) 'Honour, Reputation and Local Officeholding in Elizabethan and Stuart England', in A. Fletcher and J. Stevenson (eds) *Order and Disorder in Early Modern England*, Cambridge: Cambridge University Press.

Foucault, Michel (1967) *Madness and Civilization*, trans. Richard Howard, London: Tavistock.

—— (1970) *The Order of Things*, London: Tavistock.

—— (1977; this ed. 1981)) 'What is an Author?', in John Caughie (ed.) *Theories of Authorship*, London: Routledge and Kegan Paul/British Film Institute: 282-91.

—— (1979) *The History of Sexuality: An Introduction*, trans. Robert Hurley, Harmondsworth: Penguin.

Fraser, Antonia (1984) *The Weaker Vessel: Woman's Lot in Seventeenth-Century England*, London: Weidenfeld and Nicolson.

Gallagher, Catherine (1988) 'Embracing the Absolute: The Politics of the Female Subject in Seventeenth-Century England', *Genders* 1, 1: 24-39.

George, Margaret (1988) *Women in the First Capitalist Society: Experiences in Seventeenth-Century England*, Brighton: Harvester.

Gilbert, Sandra and Gubar, Susan (1979) *The Madwoman in the Attic*, New Haven: Yale University Press.

Goldberg, Jonathan (1982) 'The Politics of Renaissance Literature: A Review Essay', *Journal of English Literary History* 49: 514-42.

—— (1986) 'Fatherly Authority: The Politics of Stuart Family Images', in Margaret W. Ferguson, Maureen Quilligan and Nancy J. Vickers (eds) *Rewriting the Renaissance: The Discourses of Sexual Difference in Early Modern Europe*, Chicago and London: University of Chicago Press.

Goulianos, Joan (ed.) (1974) *by a Woman Writt: Literature from Six Centuries by and about Women*, London: New English Library

Graham, Elspeth, Hinds, Hilary, Hobby, Elaine and Wilcox, Helen (eds) (1989) *Her Own Life: Autobiographical Writings by Seventeenth-Century Englishwomen*, London: Routledge.

Greaves, Richard L. (1986) *Deliver Us From Evil: The Radical Underground in Britain, 1660-1663*, New York, Oxford: Oxford University Press.

Greaves, Richard L. and Zaller, Robert (eds) (1982-84) *Biographical Dictionary of British Radicals in the Seventeenth Century* (3 vols.), Brighton: Harvester.

Greenblatt, Stephen (1980) *Renaissance Self-Fashioning: from More to Shakespeare*, Chicago: University of Chicago Press.

—— (ed.) (1988) *Representing the English Renaissance*, Berkeley: California University Press.

Greene, Gayle and Kahn, Coppélia (eds) (1985) *Making a Difference: Feminist Literary Criticism*, London: Methuen.

Greene, John C. (1971) 'Les Mots et Les Choses', in Julia Kristeva (ed.) *Essays in Semiotics*, The Hague: Mouton.

Greer, Germaine, Medoff, Jeslyn, Sansone, Melinda and Hastings, Susan (eds) (1988) *Kissing the Rod: An Anthology of Seventeenth-Century Women's Verse*, London: Virago.

Grosz, Elizabeth (1981) *Sexual Subversions: Three French Feminists*, Sydney: Allen and Unwin.

—— (1992) 'Julia Kristeva', in Elizabeth Wright (ed.) *Feminism and Psychoanalysis: A Critical Dictionary*, Oxford: Basil Blackwell.

Grundy, Isobel, Blain, Virginia and Clements, Patricia (eds) (1990) *The Feminist Companion to Literature in English: Women Writers from the Middle Ages to the Present*, London: Batsford.

Grundy, Isobel and Wiseman, Susan (eds) (1992) *Women, Writing, History 1640-1740*, London: Batsford.

Haller, William (1946) 'Hail Wedded Love', *English Literary History* 13: 79-97.

—— (1951) 'John Foxe and the Puritan Revolution', in R. F. Jones *et al. The Seventeenth Century*, Oxford: Oxford University Press.

—— (1955) *Liberty and Reformation in the Puritan Revolution*, New York: Columbia University Press.

Haller, William and Haller, Malleville (1941-42) 'The Puritan Art of Love', *Huntington Library Quarterly* 5: 235-72.

Harvey, David (1990) *The Condition of Postmodernity: An Enquiry into the Origins of Cultural Change*, Oxford: Basil Blackwell.

Henderson, Katherine Usher and McManus, Barbara (1985) *Half Humankind: Contexts and Texts of the Controversy about Women in England 1540-1640*, Urbana: University of Chicago Press.

Henderson, Mae Gwendolyn (1990) 'Speaking in Tongues: Dialogics, Dialectics, and the Black Woman Writer's Literary Tradition', in Cheryl A. Wall (ed.) *Changing Our Own Words: Essays on Criticism, Theory and Writing by Black Women*, London: Routledge.

Higgins, Patricia (1973) 'The Reactions of Women, with Special Reference to Women Petitioners', in Brian Manning (ed.) *Politics, Religion and the English Civil War*, London: Edward Arnold.

Hill, Christopher (1940; this ed. 1979) *The English Revolution 1640*, London: Lawrence and Wishart.

—— (1961; this ed. 1980) *The Century of Revolution 1603-1714*, Walton-on-Thames: Nelson.

—— (1964) *Society and Puritanim in Pre-Revolutionary England*, London: Secker and Warburg.

—— (1965; this ed. 1980) *Intellectual Origins of the English Revolution*, Oxford: Clarendon Press.

—— (1972; this ed. 1975) *The World Turned Upside Down*, Harmondsworth: Penguin.

—— (1988) *A Turbulent, Seditious, and Factious People: John Bunyan and his Church*, Oxford: Oxford University Press.

—— (1993) *The English Bible and the Seventeenth-Century Revolution*, London: Allen Lane, The Penguin Press.

Hobby, Elaine (1979) 'The Fame of the Honest Margaret Cavendish', unpublished MA thesis, University of Essex.

—— (1988) *Virtue of Necessity: English Women's Writing 1649-1688*, London: Virago.

—— (1991) 'Katherine Philips: Seventeenth-Century Lesbian Poet', in Elaine Hobby and Chris White (eds) *What Lesbians Do In Books*, London: The Women's Press.

—— (1995a) 'Handmaids of the Lord and Mothers in Israel: Early Vindications of Quaker Women's Prophecy', *Prose Studies* 17: 3.

—— (1995b) 'The Politics of Women's Prophecy in the English Revolution', in Helen Wilcox *et al.* (eds) *Sacred and Profane: Secular and Devotional Interplay in Early Modern British Literature*, Amsterdam: Free University Press.

Holden, Kate (1985) 'Women's Writing and the Carnivalesque', *Literature Teaching Politics Journal*: 5-15.

Holdsworth, W. S. (1924) *History of the English Law*, vol. 5, London: Methuen.

Holquist, Michael (1990) *Dialogism: Bakhtin and his World*, London: Routledge.

Hull, Suzanne W. (1982) *Chaste, Silent and Obedient: English Books for Women 1475-1640*, San Marino: Huntington Library.

Hurwich, Judith Jones (1970) 'Debate: The Social Origins of the Early Friends', *Past and Present* 48: 156-64.

Ingram, Martin (1985) 'The Reform of Popular Culture? Sex and Marriage in Early Modern England', in B. Reay (ed.) *Popular Culture in Early Modern England*, London: Croom Helm.

—— (1987) *Church Courts, Sex and Marriage in England, 1570-1640*, Cambridge: Cambridge University Press.

Irigaray, Luce (1985a) *Speculum of the Other Woman*, trans. Gillian C. Gill, Ithaca, NY: Cornell University Press.

—— (1985b) *This Sex Which is Not One*, trans. Catherine Porter with Carolyn Burke, Ithaca, NY: Cornell University Press.

Jacob, Margaret and Jacob, James (eds) (1984) *The Origins of Anglo-American Radicalism*, London: Allen and Unwin.

Jacobus, Mary (ed.) (1979) *Women Writing and Writing About Women*, London: Croom Helm.

Jameson, Fredric (1981) *The Political Unconscious*, London: Methuen.

Jardine, Lisa (1983) *Still Harping on Daughters: Women and Drama in the Age of Shakespeare*, Brighton: Harvester.

Jay, Karla and Glasgow, Joanne (eds) (1992) *Lesbian Texts and Contexts: Radical Revisions*, London: Onlywomen Press.

Jelinek, Estelle C. (ed.) (1980) *Women's Autobiography: Essays in Criticism*, Bloomington: Indiana University Press.

Jones, Ann Rosalind (1986) 'Surprising Fame: Renaissance Gender Ideologies and Women's Lyric', in Nancy K. Miller (ed.) *The Poetics of Gender*, Columbia University Press.

—— (1987) 'Nets and Bridles: Early Modern Conduct Books and Sixteenth-Century Women's Lyric', in Nancy Armstrong and Leonard Tennenhouse (eds) *The Ideology of Conduct: Essays in Literature and the History of Sexuality*, London: Methuen.

—— (1990) 'Counterattacks on "the Bayter of Women": Three Pamphleteers of the Early Seventeenth Century', in Anne M. Haselkorn and Betty S. Travitsky (eds) *The Renaissance Englishwoman in Print: Counterbalancing the Canon*, Amherst: Massachusetts University Press.

Jones, R. F. (1951a) 'The Background of *The Battle of the Books*', in R. F. Jones *et al. The Seventeenth Century*, Oxford: Oxford University Press.

—— (1951b) 'The Attack on Pulpit Eloquence', in R. F. Jones *et al. The Seventeenth Century*, Oxford: Oxford University Press.

—— (1953) *The Triumph of the English Language*, Oxford: Oxford University Press.

Kahn, Coppélia (1986) 'The Absent Mother in *King Lear*', in Margaret W. Ferguson, Maureen Quilligan and Nancy J. Vickers (eds) *Rewriting the Renaissance: The Discourses of Sexual Difference in Early Modern Europe*, Chicago and London: University of Chicago Press.

Keeble, N. H. (1987) *The Literary Culture of Nonconformity in Later Sevententh-Century England*, Leicester: Leicester University Press.

Keeble, N. H. (ed.) (1994) *The Cultural Identity of Seventeenth-Century Woman*, London: Routledge.

Kelly, Joan (1984) 'Did Women Have a Renaissance?', in *Women, History and Theory: The Essays of Joan Kelly*, Chicago, London: University of Chicago Press.

Kibbey, Ann (1986) *The Interpretation of Material Shapes in Puritanism: A Study of Rhetoric, Prejudice and Violence*, Cambridge: Cambridge University Press.

Knowlson, James (1975) *Universal Language Schemes in England and France 1600-1800*, Toronto: University of Toronto Press.

Kristeva, Julia (1980) *Desire in Language*, trans. Leon S. Roudiez, Oxford: Basil Blackwell.

—— (1984) *The Revolution in Poetic Language*, trans. Margaret Waller, New York: Columbia University Press.

—— (1987) *The Kristeva Reader*, ed. by Toril Moi, Oxford: Basil Blackwell.

Lamont, William (1970) *Godly Rule: Politics and Religion*, London: Macmillan.

Latt, David (1978) 'Praising Virtuous Ladies: The Literary Image and Historical Reality of Women in Seventeenth-Century England', in Marlene Springer (ed.) *What Manner of Woman: Essays in English and American Life and Literature*, Oxford: Basil Blackwell.

Lerner, Gerda (1993) *The Creation of Feminist Consciousness: From the Middle Ages to Eighteen-Seventy*, Oxford: Oxford University Press.

Lewalski, Barbara (1993) *Writing Women in Jacobean England*, Cambridge, MA and London: Harvard University Press.

Lewis, Reina (1992) 'The Death of the Author and the Resurrection of the Dyke', in Sally Munt (ed.) *New Lesbian Criticism: Literary and Cultural Readings*, Hemel Hempstead: Harvester Wheatsheaf.

Lodge, David (1981) *Working with Structuralism*, London: Routledge and Kegan Paul.

London Feminist History Group (eds) (1938) *The Sexual Dynamics of History*, London: Pluto.

Ludlow, Dorothy Paula (1978) '"Arise and Be Doing": English "Preaching" Women, 1640-1660', unpublished Ph.D. thesis, Indiana University.

Celia Lury (1992) 'Popular Culture and the Mass Media', in Robert Bocock and Kenneth Thompson (eds) *Social and Cultural Forms of Modernity*, Cambridge and Oxford: The Open University and Polity Press.

Lyotard, Jean-François (1984) *The Postmodern Condition: A Report on Knowledge*, first pub. in French 1979; trans. Geoff Bennington and Brian Massumi, Manchester: Manchester University Press.

Macherey, Pierre (1978) *A Theory of Literary Production*, trans. Geoffrey Wall, London: Routledge and Kegan Paul.

Mack, Phyllis (1982) 'Women as Prophets During the English Civil War', *Feminist Studies* 8,1: 19-45; reprinted in Margaret Jacob and James Jacob (eds) (1984), *The Origins of Anglo-American Radicalism*, London: George Allen and Unwin.

—— (1992) *Visionary Women: Ecstatic Prophecy in Seventeenth-Century England*, Berkeley, CA and Oxford: University of California Press.

McArthur, E.A. (1909) 'Women Petitioners and the Long Parliament', *English Historical Review* 24: 698-709.

McGee, J. Sears (1976) 'Conversion and the Imitation of Christ in Anglican and Puritan Writing', *Journal of British Studies* 15: 20-39.

McGregor, J. F. (1984) 'The Baptists: Fount of All Heresy', in J. F. McGregor and B. Reay (eds) *Radical Religion in the English Revolution*, Oxford: Oxford University Press.

McKeon, M. (1987) 'Politics of Discourse and the Rise of the Aesthetic in Seventeenth-Century England', in K. Sharpe and S.N. Zwicker (eds) *Politics of Discourse: The Literature and History of Seventeenth-Century England*, Berkeley and London: California University Press.

Maclean, Ian (1980) *The Renaissance Notion of Woman: A Study in the Fortunes of Scholasticism and Medical Science in European Intellectual Life*, Cambridge: Cambridge University Press.

McLennan, Gregor (1981) *Marxism and the Methodologies of History*, London: New Left Books.

Malekin, Peter (1981) *Liberty and Love: English Literature and Society 1640-88*, London: Hutchinson.

Manning, Brian (ed.) (1973) *The English People and the English Civil War*, London: Edward Arnold.

Marks, Elaine and de Courtivron, Isabelle (eds) (1981) *New French Feminisms*, Brighton: Harvester.

Masek, Rosemary (1980) 'Women in an Age of Transition 1485-1714', in Barbara Kanner (ed.) *The Women of England from Anglo-Saxon Times to the Present*, London: Mansell Information Publishing.

Mayne, Judith (1990) *The Woman at the Keyhole: Feminism and Women's Cinema*, Bloomington and Indianapolis: Indiana University Press.

Medhurst, Andy (1991) 'That Special Thrill: *Brief Encounter*, Homosexuality and Authorship', *Screen* 32, 2: 197-208.

Miller, Casey and Swift, Kate (1976) *Words and Women: New Language in New Times*, Harmondsworth: Penguin.

Miller, Nancy K. (1989) 'Changing the Subject', in Elizabeth Weed (ed.) *Coming to Terms: Feminism, Theory, Politics*, London: Routledge.

Millett, Kate (1970) *Sexual Politics*, London: Abacus.

Mills, Sara, Pearce, Lynne, Spaull, Sue and Millard, Elaine (1989) *Feminist Readings, Feminists Reading*, Hemel Hempstead: Harvester Wheatsheaf.

Milsom, S. F. C. (1969) *Historical Foundations of the Canon Law*, London: Butterworth.

Moers, Ellen (1978) *Literary Women*, London: Women's Press.

Moi, Toril (1985) *Sexual/Textual Politics: Feminist Literary Theory*, London: Methuen.

Moi, Toril (ed.) (1986) *The Kristeva Reader*, Oxford: Basil Blackwell.

—— (ed.) (1987) *French Feminist Thought: A Reader*, Oxford: Basil Blackwell.

Moore, R. I. (1975) *The Birth of Popular Heresy*, London: Edward Arnold.

Morgan, John (1986) *Godly Learning: Puritan Attitudes Towards Reason, Learning and Education 1560-1640*, Cambridge: Cambridge University Press.

Morrill, John (ed.) (1991) *The Impact of the English Civil War*, London: Collins and Brown.

Morrill, J. S. and Walter, J. D. (1985) 'Order and Disorder in the English Revolution', in A. J. Fletcher and J. Stevenson (eds) *Order and Disorder in Early Modern England*, Cambridge: Cambridge University Press.

Morris, Meaghan (1988) 'The Pirate's Fiancée: Feminists and Philosophers, or Maybe Tonight It'll Happen', in Irene Diamond and Lee Quinby (eds) *Feminism and Foucault*, Boston: Northeastern University Press.

Notestein, Wallace (1955) 'The English Woman 1580-1650', in J. H. Plumb (ed.) *Studies in Social History: A Tribute to G.M. Trevelyan*, London: Longman.

Nuttall, Geoffrey (1946) *The Holy Spirit in Puritan Faith and Experience*, Oxford: Basil Blackwell.

Olsen, Tillie (1980) *Silences*, London: Virago.

Osborn, James M. (1959) *The Beginnings of Autobiography in England*, Berkeley, CA: University of California Press.

Patterson, Annabel (1984) *Censorship and Interpretation*, Madison, WI: University of Wisconsin Press.

Pearce, Lynne (1994) *Reading Dialogics*, London: Edward Arnold.

Plomer, Henry (n.d.) *Mary Westwood: Publisher of Quaker Literature 1659*, ms, London: Library of the Society of Friends.

Pomerleau, Cynthia S. (1980) 'The Emergence of Women's Autobiography in England', in Estelle C. Jelinek (ed.) *Women's Autobiography: Essays in Criticism*, Bloomington: Indiana University Press.

Pooley, Roger (1981) 'Anglicans, Puritans and Plain Style', in Francis Barker, Jay Bernstein, John Coombes, Peter Hulme, Jennifer Stone and Jon Stratton (eds) *1642: Literature and Power in the Seventeenth Century. Proceedings of the Essex Conference on the Sociology Of Literature*, Colchester: University of Essex Press.

Poovey, Mary (1988) 'Feminism and Deconstruction', *Feminist Studies* 14: 51-65.

Powell, Chilton (1917) *English Domestic Relations 1487-1653*, New York: Columbia University Press.

Mary Prior (ed.) *Women in English Society 1500-1800*, London: Methuen.

Purkiss, Diane (1992a) 'Producing the Voice, Consuming the Body: Women Prophets of the Seventeenth Century', in Isobel Grundy and Susan Wiseman (eds) *Women, Writing, History 1640-1740*, London: Batsford.

—— (1992b) 'Material Girls: The Seventeenth-Century Woman Debate', in Clare Brant and Diane Purkiss (eds) *Women, Texts and Histories 1575-1760*, London: Routledge.

Rabinow, Paul (ed.) (1986; this ed. 1991) *The Foucault Reader: An Introduction to Foucault's Thought*, London: Penguin.

Ramazanoglu, Caroline (1993) *Up Against Foucault: Explorations of Some Tensions between Foucault and Feminism*, London: Routedge.

Ramazanoglu, Caroline and Holland, Janet (1993) 'Women's Sexuality and Men's Appropriation of Desire', in Caroline Ramazanoglu (ed.) *Up Against Foucault: Explorations of Some Tensions between Foucault and Feminism*, London: Routledge.

Reay, Barry (1984a) 'Radicalism and Religion in the English Revolution: An Introduction', in J. F. McGregor and B. Reay (eds) *Radical Religion in the English Revolution*, Oxford: Oxford University Press.

—— (1984b) 'Quakerism and Society', in J. F. Mc Gregor and B. Reay (eds) *Radical Religion in the English Revolution*, Oxford: Oxford University Press.

—— (1985a) 'Introduction: Popular Culture in Early Modern England', in B. Reay (ed.) *Popular Culture in Seventeenth-Century England*, London: Croom Helm.

—— (1985b) 'Popular Religion', in B. Reay (ed.) *Popular Culture in Seventeenth-Century England*, London: Croom Helm.

—— (1985c) *The Quakers and the English Revolution*, London: Temple Smith.

Riley, Denise (1988) *'Am I That Name?' Feminism and the Category of 'Women' in History*, London: Macmillan.

Rivers, Isabel (1991) *Reason, Grace and Sentiment: A Study of the Language of Religion and Ethics in England, 1660-1780. Volume 1: Whichcote to Wesley*, Cambridge: Cambridge University Press.

Roper, Lyndal (1989) *The Holy Household*, Oxford: Clarendon.

Ross, Isabel (1949) *Margaret Fell: Mother of Quakerism*, London: Longman.

Rowbotham, Sheila (1972) *Women, Resistance and Revolution*, London: Allen Lane.

—— (1973; this ed. 1977) *Hidden from History*, London: Pluto.

Russ, Joanna (1984) *How to Suppress Women's Writing*, London: Women's Press.

Russell, Conrad (1990) *The Causes of the English Civil War*, Oxford: Clarendon.

Sarup, Madan (1988) *An Introductory Guide to Post-Structuralism and Postmodernism*, Brighton: Harvester.

Scott, Joan W. (1988) 'Deconstructing Equality-versus-Difference: Or, the Uses of Poststructuralist Theory for Feminism', *Feminist Studies* 14, 1: 33-50.

—— (1989) 'Gender: A Useful Category of Historical Analysis', in Elizabeth Weed (ed.) *Coming to Terms: Feminism, Theory, Politics*, London: Routledge.

Selden, Raman and Widdowson, Peter (1993) *A Reader's Guide to Contemporary Literary Theory*, 3rd ed., Hemel Hempstead: Harvester Wheatsheaf.

Sellers, Susan (ed.) (1994) *The Hélène Cixous Reader*, London: Routledge.

Sharp, Buchanan (1985) 'Popular Protest in Seventeenth-Century England', in B. Reay (ed.) *Popular Culture in Seventeenth-Century England*, London: Croom Helm.

Sharpe, James (1985) 'The People and the Law', in B. Reay (ed.) *Popular Culture in Seventeenth-Century England*, London: Croom Helm.

Shepherd, Simon (ed.) (1985) *The Women's Sharp Revenge: Five Women's Pamphlets from the Renaissance*, London: Fourth Estate.

Shorter, Edward (1976) *The Making of the Modern Family*, London: Collins.

Showalter, Elaine (1978) *A Literature of Their Own: British Women Novelists from Bronte to Lessing*, London: Virago.

—— (1979) 'Towards a Feminist Poetics', in Mary Jacobus (ed.) *Women Writing and Writing About Women*, London: Croom Helm.

—— (ed.) (1986) *The New Feminist Criticism: Essays on Women, Literature and Theory*, London: Virago.

Slaughter, M.M. (1982) *Universal Languages and Scientific Taxonomy in the Seventeenth Century*, Cambridge: Cambridge University Press.

Smith, Ginnie (1983) 'Thomas Tryon's Regimen for Women: Sectarian Health in the Seventeenth Century', in London Feminist History Group (eds) *The Sexual Dynamics of History*, London: Pluto.

Smith, Hilda (1976) 'Gynaecology and Ideology in Seventeenth-Century England', in Berenice Carroll (ed.) *Liberating Women's History*, Urbana: Illinois University Press.

—— (1982) *Reason's Disciples: Seventeenth-Century English Feminists*, Urbana: University of Illinois Press.

—— and Cardinale, Susan (1990) *Women and the Literature of the Seventeenth Century: An Annotated Bibliography Based on Wing's Short-Title Catalogue*, New York, Westport, CT and London: Greenwood Press.

Smith, Nigel (1989) *Perfection Proclaimed: Language and Literature in English Radical Religion 1640-1660*, Oxford: Clarendon.

Sontag, Susan (1969) 'The Aesthetics of Silence', in *Styles of Radical Will*, New York: Farrar, Strauss.

Spacks, Patrica Meyer (1976) *The Female Imagination. A Literary and Psychological Investigation of Women's Writing*, London: Allen and Unwin.

Spencer, Jane (1986) *The Rise of the Woman Novelist: From Aphra Behn to Jane Austen*, Oxford: Basil Blackwell.

Spender, Dale (1980) *Man-Made Language*, London: Routledge and Kegan Paul.

—— (1983) *Women of Ideas (and what men have done to them)*, London: Routledge and Kegan Paul, Ark.

—— (1986) *Mothers of the Novel*, London: Pandora.

Spender, Dale and Todd, Janet (eds) (1989) *Anthology of British Women Writers*, London: Pandora.

Spufford, Margaret (1979) 'First Steps in Literacy: The Reading and Writing Experiences of the Humblest Sevententh-Century Spiritual Autobiographers', *Social History* 4, 3: 407-35.

Reprinted in Harvey J. Graff (ed.) (1981) *Literacy and Social Development in the West: A Reader*, Cambridge: Cambridge University Press.

—— (1981) *Small Books and Pleasant Histories: Popular Fiction and its Readership in Seventeenth-Century England*, London: Methuen.

—— (1985) 'Puritanism and Social Control?', in A. J. Fletcher and J. Stevenson (eds) *Order and Disorder in Early Modern England*, Cambridge: Cambridge University Press.

Stacey, Margaret (1988) *The Sociology of Health and Healing*, London: Unwin Hyman.

Stallybrass, Peter (1986) 'Patriarchal Territories: The Body Enclosed', in Margaret W. Ferguson, Maureen Quilligan and Nancy J. Vickers (eds) *Rewriting the Renaissance: The Discourses of Sexual Difference in Early Modern Europe*, Chicago and London: University of Chicago Press.

Stallybrass, Peter and White, Allon (1986) *The Politics and Poetics of Transgression*, London and New York: Methuen.

Stanley, Liz (1994) 'Recovering *Women* in History from Feminist Deconstructionism', in Mary Evans (ed.) 2nd ed., *The Woman Question*, London: Sage.

Stenton, Doris Mary (1957) *The English Woman in History*, London: Macmillan.

Stone, Lawrence (1964) 'The Educational Revolution in England 1560-1640', *Past and Present* 28: 41-80.

—— (1969) 'Literacy and Education in England 1640-1900', *Past and Present* 42: 69-139.

—— (1977) *The Family, Sex and Marriage in England 1500-1800*, London: Weidenfeld and Nicolson.

—— (1990) *Road to Divorce: England 1530-1987*, Oxford: Oxford University Press.

Tawney, R.H. (1926; this ed. 1948) *Religion and the Rise of Capitalism*, Harmondsworth: Penguin.

Taylor, Barry (1991) *Vagrant Writing: Social and Semiotic Disorders in the English Renaissance*, Toronto: University of Toronto Press.

Thomas, Keith (1958) 'Women and the Civil War Sects', *Past and Present* 13: 42-62.

—— (1959) 'The Double Standard', *Journal of the History of Ideas* 20: 195-216.

—— (1971) *Religion and the Decline of Magic*, London: Weidenfeld and Nicolson.

Thompson, Ann and Wilcox, Helen (eds) (1989) *Teaching Women: Feminism and English Studies*, Manchester: Manchester University Press.

Thompson, Roger (1974) *Women in Stuart England and America: A Comparative Study*, London: Routledge and Kegan Paul.

Thomson, John A. F. (1965) *The Later Lollards 1414-1520*, Oxford: Oxford University Press.

Tilley, M. P. (1950) *A Dictionary of the Proverbs in England in the Sixteenth and Seventeenth Centuries*, Ann Arbor: University of Michigan Press.

Tindall, William York (1934) *John Bunyan, Mechanick Preacher*, New York: Columbia University Studies in English and Comparative Literature.

Todd, Janet (1989) *The Sign of Angellica: Women, Writing and Fiction 1660-1800*, London: Virago.

Toulmin, Stephen (1961) 'Seventeenth-Century Science and the Arts', in H. H. Rhys (ed.) *Seventeenth-Century Science and the Arts*, Princeton: Princeton University Press.

Travitsky, Betty (1984) 'The Lady Doth Protest: Protest in the Popular Writings of Renaissance Englishwomen', *English Literary Renaissance* 14: 255-83.

—— (ed.) (1989) *The Paradise of Women: Writings By Englishwomen of the Renaissance*, New York: Columbia University Press.

Underdown, D. E. (1985a) 'The Taming of the Scold: The Enforcement of Patriarchal Authority in Early Modern England', in A.J. Fletcher and J. Stevenson (eds) *Order and Disorder in Early Modern England*, Cambridge: Cambridge University Press.

—— (1985b) *Revel, Riot and Rebellion: Popular Politics and Culture in England 1603-1660*, Oxford: Oxford University Press.

Underwood, A. C. (1947) *A History of the English Baptists*, London: The Baptist Union Publication Dept (Kingsgate Press).

Vann, R. T. (1969) 'Quakerism and the Social Structure in the Interregnum', *Past and Present* 43: 71-91.

Veeser, H. Aram (ed.) (1989) *The New Historicism*, London: Routledge.

Voloshinov, V. N. (1929; this ed. 1973) *Marxism and the Philosophy of Language*, trans. Ladislav Matejka and I. R. Titunik, New York: Seminar Press.

Wall, Cheryl (ed.) *Changing Our Own Words: Essays on Criticism, Theory and Writing by Black Women*, London: Routledge.

Walzer, Michael (1966) *The Revolution of the Saints: A Study in the Origins of Radical Politics*, London: Weidenfeld and Nicolson.

Watkins, Owen C. (1953) 'Some Early Quaker Autobiographies', *Journal of the Friends Historical Society* 45: 65-74.

—— (1972) *The Puritan Experience: Studies in Spiritual Autobiography*, London: Routledge and Kegan Paul.

Watson, Foster (ed.) (1912) *Vives and the Renascence Education of Women*, London: Edward Arnold.

Watts, Michael (1978) *The Dissenters. Volume 1: From the Reformation to the French Revolution*, Oxford: Clarendon Press.

Wear, Andrew (1985) 'Puritan Perception of Illness in Seventeenth-Century England', in Roy Porter (ed.) *Patients and Practitioners: Lay Perceptions of Medicine in Pre-Industrial Society*, Cambridge: Cambridge University Press.

Webber, Joan (1968) *The Eloquent 'I': Style and Self in Seventeenth-Century Prose*, Madison: University of Wisconsin Press.

Weedon, Chris (1987) *Feminist Practice and Poststructuralist Theory*, Oxford: Basil Blackwell.

White, B.R. (1983) *The English Baptists of the Seventeenth Century*, London: Baptists Historical Society.

Whitford, Margaret (1991) *Luce Irigaray: Philosophy in the Feminine*, London: Routledge.

Whiting, C.E. (1931) *Studies in English Puritanism from the Restoration to the Revolution, 1660-1688*, London: Macmillan, for The Society for the Promoting of Christian Knowledge.

Whiting, John (1708) *A Catalogue of Friends Books*, London: J. Sowle.

Whitley, William Thomas (1916) *A Baptist Bibliography: Volume 1 1526-1776*, London: Kingsgate Press.

Widdowson, Peter (ed.) (1982) *Re-Reading English*, London, Methuen.

Wilcox, Helen (1992) 'Private Writing and Public Function: Autobiographical Texts by Renaissance Englishwomen', in S.P. Cerasano and Marion Wynne-Davies (eds) *Gloriana's Face: Women, Public and Private, in the English Renaissance*, London: Harvester Wheatsheaf.

—— (1996) *Women and Literature in Britain 1500-1700*, Cambridge: Cambridge University Press.

Williams, Ethyn (1929) 'Women Preachers in the English Civil War', *Journal of Modern History* 1: 561-9.

Williams, Raymond (19770 *Marxism and Literature*, Oxford: Oxford University Press.

Williamson, Judith (1978) *Decoding Advertisements: Ideology and Meaning in Advertising*, London: Marion Boyars.

Wing, Donald (1945-51) *Short-Title Catalogue of Books Printed in England, Scotland, Ireland, Wales and British America and of English Books Printed Abroad, 1641-1700*, 3 vols, 2nd ed.

of vol. 1 (1972) and vol. 2 (1982), New York: Index Committee of the Modern Language Association of America.

Wiseman, Susan (1992a) 'Unsilent Instruments and the Devil's Cushions: Authority in Seventeenth-Century Women's Prophetic Discourse', in Isobel Armstrong (ed.) *New Feminist Discourses: Critical Essays on Theories and Texts*, London: Routledge.

—— (1992b) 'Gender and Status in Dramatic Discourse: Margaret Cavendish, Duchess of Newcastle', in Isobel Grundy and Susan Wiseman (eds) *Women, Writing, History 1640–1740*, London: Batsford

Wisker, Gina (ed.) (1992) *Black Women's Writing*, Basingstoke: Macmillan.

Woodbridge, Linda (1984) *Women in the English Renaissance: Literature and the Nature of Womanhood, 1540–1620*, Brighton: Harvester.

Woodhouse, A. S. P. (1938; this ed. 1974) *Puritanism and Liberty: Being the Army Debates (1647–9) from the Clarke Manuscripts, with Supplementary Documents*, London: J. M. Dent and Sons Ltd.

Woolf, Virginia (1928; this ed. 1945) *A Room of One's Own*, Harmondsworth: Penguin.

Woolrych, Austin (1982) *Commonwealth to Protectorate*, Oxford: Clarendon Press.

Wright, Elizabeth (ed.) (1992) *Feminism and Psychoanalysis: A Critical Dictionary*, Oxford: Basil Blackwell.

Wright, Louis B. (1935) *Middle-Class Culture in Elizabethan England*, Chapel Hill: University of North Carolina Press.

Wright, Luella M. (1932) *The Literary Life of the Early Friends, 1650–1725*, New York: Columbia University Press.

—— (1933) 'Literature and Education in Early Quakerism', *University of Iowa Humanistic Studies* 5, 2: 161–5.

Yoshioka, Barbara Gerd Samuelsen (1977) 'Imaginal Worlds: Woman as Witch and Preacher in Seventeenth-Century England', unpublished Ph.D. thesis, New York: Syracuse Unversity.

Zaretsky, Eli (1976) *Capitalism, the Family and Personal Life*, London: Pluto Press.

Index